Dear Reader,

One of the signature-type stories we tell at Guideposts is from people who have died, experienced heaven, and then returned to tell others about their experiences. We've been publishing these amazing "eyewitness accounts" of our eternal home for seventy years! Each one augments, in some way, what Scripture says about heaven.

The Gospel of John likens heaven to a mansion with many rooms (John 14:2). The Book of Revelation gives us the expression "pearly gates" and the concept that heavenly streets are paved with gold (Revelation 21:21).

Peter Baldwin Panagore, the writer of *Heaven Is Beautiful*, died while ice climbing in Banff National Park, Alberta, Canada, when he was a college student. He was catapulted into another world, where he experienced God's great love, and miraculously returned to this life. His description of heaven is not so much visual, although he does see a giant doorway or gate that shimmers and flows like a waterfall ("Only it was not water and was simultaneously translucent and transparent"). But what intrigued us about his account of his time with God was it echoed the sweetness of heaven, described in Revelation 21:4 ("He will wipe away every tear from their eyes, and death shall be no more, neither shall there be mourning, nor crying, nor pain anymore, for the former things have passed away"), and the longing that Paul expresses in 2 Corinthians 5:8 ("Yes, we are of good courage, and we would rather be away from the body and at home with the Lord").

To make sense of his mountaintop experience, Peter went to divinity school and has been a pastor for the past thirty years. He told us, "My ne̶a̶r̶-̶d̶e̶a̶t̶h̶ ̶e̶x̶p̶e̶r̶i̶e̶nce drove

me in desperation to find a way or ways to let more light in, to create more space for God inside me, to sit as close to God as I could. Because I crave even a taste that I had when I was dead, the full beauty and love of God, which is ten thousand times ten thousand greater than any touch of God, that I have ever felt here in this world."

Heaven Is Beautiful is rich in descriptions of the natural world—of stunning views of a glacier glistening in the setting sun and the night sky a blanket of bright twinkling lights. This outdoor adventure led us to select from the *Guideposts* archive "I Have Been Somewhere!", Dr. Ellen NicKenzie Lawson's glimpse of heaven while hiking in the beautiful Columbia Mountain Gorge, as a special bonus at the end of this book.

In the words of Peter: "Be of good cheer, for in the end we get to go back to where we came from, thanks be to God, who was, who is, and who shall be evermore and eternally love."

Faithfully yours,
Editors of Guideposts

Heaven Is Beautiful

·······

How Dying Taught Me That Death Is Just the Beginning

PETER BALDWIN PANAGORE

Guideposts

New York

Hampton Roads Publishing Company, Inc.
Charlottesville, VA 22906
Distributed by Red Wheel/Weiser, LLC
WWW.REDWHEELWEISER.COM

Sign up for our newsletter and special offers by going to www.redwheelweiser.com/newsletter/.

ISBN: 978-1-57174-734-1

Library of Congress Cataloging-in-Publication Data is available on request

Printed in the United States of America
M&G
10 9 8 7 6 5 4 3 2 1

For Mom and Dad

Contents

Lower Weeping Wall on Cirrus Mountain, Banff National Park, Alberta, Canada, where the author died, crossed over, and then came back to life. Photograph by Peter Valchev.

*We are not human beings having a
spiritual experience; we are spiritual
beings having a human experience.*

—Pierre Teilhard de Chardin

Introduction

"My thoughts are nothing like your thoughts," says the Lord. "And my ways are far beyond anything you could imagine."
—Isaiah 55:8 (NLT)

This is the story of how I died, why I came back, and what has become of me since.

Dying changed my life forever. I am not the same person I was before that transformative night. There are a hundred times that I wish and pray it had never happened. But it did, on March 20, 1980. I was stuck on a mountain, stranded in the wilderness, in the bitter cold, with no way down. Only by the grace of God am I here today.

The first time I told my story was five years after my accident, in 1985, to my bride-to-be on the night before our wedding. *Better late than never,* I thought. I had struggled with telling her but finally decided she needed to know what she was getting into before she married me.

After that, I never told another person—until my friend Bryan witnessed an incident in my presence.

I was the only trained responder at the scene of a bad car wreck, and I prayed over one of the men whose injuries were internal, which meant that the only thing I could do was to treat him for shock and pray. Suddenly a bolt of electricity surged through me repeatedly and into the man I was caring for. I did not know what was happening, only that somehow I was a conduit for the power of God.

Once we were back in our car driving south again, all of a sudden all the pain suffered by the accident victim was inexplicably transferred to me. I writhed and screamed in agony and screamed for many minutes, much to my friend's disconcertion and fear, until I felt and "saw" a cross that was atop a steeple by the side of the highway leap at me and somehow strike me. Just as suddenly, the pain vanished.

I know how kooky this sounds and looked to my friend. This happened when we were in divinity school together in 1986, and afterward, I felt I had to explain myself; so I told him my tale.

It wasn't until a Sunday in 2001 that I spoke of my near-death experience (NDE) again. I was the minister of the Congregational Church of Boothbay Harbor, Maine, and our community was going through great hardship. We had suffered through ten years of embezzlement by a church member and incredible fallout due to it. The people of the church were stressed, anxious, and exhausted. On one Sunday morning, just before church, a parishioner asked me "how my faith had endured unshakably" through a decade of church turmoil. His question made me stop in my tracks. He asked about my faith, and for the first time I understood the profound shift within myself. My faith? What near-death experiencer has need of faith when he *knows* God is Real? I realized it was time to finally tell my congregants the truth about who I was. Right then and there I scrapped the sermon I'd spent half a week on and stood in the pulpit, ready to share my story and why I would say I have no faith.

Alarming words to read, I know, especially coming from the mouth of a Christian minister. But that is the plain truth. My faith in God did not sustain me in the pulpit through the dark times in our church. I was sustained by something else, by something that I had learned when I died: *I know that I am known by God* and *I know that God is Real.*

In the same way that I don't believe in snow or birds or trees because I can see them and experience them with my all of my senses, knowing they're real, I do not have to "believe" in God, because God is Real. God is as real to me as snow or birds or trees. Truly, God is more Real to me than any of those things. God is the only Real there is—and that is what this story is all about.

Since finally sharing my NDE story from the pulpit that Sunday morning to a surprised and appreciative congregation, I stopped holding it in. It was time to be honest about my newfound understanding of the Realness of God. My church and I had suffered greatly during that decade of embezzlement; yet through that dark time God was always with me, and is with me now inescapably— not because of who I am, but because of who God is. I told my story publicly that first time to help my congregation begin the healing process.

Since then, I have told my story to audiences large and small, to individuals over coffee, to the terminally ill, to the grieving, and from coast to coast. I am thankful to God that in my ministry, my death and return to life have turned me into something of a reverse midwife. Instead of catching babies as they enter this world, I've eased the passage of the dying into the next and much more beautiful world.

I tell my story not to ease the dying process, for dying, I have seen so many times, can be terribly painful, or quietly peaceful, or shockingly sudden. I tell my story here for the reasons that I always tell it: to give hope that is stronger than death, to give courage to the fearful, to give faith to the wavering and faithless, to take the sting from death, to ease grief, to teach that love is eternal and that beauty beyond words awaits us all on the other side. And, I also tell it to help those like me who have had a near-death experience to find their voice, to speak their truth, and to know what I did not, and could not, know for decades: *You are not alone.* There are many like us. More and more of us return each day through the miracles of modern medicine.

Let me add that like all NDEers, there has always been a volcano in my soul to speak about this, and there still is. The strange thing is that the more I've thought about that experience in the wilderness over the decades, the more details I remember. To date, this is the clearest account. There is a saying attributed to Pierre Teilhard de Chardin that captures my inner space, the center of my experience where I live today and have lived since that day in March of 1980: "We are not human beings having a spiritual experience. We are spiritual beings having a human experience." I am proof of that.

Fear not. God is with us, intimately and personally, immanent and transcendent, and God will catch each of us because God loves each of us as if we are God's only beloved. God will catch us when the door of death opens to swallow us whole, and wholly, and we depart this shell of flesh and bone and find ourselves in the inexplicable beauty and love of God's eternal Home prepared for us.

The author two years after his near-death experience, atop the summit marker on Mount Madison in White Mountain National Forest, New Hampshire, 1982. Photograph by Don Scott.

Here is a test to find whether
your mission on earth is finished:
If you're alive, it isn't.

—Richard Bach, *Illusions*

∽ 1 ∼

Goat Foot Boys Get Gear

The first time I met Tim, I was walking the five or so blocks from my off-campus room over to the student lounge on the Montana State University campus, in Bozeman, where I was a national exchange student for the year. It was a sunny, polar-cold afternoon with a near gale blowing down from the north, and we wanted to talk about spring break. For weeks I had been trying to figure out how not to go back home to Massachusetts for break. I played with the idea of Newport Beach, California, or anywhere warm that was not home, until the day I visited the Outdoor Recreation Program's bulletin board. I was a member of the program and had helped two other fellows lead a backpacking trip for twenty-one students up into the Grand Tetons in Wyoming the previous October. I thought I might find a high adventure trip to use as an excuse to stay out west.

My folks had wanted me home in March but had come around to accepting my backpacking adventures. As a kid, I had grown up with my sister playing in the woodlands behind our house, and as a Boy Scout I had learned the wilderness and leadership skills that I needed when backpacking above the tree line. They had, over time, come to expect that at the drop of a rag wool hat I would head into the mountains of New England to backpack for days or weeks at a time, and that I might even hitchhike to get there and back. I had just turned twenty-one and felt independent and invincible.

I was in luck—tacked on the bulletin board outside the recreation office was a colored flyer that read:

Ice Climbing and Back Country Ski Partner Wanted.

Experience a necessity. Join me for eight days of snow caving in Canada's Mount Assiniboine Providial Park, followed by a day of ice climbing on the world famous Lower Weeping Wall. I am an experienced lead climber. You are experienced in winter camping, backcountry Nordic skiing, and in technical climbing. Call Tim at . . .

I tore off a tab with his name and number and pocketed it. Visiting the Canadian winter wilderness sounded like a good time to me. From his note, Tim seemed organized and seasoned, and I decided to give him a call when I got back to the Men's Co-op a few blocks from campus where I had a room. The co-op was a relatively clean boardinghouse with a big front porch, which was a great place for leaving skis or bicycles without fear of them being stolen.

I shared a room with a theater troupe friend with whom I planned to travel after spring break on a national tour to fourteen western states. That tour would take us over 24,000 miles, to perform in sixty shows with

Montana State University's Theater of Silence, a company of performers who spoke in American Sign Language and annually presented performances to the western deaf community. The fifteen performers in our troupe had been in rehearsal for months, and we were leaving to tour in early April. Originally, I had intended to stay at Montana State only through January and then return to UMass; but after auditioning for this theater troupe and landing a role, with my parents' blessing and encouragement, I had stayed out west.

I called Tim, and he agreed to meet me in the student lounge in the comfy chairs for an interview. Backcountry skiing, backpacking, and technical climbing in the remote Canadian Rockies in the dead of winter was easily twice as dangerous as summer simply because cold weather can kill. Tim had to be sure I could handle it.

While we sat in the student lounge, I told Tim about my backpacking trips and my years on the National Ski Patrol. I was experienced and had the necessary skills, but more than that I wanted Tim to know he could trust me with his life. For his part, Tim told me about his skills in the high country backpacking and climbing on rock and ice.

Tim was an experienced lead climber. This meant that he was skilled at picking the right routes up a rock or ice face and had mastered the techniques of climbing itself—most importantly, placing protection like chocks or ice screws on rock and ice for safety in case of a fall. I enjoyed technical climbing and had been doing it for about three years. I had a natural capacity for it. I liked the mental focus of climbing, the coordination needed, and the physical fitness it required. I climbed everything that looked like it could be climbed.

Tim said that he wanted to spend one of our days in Canada ice climbing. I had never ice climbed before, and had never thought much about it. Tim described the unique equipment involved in ice climbing. It sounded exciting, technical, and dangerous—just perfect for me. Ice climbing would be a new challenge, and I loved challenges, so I said, "Yes, let's go ice climbing and backcountry winter camping."

By the time we'd hashed everything out, we decided that we could trust each other. It was apparent that we could get along with each other, too. The one area where we differed was that I was a spiritual person and Tim was an atheist. We agreed not to talk about religion or God.

We began to plan our trip to spend seven days in Mount Assiniboine Provincial Park backcountry skiing and snow caving, with one day climbing the world-famous Lower Weeping Wall along the Icefields Parkway in Alberta. It would be a ten-day trip overall, including driving time. Tim had the topographic maps we needed, and we pored over them as we planned our skiing route. Over the next few weeks, we gathered our deep winter gear.

Tim owned a lot of the climbing gear that we would use on our trip, including rope, ice screws, nylon webbing, carabiners, crampons, thin line, ice axes, an ice hammer, and ice climbing boots. I did not own any technical climbing gear. I had always rented gear from my outing club at UMass, and I certainly did not own any ice climbing gear. "We'll use my rope, ice screws, carabiners, and webbing to make a harness for you," Tim said. "You'll need to find axes, a hammer, ice climbing boots, and crampons of your own."

As a penniless college student working in the school's food service flipping pancakes, I was unable to afford any more gear beyond my Epoke 900 skis, backcountry Nordic ski boots, gators, and a backpack I had bought in Bozeman using some of my student loan money. I had my gas stove (an Optimus 8R), a sleeping pad, a mess kit, water bottles, a compass, and everything else needed for safe winter camping and wilderness backpacking, except for a deep winter sleeping bag, rated to -30°F. I borrowed one from a generous friend, along with her backpacking shovel for digging out snow caves.

Eventually, I gathered all the gear I needed except for a second ice axe, climbing boots, and crampons, spikes worn on the boots necessary for ice climbing. You cannot ice climb without them. I had rented a pair once before for a backpacking trip in the Grand Tetons where we traversed and went glissading on a glacier, a very fun technique of sliding down a glacier using an ice axe to slow the descent and to stop.

I rented one axe, a hammer, and crampons and so solved most of my equipment problems, or so I thought. I still had to buy, borrow, or rent ice climbing boots. These are specially designed for ice climbing; they are constructed of stiff plastic with insulation to keep your feet warm and have ridged soles that have no flex. They are expensive; a new pair was way beyond my reach. Not having a pair nearly scuttled our trip. "Try finding a used pair of old-time stiff leather alpine ski boots from the sixties," Tim suggested. "They'll be as flat-soled, inflexible, and warm as fancy ice climbing boots." So one snowy afternoon after classes, I walked over to a Bozeman thrift shop where I had purchased wool pants and a wool shirt for our trip. The shop also carried old ski gear. Among the shoes and boots, I found what I was looking for—a pair of old, black leather, buckle-style ski boots in my size. With the boots acquired, that left one last piece of essential equipment: a second ice axe.

In those days, ice axes had straight shafts (today the shafts are more Z-shaped). The shaft is a couple feet long. At the top of the shaft is a serrated bird beak called the pick that, when swung, is used to bite into the ice. The beak sets into the ice and holds there. The shaft, with its spike at the bottom, is then leaned toward the ice so that the spike also sets firmly into the ice. The axe forms a right triangle against the ice wall. Partway up the shaft is usually an O-ring or a hole drilled through the shaft. Through this O-ring or hole a narrow ribbon on nylon webbing is tied in a loop, called the leash. My leash had a bead on it, so that when my hand was through the leash, the bead could be slipped toward my wrist, tightening it. This meant that when the axe was set properly into the ice, I could let go of the shaft and dangle safely by my wrist. It sounds much scarier and more dangerous than it actually is. Also, the leash prevents the possibility of accidentally dropping the axe.

Ice hammers look and function almost exactly like ice axes, except for a few important factors. Ice hammers are smaller, and they have much shorter shafts/handles. The nylon leash is affixed directly to the bottom of the handle instead of the middle. Ice hammers are primarily used to chip at the ice and to use as an ice screwdriver. In the latter function, the hammer is used to spin ice screws into the ice and set them firmly; here, the mechanics are actually more like a wrench than a screwdriver. Ice hammers can also bite into the ice just like ice axes; they can, just like ice axes, be set in such a way that they can support the full weight of a climber. I know this firsthand. The problem with using a hammer instead of an axe is that the climber can never let go of the hammer and dangle on the leash. A person attempting to dangle on a hammer leash causes the bottom of the hammer shaft/handle to pull away from the ice wall, causing the "beak" to release from the ice. I learned this firsthand, too.

Once we had all our gear collected, we packed for our trip. To lighten our loads while backcountry Nordic skiing, we bought expensive freeze-dried food for the week; between us, we carried enough white gas for our stove to last the duration. Our backpacks weighed about twice what we normally carried on our backs for a week walking in the high country since winter backpacking requires additional, heavier gear. In spring, summer, and fall, I carried about thirty-five pounds in my backpack. Our winter packs weighed about seventy pounds each by the time we gathered and packed everything we needed to survive and enjoy the subzero winter weather in Mount Assiniboine Provincial Park, British Columbia. I knew that this would be the most difficult wilderness challenge of my life, and I couldn't wait for it.

≈ 2 ≈

Immortal Youth

Like many families, my family had our share of trouble. I was in Montana to escape it. I'd picked Bozeman because it was far away from Massachusetts and our family crisis, which had dragged on for decades. It started when my sister Andrea was a child, and she accidently hung herself by her cowgirl hat while bouncing on her bed. Our mom had told her not to bounce on the bed, but she did. Our mom was in another room when she heard silence from Andrea's room. Mom dashed in to find her hanging by her neck on the hat string. Andrea had turned blue. They rushed her to the hospital, where the doctors put her in an oxygen tent. Our dad spent the next forty-eight hours in bed with Andrea, holding her in his arms. When she came home from the hospital, she was not the same person. A light had gone out of her eyes. Years went by, and I did not know her any other way than she'd become.

When I was fourteen, on the night of Andrea's high school graduation, she did not come home. Two days later, when she did finally return, having not called, there was a huge scene between her and my parents. The summer continued to be tumultuous. Every dinner was a battlefield. That fall, Andrea went off to the Massachusetts College of Art and Design, but she lasted less than a semester. She had been home about a week when she vanished. Mom was in a panic. She had been talking about her friends in Boston, so Dad took time off from work to see if he could find her.

One day, weeks later, I walked in to find Andrea sitting at the kitchen table. Mom was delousing her hair and boiling her lousy clothes in a pot on the stove. Over dinner, I learned that Dad had seen her in Boston Common with a bunch of hippies. He grabbed her and brought her home. Less than a week after that episode, I got home from school to find the house empty. I expected Andrea to be there and was concerned that she wasn't. My concern shifted to fear when I went to get my backpack and gear out of the attic for an upcoming Boy Scout trip. My pack was gone, along with my sleeping bag and my mess kit.

I knew she'd taken it. I was hurt because in my gut I knew she'd gone, and gone for good. I was angry too, though, because she'd stolen my new pack and my gear and I knew that I could not go camping that weekend, which meant I had to stay home with all the trouble and tension that was simmering. It boiled over that night. The next day my dad took off to Boston again, as he did every day for the next few weeks, to try to find her. He never did. It broke our mother's heart and spirit, too. The ensuing years brought tears upon tears, as the silence deepened and the brokenheartedness reached a devastating level. Each Christmas, we would get a postcard with no return address, so we knew she was alive. Each night our mom would stand alone in the dark of the dining room, holding the curtain back with one hand, staring down Church Street, quietly crying and watching for her prodigal daughter's return.

My senior year in high school, around the time I turned eighteen, in February, Andrea returned with a two-year-old baby in her arms. Our parents welcomed her back, set her up in her own apartment, and found her a job at the public library. I visited the two of them every day after school, for a month, until the day I went to her apartment and found a note on the counter. Andrea said that she was hitchhiking with the baby to the annual Rainbow Family Gathering, which was being held in Virginia that year. It was snowing the day she left. If Andrea's running away the first time broke our mother's heart, her leaving the second time, with a grandbaby on a snowy Saint Patrick's Day, drove our loving mom to a near nervous collapse.

The next year, Andrea was arrested in Oregon for neglect of her three-year-old daughter, Lumeria, and newborn daughter, Ruby. She called home, and our parents paid the bail. The kids were put in foster care. She then fled to Canada. Social services separated the two babies in good homes—one in the East and one in the West. Suffice it to say that during those years my family lived in the deepening pain of estrangement. My home university, the University of Massachusetts Amherst, where I was an English major, was too close to my hometown of Marlborough, where everybody knew us, and where my prominent family struggled to hide our plight in plain sight. Everyone I knew, and everyone who knew us, was respectful of our public silence on the subject of my missing sister. But the last place I wanted to live on earth at that point in my life was anywhere near my family. I needed to escape.

Montana was far, far away from the pain that was my family. The year I spent there was the most terrifying and wonderful year of my life.

In late summer I headed directly into the Montana wilderness, into deep nature that radiates God's Spirit and always, then as now, touches and enlivens my soul, for a month of backpacking with an old friend from England. We met up at Old Faithful at high noon on a certain day inside Yellowstone National Park. Jerry had hitched from Ohio, and I hitched from Bozeman. Together we hitched to trailhead of the high peaks inside Gallatin National Forest. In Bozeman we picked up Richard, and then hitched to the Beartooth Mountains, near Absarokee, Montana, where Jerry broke his ankle a day's hike in. We fashioned him a splint and a crutch and divided his gear between Richard and me and made our way out to the highway to get medical help. Even so, I loved the trip. At Christmas I went home for a brief visit and then quickly fled back to Montana State University for my winter trimester.

As for my sister, my family did not see or hear from Andrea again until I was halfway through my three years at Yale University in the Divinity School. By then, my beautiful and soul-filled sister was married and had been living in Jamaica for seven years. She left her husband and returned to our family home for Christmas that one year, and then she moved to South Beach, Florida, where she lived for many years. I kept in contact with her. Our parents visited with her in Florida. One night in 2007 Andrea fell asleep and went Home to God, God rest her soul, and we rested, too, because her true self rests in God's Love.

⚘ 3 ⚘

Into a Dangerous Foreign Land

That same summer, Tim's dad had given him a new Toyota sedan. And because it was new and a gift from his dad, Tim refused to let me help with the twelve-hour drive from Bozeman through Banff, Alberta, and then on to Mount Assiniboine Provincial Park. His dad had warned him never to let anyone drive his car and not to get a scratch on it, and Tim was adamant about following his dad's rules.

On March Break, just before sunset on the first day of our drive, we pulled into a roadside rest stop to spend the night. We boiled water on our camp stove and ate a freeze-dried dinner, pulled out our sleeping pads and sleeping bags, and slept on top of a couple picnic tables. We awoke in the morning with six inches of fresh powder snow covering us, but we were warm and snug in our sleeping bags.

That morning we left for Mount Assiniboine Provincial Park and arrived around noon. We parked Tim's car on a side road in a small, empty parking lot, strapped on our three-pin skis, hefted our seventy-pound backpacks, and skied across a snow-covered lake, using our compass

Mount Assiniboine with Sunburst Lake. Photograph by Kurt Stegmüller.

to head toward a log cabin that was clearly marked on our USGS topographic map.

By dinnertime we had found the *location* of the log cabin owned by the park, but strangely we could not find the cabin itself. The long shadows from the tall mountains around us cast a darkness hours before sunset. We knew time was limited and hunted for the cabin for an hour or more. When we could not find it, we skied back to the lake edge—about a hundred yards away—and using our compass skills, we triangulated our position using three mountain peaks within view that corresponded to three mountain peaks on our map. We were where we were supposed to be.

We figured out and verified the exact spot where the cabin should have been according to the map and skied back to that spot. The cabin was not there. We were frustrated and nervous. We had not brought a tent with us. Back in Bozeman, we had carefully researched and mapped our ski route, noting cabins and places to dig snow caves along the way. We'd intentionally not brought a large and heavy tent which, if we were to divide the weight equally, would have added about four pounds each to our already seventy-pound packs. Thus, the tent was in Tim's car, some ten or more miles across the lake.

Darkness was falling. We were on the windward side of the lake, so the snow was not deep on our side—meaning we would not find snow deep enough to dig a snow cave. Tim hunted for snowdrift anyway as I continued to hunt for the cabin. As we skied around the area, my ski got caught under something. At first, I assumed it was a downed tree branch. I backed off to free my ski and then dug around in the snow to find that my ski had been hooked under the charred remains of a cabin log. I called Tim over, and together we dug around until we discovered that the cabin had burned to the ground, literally only two logs high.

This was bad news. It gets very dark in the forest very quickly, especially among the mountains, and as the evening shadows lengthen, the air cools rapidly. Here it was, the first day of our adventure, and we were already in trouble. It was too far to ski back to the car, and even if we did get across the lake in the subzero cold that we knew was coming, we would never find the car in the dark. Death on our first night out became a possibility.

Again, we talked about heading back to the car, but the car was too far away and we were too exhausted from the long ski across the lake to make it back there. Our only choice was to ski along to the edge of the lake to see if we could find some kind of natural shelter.

The sun had already sunk behind the mountain peaks when, along the bank of the lake, we spotted a frozen water seep that had created an ice flow slab overhanging the lake. The ice made a small sort of cave—or, rather, the roof of what *could* be a cave if we could build walls of snow and ice around it. Under the ice flow, there was just enough room for both of us to lie down side by side with our noses just about touching the ice flow above us. It was a tight squeeze.

I have never really liked being in caves or tight spaces, but it would have to do for the night. We were happy we found possible shelter, but the clock was ticking; night was falling quickly, we were hungry, and it was getting colder by the minute. The wind was blowing on the lake, too, making the air feel even chillier. We had to act quickly to close off the open sides so we could create a warm and safe shelter. Using our shovels and our mittened hands, we cut and broke ice chunks from along the shoreline until we had enough large and thick pieces of ice and snow. These we placed like blocks alongside the flow, leaving one side open so that we could crawl inside.

The experience was quite the way to get to know and trust Tim. We both kept our heads, remained calm, and worked together with near-silent efficiency. I learned then and there that Tim was one to keep his cool in an emergency situation—and Tim learned the same about me. We bonded that night. Little did we know that the day's lesson—learning to trust that the other would stay calm in a life-threatening situation—would be key to our survival on our upcoming ice climb. Surviving in the winter backcountry takes skill, knowledge, the right equipment, and a huge trust in your partner, because your life can and will depend upon him or her. Being in the wilderness is dangerous enough. Being in the wilderness in deep winter is doubly dangerous. I silently thanked God that I was with Tim.

The author's remaining gear from 1980: aluminum gas can, green Polartec booties, plastic honey bottle, compass, blue gator, Epoke skis, and Kletterwerks backpack. Photograph by Peter Panagore.

Once we got the shelter closed off, we fired up our stove, melted ice to a boil, and "cooked" our freeze-dried dinner just before complete darkness fell. Using our flashlights, we hung our packs on trees, unrolled our sleeping pads and tucked them into our ice shelter, then unstuffed our sleeping bags and pulled them up over our bodies as if they were pants. We wriggled, like worms, feet first into the opening we'd left in our makeshift shelter.

Neither of us slept much that night. Mostly, we just tried to rest, uncomfortable but warm and safe, as tightly packed as sardines in a can, with the cold outside and the noise of the ice flow crackling above us. All night long, the lake boomed and shuddered as the temperature dropped and the lake froze ever deeper. The ice flow above us, touching my nose at times, also cracked and shifted around us. Our shelter was claustrophobic. It was disconcerting. I kept thinking, throughout the night, that the thick and heavy flow might crack off at any moment and pin us in our sleeping bags, where we would be found in a week's time or longer, frozen to death. I had never thought about freezing to death before, but I thought about it all that night—about the possibility of being crushed in place and then frozen. I believed I would feel pain if the ice were to pin us, but I also wondered if freezing to death would be as peaceful as it is portrayed in the movies.

⇜ 4 ⇝

In the Morning

Yet, we were warm and safe when the sun rose the next morning. And our spirits rose with it, renewed in equal parts by the stunning beauty around us in the morning light as well as by our clever, lifesaving use of a found shelter to survive the night.

The next several days were glorious. We skied many miles into the park and didn't see anybody else the entire time. We dug and lived in a luxurious snow cave for two nights on the way out, and two nights on the way back—it had beds, shelving, a "kitchen," a chimney, comfortable seating, and a heater (a burning candle). Everything except our heater was carved by hand from snow. It got so warm inside our one-room snow cave that we could strip down to our long underwear.

Farther along into the park, we also spent two nights in a log cabin that was marked on our topographic map. In the cabin we found bunk beds, thin mattresses, a woodstove, plenty of wood, and a supply of canned food. We celebrated our comfort and warmth by eating one can of beans.

On our sixth day of having a great time, after our last two nights in our luxury snow cave, we skied out and back toward Tim's car. Throughout the entire ski trip, the snow on the ground was about ten feet deep. Whenever we moved about, we had to keep our skis on. If I were ever to do it again, I think I would bring along snowshoes, too.

When we got back to the lake, the wind was blowing hard against our backs. There was not much snow on the lake, so we took out our ground tarps, tied the tarps to our ski poles with string, and *sailed* over the ice on our skis, back to Tim's Toyota. It was terrific fun to ski-sail on ice! We laughed most of the way.

That afternoon, once we reached the car and stowed our gear, we drove north to lovely Jasper, Alberta, to get a hot and fresh meal at a diner and to buy more food. It was the day before our ice climb on Lower Weeping Wall.

After stocking up on provisions, we left Jasper, driving south on Icefields Parkway, Route 93, and stopping at a park ranger's cabin just a few miles north of our climb. A local in Jasper had mentioned that there might be bunks available there. So, we knocked on the ranger's door and asked if he could give us bunks for the night. He could and kindly did. I think we may have cooked him dinner to thank him before heading to bed.

The next morning we signed into the ranger's logbook as he suggested, indicating that we were going to climb Lower Weeping Wall, a famous ice climb in Banff National Park. People from all over the world go there to climb. Not being an ice climber, I had never heard of it until Tim told me about it, assuring me it was really, really amazing, which it turned out to be.

Signing the logbook allowed us to enter the wilderness area where the Weeping Wall was located. Anytime hikers, backpackers, or climbers enter a wilderness area, they are supposed to sign in, indicate where they intend to go, for how long, and then, upon leaving, sign out. That way the officials can keep track of how many people are in an area so as to control overcrowding and people's safety. It is easy to get lost or injured in wilderness areas; they can be as dangerous as they are beautiful. If someone does not return from the wilderness on or near the day indicated, a search party will be mounted.

⊂ 5 ⊃

Lower Weeping Wall

Lower Weeping Wall is on the eastern side off the highway, about a hundred yards in. There was a small parking area directly across the highway from the climb. It was not too far from the Columbia Icefield, either, in the middle of that vast Canadian wilderness. Unlike the American Rocky Mountains I have seen, the Canadian Rockies rise pretty much vertically. They're comparatively geologically young; and as such, they are very high mountains that have not been eroded to the extent of the American Rockies.

Lower Weeping Wall lies on the side of Cirrus Mountain, which rises to nearly 11,000 feet about sea level. The ice climb itself was about 450 feet up, or about 45 stories tall; it is considered a water ice grade 4 or WI4, meaning that the climb is nearly vertical for thirty-two feet at a stretch, requiring continuous, exhausting climbing, along with placement of ice screws into the ice for protection. That equates to quite the climb for a first-time ice climber, but I was game, fit, and, like most young people, I believed in my own immortality and invincibility.

We were the last team to arrive at the wall that morning. By the time we hiked in on the tramped-down snow path, there were four or five other climbing teams—amounting to maybe twenty persons—already on the ice and climbing above us. We stopped and dropped our gear to watch the teams climb on the blue and white ice. The ice was beautiful: it looked like a waterfall had been flowing and then instantly froze in place. Tim took a minute to point out the abundance of blue ice on the ice flow. Blue ice, he explained, is hard ice and the best ice for climbing. We were going to have a great day, and we both chatted excitedly as we prepared for our climb.

Within about ten minutes of our arrival, a lead climber on one of the teams screamed as he fell. I'd been watching him lead up on the ice. Being first, he was the one who had climbed the highest, and he moved with a deliberate dexterity. I heard him before I saw him. He must have dropped about fifteen or twenty feet, right down past the last ice screw that he'd placed for his own protection. He had been about 100 feet up on his climb when he fell, plummeting straight down as he screamed. I had been fixing my gear when I heard him and looked up. He was on his rope, and "on belay" (meaning his partner had tight control of his climbing rope). The lead climber bounced a few times at the end of his rope, then smacked hard against the ice wall.

Nobody moved. We all held our breath as he dangled there, watching for signs of life. I felt a jolt of adrenaline course through my blood and tasted metal on my tongue. I was sure that every climber there felt that same surge and tasted that same taste, all of us prepared to spring into action.

Then, he moved . . . and righted himself. I think we collectively exhaled the breath we'd been holding as he waved his arms and shouted, "I'm okay." He had not dropped his axes. After a moment, he set his right axe, then his left, and then he kicked the toes of his crampons into the ice and stood there. We all whooped and cheered.

It had given us all a fright, the climber most of all, no doubt. For a minute I'd thought that our climb might be done before it began. My mood had shifted from joy to seriousness. I felt that everybody there had experienced that same shift, too.

As he continued his climb, we watched him ascend to the last screw he'd placed—the screw that had saved his life. He paused there and, using his ice hammer as a tool, tugged on that screw to make sure it was still secure. Satisfied, he continued his climb.

Tim and I watched him set his next screw and heard the lead climber shout, "Off belay!" His partner returned the call, shouting, "Off belay." Next, his partner shouted, "On belay," and the lead climber returned the call: "On belay." This meant that the lead climber was stopping in order to allow his partner to climb up. In other words, the partner was no longer holding the rope to protect the leader; the leader was now protecting the partner.

And so it is in ice climbing, with each holding the life of the other literally in his or her hands. Tim and I rested a bit to allow the adrenaline rush to subside. Watching that climber fall had made me nervous, and I tried to calm myself with a few minutes of meditation.

Tim was our lead climber; and it was his responsibility to carry all the ice screws up the ice face and place them appropriately and at the proper distance from one another—as protection against falling. Tim had trained as an ice climb leader with professionals, but this was his first solo ice lead. All lead ice climbers need superior skills.

There are subtle nuances to properly placing ice screws. A lead climber must pay attention to ice shatter as the screw is placed, and must "clean" the ice below the screw to ensure that the gate of the carabiners clipped to the screw does not open and allow the rope to escape.

Ice screws are surprisingly small, ranging in size from 10 cm to about 23 cm. In my day, they were placed into the ice at about a 10-degree angle, nearly horizontal. In the years since, after experimentation, it was discovered that a slight upward angle has proven to be a stronger and more secure setting. As the partner, it was my job to clean up the ice screws behind Tim by unscrewing them and carrying them clipped and dangling from my tool belt, in the same way that Tim was carrying them to set them. It is one of the sounds of climbing: ice screws, 'biners, draws, and such jingle together when carried. Tim used his hammer to screw the ice screws into the ice, while I used my hammer to unscrew each one later.

As we prepared to climb, I chose to use my one ice axe in my left hand and an ice hammer in my right hand. It seemed like a workable idea at the time. As it turned out, it was an ignorant choice on my part, maybe the worst choice I've ever made in my life.

Having checked our gear and finding that everything was in order, we wrapped long lengths of blue webbing around our legs and waists to create our harnesses, the webbing tied neatly and securely in square knots. We each picked a locking carabiner and attached it to our harness. Our lives depended on that carabiner and harness. We checked each other's harness and carabiner by tugging on them, just to make sure everything was done correctly. Next, we strapped on our crampons. Tim clipped on his collection of ice screws, carabiners, and slings (webbing lengths individually tied together in square knots). I slung my hammer on its sling over my shoulder, and picked up our coiled rope. Tim had his two axes, and I carried my one axe and my climbing hammer. The sun was shining. It was warm enough for a March day. We were excited, yet a bit trepidatious at the onset of our adventure, and very, very focused.

At the very bottom of the climb, Tim said, "I'm putting my life in your hands. I trust you." I replied in kind, and we began our ascent. Tim approached the ice, stopped, and looked over at me as I stood a few feet behind. He looked up the ice wall and then shouted, "On belay." I replied, "On belay." We were off.

The looped end of our doubled rope was tied in a bowline knot to his locking carabiner clipped to his harness. The bitter (or free) ends of our doubled rope were tied as one knot to my locking carabiner, which was clipped to my harness. As Tim was the lead, our rope was wrapped around my waist. I also held the rope in my right and left mittened hands, paying out the rope slowly while keeping a bit of tension on the line as Tim climbed up, setting the first swing of his right ice axe.

He climbed with ease and concentration, making sure that each swing of his axe bit securely into the ice, and that with each setting of the crampons on his feet his footing was secure. At about fifteen feet up, Tim stopped. It was time to place our first protective ice screw. I watched as he searched the ice just above him for a good place to set his left ice axe, then set and anchored it firmly and securely. No climber wants to burn out his or her calves, so Tim reached down with his right axe and chopped a step into the ice for his right foot; this way, he could stand more comfortably.

Now, he had to pick where to place his first screw. He chose a spot in the ice near his waist area on his right-hand side because it was easier to apply pressure with his arm. Tim cleaned the ice by chipping the bad (softer) ice away from the good (harder) ice underneath. Next, he chipped a starter hole in the ice, chipping in the same spot until he created a divot, and then he grabbed one of his screws from the harness rack hanging at his waist, put its end on the ice, pressed in, and turned it by hand. The screw bit into the ice. He grabbed the screw again and very carefully twisted it while pushing in. When he could not screw it in any farther, he used his ice axe as a wrench, turning the screw in the rest of the way, setting it almost firmly in place. A bumpy piece in the surface of the ice stopped him from turning the screw just that little bit more it needed, so he chipped it away, cleaned the ice a little extra, and then finished setting the screw securely using his axe as his wrench.

"Placing ice screws as protection is the hardest part about climbing ice," Tim had told me. Watching him above me, I started to believe it. He unclipped one the carabiners from his waist. It had a sling of webbing clipped into it, with a second carabiner at the other end. The first carabiner was clipped into the ice screw, and the second was clipped over our rope. Tim tugged the rope against the screw. Feeling good about it, he continued up as I waited below and payed out the line. At about fifteen feet above his first ice screw, Tim stopped and set another ice screw for protection. He stopped, and shouted, "Off belay." I replied, "Off belay."

I approached the ice wall and shouted, "On belay." Tim replied, "On belay." He tensioned the rope. I looked up and saw Tim and the other climbing teams. I took a breath to focus my head, and began the first and last ice climb of my life.

I started the day fresh and strong and began my climb with care, focus, and strength. When I reached the first ice screw Tim had placed, I stopped, unscrewed it from the ice, clipped it to my harness, and unclipped it from our rope. All the way up the 450-foot climb, for the entire day, we repeated this series of moves. Tim would climb and set the screws, and I would follow and remove the screws, with all the aluminum clinking and clanking from our harnesses.

By mid-morning, my right arm was exhausted because I could not rest it by hanging from the leash on my ice hammer. The muscles of my right arm would continue screaming for the rest of our climb, severely slowing our ascent. Unlike all the other climbers on the face that day, I had to stop frequently, and for longer and longer periods, to rest my right arm. You may think that I could have switched the hammer to my left arm and the ice axe to my right arm, right? Yes, I thought of that. I thought a lot about that . . . and I wished I could have done so. But that was impossible to do without falling.

Let me explain.

⤚ 6 ⤛

Just a Day Climb

When climbing, one needs to keep three points of contact at all times—two feet, and one hand, or two hands and one foot (or ice axes, as the case may be); otherwise, the climber is either dangling from two arms, or falling. Yes, one can hold on with one hand, but that takes an enormous amount of strength; and if one does do that, he or she does so only for a brief time. All of this meant that I could not switch the axe to my right hand and the ice hammer to my left. Maybe the maneuver is possible by someone far more skilled than I was, but, for the life of me, I couldn't figure out how to make the switch without falling. The hammer was in my right hand, and that was that.

As much as I wanted to switch the axe for the hammer—and I wanted it a lot—I couldn't do it. I had to hang on to that hammer with all my might every time I used it, and I used it all the time unless I was letting it dangle to rest my arm. Our climb was much, much slower by several hours than it would've been if I had been climbing with two axes. With only one, I was able to climb a little ways, then had to rest. I would climb a little more, then rest again. That's how it went all day.

Tim was anxious, as was I, because the sun was crossing the sky and we knew that every minute of delay increased the likelihood that we might end our ascent in the dark, and that would be bad. Toward the end of the day, totally exhausted because of my arm, I looked on with Tim as all the other teams completed their climbs above us and then rappelled down the three pitches of 150 feet each.

Ice climbing can be a wet sport, and I learned it the hard way that day. Whenever Tim cleaned the ice to set a screw, or chop a foothold for himself, he'd shout, "Ice!" and that ice would fall directly on or near me. It often hit me or my helmet and frequently went down the neck of my jacket, and down my back. We perspired a lot, too, of course—or at least I did.

As we climbed into the afternoon, we ate the food that we carried in our pockets for lunch and had snacks to keep our energy up. I carried my two plastic water bottles that I used for backpacking. One was quart-sized, the other a quart and a half. I drank through those carefully, measuring my water intake against my sweat outflow. Occasionally, I would pop a piece of ice into my mouth, as much to cool me down as to give me drink. We'd planned to carry enough food and water to get us to the top, since rappelling down was so quick and easy; we figured we would be down by late afternoon, and cooking dinner beside our tent well before sunset. Instead we reached the top near sunset. By the time we reached our last pitch up, I was wet to the skin, cold, and not too happy.

It was just a day climb. That is what the guidebooks say. That is what all the other climbers planned for: a day. We planned for the same, and carried only what we needed for a day climb and nothing more. We did not carry a stove or gas, or food for dinner, or sleeping bags, or any extra or extraneous gear—not even extra water or food. Nobody did. We traveled light on purpose, just like everybody else. You might guess that I've thought a lot about the mistakes we made that day . . . and I have. I attribute it to the exuberance and optimism of my youth and my false belief in my own invulnerability and immortality. In hindsight, of course, I was foolish to believe I was strong enough to climb all that way with a hammer— and I was ignorant of the hazard that choice would cause.

Meanwhile, after many hours of slow but methodical climbing, we reached the top of our climb, about 450 feet up. A climb that should have taken seven hours or less instead took us around twelve hours to complete. I say "around" because, for one, I was not wearing a watch, and, for two, my mind was focused the entire time on my task and my body, not on the passage of time . . . other than to know that time was passing, and that in passing, our situation was becoming more dangerous by the minute.

Climbing is intensely physical, but it also requires constant mental focus. This is what I enjoyed most about it: the only thing that matters when you're climbing is climbing; the rest of life completely fades away. I couldn't focus on the height, or the danger, or the fear. The fear was there for me every time I climbed, but the mastery of that fear is what made me feel alive. When climbing, there was only me—where I was, in that spot, on whatever face I was climbing. Nothing else existed except for my climbing partner and me. Here, there was nothing else to care about, think about, or consider—nothing else mattered but the task at hand. Every move must be efficient, clean, and thought through. No energy is wasted; no move is clumsy or without purpose.

When climbing, there were no concerns, no worries, no love life, no home life, no anything other than the climb itself. If my mind wandered from the task at hand or the place I was, I was putting not only my life but also my climbing partner's life in danger. Focus, focus, focus, master fear, pay attention, think only of my position at the moment and my next move—that was the name of the game.

The last section of our climb was to the small ledge on which Tim sat waiting for me, anchored into the ice by screws. The ledge was an ice-covered rock about four times the size of a twelve-seat dining table. As I crawled up over the edge, eager to rest for the first time since early that morning, I took in the view.

It was amazing. The Columbia Icefield was visible in the distance. The ice was gorgeous. But the sun was setting, and the temperature had begun to drop steeply, quickly, and steadily. Now at rest, I realized my clothes were soaked; I was wet to the skin from sweat and the ice falling down my shirt, melting against my skin. Tim was wet, too. We were very cold, but not as cold as we knew we were about to be.

⇐ 7 ⇒

Alone and Cold

We began to shiver as we watched the last of the other climbing teams reach the bottom of their rappels below. We watched as the last team of three walked back to the parking lot, carrying their gear. One guy in the last team looked up at us and waved his arms. We waved back. He waved again.

We were alone, Tim and I, high on the ice mountain in the middle of a vast and empty wilderness. A feeling of foreboding overtook me, but I fought it off just as I'd fought off all of my fears all day. We were in trouble, and we knew it. It was obvious. Neither of us carried a watch, so we didn't know what time it was; but as we watched the sun set behind the distant mountain peaks to the west, we knew we had to talk about what to do and make choices soon. We remained levelheaded, but we were out of food and water, and we didn't have anything to save our lives except our wits, skills, determination, and each other.

We were not far from the parkway, a portion of which we could see; but this was the borderland of rural eastern British Columbia, and there were no cars on the road that evening. As we sat on the ledge with our legs hanging over the side, our shivering got worse. My teeth chattered, or more accurately, clattered. My jaw was just about out of my control. The noise of my teeth hitting my teeth made me think about my skull, my skeleton, my bones, my muscles that twitched all on their own, and about how fragile the human body is.

Where was the line, I thought, between my conscious mind that controlled my thoughts and movements, and the actions of my body, which suddenly seemed to have a mind of its own, making me twitch and shake, clatter and shiver. I fought to keep control. "Shivering is good because it's the body's way of producing heat," Tim told me. He was right, of course, but my chattering teeth made it difficult to talk. Tim was shivering, too, his teeth chattering.

We had not planned on spending the night up there, but we also knew that we had to consider it as an option. We were in a dangerous situation that could turn deadly. We were exposed, vulnerable, and determined not to die.

Earlier that winter, while volunteering on the National Ski Patrol, I had forced numerous skiers off of the mountain at Bridger Bowl ski resort in Bozeman because of frostbite and potential exposure during a -50°F week. That winter I had studied up on hypothermia and frostbite, so it was still fresh in my mind. Tim's and my shivers were the beginning stage of what I knew quickly could and probably soon enough would turn into hypothermic risk of death from exposure to the cold. I told Tim what I knew and about the possible stages of hypothermia. We both needed to know what its process was so we could keep an eye on each other.

Here's what happens in hypothermia: Shivering begins, and then violent shivering. The physiological responses of the body are geared to preserve heat; we're geared to survive. Hypoglycemia, or low blood sugar, may present itself as cells decrease their consumption of glucose.

Micromuscular miscoordination comes next—movements become slow and labored, accompanied by stumbling and mild confusion. Surface blood vessels contract as the body focuses its remaining resources on keeping the vital organs warm, and the skin becomes pale and sometimes blue. As body temperature decreases, further physiological systems falter; heart rate, respiratory rate, and blood pressure all decrease. Difficulty speaking, sluggish thinking, and amnesia start to appear, and a lack of coordination and stumbling are also usually present. Cellular metabolic processes shut down.

Below 86°F, exposed skin becomes blue and puffy, muscle coordination becomes very poor, walking becomes almost impossible, and the person exhibits incoherent/irrational behavior or can even go into a stupor. The pulse and respiration rates decrease significantly, but fast heart rates can occur. Major organs may fail, but because of decreased cellular activity in stage 3 hypothermia, the body will actually take longer to undergo brain death. Lastly, one falls asleep.

There is a thing called "paradoxical undressing" that occurs in up to 50 percent of hypothermia cases. The person becomes confused and begins to disrobe because he or she feels hot, which of course increases the rate of heat loss. Wikipedia says "one explanation for the effect is a cold-induced malfunction of the hypothalamus, the part of the brain that regulates body temperature. Another explanation is that the muscles contracting peripheral blood vessels become exhausted . . . and relaxed, leading to a sudden surge of blood (and heat) to the extremities, fooling the person into feeling overheated." In my case, it felt as if my core was suddenly superheated.

Only some of this had occurred so far. We sat there shivering, discussing what to do while watching the sky go dark as the stars came out. We had a choice: We could spend the night where we were and snuggle into the mountain as best we could, or we could try to get off that mountain, and fast.

If we stayed put, rescuers would find us in the morning. One of the first rules of wilderness survival is if you get lost, stay put. We had signed the logbook at the ranger's station. The climber from the last team had seen us at the top and waved as he was leaving. We were not lost, but staying put might be the best choice, if we could survive the night. In the warmth of the morning, in the daylight, we could rappel.

On the back side of the ice ledge was a vertical wall. I think it was stone, not ice. I got up to look it over. It was about ten feet from the ledge. If we could tuck our bodies against the mountain and spoon together for warmth, that might save our lives—but we were already so cold that, even together, we thought we might not produce enough body heat between us.

The way I imagined it was with Tim against the rock face with my nose to his helmeted head, snuggled against his back for warmth with my back exposed to the weather. It did not have to be me on the outside, but that is the way I came to think that whoever was on the outside likely would die, and surely the other one might, too. We had been in the mountains for more than a week, so we knew how cold it was going to be that night.

There were no clouds in the sky. That was both good and bad. It was bad because that meant that all the heat of the day, baked into the earth by the sun—though there had been little heat that sunny day—would rise and escape into the atmosphere. If there had been clouds there would have been a thermal inversion, whereby the clouds act as a sky blanket, forcing the heat to stay closer to the ground.

There was no thermal blanket of clouds overhead, but there were thousands of stars. This was the good news. We knew that it was going to be dangerous to try to escape our situation by moving around on the cliffside in the dark. We could slip and fall off. We might stumble and break a bone. We could get lost, although that was unlikely. But with thousands of stars coming out overhead, there might be just enough light to move about. It was very dangerous to stay still, maybe more dangerous than moving about. Just sitting there and talking was starting to kill us.

We decided that if we spent the night tucked up against the mountain at the back of the ledge, using each other's bodies for warmth, we were probably going to die—and if we were probably going to die by spending the night, then we'd be better off dying while trying to get down off the mountain. So, that's what we decided to do.

I was already in worse shape than Tim. My body had begun to shiver violently and uncontrollably. It was a scary feeling. I learned that night that courage is not feeling "no fear"; courage is feeling fear and moving forward bravely anyway. We were both scared, although to keep up morale neither of us talked about it. There was no point. We knew each other very well by this time. We each knew the other was afraid, but we also knew that together we were courageous, capable, and trustworthy.

~ 8 ~

Galaxies for Light

It is sobering to see one's own death nearby. It bonds people together when you know that your very survival, your heartbeat, sits in combined hands, and in the will and determination of you and your partner. Our week in the winter wilderness had taught me that Tim had a level and a rational head. He never panicked. As it turned out, neither do I. We believed in each other. We had to. And, by believing in each other, we found the strength to believe in ourselves. We were fighters. We were a team. We aimed to get off that mountain and to survive. We were embarking on what we knew was going to be the longest night of our lives.

As we sat on the cliff talking about our choice to push on, Tim was pulling up our 300-foot rope as quickly as he could. Because it was getting dark, and because we were in a desperate hurry, Tim forgot to lay the line neatly and correctly, which resulted in a 300-foot tangled knot.

More stars came out, making it easier to see. There must have been a million stars overhead, no exaggeration. When you get far enough away from light pollution, you can see every color of every visible star in the sky—red, yellow, blue, white, and orange. On that cliff we could see millions of stars and galaxies of every color. The sky was a blanket of bright twinkling lights. It was not pitch-black where we sat, as it would have been if it had been a cloudy night. If it were pitch-black out, we would have had to stay put; but because there were so many stars in the sky, they actually provided some light by which to see. We had options. Not a lot of light, but just enough.

My eyes are very light sensitive—so much so that I must wear sunglasses or a hat when I'm outside even on cloudy days. The flip side of this is that I can see pretty well in very low light, and I could see the details of the rope better than Tim could. I was then and remain today a rope man. Rope, knots, bends, lashings, and whippings have always come easily to me. Thus, it was my job to untangle our rope. But rope handling is tactile, and I needed to feel it as much as see it to succeed. This meant that I had to take off my mittens. Untangling the 300-foot knot took what felt like hours. I don't know how long it actually took, but it was long enough to set frostbite into all of my fingertips, in particular three of them on my right hand.

Ever since that night, I must wear gloves whenever the temperature falls below fifty degrees. At forty-nine degrees my fingertips ache; in colder temperatures, they tend to dry and crack and bleed. I've also discovered over the course of my lifetime that frostbite is cumulative; since that night, whenever my fingers get just a little too cold in the wintertime, the frost damage increases.

All that night, as Tim and I sat on the ledge making choices, frostnip bit into our fingertips, and the tips of our toes and noses, and on our cheeks and earlobes. As we sat there and I worked the rope, my shivering continued to increase in violence. My body was spastic, bouncing up and down, and difficult to control, making it increasingly difficult to make my hands and arms do what I wanted them to do in order to untangle the rope.

Tim, who was not in as bad of shape due to the cold as I was, kept telling me in a calm and caring voice that my shivers were a good sign, because they meant my body was trying to keep itself warm. He was right. Hearing him say it gave me heart. I think at one point he even put his hand on my shoulder as he said it. Tim is a good guy.

We sat there side by side as I untied the knots and pulled the long line through itself, always being extra careful not to drop the rope over the edge. I could not tie one end to myself until I got close to the end of my task: to untie the rope, I had to work from both ends. This made my job easier and faster, but it also increased the risk of losing the entire line over the side. I never let the rope dangle down, as I might have done during daylight, or if I could've tied one end to myself. That meant I had to be particularly careful to lay the line safely and correctly every time I untangled or untied a section.

Tim was mostly silent while I concentrated on the line. At one point, he said, "The moon is going to rise, and when it does, we'll have more light to move about with added safety." In any case, we had to wait for the moon to rise because even though I could see pretty well in low light, Tim could not. The starlight was just not bright enough of a light source for us to be able to stand and walk safely.

Eventually, I untangled the entire line. My violent shivers and chattering teeth lasted for hours. I'm pretty sure that by the time I finished untangling and setting the rope, Tim had the violent shivers, too.

As Tim had predicted, a near three-quarter moon rose over the mountain ridge, casting a lot more light. Suddenly, we could see just about everything there was to see. We could almost see the colors of our clothing and could definitely see the valley below us, the mountains around us, the Columbia Icefield to the west—and, most importantly, the details of the mountain where we sat. I had never been so glad to see the moon in all my life. There was enough light to push on, thank God.

Tim was a rationalist, a humanist, and an atheist . . . or at least an agnostic who leaned heavily to atheism. He tolerated my faith in God, and I tolerated his lack of it. It didn't really matter all that much since we liked each other. (In the years since that day, as it turns out, quite a number of my friends are atheists. They tell me that I'm nuts, and I tell them that they'll find out who was nuts the day they die. Then, we laugh about it!) Early on, Tim and I had agreed to disagree and leave God off the table of our conversation topics. I was not the type then, nor am I now, to make it a personal mission to convert anybody. I prayed a lot that night. I did not ask to be rescued; I asked that God be present to me, and to us, as we struggled for our survival.

I coiled our rope and we stood up, staying back from the cliff's edge. Standing was difficult because our muscles were sore, tired, stiff, and beginning to malfunction because of the cold. Tim said that we had better tie ourselves together in case one of us fell, so the other might be able to save him. I took off my mittens again, uncoiled a portion of the rope—maybe twelve feet worth—and tied the rope to itself, leaving the twelve feet loose and handing the coil to Tim. He slung the coil over his shoulder, tied a bowline knot close to the coil, and then clipped the bowline to his harness carabiner. I took my end of the of the rope and tied my bowline there and clipped that to my harness carabiner. We both felt safer knowing that we might be able to save the life of the other if one of us fell . . . or perhaps that we would die together if one went over and the other could not stop his fall.

⤛ 9 ⤜

First Rappel

Tim led and I followed as we carefully traversed the narrow trail along the face to the first rappel point. The mountain face was to our right, and we could touch it with our hands, or bump against it with our shoulders. Immediately to the left of the trail was our 450-foot drop. Each step of the way was carefully placed. We moved slowly, in part out of caution, in part out of necessity due to the worsening condition of our bodies and minds. Tim had a pretty good idea where the first and nearest rappel was, because while he was waiting for me to complete my slow ascent he had had time to watch the other climbers descend. I myself had no idea where it was or what to expect. Tim said he knew where it was, and that was good enough for me. The trail was stony, icy, and snow covered. We spoke little and only as necessary: We'd already learned that it was important to conserve what little strength we had left, and speaking took too much energy.

Looking down by hanging over the edge from where we stood, we could see the landing area in the moonlight.

It was white because of the snow cover and surrounded by darkness. At the bottom of the rappel was a large, flat, and irregularly shaped landing area covered in knee-deep snow. The landing area was about twenty-five feet wide and close to the mountain. It projected out roughly the same distance, but narrowed at its cliff edge to about ten feet wide. The exertion of our walk on our traverse had warmed us up a little, but that warmth was fleeting, and we soon started shivering again.

In front of us was a small conifer tree rooted into the rock, with a trunk about eight inches in diameter. "We'll use the tree for the anchor of our rappel," Tim said. He explained that he had seen the other teams wrap a knotted piece of webbing around the tree and then slip their rope through the loop of webbing. The other teams tossed the two bitter ends of their ropes over the side. They did this instead of wrapping their rope around the tree. When I asked why, Tim said he thought it was to prevent the rope from freezing to the rough bark of the tree. It would be easier to pull the rope down to us if we slipped it through a length of webbing. That made sense, and it was the right way to do it.

If we had been in our right minds—and we were not—that is exactly how we would've done it. Instead, we talked about the cost of webbing. If we did it the way we should have, the way all the other teams had, then Tim would lose that length of webbing. Webbing was expensive for college students. We decided then and there that it was a perfect waste of a perfectly good length of webbing—and, besides, we might need that piece to survive later on. There was no way, given how cold it was and how everything was already frozen, that that rope would stick to the tree. No way. None. It was logical. We decided that we didn't want to leave the webbing behind. We decided we would save it, and instead wrap the rope directly around the tree. It is no surprise in hindsight that it was a stupid choice and one that largely contributed to my death. But Tim was convinced that it would be okay, and I believed him.

We unclipped ourselves from our rope and untied our bowline knots. Tim unslung the coil from his shoulder, laid it down on the snow, and untied the clove hitch that was holding the rope in its coil. He bent over and carefully divided the coil into seemingly equal halves, then opened a short length of line between the two halves. He put one half to the right of the tree, and the other half to the left of the tree. I watched and waited, ready to comment or intervene if necessary. Tim worked silently. He handed me the short length that represented the middle of the entire length of rope as he prepared to toss both coils over the side. My job was to hold my part of the rope to make sure that we did not lose it, because to do so meant certain death. His job was to toss the coils on either side of the tree.

He tossed. I held. It worked. I laid the line against the tree but kept a grip on it just in case. Tim looked over the edge and pulled one side of the line up to even it out as best he could. He could see that the bitter ends lay in the snow like black snakes way below us. I let go of the rope. Tim volunteered to take the risk and go first because he had tossed the line. He pulled the double line up toward him, then threaded and clipped it through his double carabiner rig that created a metal figure eight. Both carabiners were the kind that lock, ensuring that the rope would not accidentally pop out. This figure-eight rig was common enough in those days.

We looked each other in the eye just before he went over the edge. I am sure he was scared to go. I was scared to stay alone. He leaned back against the rope, making it taut, then let it slip through his mittens in a controlled manner as he leaned back and stepped to the very edge of the ledge. We watched each other's eyes. Mine said: *You can do it.* His said: *You, too.* He leaned out over empty space until he was almost parallel to the soles of my boots. Then, he took a step or two down, and I lost sight of him.

I lay down in the snow and inched my way to the edge so I could watch him descend. Tim was dangling in space with his head up and his feet down, sliding down the rope with control and stopping every so often. It only took a few minutes for him to reach the wide ledge below. When he got down there, he looked like a silhouette. I waited until he waved both arms at me—that meant it was my turn.

It was so silent up there. There was no wind. In the distance, I heard a car. I saw that Tim had heard it, too. We both looked out toward the highway and waited as headlights illuminated the roadway. I stood up and backed up against the cliff behind me. When I could see the car, I jumped up and down, waved my arms, and yelled as loudly as I could. I could hear Tim yelling below me, too, and guessed he was doing exactly as I was. But the car drove on; the driver never saw us.

With a bit of despair, I readied myself as Tim had and prepared to go over the edge. I threaded, clipped, and locked the double line into my figure-eight carabiners. I had to take my mittens off to do this. My fingers were stiff and burned with cold.

I had rappelled several times before and liked it. I liked the rush, the pounding of my heart, the focus of my mind, and the knowledge that my life depended on a rope, keeping my head, my skills, and my actions. My previous rappelling experiences had always been with my feet against a cliff, using a technique of walking down the cliffside, with my body perpendicular to the cliff and my back parallel to the ground. This was to be my first rappel in open space. I'd watched Tim make his descent so I might get an idea how to do the same before I started. I told myself that it would be okay, and that the friction created by this figure-eight carabiner rappel would easily control the rate of my descent. Tim had said it would be easy and not to worry, that if he could do it, so could I. And now, it was my turn. I felt fear, but I tamped it down by sheer force of mind, will, and my growing determination simply to survive. Besides, I had no choice. I had to go.

I took up tension in the rope, faced the mountainside, and inched my way back until I felt the edge under my right foot crampon, then stepped back to the edge with my left foot. With both feet now on the edge, I slowly and carefully leaned back out into empty space, moving slightly to the side until the tree was between my feet and the angle of my body made it possible to trust the rope, the tree, my carabiners, and myself. My back was parallel to the ground and my body perpendicular to the mountainside, the opposite of what I was accustomed to doing.

Slowly, I walked myself down, letting the rope slide in a controlled manner through my leather-mittened hands. Once I was over the edge, there was no going back up; I was committed and determined. I continued my descent, watching the ledge disappear from view until my legs no longer reached the ledge. Now, it was my turn to hang on to our rope, my turn to be free and dangling in the air with my feet pointed downward and my head toward the stars. Letting the rope slide through my hands, I stopped on occasion—just to make sure that I could stop—until I reached our landing area and Tim, who was waiting for me, holding the double rope as steadily as he could.

The snow on our landing area was knee deep and soft. I was not going fast, but I sort of landed on top of Tim and knocked him down. I rolled away a bit. Then, we lay there in the snow for a few minutes to rest and gather ourselves for our next task. I watched the stars. There were more stars than I had ever seen in my life, and the sky was so clear. Soon after, Tim struggled to his feet, and I listened as he tried to pull our rope down. I expected that it would be easy and was surprised to hear him muttering and swearing. The swearing itself was not a surprise. We were college students, after all, and I'd spent my summers working in the trades where the same word was frequently used as a noun, verb, adverb, adjective, and even an expletive. What surprised me was that Tim was swearing at that moment.

⌒ 10 ⌒

One Way Up

I tried to sit up but could not quite manage it. My muscles were stiff, and so I sort of inadvertently tipped over as I sat up. I went with it and rolled over onto my stomach, pulled my knees in, pushed up on my hands, and worked myself into a standing position, then slowly turned around to see what Tim was doing. He was pulling hard on one length of the rope, and I could see that it was not budging. He called me over.

I took a step. The snow was knee deep and normally would not have been that difficult to move about in, but I found myself teetering like I was an old man or had some kind of muscle disease. Tim watched me.

"You're moving funny," he said.

"I know," I said, "I'm losing coordination." To my ears, his words and my words sounded slurred, as if I was drunk. I sounded drunk. I walked like I was drunk. That was bad. As I walked over to Tim, I lost my balance and fell on my knees. We had to get out of there before the cold killed us, and it was killing us. It was after us, pursuing us, and I thought of it as my enemy.

The moon had begun to rise over the top of the peaks far above us, bringing us lots of light; and for that we were very glad. Tim continued to pull on the rope. He pulled harder and harder, lifting himself using all his weight. He said he thought our rope might have been wet after all and had frozen to the rough bark of the tree 145 feet above us at the cliff peak. That made sense.

I stumbled my way over to Tim. We grabbed the rope together and pulled down on it. Nothing.

We tried again with all our might and weight. Nothing.

We rested, then pulled again, and again, and again. Nothing.

We were desperate and determined, but the rope would not budge. We kept our heads. We had to get the rope loose. It was either get the rope free, or die on that ledge.

The choice was clear and unfortunate: One of us had to climb back up to the tree and free the rope. The problem was that the climb above us was a 145-foot inverted incline. In layman's terms, it was a 145-foot overhang. There was no ice on the overhang. It was all rock, and the entire underside of the overhang was in dark shadow. There was no way either of us was going to climb that—even if we had the strength, which we did not. Even if it had been daylight, and warm, and summer—which it was not—neither of us had the skills to ascend a 145-foot overhang.

We were stymied and fearful. We both sat down in the snow next to the hanging rope and looked up at the stars and the moon, and off to the valley below us. Tim said he knew how to tie a Prusik hitch, a friction hitch used to ascend climbing rope. I had never heard of it, but Tim said he'd tied the knot before, and had practiced using it a little bit. The Prusik hitch was for an emergency situation, which ours definitely was.

The added trouble for us was that our rope was not fixed to the ground, so there was nothing to tie it to on our end, and up top it was not secure; it was merely frozen in place. Ice, bark, and friction held it fast to the tree, but it was not *tied*. It was actually a loose rope when you think about it, not secured to anything. Tim planned to tie one Prusik hitch to each piece of our double line and climb up. We knew that at any moment, at any place during his climb back up—ten feet above us, or a hundred feet above us—the ice holding the rope to the tree might break loose and Tim could fall to his death.

We talked about it. Tim said that he felt responsible for our situation. It was, he said, his fault that we were there because he was the lead climber; he was the boss, and I was new to ice climbing. I did not blame him, but I thanked him for saying so. Yes, he was the experienced one, but we'd both made choices that had gotten us into this situation.

Tim was a brave man. That much I knew for sure. He was not fearless or reckless—a fearless person has no fear, and a reckless person doesn't take into account danger or the results of risk taking. Tim was courageous and calculating. He was afraid, as was I, that he might fall. But he calculated correctly that unless one of us acted we both would die.

We talked a little about what it would be like to freeze to death, sitting there, looking out at the moonlit landscape, with our eyes open until we died. We talked about what it would be like for the climbers who would certainly find us the next day, and the horror they would feel when they saw our faces and our bodies. We had no other choice: Tim had to climb.

My job was to tie the bottom of the ropes to my body and roll them as tightly as I could into my waist. By doing so, I would try to create as great a tension in the rope from top to bottom as possible, and thus hold the rope as steadily as I could while Tim ascended.

Friction hitches such as a Prusik hitch grab into a rope when a load is applied to it and release the rope when the load is removed. Our Prusik hitch involved looping a thin nylon cord around a rope. Tim cut two long lengths, each maybe eight feet long, of low-stretch 6 mm nylon accessory climbing cord. Climbing cord is very strong. He tied the ends of each length of cord together using a square knot to form two four-foot-long loops.

Tim hitched one loop to one side of the double rope, and the other loop to the second side of our double rope. These loops created two four-foot-long slings for his feet to slip inside of and stand on. "Have you tried these Prusik hitches before, and are you really sure you want to do this?" I asked Tim again. We both knew the answer. Tim repeated, yes, he'd tried this Prusik technique when he had learned how to use it, and yes, he had to climb. With his right foot in the right sling, his left foot in the left sling, and his hands on each Prusik hitch respectively, Tim was ready to begin his ascent 145 feet up the rope to the rough-bark tree. His intent was to reach the peak, peel the frozen rope from the tree, put a sling around the tree, and rappel back down to me. It was an extremely dangerous maneuver. Just before he started, and before I rolled myself into the rope, I stopped him, repeating that we'd gotten ourselves into this situation together, that it was not his fault alone. I shared the burden equally. We hugged.

I started thinking about what I had once heard from another climber: "Once you get above a certain height on a wall, it doesn't matter how high you've climbed because if you fall from thirty feet or three hundred feet or three thousand feet, it will kill you." That climber added, "It's not the fall that kills you anyway; it's the sudden stop at the end." Gallows humor.

I grabbed the rope, wrapped it around myself with one loop, took off my mittens, clumsily tied a double half-hitch, and tightened the rope around my waist. There was not much excess line. I lay down at Tim's feet and rolled and rolled until I got the rope as taut as I could get it. When he was ready, he began to climb right above me. I positioned myself to watch him as best I could.

Tim was already exhausted. We both were. And Tim had to climb unprotected. If he fell, he could die. We kept our heads, but we both knew with every breath we took that the rope could break free at any moment and Tim could fall.

The ropes jerked as Tim started up, by lifting his right foot while sliding his right mittened hand up the rope and pushing the Prusik hitch upward. He put weight on his right foot and pushed down on the Prusik cord with all his might in order to check it. The Prusik hitch held firmly in place because of friction on the rope; he had tied it correctly. "It works," he said.

Tim lifted his left foot while slipping the left Prusik hitch up the rope with his left mittened hand. The rope swayed. He waited a moment to see if the left hitch would also hold fast under his weight. It did. He began to climb, slowly and carefully. Each time he moved one hand and one leg, the rope jerked and swayed. The whole setup was so sloppy, and it swayed with each step no matter how hard I tried to keep the rig steady. I told Tim again that he was brave, and thanked him again, adding that I would do my best to steady the rope. He said nothing and continued his climb.

The higher Tim got, the more the rope swayed and twisted. It was dead silent. I waited below in the cold snow, feeling my body growing colder and more sluggish by the minute. The shivering had stopped for both of us. That was not a good sign, given the circumstances.

Tim climbed up and up, slowly, steadily, with rhythm. He got to twenty or twenty-five feet as I watched from below.

The jerking motion required to shift the hitches, maybe combined with the swaying of the rope, suddenly forced the frozen rope to break loose from the tree.

It happened so quickly. I felt the rope jerk me and unwind a bit. It rolled me a half turn until my face was in the snow. Tim shouted, "FALLING!" I was directly beneath him. He had his crampons on. I braced myself and tried to roll away as quickly as I could, but I was tied in and could not roll far. Tim fell and landed partly on me and partly on the snow. We lay still for a minute. I asked him how he was. He was unbroken and unhurt. "Me too," I said.

The rope was free. It felt like a miracle that it had come free before he had climbed very high up. I kept imagining what would have happened had he gotten farther. Tim rolled off of me. I sat up and untied the half-hitch from around my waist and gave a tug on the rope. It was free and easy to haul down until it fell down on top of us. We laughed our relief, and sat in the snow resting for several minutes. With the rope now free and in our hands, we had a chance again.

I carefully coiled the line and tied it off with a clove hitch to secure it, leaving enough line so that we could tie ourselves to each other. We rose to our feet.

❦ 11 ❧

Seen

Our climb that day was in a very sparsely populated portion of rural Alberta, Canada. In 1980, there were two million people living in all of Alberta, an area of roughly 255,000 square miles, and most of the population lived in the cities far to the south. Only one car drove down the parkway that night. We felt—and were—very alone. Even if a car did drive by, why, we asked ourselves, would anybody happen to look up to our spot and see us on this long range of mountains paralleling the parkway?

And yet, just before we tied ourselves off to each other for our next traverse to our rappel, we heard a vehicle heading south on the Icefields Parkway far below us. We stopped, watched, and waited, ever hopeful that we might be spotted. As the headlights came into view, we watched as the car slowed down and turned right into the parking lot where we'd left Tim's car. We guessed it was around midnight. We thought maybe the driver of the vehicle had seen Tim's car sitting there alone and was going to check it out. The vehicle slowly swung around and faced the mountainside, toward us, and with its head-lights still on, stopped.

We stomped to the edge of the cliff and jumped up and down, shouting and waving our arms high over our heads in the moonlight, hoping we would be seen. After an exhilarating but exhausting bit of movement, the driver flashed his headlights twice. We stopped jumping. He flashed his headlights again. We jumped again. He flashed again. He could see us!

We deduced that the driver must be the park ranger at whose cabin we'd spent a night. He must have realized that we had not signed out of his wilderness entry and exit registration log and had come to find us. We were heartened and felt a surge of joy. We laughed and dared to hope, though we were still in serious trouble stuck up on the ice climb. He could not save us, but he knew we were there.

Our exhaustion, exacerbated by our outburst of energy upon seeing the ranger's truck and our ever-advancing hypothermia made it difficult to walk. We tied ourselves to each other again for safety. Again, I had to take my gloves off to tie the knot. The cold bit deeply into my fingers. The ranger must have watched our sil-houettes as we traversed through the deep snow to the narrow icy and rocky trail that led beside the steep moun-tain face, walking with slow and deliberate steps toward our next rappel.

Tim turned to me and raised a finger to his lips, indicating that he was not going to speak unless nec-essary. As we felt our energy draining even further, we understood the desperate need to conserve our strength. Expending even a little might cause us to lose our lives. Survival was the only consideration. When he raised his finger to his lips, I told Tim, "Can't talk. Too tired. Too cold." Even without his voicing a reply, I knew that the same was true for him.

All night long we trusted each other in a way that I have never trusted anyone before or since. My life was in his hands, and his was in mine. During the hours of our tribulation, we each had withdrawn inside of ourselves out of necessity. My mind became 100 percent focused on one thing: driving my body to survival. Nothing else mattered.

We forced ourselves onward, forward. Each step took us closer to salvation at our last rappel, and then to the warmth of our tent. Yet, each step, because of the cold and our extreme exhaustion, also took us closer to death. We were balancing exhaustion and energy, fighting against our rapidly increasing hypothermia, and we both knew it. Once in a while, I looked down toward the ranger's truck. He sat there with his headlights on the whole time. He gave me hope, but I was still deeply, deeply afraid.

At one point during our traverse, I began to hear and feel my crampons scrape and clink on hard rock. The path itself was dark beneath our feet. I mostly walked by feel, with one mittened hand touching the mountain when I could. We entered the top of what appeared to be a boulder chute. The chute was our next rappel location. The top of the chute was bathed in moonlight, but most of it was in the dark shadow cast by the mountain, where the moonbeams could not reach. We took off our mittens without talking and untied ourselves.

Tim looped our rope through the iron O-ring that attached to an iron pin permanently hammered into the mountain face. We tested the strength of the O-ring and the pin for safety by pulling on the rope. As always, Tim led the way. He said, "I'll tug twice when I get to the bottom." I nodded and said nothing, watching as he disappeared among the boulders into the darkness. Once again alone, I leaned back against the mountain. I did not sit down for fear that I wouldn't have the energy to stand again. I was so cold, colder than I'd ever imagined I could be. There was no warmth in me at all. My feet hurt with cold; my hands hurt, my legs, and arms, and face, all hurt. I could feel the cold inside my brain. I kept a hand on our rope. After a time, I felt the two tugs. I tugged back twice. Tim replied with two more tugs. It was my turn.

I took my mittens off, felt the bite of the cold again, and concentrated on moving my fingers as my mind commanded them, willed them, to move, then watched them to make sure they did. I made my figure eight with my two locking carabiners and clipped our rope in. My path down on rappel was through the midst of huge boulders and crags, or at least that's what it felt like. I could not see much at all in the dark shadow cast by the mountain. I worked my way down slowly, trusting my rope, feeling with my feet, still colder than I thought humanly possible to survive, my mind still focused on a single drive: survive. I had no other thoughts.

In fact, my thought to survive did not feel like a thought at all. It was deeper than that. It was primal. All night long I kept digging deeper and deeper into my willpower, into my inner drive to live, into my inner resources, striving with a single-mindedness I had not known I possessed. I was devoid of energy. My thin body had already consumed what little fat I had, or so it felt. I felt empty, but I could keep going sheerly because of my mind and an inner strength greater than I'd known I had. I was surprised that it was there, but I imagine everyone has this and can find it when it is needed.

At the bottom of our rappel, I rounded the sharp-edged corner of the vertical cliff on my left and stepped to the narrow ledge where Tim waited for me. The ledge was narrower than the length of my boots and crampons. My heels hung over the edge. My toes touched the mountain face. My nose touched the rock.

I clipped my harness carabiner to the iron O-ring that was permanently iron-pinned into the mountain. Tim, to my left, had done the same. I looked at him. He smiled. We were safe for the moment and back in the moonlight. We turned to the ranger and waved. He flashed his headlights and, surprisingly, slowly drove out of the parking lot, turning left onto the parkway and then heading north.

We were alone again. My heart sank. We thought about this and spoke about it briefly, figuring that the ranger must have believed that we were safe enough with one single and easy rappel left, and close enough to the bottom to get there on our own; plus, he must have been tired and needed sleep. No doubt he was angry with us, too.

⌒ 12 ⌒

A Beautiful Place to Die

It was now an hour or two before dawn. Our tent, which was still packed inside Tim's car, was now 150 feet below us, ready to be set up, ready to give us shelter. We were exhausted beyond what I could have ever imagined for any human being; our energy was completely depleted. We were ravenously hungry, bitterly cold, frostbitten, blue-lipped, shivering to our marrow, yet driven to survive. I took my mittens off my frozen hands one more time, felt again the bite of the icy air in my fingers down to my bones, and tied one end of our climbing rope to my harness and dropped the bitter end into the darkness to my right, into the shadow of the chute. I pulled on my end.

Immediately, the rope jammed. I gave it a whip, hoping that would free the line. I pulled again. The rope jammed tighter and would not budge. With difficulty, my lips were barely able to move, I told Tim the rope was jammed.

It was a tricky situation. The bowline knot I had tied to connect the rope to my harness meant that the rope was too short for Tim to reach and help me pull. If

I untied the rope from my harness, Tim would be able to reach it and help me pull, but in our clumsy and frozen condition we might drop the rope. I had enough brain-power left to figure that out and told Tim, "If we drop the rope, we die." That was the bottom line. No rope, no survival. No rope, sure death.

We discussed this some, and with each word I could feel my remaining strength leave. It was almost as if I could measure my last drops of energy and see them leave my mouth. I had never before thought about how much energy it takes to think, to form words and sentences in the mind, and then speak them aloud. When one has nothing left for strength, that effort becomes clear.

We decided that we needed the rope to stay tied to me, and talked about an alternative: Tim could unclip his carabiner from his O-ring and inch along the rock face with his nose to the wall, then try clipping his carabiner into the same O-ring I was using. It was a brave and fool-ish idea. With his steel-cramponed heels hanging over the granite ledge, it was too dangerous of a maneuver for him to try to help free our rope. Without the protection of his carabiner clipped into the O-ring that was pinned into the mountain, and with no rope to save him, Tim would very likely fall to his death.

It was up to me. Getting the rope free was my job. In my weakened and failing condition, I pulled on our rope again, by myself. All night we had striven together as one force, as a team. Together, we would survive—that is what I chanted in my mind: *Together, we will survive*. It became my prayer.

And, now, that had changed. Our lives were in my leather-mittened hands. I continued to pull on the rope as hard as I could with all my remaining strength. The rope was completely jammed around the corner and lodged up in the dark. It did not budge, and my pulling may have jammed it tighter. I told Tim this. "Keep trying," he said. I kept pulling.

I thought about trying to trust the jam, thinking to swing out around the corner and try to reascend. It was a crazy thought, and when I told Tim, he told me so. The rope could un-jam under my weight, or as soon as I got around the corner; if it did, I would fall and die, and Tim, rope-less, would die too.

I had been so cold, so cold for so many hours. Then, rather suddenly, warmth swept though my entire body. For the first time since the morning before, I was actually hot. I was sweating. It was illogical. Rationally, I knew that my body was cold, but my torso and head were hot. I felt the blood drain from my arms and stop flowing toward my legs. I figured that my body knew that my limbs were expendable. I could lose my arms and legs, but my brain and heart and lungs—my core—must be saved if I was going to live.

This was a bad sign. "I'm hot," I told Tim. I unzipped my 60/40 jacket. It was crazy to open my jacket to try to cool down. I realized it was crazy, and despite feeling hot I zipped back up, or maybe Tim told me to zip up. I pulled on the rope again and again, but it still wouldn't budge. I kept whipping the rope up and down, up and down, then I pulled again. It was definitely stuck.

My mind and willpower remained hyperfocused on survival, but I stopped pulling and rested. I looked back over my left shoulder, away from the dark wall, up into the stunning beauty of the sky, and around at the gorgeous moonlit scenery in which we were immersed. At first I was afraid that I would not be able to save us, and then a surge of peace overtook me. I was no longer afraid. I was accepting my fate . . . my fate was death, and that was okay with me. I had tried. I had striven. We had striven, and we had failed.

My eyes took in what I thought would be my last view, my final sight: I could see the Columbia Icefield glistening in the moonlight. It was beautiful. I was warm. My mind was at ease. I knew the signs. A resignation and a self-admittance told me I was going to die there. I thought about my family, and how brokenhearted they would be when they found out I'd died. After my mom's breakdown, and the subsequent family suffering after my sister vanished from our lives, I wondered if in their coming grief they would be angry with me; and if their grief would crush them.

I said to myself, *This is a beautiful place to die.* And it was. I knew my death would be peaceful rather than violent. Freezing to death is peaceful, or so I had read. It is as peaceful as falling asleep, which I knew was about to come next. The rope was stuck. I was stuck. We were stuck, and there on that cliff the next morning, the first climber to arrive after first light would see our bodies. I was sorry about that and knew that we would be ruining someone's day.

Under that wide sky with its myriad brilliant, distant, and distinct stars shining and twinkling in a dozen colors, visible even under the bright moon that had risen ever higher throughout the night, I felt a complete and compelling peace about dying.

This surprised me. Feeling peaceful in the face of death felt like giving up. And I refused to give up. My willpower, my primal self, said, *NO! I will not quit. I will NOT die. Not here. Not tonight.*

The scene around us was beyond beautiful, indescribable, and I prayed again, but this time a different prayer. I said to God, and again to myself: *This is a beautiful place to die. I'm not quitting; but if I have to die tonight, I am content that it is in a most beautiful place.*

I pulled the rope again and again, and as I pulled sleep came for me. I began to feel so sleepy, so impossibly sleepy. I tried to stay awake. I tried to force myself to stay alert. I told myself, *This is not sleep. This is dying.* I dug deeper into myself to force myself to awaken, will myself to remain awake, but I was spent. I had no strength left.

As I began to fall asleep for the first time, I felt my knees buckle beneath me, and I could not stop them. I felt darkness close in around me, narrowing my vision. My eyes closed, and I could not force them back open. I felt my feet lose their footing, and felt myself fall. I swung down on my harness and carabiner and slammed, frozen face and helmeted head first, into the granite mountainside.

The hard blow against the mountain woke me. My face hurt. My head hurt. I climbed back up. Tim was speaking. I could hear him, but I couldn't understand what he was saying . . . nor did I care. I yanked on the rope. My world narrowed. My mind got smaller. I could not see or hear Tim at all, and I did not care that I could not. It didn't matter. All there was, was me, just me and the cold, the mountain, and the rope. Again I felt darkness encircle me, close in on me. I was aware of my sight narrowing, of darkness closing in like a fade to black in an old black-and-white film. Sleep overtook me, and I tumbled off my ledge.

I hit the rock face again, awoke again, and climbed up, and pulled the rope. I do not know how many times this happened—twice, thrice, or more—nor do I have any idea what Tim was doing at that time. It was all darkness to me. I lost track of time, and lost track of myself and the world around me. Darkness had closed in on me again. It was a struggle to see anything. The light of the night faded in my mind. The light of my mind faded to black. My vision narrowed. I felt my breathing slow down. Sleep was more powerful than my willpower to stay awake, than my willpower to survive. Each time I felt myself falling asleep, I dove even deeper into myself, willing myself to stay awake, but instead I slept. I fought sleep. I knew sleep was my end; yet, I could not stop it.

My years of first-aid training had helped me understand and explain to Tim the measure of trouble we were in at each stage of increasing hypothermia, and how much time we might have left as each stage encroached upon our bodies. It was macabre but necessary to keep track of our dying. Throughout the night, symptom by symptom, step by step, we watched as we strove to live, yet continued to succumb to exposure. Sleep is the end stage of dying from exposure. Hypothermia means too little heat. Sleep is death, and death is sleep. I knew that, did not want that. Every cell of my body screamed *NO!*, but I could not fight my body's demand for sleep. *If I'm going to die*, I told myself again, *this is a beautiful place to do so.*

⌒ 13 ⌒

Irresistible Pull

I felt myself slipping completely into darkness. I watched it envelop me like a sphere closing in. I could not stop it. My sight narrowed to a smaller and smaller circle of light until even that was crushed and closed by the overwhelming darkness. My body had failed me. My brain had failed. I had failed. I felt my last breath leave my body. I tried to take in one more and I could not. I had fought the closing darkness with all I had left inside me, but I was finally dying. I could feel it. I knew it. Inescapable death . . .

I could feel death. Such a strange thing it was to feel death, to feel my body fail and the world cease to be for me. The night and cold had killed me, and I was powerless to stop it. I was not the all-powerful and immortal youth I had believed I was. I was a human and I was dying, and that was life. Life will kill you.

I sensed my body fall off the ledge again, but this time I did not feel my face or head or body hit the wall. I had fallen asleep; I knew that. I was in the darkness and had fallen off my ledge; I knew that. I was confused because

I was awake in what *felt* like sleep. My mind should have faded to black, like every time it had ever since childhood whenever I fell asleep. I was in total darkness, but knew not where I was . . . except for the fact that I was not asleep. I was somehow awake inside an inner darkness. I was conscious; I was confused. *I should be asleep,* I thought. I knew that the mountain must be in front of me. It had to be, but I could not feel it, and I could not open my eyes to see it. Yet, with my eyes closed, I could suddenly see . . . but what I was seeing and what I was feeling were things I could not understand.

I saw and felt the darkness as if it was one thing: a greater darkness, a moving darkness, a living darkness. And it was moving toward me, moving at me. It came right at me, rapidly. It wanted me. It was coming for me. The feeling was like a soul-sucking vacuum, one with an overwhelming force of the most powerful gravity. Immediately, it was sucking *me* out of my body. I put up a shield of my will. I refocused all of my might to stop this thing from taking me. I did not know what it was. I only knew it wanted me. And I fought. I clung. I willed myself to stay.

But it was only a moment of will, only a moment of fight against such a tremendous power and unspeakable force. I was outmatched by a factor of ten trillion to one. My intense willpower and the inner strength I had honed through the night had gotten me to a single-minded state of bestial survival, but it seized me anyway, broke through my fragile defenses. It happened fast. It took me and I released, because I had no choice. I was like a leaf caught up in a great flood. It took me, and I felt it meant to take me. I sensed it had the intention to take, and in some strange way, deep, deep down inside myself, I knew that it must. It was not a thing. It was no thing. It had no form. It was not of this world. It had no molecules, no chemicals, no DNA, no cells, no particulars or any other thing that I could begin to describe or read about or conceive. It was no thing. Not a thing. It was other. I had to go. I could not stay.

The Power plucked me. It plucked the real me, the whole me, the holy whole soul me. Until that moment I had never fully understood the soul of me—the who/what/why that are the real whole of me. I had thought that I was body and soul. Suddenly, I knew that this was not the case. I was only soul. My body was simply where I had dwelled. I suddenly, fully, completely knew that what I was, what I am, who I am, and what I will be forever and eternally is soul. Soul was me. Soul is me. My body was not me. It never had been me. My body housed my soul, and when I was plucked from my flesh, I was still *me*.

This is the hardest part of my story to write because nothing I will say from here on out can be verified, quantified, or qualified. Why? Because on the other side I had no body, no brain, no blood, no bones, no eyes, no fingers, no toes, no culture, no language, no anything that is a thing in this world.

Without a brain, there is no language. Without language, how can one say what one saw or heard or felt? I could see, but had no eyes—or maybe I had ten thousand eyes, because I could see in every direction all at once. I could hear when spoken to, but I had no ears; furthermore, there was no voice or sound—yet, I could hear.

On the other side, there is no thing. Everything on this side, in the world in which we live, is a thing. Over there, nothing is a thing. There is no thing. Language cannot describe it. Language cannot contain it.

I am compelled to talk about it now; yet, paradoxically, I know no words can convey it. This no-thing is so present to me now as I write that it overwhelms me. I cannot escape it. This overwhelming feeling has filled my days, every day, ever since that night. In the years since my death I have done my best to say what cannot be said, to articulate what cannot be articulated, to describe what cannot be described, and think about what cannot be thought about.

Three years after my experience, I went to Yale Divinity School in order to find some language that might help me frame what happened to me. And so, here it is: God is no thing. I repeat: God is no thing. God is not a thing. Anything that can be said about God is inaccurate. Words are things. God is not. God cannot be explained, contained, described, or even seen.

⁓ 14 ⁓

The Voice

I found myself in a vast, infinite darkness, in a place that was not a place, a place that was outside of time, and eternal, a place where there is no thing—and, yet, I was a being . . . spherical, sort of, and I had life, but no breath. I was me, and I knew I was me, yet I had no flesh and no bones. It was curious, and I was unafraid. I could think, and, as best I could, comprehend that I was still me. Better yet, I had no brain to interfere with my thinking. I was *life*, or energy, or soul. I was a being. My body was a ball of soul, a being ball, a ball of being. I was I. I could see, but I had no eyes. It was as if I could see with ten thousand eyes, or one eye in every direction at once. I was floating, and yet firmly in a Vast Darkness—a Greater Darkness that extended beyond sight in every direction. But the Darkness was not dark. I could see it. I floated and was stable in the Darkness, and I was alone.

A gigantic doorway or gateway appeared, or maybe it was there all along and I'd just not seen it yet. This is what the entire experience was like: Maybe it had all been there my entire life, just beyond my vision, and I simply could not see it. (Note: I'm using words to describe what I remember, but remember I had no brain, nor had I language; neither exists on the other side.) It was timeless there—I tell my story in this order because words must be placed sequentially, but there was no sequence of events. All I experienced may have happened at once.

The gateway, the doorway was a hundred yards high and seventy yards across if I had to guess. I could see a long, arching tunnel of darkness; it was very, very dark leading from the gateway to God-knows-where. The gateway and its tunnel or corridor pierced the Greater Darkness and was contained within it but seemingly led beyond it, or through it somehow. The doorway itself was shimmering and flowing, like a waterfall, only it was not water, and was simultaneously translucent and transparent. I reached out with my being to touch the shimmer, to feel it . . . and I did. I touched the shimmer with something like a hand, but I had no hand. The shimmer was Alive. The gateway was Alive. I felt the Life in it. It was Living Energy. I felt the energy of Life flowing in the shimmer and I felt it flow into me.

Simultaneously, I heard my name called from deep, deep inside of me, and yet also from beyond me. I heard my name called, and it was not just my name Peter, or Pete, or Petie, or Petro, or any of the names I was called by those who knew me and loved me. It was Peter and more: It was my soul's name, and it was said with Love beyond imagination, beyond comprehension. It was Love that was Real, and Love that is Reality. It was my true name, my real name, and the name that revealed *me* to me. It was and is my name that only God can speak. I heard my name come from outside of myself but heard it inside myself, but it was not a word. At least, it was not spoken as a word in any way that I can say. Yet, it was me: I was in the word, and the word, my name, was who I was.

The scriptures teach us that to know the true name of a person is to have power over them. This is what happens in the story where Jacob wrestles with the angel and demands to know the angel's name. On the other side, my true name was called to me. I was called by my true name, and thus was completely and utterly in the power of the Being that called my name. I belonged to the One who made me, and suddenly I knew the truth of that and what it meant.

My name was, and I suppose still is, the essence of my being, the ground of my *self*, the light of me, and the whole of life. There were no words spoken. There was no language. There was no sound. The Voice that called my name came from outside me, and was present to me and nearby, yet distant as well. I could not see the Voice, but instead felt Its immanence and immensity. It was not my voice that I heard, nor the voice of my unconscious or my conscience. I heard the Voice of the Almighty deep inside my soul, beneath me, around me, beyond me, and the Voice filled me with my name—and, in the filling, knew me in totality.

The Voice knew me fully and completely and there was no part of me that was unknown. I was revealed, fully revealed, in all my beauty and hideousness. Nothing could be hidden; nothing of me was hidden. I had no choice in the matter. I was fully and completely known, and that was that. All of me, the whole of me, everything about me was completely contained inside my name. In saying the name, I was known. And, in hearing my name, I knew that I was known. It was my true name that only God knows, and only God can say. Every action, every love, every hate, every sorrow, every joy, every tear, and every smile was there, and there were no dark and hidden corners with me. When I heard my name, I was revealed, and I knew God was completely present.

How did I know it was God? I just knew that it was, and it could be no other. I knew because God told me so in the very calling of my name. I knew that the Knower knew me. It was instantaneously obvious that my Creator was there with me, calling my true name that I heard inside myself, inside my soul. I was creature; I knew in that moment I was made by my Maker. I was a created being made by the Uncreated.

I understood that God was right there beside me, and fully with me, although I could not see God at all. God had no being but was all Being. I could still see the Greater Darkness, and the gateway, but my sight turned within. I was on the doorstep, the threshold of heaven, and I knew to the core of my soul that it was YHWH who spoke. The Voice that spoke without sound or language communicated with me telepathically. The Voice was neither male nor female, neither old nor young. The Voice was pure and holy, and only Love, Only Love and Beauty, and Light, Almighty, Maker. There was total and complete communication without words, unencumbered by language. I heard with my soul-mind; I heard with the ear of my soul; I heard with all of my being, I heard with my soul. Seeing, hearing, being, feeling, thinking was all one to me.

My true name filled me; it in-filled me. The Voice in-filled me like a breath with a gift undeserved of Love-Hope-Joy-Beauty-Truth-Charity-Kindness-Compassion-Love-Patience-Beauty-Love, and it was all one indescribable, amalgamated combination. The gift was heaven filling up inside my soul-being, inside of me, the true and real me. I was on what I think of as the threshold of heaven, at the gateway, the proverbial pearly gate, and God gave me the undeserved gift of heaven within me. In this world of ours, here on earth, we separate Love-Hope-Joy-Beauty-Truth-Charity-Kindness-Compassion-Love-Patience-Beauty-Love into differentiated things. We individualize them. We have truth. We have love. We have beauty. We have joy. We have hope. We have charity. Each is a separate idea or action or experience, and sometimes they overlap. Not so in heaven. In heaven they are One; they are One-ness, and they emanate from the Divine who is Oneness.

I was in-filled, overfilled, completely filled, spilling over with this Oneness, this Love-Hope-Joy-Beauty-Truth-Charity-Kindness-Compassion-Love-Patience-Beauty-Love—this Unity. I became the Love-Hope-Joy-Beauty-Truth-Charity-Kindness-Compassion-Love-Patience-Beauty-Love. It was and is indescribable, and yet even with this heaven within me, I was still just me, soul-Peter—I knew who I was, and I knew that I was *known*, fully, completely, and utterly *known*, completely naked to my Maker who could see every part of me. I was naked. That is the word. Naked. Exposed. Seen. And I was loved beyond imagination, beyond comprehension.

≈ 15 ≈

My Hell

The divine in-filling flooded me with knowledge. I suddenly knew and understood so many things I had not comprehended on earth. Eventually, when I returned to my flesh body, to my earth body, I remembered only that I had once known so very much more, but that I now no longer understood or comprehended what had been shown to me in heaven. I now know only that I did once know, no longer knew, and expectedly will know once more when I die again.

And then came hell. (Again, dear reader, I tell this story as if it happened in a sequence, but time did not exist. There was no sequence there, only eternity. This is the sequence that I first told my story on that Sunday morning, and because of that I think maybe it occurred this way, though perhaps it did happen at once, which is more likely.)

Hell. I entered my own hell. It was hell inside me, my personal hell. It was, it turns out, the hell I had created for myself; or, rather, my own hell entered into me, overtook me, owned me, and filled me. It was my personal hell because I saw that I had created it second by second, minute by minute, hour by hour, day by day, month by month, and year by year while I lived enfleshed. I made my own hell, and it was horrifying.

I had not known that I had been busy creating my own hell while I was alive. I did not know I carried my own hell within me as my loathsome treasure. As I reflect on this part of my death, I see in my mind's eye the ghost of Jacob Marley from Charles Dickens's *A Christmas Carol*. Marley wore the chains he had forged in life link by link. I had forged my own hell, action by action. My birth—during which I caused my mother much pain—was not included in my self-judgment; neither was the period when I was an innocent newborn. Are we not all born the same—innocent?

Let me explain: The hell I suffered was to see, hear, feel, understand, and embody all of the pain I had ever caused during my earthly life to anyone I had known, from their point of view. I had carried their pain with me and brought their pain with me into the afterlife. How unexpected. It was a record, a file, a folder, a book of life somehow written and recorded inside my soul. God had not done this to me. God had not caused my hell. I saw that immediately. I had done it to myself. I had woven it on my own. I had burned each wrong action onto my own DVD, and yet it was also clear to me that my brokenness was simply a part of being a human being.

To cause pain to another was, or so it appeared to me, the natural order of life on earth. I was not special; I was not unique in that regard. I had just been a human and did what all human beings do to each other. We hurt each other. The hurting is sin.

I felt their pain, the pain I had unwittingly caused and the pain I had freely and often purposefully given to some persons, particularly the ones I loved—my mother, my father, my sisters, my brother, my friends, but my classmates, acquaintances, and strangers, too. They were all there—every one and every instance.

I witnessed and suffered every instance of pain, every instance of sin since the moment of my birth, in rapid and full sequence. I felt their pain, the pain that I had caused them to feel, and it was overwhelming, like a painful yet purifying fire in my soul. Every hurt I had ever caused, big or small, intended or unintended, was piled up for me to see and feel and experience. I had sinned. I had never really even understood what sin was; I had denied that sin really existed. But suddenly I knew what sin was: Sin was and is causing another to hurt. Sin was unavoidable. Sin was inevitable. Many of my sins were unintentional, accidental, actions I'd taken that I'd never known might cause hurt. I knew I had sinned, and now I understood the full meaning of this.

It is odd to me that of all the understanding I gained on the other side and have forgotten, this one thing I remember so well. Sin was the hurt that I had given or caused in my lifetime. In my own hell, I suffered all of the pain that I had cast on others, from the smallest pain to the largest, intentionally given or unintentional. Hell was not outside of me; it was not a place to go to—it was a place within. My hell drowned out the Love-Hope-Joy-Beauty-Truth-Charity-Kindness-Compassion-Love-Patience-Beauty-Love that had been in me—and left me filled with shame. Further, for each sin, each and every pain I had ever caused, I also simultaneously witnessed and felt all of my inadequate justifications, my weak reasoning, my causations for giving each individual every pain that I had given them. I was my own judge. I held the scale of my guilt, and my fate.

I saw my inadequacies—all of them. Every single circumstance was accounted for, even those in which I had harbored no ill will, had no intention to cause hurt, or had not even known that I had caused pain. These two things—feeling all the pain I had ever caused in my life juxtaposed with witnessing all my paltry justifications—led me to self-judgment . . . and I judged myself guilty. I was guilty. I had sinned greatly.

I was utterly ashamed of myself. The evidence against me, created by me, was within me, and I was overwhelmed. I had no defense. There was no defense. In the face of Great Love I was nothing, and had nothing with which to defend myself. I was guilty as charged. My reasons, my justifications, my causations for causing hurt weighed nothing on my scale when compared with the immense pain I had caused in my twenty-one years of life. I was guilty. I knew it. I believed it. My hell was repulsive and abhorrent. Hell hurt. Hell held no beauty, and no love, only truth. My hell was the most pain I had ever suffered. It was the pain of others.

And yet, there was a third simultaneous perspective even as I experienced my own hell. It was the Voice of God, the Love of God spoken to soothe my passage through hell, speaking to me and within me from outside of me but without language. It was the Voice of God that I heard, repeatedly assuring me, *I love you, Peter. I know you, Peter. I made you, Peter. You are my creature, Peter. I know all about you, Peter. Nothing is hidden from me. I have always known all about you. I know you did all of this. I see all. I see all of you. I love you. I made you. You are my creature. I love you. I forgive you. I forgive you. I forgive you.*

And suddenly, undeservedly, I was forgiven fully and completely and instantaneously. I deserved no mercy. I had judged myself guilty, and I was guilty; I was worthy of punishment. That was truth. I was soulfully ashamed of myself—perhaps that is what saved me, my shame, or perhaps not. Perhaps God, the Unseen, the Merciful, the Almighty, forgave me completely and burned away all of my sin in my own hell simply because I am beloved, just as you are beloved, just as each and every one of us is beloved. All I know is that I was made whole and holy again. All the pain I had caused vanished. My hell ended; my need for hell ended. I passed through, and because of Love, I was once more in-filled with Love-Hope-Joy-Beauty-Truth-Charity-Kindness-Compassion-Love-Patience-Beauty-Love. I was loved, and knew I was loved by the Lover.

～ 16 ～

God Is Love

Heaven and hell all happened inside my mind/soul/
being. There were neither words nor even a voice,
per se. It was all communicated directly to me telepathically. I knew I had no brain to process the information;
yet, strangely, I could think more clearly and understand
more clearly than I ever had or have since. My brain was
not getting in the way of my thinking, as it is now. I am
dyslexic with ADD; I am an American; I speak English—
and none of these attributes, or anything else, interfered
with my thinking on the other side. I was simply beloved
creature, fully known and fully loved, and I was grateful-
ness itself, and worshipful completely.

From inside my soul-self, I spoke to God without
words or language, through pure thought, and asked, *Am
I dead?*

God said, *Yes. You are dead.*

I heard this inside my soul, inside myself, but I knew
that it had been spoken to me, or more accurately *thought*
to me, from outside myself, from God who was present
but whom I could not see. How did I know it was God?

I just knew. It was self-evident. Another thing that was self-evident was that I had carried into the afterlife all the love I had given away and all the love I had ever gathered. All of that love—given and gathered—was my treasure. While there were two types of love that I had with me (given and gathered), they seemed also to be simultaneously one love.

I thought to God, *I haven't gone through the door yet, and I can't go through the door* (referring to the gateway that I somehow knew led to a deeper heaven).

God asked, *Why not?*

I should have wondered why God, who knew me thoroughly, did not know the answer to this. It seemed natural that God should ask this question of me and that I should have a chance to answer in my own way.

I answered, *My sister Andrea ran away when I was young. Andrea just vanished. She broke my mother's heart. My mother still has a broken heart. It ruined my mother's life and affected her health. My father also has a broken heart and a lot of anger because of what Andrea's running away did to her mother, to her siblings, and to him. We kept her absence a secret from everybody except family. I cannot be the one who takes another child away from them. I cannot break their hearts that way again. It would crush them, and wound them so that they might never recover. They have not recovered from Andrea. It would devastate them. I love them too much for that. I cannot go. I cannot.*

Suddenly, God took me, carried me or swept me, to a high place and showed me all of earth all at once from a great distance, and yet I could see all the people on earth individually and all at once, all together. In particular, my focus landed on my mother and father, whom I could see up close and clearly. I could see their broken, loving hearts inside of them. I could see all of their suffering and sorrow, their pain, their wounds, anger.

God said to me, *I love you.*

I said, *I know.*

God said, *I love you more deeply than your imagination could ever have conceived. I know you and love you, Peter. You are my creature. Because you are here, now you know how much I love you, and you know how great my love is.*

I said, Yes, God, I know You love me, personally and infinitely more than I could have ever conceived or imagined. I feel like your beloved, your special one, and more than that. I feel Your love as the greatest love beyond what I can even contain or hold within me.

God's love was so wide and deep, so full and sweet, so safe and eternal. It was so much greater than any love I had ever felt before, and yet somehow I knew I had always been loved in this way by God for my entire life, even when I was in my physical body and could not feel the fullness of that great love. I knew I was always beloved.

God said to me, inside me, without language, *In the way I love you now I have always loved you, and will always love you. You know.*

I knew that was the Truth. I knew I was beloved as a particular person, individually, and specially, as if I was the only one who mattered. That is how it felt, and yet it also felt that God's great love for me was not exclusive to me, that God loved every human being in exactly the same way. It felt that God is, was, and always will be love.

God continued, *In the way I love you now, and you know that I love you, I also love everyone, every human being, every person on earth, right now, always—and I love your mother and your father in this same way. Because I love your parents in the same way that I love you, in the way that you now understand I have always loved you, forever and eternally, all has been well, all is well, and all will be well with them, and for everyone, because of My love.*

I could see, sense, feel, taste, hear, and know to the core of my soul the very Truth of God's eternal love for me, for my parents, and for all of humanity. God's love was, is, and will be forever real, eternal, and lasting. I knew that for my parents, at their death, all would be well. I knew this because at my own death all was well, and love made me whole and holy, worthy, and acceptable.

None of this was my doing. All of it was God's doing, from God's love. All of my suffering had ended, and I understood that eventually, when my parents died, when they stepped outside of time, that their suffering would end too, permanently; that their sorrow, sense of loss, and anger would vanish, and joy and love and healing and wholeness and holiness would be in them, just like it was in me. My loving God had healed me, fully, totally, and completely to the core of my being. I was imbued with love and joy. My parents would also be healed upon their deaths. However, I also knew and understood that until they died their suffering in life would continue—and were I to stay on in heaven, I understood that their suffering would be ever more painful.

☞ 17 ☜

Life's a Wink and Heaven Is Beauty

Although God had no eyes that I could see, I could sense God wink at me—and in the wink show me that my entire life, the lives of my parents, and the lives and times of all humans on earth encompass just the wink of God's eye. My life and your life are as brief as the quick wink of God's eye. The illusion is that we have all the time in the world, but time itself is an illusion. We have little time. Life on this planet is brief. In that amount of time, just a wink, my life began, was lived, and ended. The same is true for you, although it does not feel that way.

I understood that time and life on the planet, in the world we call earth and galaxy and universe were not real in the way that God is Real. Only God is Real; all else is both real and an illusion. All of my life, from my birth to death, all twenty-one years of it, was a mere blink when compared with eternity. God showed me that as a creature, as one created by my Creator, as one who is made and not self-made, that all lifetimes—mine, yours, our mother's and father's, everybody's—are so fast. They start, and they are over. I know it does not seem like that on this side, in this world. Only in death, when eternity opens, when timelessness is normative, does it become clear just how brief life is. Time is an illusion. Eternity is Real. God is Real.

Even knowing that I was beloved eternally, and knowing that my parents were beloved, and that they would be healed of suffering at their death as I was healed—even knowing all of that, I said, *I still cannot stay here.*

As if Omnipotent did not know the reason, God asked me, *Why?*

I replied, *God, I'm in a college theater troupe. We leave on a 24,000-mile, 64-show tour in one week. The director of the Theater of Silence, and my communications professor in American Sign Language at Montana State University, had actually grabbed me by the shirt collar when he heard I was headed into the Canada wilderness to go backcountry camping and ice climbing for spring break and, with his face in my face, said to me, 'Peter, do not get hurt next week. There are no understudies. You can't be replaced. The show must go on. Be careful.' I promised him that I would be careful and that I would be ready for the tour.* I told all of that to God in a single thought.

With compassion and love God said, *You do not have to come Home now if you do not want to.*

I asked, *Is this heaven?* I was referring to heaven living inside my soul (and me contained within it)—the wholeness, the holiness, the being known by God with absolutely no secrets, and the safety and security of that overwhelming Love-Hope-Joy-Beauty-Truth-Charity-Kindness-Compassion-Love-Patience-Beauty-Love that was, in God's presence, my complete self. I was whole and holy in the presence of God, and as beautiful as it was, and as true as God's words were, I felt as if I had a responsibility on earth, to my parents and to my theater troupe. I was not done with life. I had commitments. I had work to complete, and family not to hurt.

God said, *Yes, this is heaven that you feel, that you are because of Me, living within you. You do not have to die now; you do not have to stay here. You can go back if you want to go back.*

I knew that to be the Truth. I said, *If I go back to earth, to my body, to my life, to my family, then the next time I die, may I come back here to this Beauty-Love, to this heaven of healing and wholeness, this mercy and forgiveness, this Compassion-Joy and Truth? If I choose to live my life, will I come back here? Will I come back to you?*

God was heaven, and heaven was God, and God was greater than heaven. The two were one, yet separate. God gave me heaven. It was beauty and love beyond compare. I did not deserve it, but I was so grateful to be there. And yet, I was bold enough to ask to leave.

God said, *Yes, Peter, my beloved, you can come back to Me.*

I said, *I choose to live my life.*

God said, *Peter, my beloved, you won't live your life.*

And with those words, God sent me away.

⟱ 18 ⟱

Alien in My Body

The next thing I knew and felt was searing pain. It felt like I was being slowly and painfully twisted, like an ice screw, back into my physical body at that point above my stomach and below my heart. I was stuffed back into my body, and it hurt. I hurt all over. I awoke. I was me, but I did not know what I was, who I was, where I was, or what I was doing. My body was dangling on my harness at an angle, and I could hear a voice shouting. I was dazed and disoriented. I did not understand anything. I was back in the world inside a body that I did not understand. I opened my eyes and looked up at the man who was screaming at me and looking right at me. I wondered, *Who is he? Where am I? Why is he yelling?*

Then, he had a hand on me, was grasping my jacket hood and pulling on me, jerking me, trying to hoist me up, or wake me up, or something. I watched him dispassionately for a time, as if I was observing him from afar, while trying to figure out what I was: What was this thing—this body—that I was in? Who was I? Where was I? What is this being—this man thing—who is yelling words at me that I do not comprehend while yanking on me?

Minutes passed, and I slowly understood that I was back in my body. Then, I recognized Tim. Bit by bit, I understood: I was Peter. I was a human being and no longer just a soul. I was on a mountain. My body hurt. I had not been hurting before.

Tim was shouting at me. He was very loud. He screamed at me, "DON'T DIE! DON'T DIE. WAKE UP! WAKE UP! DON'T DIE AND LEAVE ME HERE! DO NOT DIE! WAKE UP! IF YOU DIE, I WILL DIE."

Tim was crying, and shouting, and there was fear in his voice; but there was determination, too. I looked at his eyes, into his eyes, and saw that he saw that I was awake, and so he pulled harder on my shoulder. I clambered back up onto the ledge, disoriented. I watched him in the moonlight. He was still shouting and crying, saying, "I thought you were dead. I thought you were dead. I'm so glad you're not dead. You scared me. I was alone."

I said nothing. I could say nothing. I was having a difficult time thinking. I still didn't understand what I was or what had just happened to me. I remembered where I had been, but I didn't understand anything about it. I was perplexed, and struggled to figure out how my body worked, and even what my body was. One thing I did know was that I was not my body. I knew I was something inhabiting a body and that although it was somehow "me," it was also not me at all.

I stopped listening to Tim and focused on inhabiting this thing, this body I was in. After a while, I figured out how to move. I figured out where I was and who I was and what I was doing there. It all felt so alien, as if I were in a film against my will. I was disassociated from my body and everything around me, but I was also definitely in my body. It felt, I felt, like a contradiction. I looked down and saw the rope hanging from my harness and picked it up with both hands. It was instinctive rather than thoughtful. I turned away to look at the rope and saw it disappear around the corner of the cliff, and I pulled it hard. My hands hurt. My feet hurt. My face, my ears, my cheeks, my nose, my entire body hurt. Though I could barely make sense of anything, I pulled the rope hard . . . and the rope pulled free.

Tim cheered. The rope that had been stuck for God knows how long—hours?—suddenly on that one pull came free, and so I hauled it down, easy as could be. Tim whooped in joy. I began to remember who I was, or at least who I was as a body, and my mind started to make sense of all that was around me. Tim was talking excitedly, saying, "I thought you were dead. I thought I was going to die, too." I didn't know what to say. That I had been dead? That I had been somewhere else and in that somewhere else I had been me, but the me that I truly am, the soul me, the without-flesh me? I did not understand how to articulate my experience. I only knew that I had died, and I was no longer dead. Tim did not believe in God. How could I possibly talk with him about what I'd experienced? I could not.

Everything was different, as if I had been born again. And, in that second time, I knew that I was not real, and that the world was some sort of temporary illusion in which I was stuck and through which I was passing. I felt like I was in an alien world inhabiting a body that was not *me*, and that Tim could not see who I really was. He could only see what he thought I was.

But the rope was free, and all of those thoughts had to wait. I was no longer desperate to get off the mountain. Dying was hard, but death was beautiful . . . and the world was not. I no longer feared death, not at all. I was dispassionate about the world; I wanted to go back. I had made a choice: I had chosen this world and life here, but I knew deep down that I had made a tremendous mistake. I did not belong here. I was not from here. I wanted only to go back to God. Tim was my responsibility, though. He still feared dying. I needed to stay with him and help him, but had I been alone I know I could have unclipped. I could have just unclipped right there.

I thought about it—unclipping, leaning back slightly, and falling. The fall would surely have killed me, or killed my body. I did not want to be in this world, but I had a responsibility to Tim, to my troupe, and to my parents.

We had been standing on that narrow ledge for hours, fighting to save our lives—that much I understood. I also knew I had been dead, and that I'd been in heaven, or at least on heaven's threshold . . . but where was that? What had happened to me? How long had I been dead? I did not know.

I tried to focus on the task at hand, but it was difficult. My mind kept flying back to where I had just been. It felt as if the greater part of me was still there. I felt bifurcated, divided, not wholly in the world. It felt, it still feels, as if I had one foot here, and the other there. I knew that, moments before, I had been without a body, yet here I was in a body. I had been in God's overwhelming presence, and the Voice had spoken to me. I understood that the smartest I had ever been was when I had no brain. I had a brain again, and that confused me. I was aware that I had known and understood infinitely more only moments before than I now knew as I stood under the moonlight. I also knew that all I had just known moments before had slipped away as I reentered my body.

It was all so confusing and disorienting. I was lost, and so alone. I craved one thing: God, in fullness, in joy, and love, and truth, and beauty. I knew that I'd had all of that, and I had let it all go. *What a fool I am! What a fool I am to have come back,* I thought.

I ran the rope's bitter end through the iron O-ring that was iron pinned into the rock of the mountain cliff, and then threw both bitter ends down. "I'll go first," I said to Tim, and I rappelled our final 150 feet. Upon reaching the bottom my feelings were mixed. I was exhausted and only wanted warmth, food, and sleep. I was glad to be down, but I did not want to be there. I landed on the top of the partially snow-covered talus cone. (A talus cone is the accumulation of rocks, gravel, and dirt caused by erosion and found at the base of very steep mountains.) I waited and watched as Tim rappelled down next. After he was standing beside me, he pulled the rope down, quickly coiled it, and slung it over his shoulder. Silently, we picked our way down the steep slope to the flat, snow-covered ground.

⇜ 19 ⇝

Warden's Worry

We were still suffering from exposure, but glad to be off the mountain as we headed toward Tim's truck. His tent and our packs were still in it. I could hardly think, and barely walk. Our bodies were worn out and still dying. Tim found his keys with frozen fingers and unlocked the trunk. We resisted the temptation to rest in the car with the heater on high—heating up too quickly is a bad idea when recovering from hypothermia, and the shelter of our tent, some tea, and our sleeping bags seemed like the better choice. So we shouldered our backpacks and trudged back across the Icefields Parkway to set up camp away from the base of Lower Weeping Wall.

We unpacked the tent and, with little communication, efficiently set it up in the moonlight, found our flashlights, turned them on, and pushed our backpacks inside the tent. We climbed into the tent and unrolled our sleeping pads on the floor, unstuffed our down sleeping bags, clumsily stripped off our wet clothes, and climbed naked inside our bags. I remember thinking that our best chance would be to zip our bags together and climb in together. We did not do this, though we should have.

Holding my little yellow flashlight between my teeth, as was my habit, I unpacked and set up my backpacking stove, filled it with white gas from my gas tank, pumped up the stove's tank, and fired it up with my Bic lighter. Meanwhile, Tim zipped the tent shut, popped up the chimney vent on the tent's roof, and opened the floor vent for ventilation. That way, we could fire up the stove inside the tent without adding asphyxiation as a danger. It was a large winter tent with enough room for our backpacks and both of us. Tim unzipped the tent door and reached outside to fill our large aluminum cooking pot with snow to melt for water. I put the pot on the stove as the tent began to warm up from the roaring blue flame. We waited in silence and shivered.

I pulled out some dry long underwear and wool socks and put them on. Tim did the same. The water steamed. I dropped a couple of Tetley tea bags into the simmering pot. We did not want boiling water, only *warm* water so as to gently raise our body temperatures. We did not wait for it to steep. We filled our plastic camp cups over and over, sipping the warm tea. We melted more snow and drank a lot more tea. As we warmed up, we gnawed on hard backpacker's bread and ate spoonfuls of peanut butter squeezed from our plastic backpacker's tubes. We dipped the peanut butter in the raisins we'd bought in Jasper two days before. We huddled close together for warmth, then lay down and nodded off.

Sometime after sunup, we were warm enough and we awoke. The tent was warm. The stove was out. I refilled the tank and fired it up as Tim got more snow to melt. We drank more tea—hot tea this time—and ate instant oatmeal with a dollop of honey and some boiled raisins on top. We talked little. We were still exhausted. Every extremity of my body ached and burned.

After breakfast, we pulled on dry clothes and put on our extra mittens and cross-country ski boots, crawled out of the tent on our hands and knees, and greeted a sunny, cold, and clear morning. We were alone. I put on my dark glasses to ward against the bright sun and snow reflection, and stared up at Lower Weeping Wall. It was a quiet, windless morning. We traced our climbing route up, our traverse across, and our rappelling routes down with our eyes. My eyes lingered on the ledge where we first sat at the top of our climb, and then on the lone tree at the top of our first rappel. I looked at the overhang below that tree and the edge of the ledge where we were when the ranger saw us. The traverse to our next rappel was narrow and, given the angle, I could see little of the boulder-filled crag that was our second rappel. When my eyes got to the narrow ledge on which I died, I just looked and looked. Tim jostled my shoulder. Apparently, I had been looking for some time and he'd been speaking to me, but I had not heard him.

It was frightening to see what we had survived. I was still completely confused about what had happened. Had it happened? Was it real? Had I died? What had I experienced? Was I crazy? Had the cold driven me temporarily mad? I felt that I was living simultaneously in two places, as if I was seeing what was before me—the snow, the mountain, the ice, the trees, the climb, and Tim—with one eye, while my other eye seemed to see something beyond, and it focused there, in another world, in another dimension, in a place more real than reality. I suddenly felt bereft and homeless.

Those feelings are with me still, more than thirty years later. I knew, at the time, that I could not explain any of it to my dear atheist friend to whom I had just trusted my life and, before I died, my inner thoughts. Besides, it all seemed like madness to me. I felt that I had touched upon insanity, and surely if I spoke of it aloud to my dear friend, he would not understand. What's more, I myself did not understand—and how could I talk about what I did not understand? I felt more lost and confused than I'd ever felt in my life.

Tim shook my shoulder again. "Come on," he said.

The air was crisp, and my feet and hands were getting cold again. They hurt again. They would hurt again for the rest of my life—every day that the temperature dropped below fifty degrees. That pain functions as a constant reminder of that day.

I was warmer, but my core was still cold. We decided to get on the road as soon as we could. We pulled everything out of the tent, stuffed our sleeping bags, packed our gear, collapsed the tent, then packed that too. Tim and I shouldered our backpacks and our climbing gear for what we thought was the last time in this wilderness, and walked out on the snow-packed path to the side of the Icefields Parkway. We dropped our backpacks by the roadside. Tim walked over to the car while I waited. It started up right away. He drove it over and left it running so that it would be warm when we got in.

As we loaded our gear into the open trunk, we heard a pickup truck coming down the highway. It was the first vehicle we'd seen that morning. The truck pulled up right behind us and stopped. It was the ranger—our ranger. He got out. We waited for him to approach and said hello.

"Boys, were you the two guys on the mountain last night?"

"Yes, sir," we said.

"I watched you last night from my truck in the parking lot. You saw me?"

"Yes, sir, and thank you. You gave us hope."

"I came down here this morning to see if you were alive, or if we had to go get the helicopter to recover your bodies off the mountain. I'm glad you survived. You two take care now," he said, shaking his head.

We shook hands, said good-bye, and then the ranger turned back to his truck, got in, and drove back north. He left us quietly pondering the truth of what he had said. We might have survived. Or, he might have had to dispatch the helicopter and team to recover our bodies; we would have made the news as the two dead climbers from Montana, and our parents would have been broken-hearted. We were humbled by his question and shaken by his statements.

We climbed into Tim's car and drove south. We did not talk much. We were both too exhausted. I offered to drive again. Tim said no, that his dad would not let anybody drive the car except him, adding that I knew that already and shouldn't bother asking again. That much had not changed. But I was changed. I was a different person. I was not the same man I'd been just the day before.

I knew I was Peter Panagore. I had all of my memories and feelings about the people I loved, but I no longer knew who—or what—I was anymore. I was from another dimension, another place. Earth was no longer my home. The part of me that was still in heaven was the real part of me; the part of me on earth was the lost part. I did not want to be in this body; hence, I did not want to be alive. Everything around me, everything I could see was flat, black-and-white, cartoonish, two-dimensional, and—despite the great beauty of the Canadian Rockies that morning—everything looked ugly and crass.

⤳ 20 ⤳

Bad Ride and Jail

I rode shotgun and watched the world out the window in silent reflection until I fell asleep. Sometime after dark, I awoke still in the car. I looked out the window into blackness then looked over at Tim. There was a jazz cassette playing in the tape deck. We had been listening to jazz since we left Bozeman. Jazz was new to me, and I liked it. Jazz still speaks to me, and for me, thanks to Tim. I looked at the road ahead as we sped south. Tim must have been really exhausted, because he had slept as little the night before as I had and had not slept at all during the day. The road ahead was dark except for a pair of headlights coming toward us . . . coming directly at us.

"Tim," I said, "I think you are on the wrong side of the road. Those headlights are headed straight at us."

Tim said, "I'm not on the wrong side of the road. You just woke up. You don't know what you are seeing."

I scanned the road intensely, believing him. But I was sure of what I was seeing; he was wrong. We were in the wrong lane.

"Tim!" I shouted, "You ARE on the wrong side of the highway!" It was one of those two-lane highways—one lane northbound and one lane southbound, with a very faded double yellow line between them.

"SWERVE!" I shouted.

At the last second Tim swerved into the safety of our lane. The other car sped by us with its horn blaring. Tim apologized.

"Are you okay? I asked. "You must be very tired. Pull over. I can drive; your dad will never know. I slept. You haven't."

Tim said, "No, I'm okay now. Go back to sleep."

I knew Tim enough to know that arguing would not help. He was stubborn that way, but that stubbornness was also the source of his inner drive, which had helped keep the two of us alive the night before. I trusted him, and went back into a dreamless sleep.

The next time I awoke was to the sound of a Royal Canadian Mounted Police constable's siren roaring up behind us, with its cop car lights flashing. I opened my eyes to see the last of a small town's center fly past us—houses in a row, all with snowy yards. It was just after dark when Tim pulled over to the edge of the road, stopped the car, and rolled down his window. The Mountie told us sternly that we had sped through his town going thirty kilometers per hour (about nineteen miles per hour) over the speed limit. Tim had not even seen the town, he said, and apologized. The Mountie admitted that it was a very small town, one of the do-not-blink towns that you may miss even as you drive through. We had missed it.

The Mountie said, "May I have your license, registration, and insurance card, please?"

Tim took out his wallet as I fished in the glove box for the registration and insurance card that were neatly organized in a folder and handed them to Tim. Tim handed the three items to the Mountie. The Mountie was quiet as he looked over the documents.

He said, "You're Americans. We've had bad experiences with Americans after we ticket them. They say they will pay when they get home, but once they cross the border, they never do. I'm going to give you a speeding ticket, and you have to pay for it right now—right here and right now. Wait for me."

The Mountie turned around and walked back to his cruiser. Tim rolled up the window because it was cold outside. We talked about the ticket. We did not know how much it was going to be, but we did not have much money on us, only enough to pay for gas to get back to Bozeman and to buy a pizza for dinner. We decided that we would take the ticket with us, and the Mountie would just have to trust us. Tim was watching in the rearview mirror and saw him get out of his cruiser.

"Here he comes," Tim said, and he rolled down his window again. The Mountie handed him the ticket. Tim looked at it and showed it to me.

Tim said, "We're not going to pay this now. We can't pay for it now. You'll have to trust us. We have just enough money on us to pay for gas to get home. We promise to pay it. My dad will pay it."

The Mountie said, "No. You pay for this ticket right now. We don't trust Americans."

Tim said, "We can't pay now. We won't pay."

I leaned over Tim and agreed, saying, "Please. We had a terrible, terrible night last night. Can't you give us a break? We promise to pay. It's just, like Tim said, we can't pay now if we want to get home. We do not have enough money."

The Mountie's face hardened as he ordered, "Take the keys out of the ignition. Close the windows, and both of you get out of the car, slowly, with your hands where I can see them."

We did as he ordered. We wondered what was going on and asked him when we were out of the car. He said, "You are both under arrest for speeding and for refusing to pay the fine. I'm taking you back into town. No questions. Lock your vehicle. Get into the backseat of my car."

We walked toward his cruiser; he followed, walking closely behind us. Tim opened the door and we got into the backseat as the Mountie held on to the car door. He put his hand on my head as I got in, pushed me down a little, then closed the door behind us. I tried the handle. There was no door handle. There were no handles for the windows either. And there was a wire cage between the front seat and the backseat. We started to talk to the Mountie when he got in the car, but he ordered us to be quiet. We shut our mouths. It was a short ride back into the sleeping small town. He radioed ahead saying that he was bringing us in.

What had we gotten ourselves into now? He parked next to a snowbank outside of a well-lit municipal building, got out, and let us out. He marched us inside the constable's station in front of him, through the front office, passing the officer on desk duty who nodded knowingly to our Mountie, gave him a key, and glared at us. He then marched us into the back room, where he unlocked the barred cell and ordered us inside. We were scared and hesitated. "Get in!" he ordered. We went in, and he shut the cell door behind us. It locked with a metallic click and the turn of the key that the deskman had handed him.

He said to us, "Now is the time to talk. I arrested you two because you refused to pay your legal fine. We've had trouble with Americans not paying their fines. We're not letting you go until you pay. It's as simple as that. You talk about it while I go get a cup of coffee."

He walked away, and we were alone. I do not remember how much the ticket was for, but Tim still had it in his hands. We looked at it, read it over. We did not have enough money to pay the ticket, period.

Tim and I both carried our money in two places. It is a trick many travelers use. We each had a wallet with cash, and we each had emergency cash stashed away inside our smelly hiking boots—just in case we were robbed. Alone in the cell, we opened our wallets, pulled out our cash, and pooled it. It was not much, maybe twenty or thirty American dollars. We called out to the Mountie, and he walked back to us, sipping his coffee. We showed him the cash we had, emptied our pockets, and showed him our empty wallets. "It's all we have between us," we lied. The Mountie told Tim to hand him the cash, and then he counted it. "It's not enough," he said, "but it'll have to do."

He unlocked the cell and let us out, and offered us coffee, which we politely accepted, even though I did not drink coffee at the time. "I'll drive you back to your car, boys," he said. He was all smiles and friendliness now. It was a quiet ride back. As he let us out of his cruiser, he said, "Drive slowly and stay out of trouble, boys."

"Yes, sir," we said in unison.

I dumped out my coffee in the snow outside Tim's car, and we drove on. By the time we got to Calgary we were hungry, so we pulled off into that shining light of a city. After calculating money for gas and food, we figured we had enough boot cash between us to eat a cheese pizza for supper and just about get back to Bozeman. So we pulled into the first pizza joint we saw and ate hungrily at a Formica-covered table under neon lights. It was a noisy place and a harsh culture clash for us. Tim was talkative. I was not.

Our encounter with the Royal Canadian Mounted Police had not fazed me. I was deeply, emotionally disturbed by our extreme ice climbing adventure, and becoming ever more so, troubled and confused to the depth of my spirit by my encounter with heaven and God. I had thought that maybe, when I woke up, the feeling of being in two places at once might go away. It had not. It haunted me. I was pensive and quiet. Tim tried to cajole me back to my good humor by saying all was well because we had won; we had beat the mountain. He commented on the culture shock of the quiet wilderness compared to the bright lights of the big city. He said he was sorry about being in the wrong lane and about our police encounter. I said it was okay. I was overwhelmed and reeling but could not explain why. I did not smile. I could not talk. Tim tried, but eventually, over our pizza, he gave up and left me alone.

Wrecked

Back in the car, I fell asleep again. When I awoke, we were still on that two-lane highway, headed south in the dark. I looked ahead and again saw a pair of white headlights headed straight toward us, about a half-mile away. Other than the car lights headed directly at us, the road was empty.

Calmly, I said, "Tim, you are on the wrong side of the road again."

"I am not," he said. "You just woke up. You don't know what you are talking about. We are doing fine. I am right where I am supposed to be. Go back to sleep."

"Tim," I insisted, "You're on the wrong side! You're in the wrong lane!"

"I am not!" he said. "Go back to sleep!"

I thought he was wrong, and rather than argue and risk our lives again with a head-on collision, I reached out with my left hand and grabbed the wheel.

Tim looked over at me with his eyes wide. "NO! Stop!" he shouted.

I did not listen to him and instead I jerked down on the steering wheel, forcing the car to the right.

Tim screamed at me, "Noooo!"

Tim was right, and I was not in my right mind. The car leaped to the right and into the emergency lane. I felt the tires on my side hit the gravel just above the edge of the roadside ditch. It felt like the car went up on the two wheels of its passenger side, and maybe it did, just a little. Tim was screaming at me, "What have you done?!" I was screaming, too.

Time slowed down. All the objects in the car drifted past me in a sort of suspended animation—a book, two or three cassette tapes, a crunched up bag, a pencil.

Tim jerked the wheel to the left to compensate. We rocketed to the left, across the centerline, this time seemingly landing on the two wheels on the driver's side. The car was strangely tipped and lurching and completely out of control. I watched as the headlights and front end of an eighteen-wheeler materialized directly in front of us, only feet away, aimed directly at us. Our car and the truck were both doing fifty-five miles an hour. The objects in the air seemed to almost freeze in space. Tim and I kept screaming. Tim saw the truck and jerked the wheel too hard to the right.

He shouted out, "My dad is going to kill me if we wreck the car!"

We missed the front end of the semi by inches. In those few moments, I plainly saw my entire life flash before my eyes, just like they say it does—like a movie. It was superfast and very clear, starting when I was a baby and running right through my entire life, day by day. It was completely unlike what I experienced the night before when I was in hell. This was like watching a reel of my life with sound, flashing rapidly across my inner vision. It blocked out my view of what was actually happening around me inside and outside of the car. It was complete, and yet also extremely fast, brief.

Tim jerked the wheel back to the left because he had overcompensated to the right, or maybe the car was somehow caught on its right side wheels and jerked itself back to the left—because we were about to crash over the side and into the ditch. We swung to the left and hit hard, front-end first on my side against the skidding double rear wheels of the flatbed of the semi.

We hit at an angle in a horrendously violent crash. There was a loud squeal of the semi's locked up and smoking wheels. We both jerked forward hard against our seat belts. Tim hit the steering wheel with his head. I watched the double wheels crush and explode the front end of Tim's car. Metal and plastic went flying. I watched through the windshield, sure that I was about to die and afraid of the pain that was coming, as the steel of the flatbed came at my head even as I helplessly felt it swing forward and hit the dashboard.

Our seat belts locked up. Mine stopped me from flying from my seat through the windshield, where I surely would have crushed my skull against the edge of the flatbed steel that stopped only inches from the other side of the windshield. My head bounced off the dashboard. And then everything stopped.

It was silent. We were still. The front end of the car was completely destroyed, shredded. Parts fell off as we sat there. I stared at the steel edge of the flatbed just on the other side of the windshield. The car's engine was mangled; it had absorbed most of the shock of the impact. Miraculously, Tim and I were pretty much unhurt. I had bruised my chest and whipped my neck but seemed otherwise okay. Then Tim exploded in anger. He started shouting all sorts of expletives at me, screaming that his dad was going to kill him because his car was wrecked. Tim was right, of course. I had wrecked his car.

"Tell your dad that it was my fault. I'll tell your dad because it was my fault," I said.

"Just shut up, Peter," he said.

The truck driver was pounding his fist on the roof of the car, shouting at us, asking if anyone was hurt. We both got out of the car on the driver's side because I could not open the passenger door—it was destroyed. We stood around as the truck driver shouted at both of us, but mostly at Tim, because he thought it was Tim's fault, and from his own fear and anger that he might have killed us. He was shaking, and so were we.

"It was my fault," I stuttered. "I grabbed the wheel. Tim didn't do it. I did. I was asleep and I woke up confused and I grabbed the wheel and I jerked it down."

Pointing at me, the trucker asked Tim, "Is he telling the truth?"

"Yes, he is," said Tim.

"It was my fault," I repeated, and stood there humiliated by what I had done.

After a few minutes, a Canadian Mountie arrived with lights flashing and sorted out what had happened. Traffic was backing up in that rural stretch of highway. The semi was in its lane headed north, and Tim's car was stopped across the southbound lane. Together, both vehicles blocked the entire road. After hearing from the trucker, Tim, and me about what had happened, the Mountie ordered us to try to push Tim's car off the truck, back across the road, and onto the shoulder, so that traffic could get moving again. I went under the flatbed to push from the front end; Tim and the truck driver pushed from over by the driver's door as the Mountie stood on duty surveying the scene and stopping traffic.

It was dark underneath the flatbed, and the Mountie was in a hurry to get us to move the car. He shouted at us in an angry voice, "Push that car out of the way." It was cold out. I was a mental and emotional mess by this point. I blindly put my hand on what was left of the hood of the car without thinking there might be sharp edges or broken glass, or that I should have been wearing gloves. We pushed hard together. The fleshy part of my right hand, between my thumb and palm, sunk into a sharp edge of metal. I felt it cut me, deeply, but I kept pushing anyway and I let it hurt. I had this idea that I deserved the pain and the wound and the blood for having wrecked Tim's car, and for having nearly killed us in a violent wreck.

The car rolled off rather easily from the highway and onto the gravel shoulder. The trucker kept repeating, "Thank you God, thank you God, that nobody died, or got badly hurt, and that my semi was undamaged."

"My dad's going to kill me," Tim said, looking right at me. And then he stopped talking. He was livid, and he was right. The wreck was my fault, and his dad was going to be very angry with him. I felt like a jerk. We were both pretty shaken up, especially considering everything that had happened in the last twenty-four hours. The Mountie got all the legal information he needed— license, registration, insurance, and listened to our story of the crash and why we were in Canada. He did seem to care when I stuttered again and again, "It wasn't his fault. It was my fault. I did this."

He asked us, "What are you going to do now? Where are you going to sleep?"

We didn't know. "It's a clear night," I said. "We have a tent. Can we set it up over there?" I pointed to the side of the road. "We can roll out our sleeping pads and bags off of the side of the highway, sleep there for the rest of the night, and figure out what to do in the morning."

"No, that's a bad idea," he said. "There is a small hotel in town. Get all of your gear and everything you may ever want out of the car. Clean it out. It's a total wreck. It will never drive again." We cleaned out the car.

By this time, a second Mountie had arrived and was directing traffic around the accident scene. The first Mountie opened the trunk of his car for us to load our gear. He continued talking to Tim and the trucker. The temperature was dropping, and I was shaking and shivering. Tim told the Mountie that we did not have enough money to pay for a room in a hotel. The Mountie said, "I don't care if you have any money or not, because no matter what you will not sleep next to the highway." He insisted that he would drive us to the hotel, adding that if we had any other ideas besides going to the hotel that he would arrest us and lock us up. That settled it. We had already spent time that night in a Canadian jail and did not want a repeat event. Neither of us told the Mountie that we'd already visited a cell that night.

I finished cleaning out Tim's car and loading our backpacks, tent, skis and poles, axes, rope, a dozen ice screws, assorted carabiners, and nylon webbing into the trunk of the Mountie's cruiser. I also collected all of Tim's valuables from inside the car—his cassette tapes, a book, and other things, plus all the stuff from his glove box. I felt like I owed it to Tim to do the cleaning. Then, for the

second time that night, we climbed into the backseat of a
police car. Once more, we were locked in the backseat of
a police car, side by side. He drove us to the hotel. It was
a silent and short ride, just a couple miles. My hand was
bleeding and pulsed with pain from the cut I got when
we pushed the car off the road. I said nothing about it
and applied direct pressure to stop the blood, wrapping
it with my bandana to try to keep my blood off of the car
upholstery. I figured that I deserved it.

✐ 22 ✐

Beggars

It was probably after midnight when we walked into the hotel lobby. A log fire was burning in the lobby, and there was red wall-to-wall carpet covering the floor. Behind the dark wood check-in counter the hotel manager eyed us suspiciously as we walked in, looking like exactly what we were at that point: two scared and dirty mountaineers. Our backpacks towered behind our heads and axes and rope hung over our shoulders. There were other people in the lobby, and they watched us and assessed us silently. We had stopped for a moment outside of the hotel to stick our cross-country skis and poles into a snowbank outside the front door. The Mountie told us that they would be safe there because it was a crime-free town.

I had the immediate impression that it was a decent hotel, and that unwashed, longhaired, backpack-carrying hippies with cross-country skis were not welcome. Tim and I shed our packs by the door and approached the desk. The couple of guests who loitered in the small and homey lobby backed away from us. We told the manager that we had just totaled—that is, I had just totaled—Tim's car, and that the Mountie who was with us had ordered us to come to the hotel even though we didn't have any money to pay for a room.

"No money, no room," the manager said. "You can leave. Get out. You're disrupting our lobby and disturbing our guests. Please leave right now."

"Mister," Tim begged, "this Mountie is going to arrest us if we leave. He told us so. He'll put us in jail as vagrants if you do not let us stay here for the night. Peter totaled my car, and we have nowhere to go. Please let us stay here."

"I don't care what happens to you," the manager replied. "What's that to me? You'll need to pay to stay here or get out. We're a hotel; we're not a charity. On second thought, just get out of here now!" He pointed to the door.

We looked at the stern-eyed Mountie who had his arms crossed over his chest. He did not look happy. Tim and I looked at each other, and Tim begged again, "Please, we just went through a frightening car wreck, and last night we nearly died of exposure while ice climbing up near Jasper. We need your help. We're college students from Bozeman."

"I don't care what happened to you, who you are, or where you are from; get out," he said.

The guests watched and listened to our little drama. I think they were sympathetic. I pleaded, "J-j-j-just let us u-u-unroll our s-s-s-sleeping bags over b-by the fireplace on the f-f-loor and let us spend the night. We p-promise to be up b-b-before daylight and out the d-d-door b-before your guests are up in the m-m-morning."

The hotel manager chuckled at my stutter and said he had had enough of us. "GET. OUT," he said once more.

Thus, our negotiations with the manager were over, and we resigned ourselves to being arrested for the second time that night. We turned away from the check-in counter and walked toward our backpacks. We both looked at the Mountie in his red uniform, high leather boots, leather belt, and leather shoulder strap. He had been leaning against the wall near the front door, watching and listening. He removed his wide-brimmed hat, held it in his hand, and then he took a step toward us.

This is it, I thought. *Jail.* I was expecting arrest when he spoke up and said to the hotel manager, "John, I think these are good boys who have had a lot of trouble last night and again tonight. This one wrecked the car and he wasn't even driving. Why don't you just let them sleep on the lobby floor tonight, as a favor to me? I'm sure they will be out at the crack of dawn. Right, boys?"

We nodded yes.

"If they're not," he continues, "you call me. I'll still be on duty, and I'll come get them and arrest them. Okay, John? Okay, boys?"

We nodded again and said, "Yes, sir." He handed John his card, and John reluctantly agreed.

"Thank you, sir," we said to the manager scowling at us. We thanked the Mountie too, who gave us a kind grin as he said goodnight. "Get some rest, boys, and don't let me find you here in the morning."

"You won't, sir," Tim said, and I nodded in agreement. The Mountie then turned and left us there.

We ignored the other guests as we unstuffed our sleeping bags, rolled out our sleeping pads close to the fireplace, and without changing clothes slipped into our sleeping bags, side by side, and fell immediately into an exhausted sleep.

The next morning we woke at dawn because the hotel manager made sure of it. "Get up, you two," he snarled. We got up, packed up our gear, shouldered our packs, and thanked him. He grunted and looked away.

Tim asked him if there was a bus station and a bus that was headed south.

"A bus? I thought you said you had no money? You hippies. There's a bus headed south this morning, but it costs money, and you don't have any money. I'm sure they won't let you on the bus for nothing. It will stop just up the road in about an hour outside a shop."

For some reason, maybe it was the look on our faces, the manager's face softened a bit and he handed Tim a bus schedule. We thanked him again, stuffed our sleeping bags, rolled up our pads, packed them away, shouldered all our gear, and went out into the cold, rosy dawn. We stopped to strap our skis and poles to each other's backpacks in a helpful way, and I could tell that Tim, while still angry with me, still liked me enough to be helpful.

The town was quiet and pretty. The night before, after the wreck, we had had no idea where we were, what town we were in, or what the town looked like. It was situated just off the highway, on a parallel side road, which probably had been the main road before the highway was built. On the far north end of town stood a tall grain silo. We were in farm country. There were a few well-painted houses set closely together, some shops, and a grocery market. There weren't any cars on the road or on the highway. The bus stop was indeed outside one of the small shops. Tim and I stood in the hotel parking lot looking around and talked about what to do next.

It was then that I discovered I had developed a strong stutter. When I was talking to the Mountie and the manager the night before, I had figured that my new stutter was temporary, a result of my nerves, and would be gone in the morning. Instead, every sentence I uttered I stammered. Tim was annoyed. I could see it in his face, and I was shocked.

"W-w-what the . . . ?" I said. I had never stuttered in all my life, not once. I stammered my way through our conversation as we looked at the bus schedule, reviewed our options, and measured our money. We had lied a little to the Mountie and to the manager. We had stashed some of our cash inside our boots. I was feeling humble, embarrassed, and ashamed for having wrecked Tim's car.

"Tim," I stammered, "I am so sorry for what I did. I know your dad is going to be so angry. You tell him it was my fault. You tell him that. If he wants to talk to me, I'll tell him that too."

Tim just shook his head slowly, and looking at the bus schedule, said, "There's a bus leaving in an hour. It looks like it will go right through to Bozeman with a few stops along the way."

"You take the bus. I wrecked your car."

We pooled our money. All together it was enough to get one of us back to Bozeman.

"You take the bus. I'll hitchhike." I had been hitchhiking since high school. My Catholic prep school had been two towns west of my city, and on occasion I'd miss the bus home and have to hitchhike. This practice eventually led me to hitchhiking between UMass and my home, and then up into the mountains of western Massachusetts, New Hampshire, Vermont, Maine, Montana, and Wyoming for backpacking and hiking trips. I was an old hand at hitching rides.

I stuttered out, "I'll be s-s-safe enough."

Tim eyed me curiously, and kindly, and then said, "Let's split the gear."

We split the gear between us, with Tim taking the large and clunky items: four skis, four ski poles, two ice axes, dozens of ice screws, and his ice hammer. We had already divided the tent parts between us. I took our climbing rope, one axe, my two hammers, my stove, and the rest of my gear.

"I'll need to make a hitchhiking sign," I stuttered, and I walked back into the hotel and stammered to the manager, "Pretty please, may I have a piece of cardboard on which to write 'Bozeman,' and may I also borrow a marker with which to write it?"

He smiled knowingly, almost kindly, and handed me a thick black marker and a piece of cardboard that he retrieved from a back room. I wrote Bozeman, MT in big, bold black letters on the cardboard, thanked him again, and walked outside to join Tim.

We chatted a little about his bus route, and I discovered that when I stuttered, if I stopped talking and started over, I stuttered less.

Tim said, "I am unbelievably angry with you for wrecking my car. My dad told me not to let anyone ever drive it and I didn't and now what am I going to say to him? He spent a lot of money on that car. He trusted me. He is going to kill me."

I repeated, "I'm sorry. It was my fault."

Tim said, "After this, when this is all over, I don't ever want to see you again."

I understood why. My time in my own hell gave me a clear understanding of how much pain I'd caused him. I was feeling heartily sorry. Meanwhile, I was still deeply confused and struggling with being a human being, being inside a body, having a brain, and having fingers and toes and a nose and cheeks that hurt from frostbite. I was lost. I did not understand what had happened to me on that ice face. Internally, I was trying to negotiate this world that I found myself in. I knew I was not from here, but where was it I had gone? What was that place? Was it real?

I felt as if I were standing in two worlds at once; one foot here, one foot there, one foot on earth and one foot in heaven. My mind would not focus. This world of blood and bone and sunrise and Tim—all were ugly and not right. Where had I been? What was I? What was this place, this world? I did not belong here. I was not from here. This was not my world. What had happened to me? Who was I? What was I? Where was I? Heaven, that other place that was no place, was where I knew I belonged, was where I was from and wanted to go back to. My soul was on fire, leaping from my body, disconnected from my body, and attached to the other side. I was lost. This world felt completely unreal. Heaven had felt Real. It was the only Real. Only God was Real. I was not even real—at least, my body and brain were not real. Only my soul was real, and it belonged to God, was made by God—I didn't even own my soul anymore. Heaven felt as if it was the only Real.

I craved the love I had felt there. I missed God. I missed the beauty. I had been in paradise, in bliss, in heaven and wholeness, and healing and love and beauty. What had it meant when God said, *You won't live your life?* Maybe now I was getting it: I was not living my life. My life was gone. I felt alien. I felt other. It was as if my vision was split in two—between this world and the world beyond. It felt as if I had two eyes—an inner eye that only saw a drop, a touch, a taste of what I had lost when I chose to come back here, and that drop, that touch, that taste was all I wanted. I regretted my choice to return to my family, to my mom and dad, to return to this earth, to this world, and to my body. What had I done? I had made a mistake. I should never have come back. Why had I come back? I silently said my first prayer to God: *Take me back. Take me Home. I made a mistake. Take me Home now, please.*

God did not grant me my request.

Little did I know that prayer would become my daily prayer for decades. My feeling of being an alien and feeling split between two worlds would remain my experience of reality forever. I was shattered emotionally, spiritually, psychologically. Was it any wonder that my traumas had resulted in a stutter?

Meanwhile, back at the bus stop, Tim had been speaking to me. "Why aren't you listening to me? I said that when I get back to Bozeman I will leave your skis and poles on the front porch of the Men's Co-op. And please, Peter, after you get back, just leave my gear in a corner on the porch for me to find. I'll pick it up at some point. I don't want to see you again. Good luck hitchhiking." We shook hands and parted in a strangely friendly, trusting, and yet broken way.

≈ 23 ≈

Not My Body

I turned and walked north toward the highway access road that was a half mile away. It was a beautiful dawn. A rosy-colored sky edging its way to blue brightened above me. I stopped to watch the sky for a time before continuing on and pondered how plain it all was. How uninspiring, how coarse, unrefined, and repulsive even the beauty of a sunrise now seemed compared with the utter and unspeakable Beauty of God. Inside me, the beauty of heaven was real. Even though I could no longer fully feel it within me, I remembered the beauty and love clearly. The memory was so strong, so vivid, that it and the sense of heaven inside me would color my vision of this world for decades to come.

Years later, it struck me: How could it be that I remember any of this? When I was dead, I did not have a body or brain. Without a brain, how could I remember anything of the experience? Aren't memories stored in cells inside the human brain? The only explanation I can think of is that my consciousness, my soul-self (which is my Real self) has a memory that is separate from my body's brain and memory. Somehow my soul interacted and interacts with my body and brain, causing me to remember a soul-memory.

That morning a heavy snow cover of a couple feet blanketed the ground. The main street, the sidewalk on which I walked, and the highway had been plowed clear. There was no wind; all was still. I walked through the quiet town, passing the grain silo on my left. A car went by. The driver stared at me as if I was an oddity, which I guess I was. My long hair stuck out from under my gray wool cap. My orange backpack was packed full and festooned with our blue climbing rope and ice axes. I am sure the look on my face must have been the oddest part of me if it, or any of what I felt inside, showed at all. I felt lost, bewildered, upset, sad, angry; and yet, some of the light that was not (and is not) mine must have been glowing within me, and shining out of my eyes. Over the years, many people have commented on my eyes, saying that they see light in them. That may be true; but, if it is there, it is not mine.

On the snowy shoulder of the highway, I took off my backpack, leaned it against the snowbank, held up my cardboard sign that said BOZEMAN, MT, and waited. As I said before, I was a veteran hitchhiker. Truth be told, the first time I hitchhiked was because I had detention after school for mouthing off to one of the Xaverian Brothers at my all-boys Catholic high school and had missed the bus home. I hitchhiked that day just so I didn't have to call my parents for a ride and tell them I'd had detention.

On that afternoon in 1973, at the age of fourteen, I picked up my heavy St. John's book bag, adjusted my necktie, stood by the side of the road next to St. John's

High School, then hitched the fourteen miles through three towns to my home. Over the years since that detention day, I would often get rides with World War II veterans with their eternally flat-topped haircuts. They would pick up a longhair like me because of hitchhiking karma. They all told me tales of getting back to the States aboard a warship, either from the European or Japanese Theater, and then hitchhiking across America to get back home to their moms, wives, or girlfriends. Those vets told me they felt a duty to other hitchhikers that they needed to repay a debt they felt they owed. It was from one of those fellows that I learned the useful trick of using a piece of cardboard as a hitchhiking sign and to write my destination on it—or, better yet, to write "Home to Mom" on it. A sign had always worked better than my thumb. "Home to Mom" always worked, too, but only if I was actually going home to see my mom. Now, I held up my "Bozeman, MT" sign, sighed, and waited.

But my mind kept up that whirling: *Who am I? What am I doing here? Where am I? What am I? Was it real? Was I real? Did I die? Am I alive? Did this really happen? What is reality? Am I crazy? Can I tell anybody that I died?*

I tried saying, "I died, and I am alive again" out loud. It sounded nuts to me. If it sounded nuts to me, and I was the one who had experienced it, it would definitely sound crazy to most anyone I told. They'd think, *This dude is bonkers!* So, standing there on the shoulder of the highway in the morning light, I decided right then to never say a word about it. I would never tell my tale.

Who would believe me, anyway? Who had even heard of a near-death experience in 1980? I had never heard of such a thing and had no idea how to explain what had happened to me. Besides, I did not think about it as near death. There was nothing near about it. It was death. I had died. I had been taken. I had been "near" death once before when I was about eight years old. I was drowning in a river, and I went under for what I believed was the last time. I felt myself blacking out. Just then, I was pulled out of the river by the strong arms of an unknown man. That was "near" death. I could have died, but I did not die in that river.

I died when I was twenty-one, but I did not start using the common term—near-death experience—until many years later. On the day after our car wreck with that eighteen-wheeler in Canada, I had no cultural or historic or literary reference points about what dying was actually like. I had read nothing about it. All the people I knew who died had stayed dead. Not one had come back. As a boy, I had been to plenty of wakes with my Dad and had seen enough dead people to know what death looked like from the outside. But what did death look like from the inside? Other than my experience two nights before, I had no idea.

The only thing I knew about dying and coming back came from the Bible, from the Gospels about Jesus and Lazarus. Jesus prayed to God, then called out to Lazarus, "Lazarus, come out!" The dead man came out wrapped in his death shroud. That is all I knew about what we now call near-death experience. I knew Lazarus had died and had come back. If Lazarus had anything to say about it, it was never written down.

Over and over again for many months to come I repeated those questions to myself: Who am I? What am I? Where am I? What is God? Where is God? How can I feel like I am in two places at once, with a part of me in heaven and part of me on earth? Part of my problem was that when I was dead I had known the answers to each of these questions; moreover, I had known the answers to a great many more questions—questions I hadn't even known I'd had. I had known so much more when I was dead. Truths had been revealed to me, but ever since I'd come back into this world, I could not and still cannot remember any of the answers. I know only that I had known, that I no longer knew, and that I might not know again until I died again. It was frustrating.

Hitchhiking to Bozeman, Montana, at dawn that day, I decided I'd never tell anybody about what had happened that night on the Lower Weeping Wall. I'd keep that secret, in part because I did not understand it, in part because I had no words to describe the indescribable, and in part to keep myself from being judged. I was scared that nobody would believe me. Even worse, I feared that if I told my story, people would think that I was really and truly insane. So I would keep my death a secret.

I knew I could keep a secret because I'd been keeping secrets since I was fourteen years old. Because of Andrea, keeping secrets had become normal for me. I could keep my mouth shut, could lock down inside and hide a part of me. I was good at this, and strangely, this skill of secret keeping would become quite useful when I became a pastor. Pastors are secret keepers, or at least they should be. I kept parishioners' secrets and still do; I will always keep the secrets shared with me by my congregants about their personal pain, tribulations, and tragedies. It is a role I handle well.

I decided that morning that I would tell the rest of my story—the snow cave, the climb, the exposure and frostbite, the car wreck—all of it, except for the part about my death. That, I would keep to myself—or, rather, as I discovered, between God and me. Of course, keeping secrets, keeping a part of oneself hidden, takes effort and energy, and there is a cost for that.

☞ 24 ☜

Stammering to Bozeman

On the shoulder of the highway I leaned my back-pack against my legs and held my sign up as cars and trucks whizzed by me. The day was beautiful, yet it did not seem beautiful to me. The entire world looked flat and uninspired since I returned to this life. Beauty seemed ugly and drab, sort of two-dimensional and cartoon-like. Compared to the beauty of heaven, everything was just less-than. I was reeling inside, still feeling displaced, disassociated, and disoriented, when a red Fiat, a two-seater convertible, pulled over just beyond where I was standing, and tooted. I shouldered my backpack and hur-ried over. The driver leaned across the passenger seat and rolled down the window. He said he could take me across the border and all the way to Missoula, Montana.

I stuttered, "Gr-gr-great."

The driver said, "I think we can fit your pack in the trunk if I put my suitcase behind the seats." He got out to open his small trunk, and moved his suitcase into the small space behind the front seats. I put my backpack into the trunk, closed it, and got into the car. Holding out his hand, he introduced himself as a professor from the University of Montana in Missoula.

"I'm Pe-Peter," I stuttered, "I go to MSU in Bozeman."

"You look like a student," he laughed. "That's why I picked you up." And off we drove. He chatted about philosophy and history and literature for a while, describing his work, all of which I tried to listen to but have long since forgotten because my mind was all topsy-turvy.

He glanced over at me as he drove, and said, "You look terrible. Are you okay?"

I was silent for a few minutes as I thought about what to say and how to say it. I kept shifting around in my seat, my body twitchy and uncomfortable. He let the silence sit until I slowly told him that I'd awoken that morning with a stutter I'd never had before, coming as a result, I thought, from the car wreck the previous night. It took me a while to say anything at all. I did not like my stutter, and I was trying to come to grips with it, on top of everything else. The professor was patient with me and allowed me to tell my tale, starting with skiing across the frozen lake with Tim a week before, finding the burned-down cabin, the snow cave, the ranger's cabin, the ice climb, the frostbite, the exposure, the falling asleep on the cliff, our self-rescue, the jail cell, the car wreck, and the hotel. I told him the whole tale minus the crazy part about my death and dying, hell and heaven, God and Love, and about how coming back to this now-unreal world left me feeling completely undone.

I discovered that I was able to tell my story about the ice climb and the car wreck without telling the whole of it. I was able to keep out the most important part. I had a new secret. But deep inside me a pressure was starting to build to speak about what had happened—I could feel it. I found out that morning that I was going to have to battle with it, this thing that wanted and demanded to be spoken aloud even though I never wanted to speak of it for fear of ridicule. I was an expert at compartmentalization, and I would win, or so I believed.

The professor listened to my entire story without interruption, and then we drove a long way in silence as I stared out the window at the passing scenery and tried to get a grip on myself.

The professor interrupted the silence. "We need a plan to cross the border into the States."

"Why?" I asked.

He said something about having crossed into Canada alone, and that the border guards might have questions about his having a young man with him. He was kind and considerate and had a good heart, and I could see the Light of God reflected in him; I felt it in him. He was the first person in whom I saw the Light of God reflected so clearly and so obviously, and he would not be the last. The Light was so plain to see I wondered that I had never seen it before. His eyes shined and I felt the Light, the Love, radiating from him. I was even more amazed that he seemed completely unaware of it. As they say, the eyes are the windows to the soul. In the years since that day, and through my practices of prayer and meditation, I have come to the place where if I place my hand near the hands of another person, or over their hearts or back, I can feel the radiance of their souls with my soul. It feels like a hum in the palm of my hand, or like a radiant warmth. The professor seemed heaven-sent.

He said, "We'll get off this main highway and start taking smaller highways as soon as we can. We'll have an easier time of it at a smaller crossing that I know." He handed me his road map. "You'll have to navigate. You're a backpacker so I assume that you can read maps. Can you?"

"Yes, I can," I said.

"Good. The crossing is a little out of the way." At the next exit, we pulled off and then he pulled over, took the map back, and flipped through the pages. "This one," he said, pointing to a road and a marked crossing on the map. "Find us our best route."

"Okay. Let's go. I'll n-n-navigate," I stuttered. And off we went. It was a quiet ride, as there wasn't much that I could say aloud. Lots of things were running through my head, and the distraction of navigation was welcome. An hour or more later, we approached the border.

"Are you ready?" he asked.

"I am," I said.

We stopped at what was obviously a lonely outpost for the border guard and rolled down our windows. Two border guards heard our story. "Get out of the car," one ordered, "and go wait inside our waiting room. Leave the keys in the car."

We did as ordered and watched them search the car. They searched it rather thoroughly—under the seats, inside his suitcase, and in the trunk. When they opened the trunk and saw my backpack with all my climbing gear, they came to get us. "You're all set," one guard said, adding, "Welcome home." We smiled and thanked them, then drove across the border and into the small town of Sunburst, Montana.

More hours passed as we headed south. We said little and only stopped for fuel along the way. I refused his offer to buy me food. I was fine, I said—I lied. He had already been so kind to me that I could not accept his offer of food, too. I slept some as we drove toward

Missoula, and when I awoke, he entertained me with his stories and cassettes.

Just outside Missoula, the professor pulled over to the side of the highway near the off-ramp. He invited me to his home for dinner, promising that he would get me back on the highway the next morning after a meal, a shower (I really needed a shower after more than a week without one), and a good night's sleep. I thanked him but gently refused. It was not the first time a kind Montanan had offered to let me spend the night in their home. I stuttered, "Good-bye, and thank you for your kindness." Whoever he was, for I have long since forgotten his name, I thank God for him.

⁓ 25 ⁓

Kind Cowboy

I walked a distance along US Route 90 southbound, positioned myself on the on-ramp, and held up my sign. My next ride, which I do not remember much about, dropped me just north of Butte, Montana, on the highway just before the off-ramp into Butte. That driver drove on into Butte, and I was still headed south. It was late in the afternoon. In those days, the population of Montana was roughly 1.7 persons per square mile, which meant that the state was seriously underpopulated. It was about an hour before the first car drove by, but it was headed into Butte. I waited for hours, watching for a single vehicle headed toward Bozeman. No one, not one, headed south past Butte. Every one of the few cars and trucks that did appear on the highway pulled off and headed into Butte.

I was beside myself, barely holding my mind and self together. Still shattered emotionally, psychologically, and spiritually, I was a wreck, and I wept. The sun had set, and night was falling. I knew I either had to get a ride or I was going to spend the night alone on the side of the road huddled in my sleeping bag and nearly out of my mind. I was determined not to do that, so I repositioned myself just north of the off-ramp into Butte and took out my flashlight. It was a long off-ramp, maybe a couple miles long into Butte. It took another twenty minutes in the fading twilight before I spotted a pair of headlights slowing down for the off-ramp. It was a pickup truck moseying down the highway. I waited until the truck got pretty close, and then, waving my flashlight, I stepped out into the highway into his path, raising my arms above my head. I flagged the driver to stop just inches from my chest. I nodded to him, and he, in his cowboy hat, nodded back. He rolled down his window and asked, "What seems to be the trouble, young man?"

I stuttered, "I'm stuck out here. I was in a bad car wreck up north of Calgary, and I'm trying to get to Bozeman and back to school. If I have to spend the night on the road, I'd rather do it closer in to Butte. Would you be kind enough to give me a ride into Butte?"

He studied my face and said, "Sure, I will. Toss your pack into the back there, and climb on into the cab." So I did. He had the Light in his eyes, too.

He asked me about the wreck. As quickly as I could, I told him with my stutter and a few tears that I struggled to hold back. I told him just about everything, except the parts about my death and hell and heaven, summarizing the whole thing in about ten minutes. He listened patiently, and then said, "Have you eaten?"

"Not since the night before last when I had pizza in Calgary."

"I'm taking you to dinner at a diner then, and I won't take no for an answer," he said. I declined, thanking him for his kindness, but he took me there anyway. Hungry as I was, I accepted his offer when we reached the parking lot. We sat across from each other at a table for two. He told me to order anything I wanted, and so I did. As I ate and talked, he listened and sipped his coffee with cream. He ate nothing.

After I had a slice of pie, which he insisted I have, and with me feeling significantly better, he asked if I intended to hitch to Bozeman that night. Since I was feeling better, I said I did. "Come on," he said, "get in the truck. Let's go." After driving for a bit, we stopped at a bus station.

"I'm buying you a bus ticket to Bozeman," he said. "Your dad would do the same for my son if he found him stuck, hungry, and far from home, and you had better not argue about this."

It makes me tear up to this day when I think about that cowboy. I do not know who he was, but I remember him and thank God for his kindness. I stood next to him at the ticket counter while he made the transaction—a cowboy and a dirty hippie. He handed me my ticket and said I had better call my mother to let her know that I was okay. Before I could say I did not have a dime to make the collect call, he handed me a quarter. I shook his hand and again thanked him for his kindness. I wanted to hug him, but that felt like I was overstepping somehow. He simply smiled and said, "It's a pleasure to meet you, young man. And remember, God loves you."

Wow, I thought, *he must be some kind of angel*. The kindness of strangers has never ceased to amaze me.

The bus station was typical of bus stations everywhere in America in those days: fiberglass benches, a dirty floor tramped with melted snow, weak yellow lighting, and vagabonds like me. A pay phone hung on the wall. I put in my quarter, dialed the operator, and asked if I could place a collect call. My mom answered. The operator said to my mom, "Would you like to accept a collect call from . . ." and to me the operator said, "Say your name." I stuttered out my name. Mom accepted.

"What's wrong?!" she said. "You're stuttering? Are you okay?"

I told my mom through my stutter and tears that I was okay and unhurt, other than a cut on my palm that I had butterflied shut with my first aid kit and had bandaged over, and of course there was my new stutter. I told her about the car wreck, and how I had caused it, and how I had awoken that morning with a stutter. I told her that Tim had taken a bus, that I was hitching, and that a kind cowboy had bought me dinner and a bus ticket to Bozeman from Butte, where I was now in a bus station, and about how he had helped me make this call. I told her I would call her when I got back to the Men's Co-op.

She cried a little, and then put Dad on the phone. He was concerned but glad when I assured him I was okay. I wanted to tell them both what had really happened to me. I wanted to tell them that I had died, gone to heaven, seen them from there, seen God's love for them, had gone through hell, had been forgiven and loved. But I did not have the words to describe what I had experienced—and besides, they were already worried about me and my wild wilderness lifestyle, and they had other worries of their own. I could not tell them. They would think I had finally gone crazy or that I was on drugs. Unformed as my thoughts were, it was still on the tip of my tongue, still wanting to be told, but I stuffed the story down and said nothing about it.

My dad said, "Your mom and I love you. Take care of yourself and call us when you get to Bozeman."

"I will," I said. "I love you, too." We hung up. I was still feeling miserable, but at least I wasn't hungry. and I was grateful to the cowboy, and to my mom and dad, so I found a seat on a fiberglass bench, sat down with my backpack leaning against my legs, hung my head down, and tried to keep myself from crying.

About an hour later the bus to Bozeman arrived. I put my backpack in the luggage compartment under the bus, boarded with all my fellow passengers, and fell asleep. I awoke in Bozeman, got off the bus into the cold night air, shouldered my backpack, and hiked several blocks to the Men's Co-op.

In the living room, a few of the guys were sitting on the overstuffed and tattered chairs and sofa watching TV. They all said hello and asked me how my trip was. I stuttered, "It was great. I'm going to bed." My roommate, Mark, was already in our room, in bed and asleep. He had a fire going in our fireplace. I needed that. I leaned my pack against a clear space along the wall, found my thermal pajamas under my pillow where I had left them the week before, put them on, sat down on my mattress, which was on the floor, tried to pray, and found I could not. I crawled under my covers and watched the fire in the fireplace. Its crackling, sparks, and flames soothed me. I watched the flames for quite a while, and finally, safe and warm in my bed, I drifted off into a dreamless sleep.

❦ 26 ❧

Good-Bye, Tim and the Theater

The next morning, just as I opened the front door and stepped onto the porch to walk to class, Tim walked up the front stairs carrying my cross-country skis and poles. He said nothing as he leaned them gently against the house. "I'll be right out with your gear," I said, and went back inside and downstairs to my room to get his gear that I had piled up before heading to class. Back on the porch, in the chill morning air, I gave him his rope, ice screws, and the part of his tent that I'd carried.

Tim told me that he had telephoned his dad and that his dad and he were both angry with me. Tim then said he did not want to see me again, though that was already likely since I was leaving in a week for a ten-week national theater tour. I apologized to Tim once more and added that our paths would not cross on campus because I was leaving soon. By the time I returned, the trimester would be almost over and he might be gone. We shook hands and even smiled a bit. After all, we had been through quite a lot together.

Tim picked up his gear, slung the rope over his shoulder, looked me in the eye with a mix of anger, friendship, love, and trust, and then walked down the steps. He was headed back the way he had come, toward the university. I sighed and went back inside the co-op to wait a few minutes so that we wouldn't have to walk the same route so closely together.

After the theater tour ended, months later, and I was back in Bozeman for a few days, Tim surprisingly showed up on the Men's Co-op porch one afternoon. I happened to be home at the time, packing to leave for Massachusetts. Tim had come by to say that he had thought a lot about the car wreck, about our climb, and about our week snow caving together. He said that, upon reflection, he had forgiven me for wrecking his car. He had come to understand that, although I was at fault, it had happened because we were both a mess. I thanked him, and to this day I appreciate his forgiveness more than I can say. That was the last I saw or heard of Tim.

The morning Tim left my skis for me on the front porch, I walked alone to my one and only class that trimester. It was in the Communications Department, and the class was called "The Theater of Silence." We had been in rehearsal for a national tour since the autumn of 1979. It was theater for the deaf. During the spring and summer of 1979, back in Massachusetts, I had helped my friends organize and run a Friday night coffeehouse in the basement hall of a Roman Catholic church twenty miles from my home. I performed as a clown. The coffeehouse was packed every Friday night with youth from the surrounding towns and cities. We had a live band, popcorn, poetry, and an open mic. That summer, I had begun clowning just to be part of the entertainment. My makeup and costume were so complete that nobody knew who I was. I kept my identity hidden. That was a delight for me.

When I arrived at Montana State University in the autumn of 1979, I had planned on continuing my English major and adding classes to my as-yet undeclared minor in anthropology. When I got to the Bozeman campus, I did as my college advisor at UMass had advised: I called him to discuss my MSU courses. He told me that I had to take a Shakespeare class for my major that autumn because I would not be able to take it the next year from UMass. I discovered that the Shakespeare class met at the same time as my dream class in Native American anthropology. That anthropology class was part of the reason I had picked MSU in the first place. This left me one course short of a full load.

As often was the case, a cute woman solved my problem for me: she mentioned that she was taking a sign language class in the Communications Department. I thought, *Why not?* and signed up. On the first day of class, the professor and chairman of the Communications Department, Dr. Jack O., told the class that there would be auditions for the Theater of Silence in two weeks. The Theater of Silence was Jack's baby. For the previous ten years, Jack had taken actors on a 24,000-mile, 64-show, spring tour across fourteen western states. The show was performed in American Sign Language and was primarily for deaf audiences. Jack said that the planned 1980 tour would play small towns, big cities, and universities, and include a shakedown tour in Alberta and British Columbia. It was an open audition. Bill, a profoundly deaf pantomime, performed for the class that day along with a couple of actors from the year before. I thought, *Why not? I'm a clown, and I can learn the art of mime from Bill.*

I called my parents that night and asked them what they thought. I had planned to attend Montana State University for just the fall trimester. If I got into the show, I would stay in Montana until June. My parents encouraged me to audition. I worked up a routine with the help of that same cute woman. I auditioned, and to my surprise I was selected. For all of that academic year I was at MSU the actors in the troupe worked with Jack to put together a cabaret-style show with music, dancing, acting, and mime—all in American Sign Language. It turned out that I was a natural at performance and sign language.

When I returned from ice climbing, our troupe had only a week to polish up the show before our scheduled tour was to begin. Before my trip to Canada, I had promised Jack that I would be a driver for the fifteen-passenger van and for the pickup truck that pulled a trailer. The van would transport all the actors and crew; the pickup would haul the large box trailer containing all our costumes, makeup, luggage, stage lights, and sound equipment.

At rehearsal that first day back, I kept my stutter a secret by speaking only in sign language. It was an easy thing to do. We all signed all the time anyway because it would have been impolite to speak with Bill there. Using American Sign Language, I told Jack, the actors, and the crew about the car wreck with the semitrailer, and ended by saying that I was just too shaken up to drive. The other drivers were angry with me, and rightly so, because it would mean more driving and less rest for them. "What can I do?" I stuttered out loud and signed at the same time. "I'm a wreck."

Silence filled the room. Bill asked in sign what everybody was staring at. One of the women signed to Bill and said out loud, "Peter has a stutter. He didn't have a stutter before." Adding to me, "Peter, is your stutter real?" I nodded my head yes as I fought back tears and signed yes with my hand. Nobody knew what to do or what to say until Bill signed with a jerky hand motion, indicating a mimed stutter: "He doesn't stutter in sign. So it won't hurt our performance." That relieved the tension, and everyone laughed. Jack said they would figure out a new driving schedule and that he, and everyone, was glad that I was unhurt. By the time the tour was over I had mastered my stutter enough to get by without showing it too much. My stutter still comes out if I get too upset, anxious, or nervous, though.

The troupe had no idea how messed up I really was. I used the car wreck and my stutter as a wall to hide behind. Nobody asked any more questions of me, not even a "How was your trip?" This was okay by me. I did not want to talk about it. My inner world, unseen by them, and unrevealed by me, was one of dislocation. Every movement of every day had become an interior battle to stay rooted in the world. I was in the gym with these people, talking with them, but half of me was still in heaven—or, rather, it felt like more of me was Over There than standing in the gym with them. I felt constantly on the verge of jumping out of my skin and could barely sit or stand still.

Our president, Susan, called our meeting to order. I lay on the floor and tried to keep still; but before long Susan interrupted the meeting and said, "Peter, I know you're not feeling well, but will you please stop squirming on the floor?" I tried, but my body felt like an itchy wool suit, and I wanted it off. I squirmed, but I tried to keep still. I was moving to keep my sanity, such as it was, in place. The more time that passed, the more difficult being in the world was becoming.

Rhanda and Kerri, both my dear friends and actors in the troupe, gave me hugs. I was glad they did. Their hugs and love grounded me in the world a bit; throughout our theater tour, their friendship and love and our closeness kept me sane. They both knew I had changed somehow, but I never explained why.

Decades later, in Facebook conversations with Kerri, I finally told her what had happened to me and why I had changed so much back then. She replied that, in all her life before then and since, I'd been the only person who taught her about unconditional love. Even in those early days after I died, love seemed to be all I had. I really had nothing else. I'd been stripped of myself somehow, had become empty, and so I clung to love inside of me. I clung to God; I clung to the love of God—and that love apparently clung to me and showed through me. I knew that it was not me. It was not my love; I could not own it or claim it. It simply came through me, and that is all.

I had that feeling of standing in two places at once, with a foot here and a foot there, with one eye seeing here and one eye seeing Over There. It was more than a feeling—it was and is an inner reality for me that has remained unchanged for decades. It is still with me to a large extent, but it is not as disturbing as it was during those first months and years after I died. Since then, I've become more adjusted to the confusing sense that

I'm simultaneously in two places. It feels, in a way, like I am inside the Matrix from the film—only instead of our reality being run by an evil machine, a loving God creates our reality. I know that this world is not the highest reality, but it is one that I can't escape; I'm just here until God takes me Home.

≈ 27 ≈

Travels in the Small Outside
and Vast Inside

Traveling 24,000 miles with the Theater of Silence that spring actually allowed me a lot of time alone. Instead of riding inside the fifteen-passenger van with my fellow actors, I opted to bring along my down sleeping bag and backpacking sleeping pad and set myself up, alone, in the back of our theater pickup truck towing the trailer with all our gear. I wanted and needed to be alone, and riding in the back of the pickup offered me that. I was no longer good company anyway, because my feelings of dislocation and my stutter made it hard for me to feel companionable. I spent nearly our entire long and slow drive through those fourteen states outside in the pickup and kept mostly to myself.

It turned out to be a great way to see both the wild and the urban western United States. Once in a while, one or two of my actor-friends would join me in the back of the truck, but only in fair weather. I stayed out there no matter the weather. My long hair, my odd behavior, and my East Coast ways set me at odds with a few of my fellow thespians; it was better that I be alone. Most of the time I had the opportunity to ponder what had happened to me, to meditate, and to pray.

Through reflection and prayer, I discovered that what I wanted most of all was to be dead again, to go back to heaven. I had made a huge mistake; I did not want to be in this world. I was not suicidal, but I wanted and needed to go back to heaven instead of living in this world that seemed so two-dimensional by comparison. The beauty there made everything here—even the vast and varied beauty of the American West—seem plain, flat, and uninspiring. Even so, from the back of the pickup truck I observed many incredible sights: the Rocky Mountains from Montana to Arizona, the Black Hills of South Dakota, Snake River Canyon in Idaho, the desert of New Mexico, Death Valley, the Pacific Ocean, redwood forests, the lush Northwest, huge herds of antelope, incredible sunsets after Mount St. Helens erupted, and every major city in the American West. All of it was stunning to see, but somehow it was simply less, flat somehow, and unappealing. All I wanted was to go Home. Thus, it was in the back of the pickup truck that I began praying.

"God, I made a mistake. I don't want to be here. Take me back. Let me die. Kill me now. Take me home. I don't want to be here. TAKE ME HOME!" This became my new prayer, my daily prayer for decades. It is a prayer and an attitude that is still with me, although during the last several years to a lesser degree.

I had learned meditation when I was a senior at St. John's High School in Shrewsbury, Massachusetts. My senior year religion class teacher had gone on a private retreat to St. Joseph's Abbey, the Trappist monastery in Spencer, Massachusetts, where the monks taught him how to meditate in the traditional contemplative style called centering prayer, or prayer of the heart. My teacher was enthralled by meditation, so one day he pulled down the shades in our classroom, closed the doors, and taught the class what he knew. I was hooked on meditation from that day on and have practiced ever since.

In general, meditation is the practice of quieting the mind, lifting the heart, and listening to God, or listening for God. Meditation in prayer opens the door to stillness and allows me to experience a tiny taste of heaven here on earth. By the time I had died in 1980 I had been practicing meditation for about four years. After I came back, meditation became my lifeline to God, and my stability in this world.

In order to still the mind, those who meditate often repeat a prayer, personalized mantra, or short chant. Back in the summer of 1979, eight months before climbing Lower Weeping Wall, while backpacking in Gallatin National Forest in Montana with my British buddy, Jeremy, and after years of meditative practice, I had finally struck upon what would become my first and second meditation prayer chant. The first was the name *Jesus*, broken into two syllables: *Je* on my in breath and *sus* on my out breath, repeated over and over until the words fell away and one was left only with breath and gentle focus. The second meditation, and the one I still use today, is the Jesus Prayer:

> Lord Jesus Christ, son of God, have mercy on me,
> a sinner.

The Jesus Prayer, through decades of regular practice, has burned itself deeply into my mind. It plays like an endless tape loop in my subconscious, in the basement of my mind, making it a simple thing nowadays to open the cellar door and let it fill my active thoughts; such is the benefit of long and dedicated practice. My meditative prayer practice has sustained me through the years. But back in the spring of 1980, when I was touring the United States in the back of a pickup truck, I plunged deeply into meditation and prayer because I was desperate for a direct and yet unattainable reconnection to God.

❧ 28 ❧

The Sinner and the Dream

I judged myself poorly. I was guilty, and obviously so. It seemed to me then, as it does now, that sin is causing pain to others. It's that simple. Sin is the hurt we inflict on others, intentionally or unintentionally. This entire world, and by that I mean the entire known universe we live in (and the unknown, for that matter), exists because it has brokenness; without that brokenness, it would not exist.

I also know that God is perfect. God is the only perfect there is. If God alone is perfect, nothing else can be perfect. This world, including all of the known universe and earth, is by nature of its existence imperfect. It exists because of imperfection. If it was perfect, it would not be what it is. If it was perfect, it would be God. That it is imperfect is not wrong or bad or evil. It just is. If it were not imperfect, it would not exist. To exist, this world (meaning the entirety of this universe) must be broken. Sin, it seems to me, is part and parcel of being a human being. To be human is inevitably and unavoidably to cause pain to others, especially those we love. God knows this—at least, God knew this about me.

People often ask me if dying has made me a better person. I think what they mean is, Do I still sin? Do I still hurt people? The answer is, yes, I still hurt people, and I still sin. Oddly, I am pretty much the same person I was before I died, even though the experience changed me radically. I am still, like you, a frail human being. I am still a creature made by God and, therefore, wholly imperfect. I have sinned; I sin, and I dare say, so do you. I am certain I will sin again. I do pray that when I die again God will forgive my sins as before. I pray that my shame upon meeting God again will allow God's love to reign inside me. I believe God will forgive me again: because God is love, and because God told me I could return to the heaven that was within me because of God's love for me.

I am certain that there are many of you who have been unmistakably touched by God. You know it when it happens, and you are irrevocably changed. I simply know that God is Real. I do not have to believe that; I know it. God is Real. God is Real and the only Real there is. I just know now, and have known for decades, that God knows me, thoroughly, through and through, every bit, every word, every thought, every emotion, and every action. Believe me, I have tried my hardest to escape from God. I have run as hard and as far as I could. I did not want this life as I have it. This life came with this bifurcation of me. I am split in two. I wanted to return to my old life. Yet, even as I ran from God, I simultaneously dove into God. I just held part of myself back until God wore me out, until I finally understood that resistance was futile. Why did

I try to run? I was afraid that God would consume me. I was afraid that I would no longer be me. I know it sounds crazy, but I am used to that.

When I could not run any longer, I simply gave myself up to God. So far, I am not consumed.

Hitching East

Back in 1980, sadness and confusion were my dominant feelings, and that sadness traveled home with me from Montana to Massachusetts. My best high school buddy, Steve, had driven westward all the way from Massachusetts in his little red pickup truck to collect me and my bike, skis, clothes, and gear and take us home to Massachusetts. Just east of Bozeman, Steve's pickup threw a rod, which killed the engine.

Steve wound up hitchhiking to the Men's Co-op. We decided that the truck was worthless and we would just hitchhike home, so I packed all of my stuff in boxes and mailed it back east. On the day before our departure, quite suddenly, Steve developed a debilitating sharp pain in his lower right side. We did not know what it was. I'd already moved out of my basement room and was sleeping on a mattress up in the attic. Steve lay down in that attic room, unable to rise for three or four days and nights. Not knowing what to do or what the problem was, I fed him massive doses of vitamin C. After a few days, he felt better. Of course, as you may have suspected, it turned out to be appendicitis. A week after we got home, he had a relapse and required emergency surgery.

It took four days and nights to hitchhike home. Our first leg was a ride across Montana with a family who took us hours out of their way into Wyoming. They were coming back from a hospital. The young fellow in the backseat had a brand-new plaster cast from his ankle up to his thigh, and he rested his leg across our laps for the eight-hour drive.

At a truck stop in Sheridan, Wyoming, we learned that dozens of hitchhikers had been stuck there for days and days. We walked to the end of the hitchers' line, held up our Home to Mom sign, and had a ride in a semi in less than ten minutes. The other hitchhikers all gave us the evil eye. That truck driver even bought us both dinner at the truck stop. He had a doctorate in philosophy and was a fine conversationalist.

In Nebraska, we had a ride with a speedy driver who had already collected eleven tickets since he'd left Oregon a couple days before. He said he had no intention of paying a single ticket.

In Iowa, our pickup truck driver learned that we had never seen his beautiful state and insisted we take back-country highways so he could show it to us. He was right; Iowa is amazingly beautiful.

In Cleveland, a crazy ice cream truck driver took us on a rush-hour romp ten miles in the wrong direction and left us in the middle of a desolate and gang-ridden urban landscape. It was after dark. We saw that it was dangerous, but we had no choice but to hitch on that perilous road.

The first car that rolled up approached slowly. It was a big, souped-up Buick lowrider blaring Spanish music with all the windows down. Inside were four gang members, all wearing red bandanas tied around their heads. They laughed when they saw us, and one of them asked us what we were doing there. We explained about the crazy ice cream truck driver. They told us that we were in gangland and it was dangerous here for us. We said that we had just figured that out and they laughed. We could see they liked us. They talked amongst themselves in Spanish, and then the man in the passenger seat said that we could get hurt if we stayed there, and thank God they found us first.

They said there was a bus station a couple miles from there, and that we had better go with them if we wanted to stay alive. They offered to drive us to the bus station and opened a car door and popped the trunk. The driver said, "Do you trust us, man?" What choice did we have? It was a dangerous neighborhood. They had guns. I could see one. Steve and I shoved our backpacks into the large backseat and climbed in. Three of them sat up front, and one sat in the back with us. They were nice to us. It took me by surprise. Angels come in all sorts of disguises. It was not the first nor the last time in my life that gang members would be kind to me.

We all laughed and enjoyed our time with them. They drove us to the bus station, and warned us to stay inside, because it was dangerous outside. They waited for us to enter the station, and then waved and laughed as the driver leaned on the horn before they peeled out and sped away. They are probably still telling stories about the crazy gringos they picked up hitchhiking in a bad neighborhood.

We bought a bus ride out of Cleveland to Rochester and eventually landed on the side of the highway hitching east again. We made it to Albany, New York, where we slept the night in our sleeping bags just off the tarmac at the curb at the Albany tollgate.

Our last ride—in a BMW—took us across Massachusetts. The driver was headed to Boston. Ravel's Boléro was playing in his tape deck. It was the day I would learn to love classical music. Our driver kindly dropped us at the front doors of our respective family homes—Steve in Bolton and me in Marlborough. Naturally, I had not told my parents I was hitchhiking home from Montana. They were surprised enough when a BMW pulled up that they came outside to see what was going on. I thanked my driver, who kindly complimented me to my parents.

Being home did not help me clarify things much. My older sister Andrea was still missing. Melissa, her toddler daughter, had been adopted by my parents, and was now my sister. I carried my inner darkness and confusion in silence, hiding it as best I could. I do not know if my mom and dad ever noticed that I'd changed. We never talked about it. If they ever asked, I never said anything, so how would they know? Besides, their world was busy with a new child in the house.

Over the next few months I found myself living more in heaven than on earth. I was in the world but most certainly not of it. Church, religious education, meditation, chanting, and prayer had taught me that God can be found within. So that is where I looked, that is where I went.

The Book of Revelation 3:21–3:22 says, "I stand at the door and knock. Open the door and let me in." The only special and safe and calm space I had was my inner space, my inner world. My inside was the cause of my turmoil, and that leaked into my outside world.

To calm myself, I'd chant in my mind, "Lord Jesus Christ, son of God, have mercy on me, a sinner." Either that or I'd close my eyes and pray myself to stillness, if I could. I had learned to dive inside of myself, as if compelled, as if the only salvation for my sanity was to seek God, and so I continued with that practice back on the East Coast: I isolated myself as best I could by diving inside my mind, breath, and soul.

In Massachusetts, I was less connected to people. I found them confusing because they could not see what I could see—that life was brief, death was always close, the world was an illusion, and only God was real. I could see the light inside people, feel it from them. Some had the light stronger than others; everybody had it, but nobody seemed to know it except me.

I told no one what I saw or felt. I kept my mouth shut. My dad used to call me "Silent Pete" when I was a kid growing up. After I returned from Bozeman, he started calling me "Silent Pete" again, in a good-natured way, besides, silence was better than a stutter. He was right: I had nothing to say because I had no words to describe what I'd been through. During the year that followed I slowly learned to control my stutter.

～ 30 ～

ZooMass

The summer after I returned to Marlborough, Massachusetts, I also returned to my special white pine tree in the woodlands behind my parents' house. There, I practiced my sitting meditation while I leaned against its pitchy rough-barked trunk. I did not date. I did not go out. I worked as a laborer at the same contracting company I'd worked for the summer before. I read literature for escape and kept to myself as much as I could.

In the fall, I went back to UMass Amherst again— ZooMass, as we called it—and enrolled in a pantomime class. My instructor, Jody, had studied under Tony Montanaro, who studied with Marcel Marceau in France. I felt part of quite the artist lineage to be a student in Jody's class. The most important thing, though, was that Jody taught us yoga every day to warm us up for mime. Jody taught us that yoga is not just to stretch and strengthen our body, but it is also to focus our mind and open our soul to God.

That semester I also took a course in the Comparative Literature Department called, "Comparative Mystical Literature East and West." I was hungry for God, who, for me, had no name that could ever be said. I needed more than the traditional church could give me. I needed God directly—not mediated, not tamed, but wild and living, present and experiential. I read so that I might learn if there was anybody, dead or living, who could tell me how to go Home without taking my own life. I needed heaven within me.

It turns out that across the globe, for centuries, men and women whom we call mystics and contemplatives have pursued God, and many of them had written works that described their indescribable experience. I quickly learned that it was much smarter to read the ancient writing of the mystics and contemplatives than it was to read any modern writer on the subject.

My death had left me knowing that God had no form, was no thing, was beyond form, and had created all things, including me. No concept, no idea, no words, could contain God. Therefore, I needed every concept, every idea, and every ancient word to try to make sense of what had happened to me. I have always been a spiritual person. I was spiritual as a child, even mystical, in the ancient sense of the word, as I would later discover in my reading. God had always had a grip on me when I was growing up, and this remains true.

This class opened my eyes to the world of people who, while not exactly like me, were close enough in kind. I began reading many deep and serious spiritual writings from around the globe. I read voraciously, hoping to find anything that might help me understand where I had been and what had happened to me.

The class ended with a voluntary, weekend-long silent retreat at St. Joseph's Abbey. It was at the same Trappist Abbey where my high school religion teacher had learned the meditation practice he'd taught me years before, the practice of which had sustained me. My entire class was invited to attend the retreat along with our professor, a deacon in a Catholic church and practitioner of meditation. He'd begun our class that fall by saying it was a class for serious scholars and that we'd get no credit for navel gazing.

At the retreat, we practiced navel gazing. We sat or walked in silent meditation for the entire weekend. There was no talking at all. The monastery allowed us one visit with the novitiate and guest master, Father Theophane Boyd, who looked a lot like Ichabod Crane dressed in brown and white monk's robes. He was very tall and very skinny, with bony, thin, and prominently knuckled fingers that could probably palm a basketball. His Adam's apple protruded like a Granny Smith and moved up and down his throat whenever he spoke. His hair was gray, long, shaggy, untamable, and stuck out in various directions. His clear blue eyes were like laser beams that read a soul just by looking into another's eyes and penetrating the heart. When he looked at me, my heart caught fire. I could see the fire in him, and I believed he could see it in me.

He spoke about life in the monastery and about spirituality in general terms. During the question and answer period, one of my classmates, David, asked him, "What is it like to be you?" Father Theophane Boyd was seated in front of us, and we were at his feet. He closed his eyes and rocked his upper body back and forth slowly as he considered how to answer. He opened his eyes and said, "I used to be asleep, and now I am awake." This man radiated light. Being in his presence was like being among the illuminated. Being awake, like him, became my goal.

I returned frequently to the monastery in the subsequent years, seeking his counsel and direction. I adopted him as my spiritual advisor, and he tolerated me.

I used to be asleep, and often I wish I could just go back to sleep.

⤢ 31 ⤡

Today

Today, some thirty years later, I sit in Maine in my studio listening to the sound of the sea crashing on the rocks and the nearby foghorn and bell buoy. As I write, a deep and old sadness touches me. It scares me a little. This sadness is familiar and similar to how I felt in those first days and months in 1980. It is a feeling of divergence. I am always in two places at once. It is like I am a river that splits in two, with one branch heading one way, and the other heading another way, giving me not one experience of life but two simultaneously. That feeling never leaves me.

The branch that weaves through life here always changes. The branch that leads to There never changes. *There* feels like a deep truth, a centering of a sort, a love inexplicable; yet, at the same time, it feels like a sad, unrequited love—a love that is always there, but just out of reach. I have this strong desire for the only One who can love me the way I know love can feel. I belong to God.

There are times I wish that was not true, but it is true and I cannot ever escape that. My wife says that has made our marriage difficult. She says it is probably true of all marriages where one partner has died and come back and the other partner has not. I live in a constant state of nonattachment. Not detachment. I am not aloof. I am simply not fully connected here, and that, of course, includes everything, even my marriage.

But I am here. And I am married and have two grown children whom I, like all parents, love more than life itself. I had not planned on having kids, but God had other ideas. I had not planned on marrying, not at least until I met my wife at a meeting in Boston where she was a presenter and I was in the audience. I was working my first real job after UMass as a legislative aide for a Massachusetts representative. She was working for the Massachusetts Department of Health. It was her job to speak with me about pending legislation that mattered to her department. We arranged to meet to discuss it, and I went back to my office and told my representative that I was smitten. He warned me not to mix work and love, but it was too late for that. I asked her out, and on our wedding day my representative forgave my indiscretion of dating someone from work.

Before our wedding it got rather complicated because I was seeking a way into Saint Joseph's Abbey. I had been going on retreat there regularly and had decided that I wanted to be a Trappist monk. It seemed that those monks lived in the light of God, and I craved that light. I felt that I did not fit in this world and that I might fit into the monastery. Falling in love complicated that.

I decided that I would delay a monastic life by going to divinity school for a two-year master's degree with a focus on the history of Christian contemplation and mysticism. As an undergraduate I had already interviewed with Princeton, and so I interviewed at Harvard and Yale. In the end, I chose Yale and planned on continuing my education in a doctoral program after earning my MA. While I was there, the dean of admissions took a shine to me and convinced me to switch to the three-year Master of Divinity degree and to consider joining the United Church of Christ with an aim toward ordination. Upon graduation I was invited to preach at a wider church gathering. After my sermon, a reverend approached me and told me he was seeking an associate minister and he would be pleased if I applied. I did, and landed a three-year extended interim associate minister's job in a suburban New Haven church. I later served four years as a minister and preacher on an island off the coast of Maine, Deer Isle, and then in the resort town of Boothbay Harbor, Maine.

One day years later, in 2001, I told my NDE story publicly for the first time from the pulpit in Boothbay Harbor. I had told it only twice before: once to a dear friend, at divinity school, in 1986, whose face betrayed to me his love, kindness, confusion, and concern for my mental well-being, and who swore secrecy to me; and, previously, on the day before I married my fiancée in 1985.

That first day I shared my story publicly from the pulpit, I needed to try to explain to them why I had done what I had done—and on that day I tried to frame language to describe the indescribable, speak the unspeakable. I had been the minister at the Congregational Church of Boothbay Harbor, Maine, United Church of Christ for about nine years. We recently had ended our very hard times over our decade together, which is putting it kindly and mildly. Over a time period of about thirteen years, a total of $200,000 was stolen from the church where I was pastor, and $3,000 was stolen from me personally. When it became apparent that something was up and I started asking questions, I was personally attacked and very nearly forced out of the church and threatened with being defrocked. A secret cell within the church controlled the board of trustees and the finances and isolated certain deacons and loyal friends, and it nearly destroyed our church and our congregation.

But we succeeded in overcoming and thriving as a body despite what had happened to us. On one Sunday morning, just before church, a parishioner asked me "how my faith had endured unshakably" through a decade of church turmoil. On that Sunday morning in 2001, I knew I did not have any faith, because what near-death experiencer has need of faith when he knows that God is Real? I wondered if I should finally tell my congregation the truth. My faith? I had none. It is a strange thing that I decided on the spur of the moment to finally admit the truth to my parishioners. I decided to tell them the truth about me: I had no faith. I have no faith. I have not had faith of any sort or believed in God ever since that dark March day and night on Lower Weeping Wall in 1980. I decided to come clean and tell my congregation just how it was that I endured nearly a decade of angst, and personal abuse, and trusted God that I would—and that we would—endure and heal, if only the truth were found out and told.

On that Sunday morning, I pondered how I might explain to my people how God is Real, and that while I had no faith, I know that I am known by God, and beloved. I have no faith, because on that night in March of 1980, my faith was taken from me. Before that, I had been a faithful person all of my life, a believer, a Christian by birth and upbringing, and then a born-again Catholic Christian active within the Charismatic youth movement. I had spoken in tongues. I had heard interpretation of tongues at prayer meetings. I had been slain in the spirit. All of that was gone in the blink of an eye and replaced with knowing that I am known by God, and knowing that God is Real. One does not have to believe in what is Real. What is Real is Real; it requires no belief and no faith. I am no longer blind. I no longer have to take the leap of faith I had taken.

So, there I was that Sunday morning, nearly two decades into being a church minister preaching to my congregation about the need for belief and faith, and yet I had none. I faced a choice that morning: tell the truth or lie.

For my part in the healing of this church, I found myself needing, truly feeling compelled for the very first time, to speak aloud my truth, tell my story, and be unafraid of what people might think of me. For decades, I had feared that if I told my story, people would think that I was crazy, insane, or just a fool. That morning, my fear vanished. Suddenly, I no longer cared what people thought of my truth, so I decided to answer this parishioner's question spontaneously, and from the pulpit.

Why then, and why so publicly? It was necessary— because the time was right, and because God had made it impossible for me to ever feel abandoned, to ever feel alone, to ever feel lost in my soul, ever, and that pressure inside me that started on the morning that I had awoken with my stutter had never left me; the internal pressure to speak had only continued to become more and more intense. Since I came back from death, I have not felt alone, not for a moment. Oh, plenty of times I have wanted to feel alone. And plenty of times I have not wanted to feel God as real and present, but I've had no choice in that matter. For that, I've felt lost here on earth and in this world ever since the day I got back. I am lost today. I was lost yesterday. And I know I will be lost tomorrow. I am displaced. I am alien. I am not from here . . . but, then again, neither are you. The only difference is that I know I am not from here. Unless you have died and come back, you do not know. Trust me, God is Real; you will go Home, and it is beautiful.

The night I died has always felt like a blessing and a curse: The blessing is that I know I can never escape the sight of God; yet, that is the curse too. I do not believe this. I know it. There is a difference between believing and knowing. I *know* where Home is, and I long for it. That night on the mountain I learned that I had a new Home, which was my old Home, my first Home, my only Home, my real Home, and that Home is the one and only deep desire of my heart. (And, that is why it is difficult to love a near-death experience survivor—my heart fully belongs to another.)

My wife is a saint—patient, tolerant, understanding. She understands and accepts that she will always be second in my heart. I wish it were not so, but it is. Although I love her and my children, my heart is over there, on the other side. My Home is heaven. It is your Home too. It is where I am from and to where I am going when I die again. It was promised to me.

So, I told my congregation about my lack of faith that Sunday morning, instead of preaching the sermon I'd prepared with over twenty hours of work—reading, research, writing, and editing. I told them because I felt they needed to know why I hadn't quit in the midst of the worst of our church's turmoil, and why during one of the darkest times of my life, I continued to pray, and actually dove even deeper into God. Why? Because God is all there is to me. God gives me strength even in my weakness.

I waved my sermon manuscript in the air and said, "I prepared a sermon for today. It took half of my week to prepare it, and here it is. But I am not going to preach this today. This morning, just before church, I was asked how I had endured terrible treatment here while we sought to solve the problem of our finances and discovered it was actually embezzlement. How did I endure? Let me tell you a story. This is the first time I am going to tell this story, and truly I don't want to tell it, but I feel I must. I kept a secret for twenty years. But if you want to know the truth about my strong faith, well, the truth is, I don't have any faith. Here is why . . ."

I then began telling my tale aloud to an attentive crowd who loved me, and in whose presence I felt safe enough to tell the truth of how I lost my faith and gained a love of God. That day, and every day since whenever I have told my story—and I have told it hundreds of times to audiences small and large—the hardest part of the telling is explaining my journey to the other side. I went through the fire once, and I expect to pass through the fire again.

On the other side, there is no time. Time does not exist. Time exists here. Time moves forward here, and we can look back in history and think about time. Time is entwined in nature, in the physics of this three-dimensional world. In time, there is a sequence of events. Here, one thing happens, and then the next thing happens, and then the next. On the other side time does not exist. Nothing happens in sequence. So, did everything happen all at once to me there? I do not know. It is eternity over there. Not forever. Forever is a measure of time. Eternity is outside of time.

Furthermore, as I have said before and will say again, there are no words, no things, no body, no brain, no culture, no history, and no language. Here, in this world, in our world of height, depth, width, and time, there are things. Everything here is a *thing*, including this book, and you, and me, and rocks, hills, words, brains, molecules, particles—even the Higgs boson is a thing. Everything is a *thing* here.

On the other side, there are no things. No *thing* exists there. No time. No things. Nothing. No thing. The most difficult task in telling this part of the story, the most important part of my entire story, is finding words to describe the indescribable. Words are things, too. Words describe things; words are symbols of things. We often think in words; and, more often, we think in symbols and images, emotions and memories, and they are all *things*. I am belaboring this point to make a point: Heaven and God are indescribable. Yet, I feel the fire within me to describe what cannot be described. It is weird to be me. I'm sure of that. For anybody who has died, crossed over, and come back to life here in this world, life is strange, and alien.

These days, I serve God on broadcast and cable television, FM radio, and social media as a sacred storyteller in Maine and beyond as the minister of First Radio Parish Church of America (DailyDevotions.org). God has given me a media platform to speak the truth that God is Real and Love is Real and that in dying we find life. From the first morning after my near-death experience I have felt an inner compulsion to tell about it. I locked that compulsion inside me, but in there it grew stronger and stronger, and demanded to be told, but I was a rebellious sort, and refused. I feel that I must tell it now.

It doesn't make me feel good to tell it. To tell it I have to go back into the dark places in my life. Telling my story usually makes me cry. I wish it didn't, but it does. I tell it to give hope. I tell it because God compels me to tell it. I am driven to tell it. I think that this story is one among many that are coming from the near-death community meant to raise the sight of the world to love, to give hope to the dying, and comfort to the mourning.

I am humbled by my situation, and I hope that the messenger is never confused with the message. I am an imperfect and broken person; only God is whole and holy. Love is what I preach, and I pray for and hunt for that full feeling of Love I experienced when I was in heaven. It is always there, filling me, yet also just out of reach. Though I immediately forgot most of what I knew and understood about life and love once I came back to this world and my body—I still sense that what I know now, today, about heaven is a mere fragment, a shard, of what I knew there—experiencing it left me with a desire for the One, a drive for God, and so I strive to open my heart as wide as I can and shout in prayer, "God, here I am. Notice me!" I know that I am noticed. It feels that way, but it is just a tiny fraction of what I knew on the other side, just a droplet that I feel. What I want is to be immersed in the river.

~ 32 ~

Being Here and Going There

I am often asked if dying and coming back influenced my decision to get ordained. The answer is yes and no. In some ways, I have always been on this path. I've had a strong interior spiritual call since I was a young boy. I'm sort of an accidental clergy member; I did not intend to remain at the pulpit, but I kept finding work that had to be done, so I did it. Also, the intensity of my spirituality increased dramatically after my near-death experience, and I knew of no other way I could get away with spending hours each day in yoga and meditation and call it work. The work of ministry has allowed me the honor of sitting and conversing with many who are dying, and many who have died. And I feel better equipped to help because of my experience.

The best part of my ministry job has always been sitting with the dying—talking, praying, and simply being with them, being real, authentic, and truthful. I've found that, when I've shared my story, even if very briefly, expressing my assurance of eternal life, my hope, my knowing that I am known, has helped ease hundreds into death, and into Love-Hope-Joy-Beauty-Truth-Charity-Kindness-Compassion-Love-Patience-Beauty-Love.

I have been an unconventional pastor because I am an unconventional person, one who has at times run afoul of certain parishioners who had their own ideas of clerical propriety and dignity. I have never been good at either of those things. Inevitably, some of these parishioners have become gravely ill, and—whether they like it or not, whether I liked them or not—it has been and will be my duty to visit them and help their passage across. Once someone reaches the stage where he or she sees death coming, we have become the fastest of friends.

I said it was an honor to sit with the dying, and it has been, every time. Part of this is because people often become more honest in their deaths; but more so, as the time nears, it is because the veil that hides heaven from the eyes of humans sometimes begins to lift. In the old days, when Auntie Mabel was dying, she might say, "I see an angel" or "I see my husband (or my mother)." The attendant might say, "No, dear. There is no angel here," or "No, dear. Your mother (or your husband) has been dead for ten years. She (or he) is not here." These days, nurses, doctors, and clergy just let those who are dying express what they believe they are seeing, even if no one else can see it. Who is to say that what they see is not real, and that an angel or a deceased family member is not in the room? The veil between heaven and earth is lifted more often than we know.

For weeks after a funeral, it has been my job to visit the grieving mother, widow, husband, or child. Often, in hushed tones, they would lean across the kitchen table and say words such as these: "Peter, this is going to sound crazy. This morning when I came down for breakfast, there was Tom, standing right there by the sink with his back to me. I was shocked. He turned around, looked me in the eyes, and said, 'Don't worry, dear. I am okay. I'll see you again.' He smiled and then vanished." A hundred times or more, I've heard such stories from the grieving. Maybe you have a similar story or have heard one like it. If the afterlife is real, and I am here to tell you that it is, then why wouldn't your loved one want to tell you that she or he is okay and all is well?

If you are dying right now, or fear dying, or love someone who is dying, then please, let me tell you this: You are not your body. You are your soul. Your soul inhabits your body. When you go across, or when the one you love departs, the soul does not die. Only the body dies. The real you does *not* die. When you die, you will carry with you—yourself—the *you* who is you, plus all the love you have given away or shared, and all the love you have gathered. All the bits and pieces of love you have given or collected are in your soul right now, and they are yours to keep. They are your treasure. Jesus said, "Store up treasure for yourself in heaven, where moths and rust cannot destroy and thieves do not break in and steal" (Matthew 6:20). He was right. Every act of love accumulates in your soul. No one, and nothing, can take these from you or destroy them. Love is eternal, and love is inside you.

You also get to carry all the pain you have caused, and whether you choose to believe me or not, that pain is sin. We all sin. I still sin, probably every day; but I love every day, too, and I know that God is merciful and forgiving—thank God.

You will carry your memories, your self, your mind, and your soul into heaven, a heaven where there is no pain, no boredom, no suffering, and where there is love and beauty beyond comprehension. God is all-loving and knows you thoroughly already, from before you were born, even before you were knit in your mother's womb. God created your innermost being. God knew you, and knows you (Jeremiah 1:5; Psalm 139:13).

You are loved. You are beloved in particular. You have always been loved; you will always be loved. You are loved with a love beyond imagination, with a power of love beyond comprehension, a thousand times sweeter than the sweetest love you have ever felt. Love is how you were made. Love is how you exist. You will not end. When the trumpet blows for you, you will transform in the twinkling of an eye (1 Corinthians 15:52) and find yourself in the presence of God, who is Love and Mercy and Truth and Beauty. Be prepared to be loved and to be welcomed: you are going Home. Death is only a doorway. When your time comes, as it must, walk through that doorway and love God. Trust God. Believe. That's all you have to do—simply believe. You can believe in God, because God is Real. This life is simply one bridge in between.

My job is to bring hope. I hope you have hope now. God is Real. Heaven is Real. God is LOVE. We are not from here; we are from There. Our end is our beginning. We go back to where we came from. This life is simply one bridge in between.

Do we all go to heaven? That is not my call, nor is it yours. That choice is God's, the Loving, the Merciful, the Forgiving. I certainly think so—or, at least, I think we all get the chance. I am rather sure I got in because I was ashamed of the pain that I'd caused, but mostly because God is forgiving.

It is true that all is well. All has always been well. All will be well. It is true that all is well because God is Love, and life is but a wink of God's eye.

My desire to die has abated some in recent years. This is not to say I was ever suicidal; I was not. Philippians 1:23–24 probably says it best for me: "I am hard pressed between the two: my desire is to depart and be with Christ, for that is far better; but to remain in the flesh is more necessary for you." 2 Corinthians 5:8 conveys my point well: "Yes, we do have confidence, and we would rather be away from the body and at home with the Lord."

From where I stand, human beings are made of at least two parts—the body and the spirit/soul. The parts are connected to each other in this world, but unconnected in the next. In this world, through prayer, through meditation, we can access the spirit/soul and learn of its existence; we can empty ourselves of ourselves and get out of the way of God, out of the way of God's grace/love, so it can infuse us and lift us. Why the wait? Not because of any purity of ours, or because of our meditative focus, but because only God can do it. Our job is to get out of the way.

That is what meditation does. Meditation teaches that I am at my best when I am at my least. Meditation gets me out of the way. Meditation fills the belly with light. It's like gathering a thin silken thread of light, then winding that into a cocoon inside my belly. Every day, I wind more thread onto my spool, and during the day I can unwind it to give it away. Meditation is like sipping from a bottomless cup and swallowing the water of life, which fills a reservoir in my belly, giving me a bellyful each day—and then, I give the water away. The water gives me strength. It shows me the way. It reminds me that I am not from here. I long for the day when I will finally get to return Home.

Meditation simply opens the inner door, over and over and over, and lets the Light seep in. As for God's part, God can swing open wide the door and let in all the Light we can stand within us, within the human body, and not shatter from joy. Or, God can swing wide open our inner door and lift us through heavens even unto God himself, in a beatific vision of God, or near enough to see the Light or hear the music that sings the soul into being. We need not die to be lifted to God, but it helps. Dying is the shortest route Home; it opens the door the widest. It is a door that rarely swings both ways. Usually, it is one-way, and it closes behind us.

What form of meditation should you practice? The one that is rooted to your faith tradition. In this life, in this world, we can open our door to God through prayer, community, kindness, and love in action in a thousand small ways or a thousand large ways. All of these allow us to get out of God's way, allow God's Light and Love to seep into us, and into the world. God is Real. God is Love. God loves you, personally and particularly.

Where are you from? You are from where I'm from— heaven and God. I am not from here, and neither are you. We are both, we are all, from heaven—every human being upon this planet. Heaven is our beginning, and heaven is our end. We are souls first, and bodies second. We belong to God, who is Light and Love, Mercy, Joy, and Beauty beyond belief, beyond imagination.

God is Love. God is Love. God is Love. Death is a door. All is well. All has always been well. All will be well. All will always be well—because of God's Love. Never forget that.

Mount Madison summit. Presidential Range, White Mountain National Forest, New Hampshire, October 2010. Photograph by Don Scott.

Acknowledgments

My tolerant and loving wife, Michelle, deserves the most thanks. She has endured years of my eccentricities that come from being a near-death experiencer. My two children, Lexa and Andy, also deserve honor and praise for having endured a dad for whom death and dying are regular dinner conversation and for having the misfortune of having been raised as pastor's kids in a small town through no fault of their own.

I am grateful to my literary agent, Stephany Evans of FinePrint Literature, who put up with my peccadillos for months upon months while working with me on my proposal and for shopping it around until she found the right publisher.

Thanks to Greg Brandenburg, associate publisher at Hampton Roads, who read my manuscript straight through one Saturday morning and then took a chance on me. Big thanks to my copyeditor, Susie Pitzen, who makes me appear to be a better writer than I am.

I'd like to thank my board of trustees at First Radio Parish Church of America/DailyDevotions.org for allowing me the time I needed to write this book and Lorraine Lamont, who helped with early copyediting.

And my friends, who loved me and tolerated me when I was lost and trying to figure out what had happened to me even though I did not tell them what had happened: Don S., Steve M., Steve C., Douglas G., Kerri K., Rhanda J., Bill L., and Charlie C.

About the Author

Peter Baldwin Panagore earned his BA in English from the University of Massachusetts and a MDiv from Yale University. He was ordained in the United Church of Christ and served churches in suburban Connecticut and Maine. He is the writer, on-air talent, and host of a daily two-minute broadcast on two Gannett Company-owned NBC stations in Maine, reaching an audience of 350,000 a week. He is the fifth minister of First Radio Parish Church of America (founded in 1926). Visit Peter online at www.dailydevotion.com.

Afterglow

As I reflect on what happened to me the night I died, God unfolds more truth and understanding about what I experienced. One of the things I've had to overcome was my anger at God that I couldn't and wouldn't live *my* life. With the gift of my near-death experience came the curse of being separate, estranged from, and outside of all humanity. I did my best to seek God and to run away from God at the same time because I couldn't reconcile the inescapable feeling of having one foot in heaven and one foot here, of one eye seeing there and one eye seeing here, all the time. I lived with a consistent and great sorrow deep inside my heart because I could see clearly the one desire of my soul, and that desire was to be utterly in the presence of God as I was when I died. It is as Paul said, "For now we see only a reflection as in a mirror; then we shall see face to face. Now I know in part; then I shall know fully, even as I am fully known" (1 Corinthians 13:12). My heart lives there, though my body is here.

But then I began developing a reputation in my small town as the one to call when death is near. I began to spend a lot of time at bedsides, in hospice situations, and at funerals. People don't know or understand why I can help the dying; they just know I can. I simply tell the truth to the dying—that God loves them, and to fear not and trust Him—and I think the sincerity of my words and the presence of God that flows through me touch them in their souls. I call myself "a midwife for the dying."

As I helped people pass from this life to the next, my heart emptied of the anger that I held against God for all those years. I see now that my calling, my "not living my own life," is to do my best to point at God, Who is the Eternally Loving One, the Creator from Whom all humanity and all life and this world springs, and in my own small way try to point the way home for those with ears to hear and hearts to seek.

Over the years, and in the years to come, I expect that there will be more learning for me as I reflect on the night I died, more truth to come, and more understanding. All in all now, looking back, I am gratified that I returned. It was better for my parents. I have beautiful, loving children and a wife who understands I live in between two worlds and am not fully in either one.

This book and my time with the dying are the most important works of my life. It is a summary of all that I am in the hope that it will lead you to believe.

I Have Been Somewhere!

by Ellen NicKenzie Lawson, PhD

I woke up that morning in my partially furnished rented house. Tiptoeing through the living room, I could see Joshua, my nineteen-year-old son, sacked out on a futon in an otherwise empty bedroom. It was Memorial Day weekend a year ago, and he had come out from the East to visit, relieving me of the loneliness I often felt living by myself in this logging city. I had moved to Longview, Washington, to teach history at a small community college. I loved my job and enjoyed the dramatic scenery of the area—snow-capped Mount St. Helens, the towering trees—but it hadn't been easy starting over in my late forties.

Because it was Sunday, Joshua and I went to church. Throughout the service, I kept thinking of the dream I had had the night before and the sense it gave me that something positive would happen to me. The sky was gray and overcast, and the roads slick from the night's rain, yet the day held promise.

That afternoon after doing some work in the garden, I announced, "Let's go for a hike." Joshua and I had read of some hot springs on Wind River in the Columbia River Gorge, about a sixty-mile drive from my home and "an easy half-mile walk from the road," our guidebook stated. We filled our backpacks with bathing suits and towels, put on sweatshirts, and drove to the head of the trail. On the way, I listened to a tape Joshua had made of his favorite songs—some classical, some pop tunes, all of them an expression of who he was and what interested him. I glanced at my handsome grown son, now in college. His long brown hair curled over his ears; his gray-blue eyes had the clear gaze of a budding philosopher.

We parked at a small area above the river where there was a registration desk with directions to the springs. I could see it was no easy hike. Thirty-foot cliffs dropped off to the rushing river below. Our route would take us across giant boulders, down a steep slope, and through muddy patches of an unmarked trail.

Walking gingerly, we made our way down the slope. I stayed close to the ground, holding on to rocks and trees to steady myself. This was tiring, and I began to doubt the wisdom of making this late-afternoon hike. After a half hour, I already wished we were there.

It was 5:00 PM when we reached the springs, the brilliant blue water steaming in the air. I sank into the warm sulfurous pool, tantalized by the sharp smell that mingled with the scent of cedar trees. Months of worry seemed to melt from me as I closed my eyes. Joshua relaxed too. All too soon it was time to go back. I was concerned about reaching our car before darkness and taking the difficult trail up.

Going back, we followed the cold rushing river over boulders and rocks. "Mom, I'm going on to find the trail," Joshua said, darting ahead. I started up a narrow ridge with a steep drop-off on one side, thinking it was the trail. I was too tired to realize I wasn't following Joshua. The hike and the hot springs had left me so relaxed I felt like a rag doll. Across the river, I noticed a couple in the distance and asked myself what they were doing. They can't get to the springs from there. They must be confused.

Just then I slipped on the muddy soil and fell to the ground. I slid backward, grasping wildly for a rock or root—any handhold. Nothing. I went over the edge.

Time slowed down for me. The air whooshed around me; the cliff rushed by. "Help!" I screamed. Reaching out, I desperately tried to grab something, anything, on the rock wall to stop my fall.

I looked at the sky. I knew down below there was nothing but rocks and the river. I'm going to die. I would either be crushed on the ground or drown in the cold water. "I'm dead!" I screamed. There was no way I could survive.

My body bounced over the boulders and came to rest at the water's edge on a pile of rocks. I was bruised and bleeding, but all I really knew ...

I'm staring at a beautiful golden screen. It takes up my entire field of vision. Behind it, filtering through, is a yellow light. The yellow light glows, filling me with inexpressible peace and joy. I want to be with the light forever. I am transfixed by it. I have never been so happy. Then there is a blip on the screen far over to my left. I am irritated because it distracts me from the beautiful golden screen. I turn my eyes from it, but it doesn't go away. It keeps pulsing, getting bigger with each beat, overtaking the former image like one TV picture crowding out another. Now within the blip I can see my son's face and he looks unhappy.

Why is he so unhappy? What's wrong? I must find out. Even if it means giving up the peace and joy I feel, even if it means turning away from the beautiful golden screen.

I shift my attention away from the light and focus on him. It takes all the strength I have because the pull of the light is so strong. It takes a conscious effort, so I know I'm not unconscious. I have been knocked out before, but this is different ...

Instantly, I was awake. I have been somewhere. Suddenly, I felt enormous pain. I groaned. For the first time, I realized I had fallen off a cliff. I could move my neck, hips, and feet. Thank God, I was alive and not paralyzed. Joshua was by my side, almost hysterical with fear.

"I've been somewhere!" I told him. He cried, not understanding, simply relieved to know I was alive. He gently slipped a sweater under my head. Blood poured from my face. I couldn't move my left arm. Joshua leaned over and talked to me to comfort me.

Across the river the man I had seen earlier scrambled up the hill for help while the woman called to Joshua to stay with me and make sure I was warm. The region was remote, and it would have taken someone a long time to reach a phone from our side of the river, but from that side it was a quick trip.

In about twenty minutes, a hiker came by and administered first aid as I drifted in and out of consciousness. Then volunteers from the Skamania Fire Department arrived. They strapped a neck brace and an oxygen mask around me. They raised me on a stretcher, and six men hiked me up the slope, sometimes slipping on the wet trail.

At the top of the hill, I was lowered into an ambulance and driven to a helicopter. I was flown to Legacy Emanuel Hospital in Portland, Oregon. I was in shock, shaking from the cold, groaning from the pain, but I thought, *I have been somewhere*.

In the hospital, I had a CAT scan. No one could believe I hadn't suffered any spinal damage. I had a crushed arm and I needed stitches on my forehead and chin. Two teeth were broken. I also had a punctured intestine, but I wasn't paralyzed.

At midnight, a surgeon had to operate on my smashed arm. I asked Joshua to get the tape recorder and the cassette he had made of his favorite songs. I was retching; they couldn't give me any general anesthesia. "I'll listen to the tape," I told the doctor and nurses. I sank in and out of awareness while they set the bones in my arm, inserting a plate and screws. Several times I shouted, "Turn it up louder!" or "Rewind the tape!"

The next day a reporter from the local newspaper called me for an interview. "I was blessed," I told him. People visited me in the hospital, Joshua was an almost constant presence at my side, and members from my church were praying for me. When I read the newspaper, I saw the reporter had quoted me as saying, "I was lucky." *No*, I thought, *he got it wrong*.

At home, while recovering, I kept recalling the brilliant yellow light I had seen. Taking out a piece of paper, I sketched a picture of the beautiful golden screen. I didn't want to lose the image of peace and joy. I made an effort to get in touch with the couple on the other side of the river but never succeeded. It was as though God had put them there for a reason. I also realized how fortunate I was in the way I fell. I had hit the rock on my side. If I had landed on my back or head, it could have meant paralysis or death.

Then one morning, a few weeks after the accident, as I was lying in bed, my eye caught the icon I use regularly in my prayers, one of the few things I had brought with me when I moved across the country. Propped against one bare wall of my bedroom, it was about the size of a large postcard, showing Christ against a background of rich gold leaf. Every morning when I looked at it, I pictured Jesus listening to me.

Suddenly, I made the connection: Christ, the yellow light and the golden screen. When I was near death, that's what I had seen! The overwhelming peace and joy came from Him. I had been somewhere—at one with a heavenly light. Because of it, I no longer fear death. I feel blessed. Thanks be to God.

A Note from the Editors

We hope you enjoy *Heaven Is Beautiful* by Peter Baldwin Panagore, specially selected by the editors of the Books and Inspirational Media Division of Guideposts, a non-profit organization that touches millions of lives every day through products and services that inspire, encourage, help you grow in your faith, and celebrate God's love in every aspect of your daily life.

Thank you for making a difference with your purchase of this book, which helps fund our many outreach programs to military personnel, prisons, hospitals, nursing homes, and educational institutions. To learn more, visit GuidepostsFoundation.org.

We also maintain many useful and uplifting online resources. Visit Guideposts.org to read true stories of hope and inspiration, access OurPrayer network, sign up for free newsletters, download free e-books, join our Facebook community, and follow our stimulating blogs.

To learn about other Guideposts publications, including the best-selling devotional *Daily Guideposts*, go to ShopGuideposts.org, call (800) 932-2145, or write to Guideposts, PO Box 5815, Harlan, Iowa 51593.

Find more inspiring true stories of how God reaches out to us in
Mysterious Ways

A bimonthly magazine from the editors of Guideposts

Learn more at
Guideposts.org/MysteriousWays2015

To receive weekly stories about those inexplicable, chill-down-your-spine experiences that are more than mere coincidence, sign up for your FREE e-mail newsletter at Guideposts.org/newsletters.

Join us on 🅵 **MysteriousWays**

"A warmly winning second-chance novel."

—*Christian Science Monitor*

the beach street knitting society and yarn club

A NOVEL

Gil McNeil

Gil McNeil is the author of *The Beach Street Knitting Society and Yarn Club*. She lives in Kent, England, with her son, and comes from a long line of champion knitters.

needles and pearls

needles

AND

pearls

Gil McNeil

voice

HYPERION / *New York*

First published in Great Britain as *Needles and Pearls* in 2008 by Bloomsbury Publishing, Plc.

Library of Congress Cataloging-in-Publication Data

McNeil, Gil
    Needles and pearls / Gil McNeil.
        p. cm.
    ISBN: 978-1-4013-4129-9
    1. Knitting—Fiction.   2. Single mothers—Fiction.   3. England—
Fiction.   I. Title.
    PR6113.C58N44   2010
    823'.92—dc22   2009054273

Hyperion books are available for special promotions and premiums. For details contact the HarperCollins Special Markets Department in the New York office at 212-207-7528, fax 212-207-7222, or email spsales@harpercollins.com.

Design by Jennifer Ann Daddio/Bookmark Design & Media Inc.

FIRST EDITION

10   9   8   7   6   5   4   3   2

For Joe

contents

needles and pearls

two weddings and a year after the funeral

February

It's half past seven on Sunday morning and I'm sitting in the kitchen knitting a pale pink rabbit and trying to work out what to wear today. All those programs where women with tired hair and baggy trousers emerge a small fortune later with a new bob and a fully coordinated wardrobe never seem to give you tips about what you're meant to wear when you visit your husband's grave on the first anniversary of the funeral. Especially when you've got to combine it with lunch with Elizabeth, the artist formerly known as your mother-in-law, who'll definitely be expecting something smart, possibly in the little-black-suit department, or maybe navy, at a pinch. And since I haven't got a black suit, or a navy one, come to that, I think I might be in trouble.

Perhaps if I'd actually got some sleep last night things wouldn't feel quite so overwhelming, but the sound of the wind and the waves kept me awake, which is one of the disadvantages of living by the seaside; it's lovely in summer, all beach huts and day-trippers coming into the shop when it starts to drizzle, but I'm starting to realize that winter can be rather hard going. It's all freezing mists and gales, and when there's a storm down here, you really know about it. Maybe if the house wasn't ten minutes from the beach I might not have quite so many dreams where I'm shipwrecked and trying to keep two small boys afloat.

I finally managed to drop off around two, and was promptly woken by Archie shuffling in to let me know he'd had his space-monster dream again. Which is something else that's not quite as good as it sounds on the packet: how five-year-olds manage to combine being far too grown-up to wear vests now they're at Big School with still needing night-lights and special blankets as soon as you've got the little buggers into their pajamas. Not that Archie really goes in for special blankets—unlike Jack, who's seven but is still firmly attached to the fish blanket I knitted him in honor of his new seaside bedroom—but he's still perfectly happy to wake his mother up in the middle of the bloody night to talk about monsters and the possibility of a light snack.

I'm writing another version of my never-ending Things I Must Do Today list, while the rain pours down the kitchen window in solid sheets. We might not be able to match Whitstable for stripy sweaters and artistically arranged fish-

ing nets, but we can certainly match them for pouring rain. We do have an art gallery in the High Street now that goes in for smart window displays involving a large wooden bowl and a spotlight, so we're starting to get there; and what's more, we've got houses that normal people can afford, and a rickety pier and newly painted beach huts that don't get sold in auctions for more money than most people paid for their first house. Gran's been renting hers for years, which reminds me, that's something else to add to my list: I need to take another towel down next time we go to the beach; we took Trevor the annoying Wonder Dog for a walk yesterday, and Archie ended up in the sea again.

I'm making a pot of tea when Archie comes downstairs, with his hair sticking up in little tufts, wearing his pajamas, and the belt from his dressing gown, but no actual dressing gown.

"It's no good just wearing the belt, you know, love. You'll get cold."

"No I won't. I like it like this, it's my rope, for if I need to climb things. And I'm not having Shreddies for my breakfast. I want a sausage, just sausage. I don't have to have Shreddies because it's the weekend. At the weekend you can say what you want and you just have it."

How lovely; I think I'll order eggs Benedict and a glass of champagne. Or maybe a nice bit of smoked haddock.

I'm rather enjoying my Fantasy Breakfast moment while Archie looks in the fridge and starts tutting. "We haven't got no sausage."

"I know."

"Why not?"

"Because you said you hated sausages when we had them for supper last week."

He tuts again. "I was only joking."

Jack wanders in, looking grumpy. "I don't want sausages. I want jumbled-up eggs."

Apparently I am now running some kind of junior bed-and-breakfast operation. Perhaps I should buy a small pad and a pencil.

"Well, since we haven't got any sausages, what about lovely scrambled eggs, Archie, before we get ready to drive to Granny's?"

"Yuck. And anyway last time you made them you put stupid cheese in and they tasted absolutely horrible."

"Well, it's Shreddies or scrambled eggs. That's it. So make your mind up."

He sighs, while Jack stands in the doorway looking like he's still half asleep.

"Did Daddy like cheese in his scrambled eggs?"

Bugger. There's been a lot less of the Did My Lovely Daddy Like This? lately, but I suppose it was bound to re-surface today.

"Yes, love, he did."

"Well, I want mine with cheese then."

Archie hesitates. "Well, I don't. He liked them without cheese in too, didn't he, Mum?"

"Yes, love."

"And there's no sausages?"

"No."

"Are you sure?"

Does he think I'm hiding a packet inside my dressing gown or something?

"Absolutely sure, Archie."

"Well, I'll have jumbled eggs, with toast. But not the eggs on the toast—toast on another plate."

Christ.

E llen calls while I'm washing up the breakfast things.

"You'll never guess what. Ask me who's calling."

"I know who's calling, Ellen. It's you, Britain's Favorite Broadcaster."

"Yes, but ask me anyway. Just say, 'Who is this?'"

"Who is this?"

"The future Mrs. Harry Williams. He asked me last night, when we were having dinner. On bended knee and everything—he'd even got the ring. Tiffany. Serious diamonds. The works. It was absolutely perfect."

"Oh, Ellen, that's brilliant."

"I know, although why he couldn't have done it on Valentine's Day is beyond me. He said he wanted to wait until his leg was out of plaster, in case he got stuck kneeling down, but I think he just couldn't cope with the hearts and flowers thing."

"That sounds fair enough."

"I've always had a crap time on Valentine's Day, so it would have made up for all those years when I didn't even get a card."

"You always get cards, Ellen. For as long as I've known you you've always got loads."

"Only from nutters who watch me on the news, not proper boys."

"Well, now you've got a proper boy, and the ring to prove it."

"I know. Christ. I still can't really believe it."

"Tell me everything. What did he say? What did you say? Everything."

"I tried to play it cool, so I said I'd get back to him once I'd reviewed my options, but then the waiter brought the champagne over and I just caved. Who knew he'd turn out to be the future Mr. Malone? Isn't life grand?"

"I suppose we'd better stop calling him Dirty Harry now. It's not very bridal."

"Oh, I don't know: Ellen Malone, do you take Dirty Harry as your lawful . . . I quite like it."

"What's the ring like?"

"Fucking huge."

"Clever boy."

"So will you be my bridesmaid then?"

"Don't thirty-eight-year-olds with two kids have to be matrons?"

"Bollocks to that—it's too *Carry On Night Nurse*. I want you to be my bridesmaid; I'm thinking pink lace crinolines. With matching gloves."

"Oh, God."

"Or possibly Vera Wang."

"That sounds more like it."

"And the boys in kilts."

"Harry, in a kilt?"

"No, you idiot, my godsons."

"My Jack and Archie, in kilts?"

"Yes. What do you think?"

"I think it depends on how big the bribe's going to be."

"Huge."

"No problem then, although we'd better not let them have daggers in their socks or it could get tricky. Have you told your mum and dad yet?"

"I'm building up to it. Actually, it's going to be one of your main bridesmaid duties, stopping Mum trying to turn this into a family wedding. I hate most of them anyway, and they hate me. I just want people I really, truly like."

"So no need for a big church then, since there'll only be about six of us."

"Exactly. Here, talk to Harry."

"Morning, Jo."

"Congratulations, Harry."

"Thanks, darling, and you'll do the bridesmaid thing, because I'm counting on you to calm her down."

"How exactly do you think I'm going to pull that one off?"

"Drugs? One of my uncles knows a bloke who can probably slip us some horse tranquilizers; that should slow her down a bit. You'll have to do something or I'll be forced to make a run for it."

"Don't you dare. Anyway, she'd find you."

There's a scuffling noise, and Ellen comes back on the line.

"Harry's just fallen over."

"Has he? How mysterious."

"I don't think his leg's completely up to speed yet."

"No, and it won't be if you keep pushing the poor man over. He's only just had the plaster off."

"He tripped. Look, I'd better go, darling, he's making toast and he always burns it."

"Put a new toaster down on your wedding list then. A Harry-proof one."

"Christ, I'd forgotten about the wedding list. God, the amount of money I've spent over the years on bloody lists. Brilliant: it's finally payback time."

"John Lewis do a good one, I think."

"Please. I'm thinking Cath Kidston, the White Company. Actually, I wonder if Prada do a list—I bet they do—and I'm thinking registry office, like you did with Nick, so my mum doesn't get the chance to cover the local church in horrible satin ribbon."

"That might work, you know, like that man who wraps up whole mountains."

"Yes, but Christo doesn't dot mini-baskets of freesias everywhere, or make everyone wear carnation buttonholes. God, I wish I could see you. Why don't you come up here for the day and Harry can limp round a museum with the boys while we start planning?"

"I'd love to, but I've got lunch with Elizabeth and Gerald."

"Oh, Christ, I'd forgotten. Sorry, darling."

"Do I have to wear black, do you think?"

"Of course not, sweetheart. Wear what you like."

"She wanted us to go to the morning service at the church, but I said we couldn't get there in time, so they'll all be in their best Sunday outfits. James and Fiona and the girls will be there too. God, I bet they all have hats."

"You could always wear your bobble hat."

"So they look like they're off to Ascot and I look like a tramp?"

"Just wear what you feel comfortable in."

"You don't think turning up in my pajamas will look a bit odd?"

"Not if you top it off with a woolly hat; very bohemian and deconstructed: Björk, with a hint of grieving widow. What about your black trousers, the ones you wear with your boots?"

"I've already tried them, but I can only get the zip done up if I lie on the floor. I think they must have shrunk."

"Shrunk?"

"I think I may have been overdoing it slightly on the biscuits when I'm in the shop. And it's bound to rain. Do you remember how much it rained at the funeral? I thought the vicar was going to fall in at one point, or Archie, and Christ knows how much therapy you'd need after falling headfirst into your dad's grave. Quite a lot, is my guess."

"The bastards would probably make you sign a direct-debit form before they let you in the door."

"Do you think I should take flowers? The boys have written letters and drawn some pictures."

"Sweet."

"They spent hours on them. Jack's done one of the new house, to show him where we're living now, and Archie's done one of Trevor, and a boat. But I haven't got anything to take."

"Darling, you should have reminded me. Look, I can drive down. What time are you leaving?"

"No, it's fine, I'm just fussing. Flowers will be fine. I'll get some at Sainsbury's on the way, and you have a lovely day celebrating with Harry. I'll call you when I'm back."

"Sure?"

"Definitely."

"But?"

"Nothing. It's just I feel such a fraud. I should be the grieving widow, but I'm still so furious with him. I thought I'd be into the acceptance thing by now, or maybe even forgiveness, but I'm not. I mean I forgive him about the affair. It's weird, but I'm really past that. Maybe my mini-moment in Venice with Daniel helped me with that one, sort of put everything into perspective, and stopped me feeling like a total reject."

"I'm sure it did, darling."

"But I still can't forgive him for planning to leave the boys. I'm nowhere near closure on that one. Nowhere near."

"Of course you're not. Why would you be? Christ, he finally gets promoted and you think you're off to a new life as the Wife of the Foreign Correspondent, but it turns out he's having an affair and wants a divorce, and the night he tells you he manages to kill himself in a car crash. Why would you have closure on something like that? It'll take years."

"Thanks, that's very encouraging."

"Darling, you're doing great, fantastic, actually. Instead of going under you've got on with it, with all the debts and the second bloody mortgage he didn't even bother to tell you about. You've sold up and moved to the back of bloody beyond so you can work in your gran's wool shop, and before you say it, yes, I know it's your shop now, and you've

made a brilliant job of it and you're new best friends with the Diva and everything. Official knitting coach to Amazing Grace, but still. I'd be fucking furious with him. In fact it's a good job he crashed that car because I'd have killed him myself if I'd got my hands on him. Bastard."

That's one of the best things about Ellen: she's so brilliantly partisan. She never sees both sides of the argument, or tells you to calm down and think about it from someone else's point of view. And she was so great last year, with the funeral and everything. Christ knows how I'd have got through it without her.

"I know, Ellen, but it was partly my fault, you know."

"Oh, please, not the guilt-trip thing again. How could it possibly have been your fault?"

"I should have known, about the money. I should have worked it out. And if I'd been less wrapped up in the boys, maybe I would have noticed how bored he was getting. When I think about it, I could see he was unraveling, but I tried to ignore it. He got so furious when I tried to talk to him about it, so I left it."

"And I suppose it was your fault he was shagging the teenage UN worker, was it?"

"She was twenty-six, Ellen."

"Twenty-six, sixteen, makes no difference, just better clothes. Now pull yourself together, darling. He fucked up, big time. And it wasn't your fault, but you're left picking up the pieces. It's bollocks whichever way you look at it."

"I suppose so. Although I love living here now."

"I know you do, Pollyanna. You've always been good at seeing the bright side . . . what's that lemon thing again?"

"If life deals you lemons, you just make lemonade."

"Christ."

We both start to giggle.

"What a load of rubbish—it sounds just like something your Diva would say, like her line about how people can only turn you over if you let them; it's all in your karma."

"Yes, but I think there's some truth in that, you know."

"Oh, definitely. It's very good karma if you're incredibly rich and freakishly thin and your last three movies were hits. Not quite so easy if you're working in Burger King and the onion rings have just got flame-grilled into oblivion."

"True."

"How is our Amazing Grace, by the way? Is motherhood suiting her?"

"Very much, last time I saw her. And she's looking even more fabulous than before she had the baby, sort of glowing. I know it sounds like rubbish, but she really is. And the baby's gorgeous. I'm doing a new-baby window display for the shop; I've been knitting baby things for days now. It's been a bit weird—it reminds me of knitting when I was pregnant with Archie, which hasn't exactly helped."

"You'll be fine today, you'll see. Now are you sure you don't want me to come down?"

"Sure. You're right. It'll be fine, and at least there's been some good news today."

"What?"

"My best friend's getting married, and I'll be in peach Vera Wang with gloves and a bobble hat."

"Call me when you get home, promise?"

"Yes."

"And if Elizabeth gets too annoying, just hit her. Pretend you've gone into widow hysterics and deck the old bag. You'll feel so much better, trust me."

"I must just try that."

"Hurrah. God, I really wish I was coming down now."

They're just getting back from church when we arrive, and Elizabeth is having a light bicker in the kitchen with Fiona about how long the joint needs to rest before Gerald can start carving. It's still pouring with rain, which doesn't bode well for our graveside moment after lunch, and Gerald hands me a rather epic sherry; for some reason best known to himself he seems to think I'm likely to start kicking up if I don't have a full glass in my hand at all times, possibly because Nick's usual tactic for getting through a Sunday lunch with his parents was to get completely plastered. Which is a perfectly sensible plan if you're not the person who has to drive home, and keep two small boys amused in a house full of china figurines and very pale carpet. Christ, this is going to be a long afternoon.

Fiona, wearing her floral pinny, has found a documentary about chimpanzees for the children to watch, and she settles them on the sofa for a quiet ten minutes before lunch.

"Now not too loud, girls, because Daddy's reading his paper."

I feel like I've been catapulted back in time into the middle of a 1950s Bisto commercial.

Lottie and Beth look rather anxiously toward James,

who's knocking back the whiskey while he reads the papers and makes Disgusted of Tunbridge Wells noises whenever he comes across anything he doesn't approve of.

"Are there any cartoons?" Archie's doing his Best Smile.

"No, Archie, but I'm sure you'll find it interesting. We love wildlife programs, don't we, girls?"

Lottie and Beth nod, although Lottie doesn't look particularly enthusiastic.

"I do try to ration cartoons, don't you, Jo? Some of them are so violent, aren't they? Awful. Now I must pop into the kitchen and see if Elizabeth needs a hand."

"Is there anything I can do?"

She gives me the kind of look you'd give a teenager who's just offered to rewire your house. My domestic skills have always been awarded nil points by Fiona and Elizabeth; I just don't think I pipe enough rosettes on things to meet their exacting standards.

"It's all under control. You just sit and have a rest after your drive."

James makes a choking noise and reads us a few lines from his paper about a woman who's suing her bosses for millions for harassment. "Just because they took a client to a club where she didn't feel comfortable. Dear God, what is this country coming to?"

James is in middle management in financial services, and slightly to the right of Attila the Hun.

Fiona tries a little laugh, which sounds rather nervous and high-pitched. "Now, darling, don't let's get started on politics."

Oh, dear. I just can't resist.

"What sort of club was it, James?"

He looks at the paper and reddens slightly. "Some sort of dancing one."

"Lap dancing, by any chance?"

"Possibly, but for heaven's sake, horses for courses and all that. Nothing to go to the lawyer's about—it's only a bit of fun."

"So if all your bosses were women, and they took you to a club where the boys were dancing about in leather trousers, with a finale that involved lots of baby oil, you wouldn't mind?"

Fiona's gone rather pale and tries another little laugh.

James gives her an irritable look.

"I think women should realize that it's a big, tough world out there, and we all have to do things we don't particularly enjoy. I had to take a load of Japanese clients to dinner a few weeks ago, sitting cross-legged on the floor for hours, but you don't see me suing anybody."

"And he had terrible trouble with his knees the next day, didn't you, darling?"

He turns to glare at her, as Archie wanders over for a cuddle.

"What's lap dancing, Mum?"

"A rather sad sort of dancing, love."

"Do they do it at discos?"

"Not really."

"We have discos at our school."

"I know, love."

Please don't let him ask me for lap-dancing tips. I'm not really sure it's what the PTA had in mind.

"I can do all sorts of dancing. Sometimes I go round and round until I get dizzy."

"I know. But don't show us now, all right? You might break something."

He giggles, and Fiona looks relieved to be back on safe territory. "I meant to tell you, Jo. The girls are doing so well at their ballet classes, Beth was chosen to do one of the solos in the last concert, actually, weren't you, darling?"

Beth simpers and nods.

Lottie rolls her eyes. "And I was a toadstool."

"Were you? That sounds like fun."

She grins. "I'll show you, if you like, Aunty Jo, but you'll have to take your boots off."

Fiona doesn't seem keen.

"Not now, darling. Lunch is nearly ready."

Archie sighs. "I'd like to be a toadstool. Can you show me too?"

Beth makes a sniggering noise. "Toadstools are only for people who aren't very good at ballet. I was a deer. I can show you, if you like, Jack."

Jack looks rather panicked. "A what?"

"A deer. Like in *Bambi*."

Archie's delighted. "Yes. And then we can shoot him."

After a last-minute crisis with the Yorkshires, which seem perfectly fine to me but apparently haven't risen properly, Elizabeth calls us in to lunch, looking rather tense. Gerald's swaying slightly as he carves the joint: perhaps that second sherry wasn't such a good idea after all.

"Would you like horseradish, Jo?"

"Thank you."

Elizabeth passes me a small china jug. "I do think proper horseradish is so much nicer than those terrible jars, don't you? Fiona made this. It's one of our Women's Institute recipes."

"Lovely."

Fiona smiles. "It's ever so easy really."

"I don't like horseradished." Jack's looking rather anxious; he's already had two Brussels sprouts launched onto his plate against his will.

"You don't have to have any if you don't want it. Just eat up your lovely carrots. And try a sprout, love; you might like them now. But if not, just leave them, okay? Nobody will mind as long as you try a mouthful."

Actually, Elizabeth will mind, since she's definitely from the You Have to Eat Whatever Is Put on Your Plate school of thought, but I don't really go in for force-feeding children, not least because it's totally counterproductive.

"Christ almighty."

We all turn to look at James, who's started coughing.

"Horseradish. Bit strong." His eyes are watering.

We all taste our horseradish, and then wish we hadn't. Bloody hell, the tip of my tongue's gone completely numb.

Fiona's looking totally stricken. "I'm sure I followed the recipe."

Gerald coughs and pours himself some more wine.

Time to change the subject, I think.

"The beef is delicious, Elizabeth. Archie, don't lean back on your chair like that, or you'll tip over."

"No, I won't."

"Archie."

"I never tip over. Jake Palmer fell right off his chair at school when we were having our lunch, and he spilled his water. But I never do."

"Archie, just sit properly, please. Do you want your meat cut up?"

He gives me an outraged look. "No, I do not. I'm not a baby."

"Well, eat properly then, please."

Elizabeth smiles at him encouragingly. "There's jelly and ice cream for boys who eat up all their lunch. Nice clean plates, that's what Granny likes to see."

I think she's trying to be helpful.

Archie looks at her. "And girls too?"

"Sorry, dear?"

"And Beth and Lottie can have ice cream, if they eat up?"

"Yes, dear."

He looks at his plate. "And can you just have ice cream, if you don't eat all of it?"

Gerald laughs. "Good point, my boy, excellent. Negotiate, that's the thing. Now then, who's for more wine?"

"Nicholas loved jelly and ice cream when he was little. It was his favorite pudding." Elizabeth is looking tearful now, and I don't think it's just the horseradish.

Oh, God, here we go.

"Granny, did you know when monkeys want to do sex they wee on all the trees? It was on our program."

Elizabeth chokes slightly, and Lottie starts to giggle.

"Archie, I don't think that's a very nice thing to talk about at lunch."

"Monkeys don't know it's not nice."

"Archie."

He sighs. "I don't even like jelly."

B y the time we're trudging through the field toward the church, I'm feeling very close to slapping someone, most probably myself for landing us with a family escort for what should be a quiet moment for the boys. Bloody hell. Elizabeth is seriously sulking now because Gerald said "bugger" after his fourth glass of wine, and she's been trying to get me to deliver Grace Harrison as her VIP guest at the next Golf Club dinner, and I've had to tell her that I think it's a bit of a long shot. Fiona's still trying to recover from the horseradish debacle, and James is having a long conversation about golf, mainly with himself. Everywhere is still soaking, and my boots keep sinking into the grass, but at least it's finally stopped raining as we climb over the stile and walk into the churchyard.

Jack's holding the letters and pictures in a plastic bag, and he starts to go rather pale as we get a few yards away from Nick's grave. There are yellow tulips in the black marble vase at the bottom of the headstone, and a small bunch of roses.

Fiona coughs, very quietly. "The roses are from the girls. We put them there earlier."

I nod. I'm not sure I can actually speak just yet; it's such a shock, seeing the grave again. Jack puts his hand in mine

and we move forward and I bend slightly to put my flowers down, but they don't look right in their cellophane wrapping—it's like Interflora have just made a special delivery or something—so I kneel to take them out of the wrapper, getting wet knees in the process. Jack and Archie are now standing on either side of me. They seem much smaller and quieter than usual.

"There, that's better. You can put your letters on top of the flowers now if you'd like to, and your lovely pictures."

They put their folded-up letters and pictures down very carefully as Elizabeth walks toward us and starts rearranging the tulips. "Shall we pop into church now and say a little prayer?"

"I think we'd like to just stand here quietly for a minute, if that's okay. You go ahead, though."

Fiona and James head off toward the church with the girls and Gerald, while Elizabeth hesitates. "I thought a prayer might be nice. Wouldn't you like to say a prayer for Daddy, Jack?"

Jack's starting to look tearful now. Bloody woman.

"Elizabeth, I think we'd like a moment on our own, if that's all right with you."

In other words, bugger off, you old bag.

I put my arm around Jack, and we walk toward the wooden seat under the tree in the corner of the churchyard.

"It's wet, Mum."

"I know, love, but it doesn't matter, we've got our coats on. Let's sit down and have a cuddle."

He smiles.

"How will Daddy see our pictures?" Archie's sounding rather shaky too.

Actually, I'm not sure I can do this. I don't know the right things to say, the magic words that will make it all right for them. Christ, this is so unfair. Why should they have to worry about how their dad will get to see the pictures they've just put on his grave? I hate this. I really hate it.

I put my arms around them. "I think the important thing is that Daddy knows how much we love him."

Jack nods.

"Let's keep cuddling for ages, shall we? I think we need a special big one, because my cuddle bank's nearly empty."

They both snuggle in and I kiss them and they pretend to mind.

"Would you like to go into the church and say a prayer? We can, if you like."

Jack seems to be considering this for a minute. "No thanks, Mum. I think this is better, don't you?"

"Yes, I do, love."

Archie snuggles in. "We're cuddling for Daddy, aren't we?"

"Yes, love."

"And then we can go home?"

"Yes."

"But only after Lottie has shown us her toadstools."

"Yes."

"And we've got cake for tea?"

"I think so. Granny said she'd made a special one."

Jack nods. "She said she made the one Daddy used to like best when he was little."

They both snuggle in tighter.

I'll never forgive him. I know it's not his fault, and it was just bad luck, and it's a terrible waste and everything. But I'll never bloody forgive him.

A rchie falls asleep on the drive home and is extra grumpy when I wake him up, but there's no way I can carry him into the house like I used to when he was little, so we do the guided-shuffle-with-whining routine instead, as I steer him toward the stairs.

"It's not fair. I haven't even had my supper yet and I was looking forward to it."

"You can't be hungry, Archie. You had crumpets and two slices of cake at Granny's."

"Yes, but that was ages ago. I need some supper, I really do, Mum."

"Well, let's get you in your jimmies and then we'll see."

He tuts.

There's a megabicker in the bath about who kicked his brother's leg on purpose and who did it by accident, and a fair amount of water gets sloshed on the floor until I promise that toasted cheese might be available for anyone who isn't screaming. Peace is restored, and at least I've got the mud off Archie's face, which he collected during overenthusiastic toadstool maneuvers.

They're both sitting at the kitchen table with damp hair when Gran arrives. She's got a packet of chocolate buttons for each of them. They'd usually reject buttons as far too babyish, but tonight they seem willing to make an exception.

"Eat them all, Jack; no saving any for later. We've got to do your teeth after supper, don't forget."

Jack likes to make his sweets last as long as possible, not least because it torments Archie. He's busy arranging his buttons on his plate while Gran puts the kettle on and I slice cheese.

"So how was Her Majesty then, pet?"

Gran's never been that keen on Elizabeth.

"She was fine, a bit of moaning about not seeing enough of us, but when I said she was welcome here any time, she backed right off. I think she wants us to trek over there every weekend, but I've told her that what with the shop and everything I just can't do it. We had a few more tearful My Perfect Son moments, though."

Gran glances at the boys, who are engrossed with their buttons, and starts to whisper. "I could soon put her right on that one."

"I know, Gran, but what's the point?"

"She ought to know what you've had to put up with, and then maybe she wouldn't be so high and mighty, but least said, soonest mended, I suppose." She turns back to the boys. "Did you have a lovely day at your granny Mackenzie's then, Jack?"

"It was all right. I had to eat my sprouts, or you couldn't have ice cream, but Mum ate one of them when she wasn't looking. And we took our pictures to Daddy, only the ground was all wet. But it doesn't matter, does it, Gran?"

"No, pet, it doesn't matter at all."

Jack nods.

"Granny made a cake for our tea, but Jack didn't like it, because he's a silly baby."

Jack glares at Archie.

"I just don't like cake with bits in, that's all."

"They were nuts, not bits. Stupid."

"The toasted cheese is nearly done. Who needs more juice?"

They both put their hands up, which makes Gran smile, and we're just settling down for a fairly peaceful supper when there's the unmistakable sound of scrabbling and barking by the back door. Sod it. Bloody Trevor has come round to play.

"Please, Mum. Please." They both turn toward me looking desperate.

Bugger.

"No way. You're not going out now—it's too cold."

Trevor starts leaping up at the kitchen window, barking enthusiastically.

Double bugger.

I close the door to the passage while Gran opens the back door, and Trevor launches himself into the kitchen like a hairy Exocet missile, helping himself to a slice of toasted cheese and knocking Archie over.

Bloody hell.

"I'll put the kettle on for Mr. Pallfrey, shall I, love?"

"Thanks, Gran. Archie, don't let him lick your face, I've told you before."

"I can wash it."

"I know, but— Oh, never mind."

Gran opens the back door to Mr. Pallfrey, who's out of breath, as usual. "I'm sorry about this. We were just out for our walk and I think he spotted your car was back. He missed you earlier. He kept whining and standing by your gate."

"Cup of tea?"

"Well, if you're sure, dear, that would be lovely."

After what seems like an eternity of stroking and patting, Gran takes the boys up to bed with the promise of an extra story. Mr. Pallfrey's trying to get Trevor back out of the kitchen door, but he's lying on the floor pretending to be asleep; only he keeps wagging his tail, which is a bit of a giveaway.

"He does love your lads." Mr. Pallfrey tugs on the lead again, and Trevor slides about half an inch across the kitchen tiles. "I'm ever so sorry about this—he's never done it before."

"What about if we turn the lights off and go and sit in the other room?"

"He might panic and break a few things. I tried it at home once, when he'd eaten one of my slippers. Thought I'd give him a spot of cooling-off time."

"And what happened?"

"He broke two chairs in my kitchenette. He just doesn't know his own strength, that's the trouble."

I can't help wishing Mr. Pallfrey's daughter, Christine, had gone for something less donkey-size when she decided she wanted a dog; maybe a nice little spaniel, something you could pick up when it was being annoying. But the boys

adore Trevor the Loony Lurcher, and there's no going back now. He pops in most days for a game of football in the back garden, and they're forever on about taking him for walks. So it's completely bloody hopeless.

Mr. Pallfrey's now pulling a completely prone Trevor toward the door. "He weighs a ton when he's asleep."

"I bet he does, but he's not really asleep, is he?"

Christ, we'll be here all night.

"No, but he's made himself go all floppy."

"What about if I tip a cup of water on him?"

Mr. Pallfrey looks at me with a glimmer of admiration in his eyes. "That might work."

Sadly, Trevor's not quite as stupid as he looks, and when I'm standing over him with a cupful of water, he sits up and licks my arm, which is a bit of a shame really because I was quite looking forward to pouring water on him.

"It's home time, Trevor."

He lies back down again.

"Do you want a drink, Trevor?"

I trickle a few drops of water onto his back, and he turns to look at me. I think we understand each other. He moves toward the door, still half lying down and looking like he's sulking, or he's lost the use of his back legs.

"Thanks for the tea."

"You're welcome. We'll probably see you tomorrow?"

"Yes, and I was meaning to say, I'm on the committee for the Seaside in Bloom, and they've put me down for front gardens and tubs for our street, so I was hoping I could count on you?"

Christ.

"Count on me for what?"

"Just a few flowers. You did say you wanted to make a start on your garden this year, didn't you?"

"Yes, but I just meant getting rid of the nettles, that kind of thing."

"You leave that to me; I'll sort you out a few plants. I've got some lovely geraniums wintering in my greenhouse—they'll look a treat—and I'll do you a couple of trays of bedding. I always do a few."

"Well, if you're sure. Only—"

"It won't be anything fancy, I'll—"

Trevor's obviously had enough chitchat and suddenly leaps toward the door, pulling Mr. Pallfrey down the path at quite a pace.

Damn. I think I've just agreed to take part in some sort of gardening competition, and I'm already down for a special window display in the shop for the Best Seaside Town (Small) competition. We won the silver medal last year and everyone's desperate for gold this year, so I've already had half the Parish Council in the shop giving me handy hints. It never rains but it pours, as Gran would say.

She comes back downstairs giggling. "He's such a card, our Archie. The things he comes out with. He was telling me he might need a drink of water, but he's not made his mind up yet, so he'll let us know, but if he could have a bell it would save him getting up. I don't know where he gets his ideas from, I really don't."

"He means the little brass one Betty gave us for Christmas. He saw it in a film, I think, someone lying in bed ringing a bell so the servants could pop up with a nice little snack. He's been after one ever since."

"You'd be up and down all night."

"I know, which is why I've hidden it."

"Good idea, pet. Let's have another cup of tea, shall we? Reg should be here to pick me up soon. Unless you want to go on up to bed?"

"At ten past nine?"

"You look tired."

"I am, but I'm not going up to bed this early—it's not that bad."

"Good, because I want to ask you something."

"What?"

"Sit down first."

"It's not the Lifeboats again, is it, Gran? Only I really haven't got the time."

"No, I've sorted that out with Betty." She sits down, looking rather nervous.

"There's nothing wrong, is there, Gran?"

"No, not at all. It's just . . . well . . . the thing is, it's Reg. He's asked me to marry him. And I've said yes. And I hope you don't think it's silly at our age, only he's such a lovely man, and it'll be nice to have a bit of company in the evenings. And, well. There it is. What do you think?"

Bloody hell.

"Oh, Gran, I think it's lovely."

"Do you? Really? Oh, I'm so glad. Only you don't think your grandad would mind, do you? I've been fretting about

it, and he was such a lovely man, you know. A real gentle-
man."

"Gran, it's been over fifty years."

"I know, pet, but it doesn't feel like that long." She looks
down at her wedding ring. "I'll not stop wearing my ring,
you know. I've told Reg, I'll have it altered so it fits my
other finger."

"That's a lovely idea."

She smiles.

"So you're pleased then?"

"Yes. Cross my heart. When did he ask you?"

"This morning. When he brought the paper round he
said he wanted to wait until we were out for a meal, and do
it properly, but he couldn't help himself. He was so nervous,
bless him."

I get up to give her a kiss, and she holds on to my hands.

"We've decided to have a proper wedding, in the church.
I know it's daft at my age, but I never had one with your
grandad—we didn't have the money, and what with the
war—and Reg was the same; they were saving up for a house,
so it was just a tea at her mother's. So this time we want the
full works, except I'll not have a dress, I'll have a suit, and I
thought I'd ask Betty to be my matron of honor, and you can
be my bridesmaid. What do you think, pet? I thought the
boys could be page boys—I've seen some lovely little velvet
suits in one of my catalogs. Although heaven knows what
your mother's going to say."

"Something unfortunate, probably."

"Yes, well, she doesn't have to come if it doesn't suit. I'm
going to tell her. If she can't be nice, she can stop in Venice.

I'm not having her upsetting everyone like she usually does."

"She doesn't mean it, Gran."

"Oh yes, she does. I don't like to say it about my own flesh and blood, but she's a right little madam, she always has been. And it's not from my side, I can tell you. Your grandma Butterworth was the same, always wanting to be the center of attention. When she died, I felt like putting the flags out, I really did. I know it's a terrible thing to say, but when I think of the years I spent stuck in that shop with her moaning on at me, well, I'm surprised I managed to stick it. Mind you, I had nowhere else to go."

"I know, Gran."

"Still, that's all over now, and you're here, and the boys, so I'm glad I stuck at it now, I really am. We thought we'd sell Reg's house and live in mine, and that way we'll have a bit of money to treat everybody."

"Or you could treat yourselves. You could go on another cruise, a honeymoon one."

She blushes.

"Reg has already been on at me about that. He's getting all the brochures, and they do some lovely ones, with suites and balconies, although I'd be worried if there was a storm. You could get drenched if you left your door open. And they cost a fair bit, and I'm not sure we'd get the benefit, what with my head for heights. But we'll see. Now I want to tell your brother, but could you dial the number for me, only it always goes wrong when I try to call him. I thought I'd ask him if he'll give me away. Do you think he'd like that?"

Vin's a marine biologist, and usually on a boat somewhere, so he can be pretty hard to track down.

"Of course he will. He'll be thrilled."

I'm sitting by the fire with my To Do list, and trying to
visualize where Jack's PE kit might be, when Ellen calls.

"So how did it go?"

"Less traumatic than I thought really. Fiona made some
nuclear horseradish, so there was slightly less of the I'm a
Perfect Housewife and You're Not routine than usual, and
Elizabeth got pretty tearful, but apart from that it was fine.
Weird, but fine."

"Weird?"

"There's something weird about visiting graves, trying to
work out what to say to a marble headstone and some wet
turf. They should have phone booths or something, like in
prisons, so you could put your hand on the glass and talk
into the phone. Except there'd be nobody on the other end."

"Isn't that what therapists are for?"

"I used to call his work mobile, in the first few weeks,
just to hear his voice. It made it all more real somehow, but
then one day there was a this-number-is-unavailable message. Personnel must have canceled the contract."

"Mean bastards."

"Well, he was hardly going to use it, was he? I suppose
it didn't occur to them I was ringing it occasionally. Anyway, never mind about that, I've got some really good news,
for a change. Gran's marrying Reg. Isn't that sweet?"

"Bless."

"I know. She's so excited, and Vin's going to give her away, and I'm meant to be the bridesmaid. The whole town will probably be there, which is the only tricky bit really, because you know what you were saying about pink crino-lines, well, that's exactly the kind of thing she's going to want."

"I've been looking at websites this afternoon, and you wouldn't believe some of the wedding kit out there. It's like there's some terrible conspiracy going on: perfectly nice sheath dress, let's add some net and a sprig of embroidery and totally fuck it up. And the veil thing is so weird. I might have a tiara, though. And maybe floral would work for your gran—there are some half-decent floral bridesmaids' outfits out there."

"I can see you with a tiara. And floral sounds lovely."

"Yes, but not in mimsy colors—acid greens, purples, that kind of thing. No Laura Ashley."

"Perish the thought."

"God, there's so much to do."

"It'll be lovely, Ellen, and we've got ages, you'll see. We'll do a plan this weekend. It's all going to be perfect."

"Promise?"

"I promise."

"Good. So what have you got on this week apart from paying homage to the Diva?"

"I've got to go into school tomorrow for another session with the staff on the knitting thing. Lesson plans or some-thing. And Annabel Morgan's still giving me the evil eye."

"What have you done to her now?"

"Nothing, but she thinks being president of the PTA

means she should get to choose which parents get hijacked into doing school projects, and I'm definitely not on her list."

"Just ignore her."

"Yes, well, that's easier said than done when she keeps barreling across the playground with a mad grin on her face and asking me about my plans. She wants a written outline, for her files."

"That's easy, darling. Just do it in management speak."

"On knitting?"

"Yes. Overarching skill development, creative empowerment, that kind of stuff."

"Cross-curricular multidisciplinary learning goals?"

"Perfect."

"Great, well, that's Monday sorted. And I've got dinner with Martin on Friday."

"Good old Dovetail."

"Yes, and stop calling him that—those shelves are really useful. I'm thinking of asking him to do me some more for downstairs so I can have more stock out."

"So you're taking him out to dinner to talk about wood again?"

"Yes, I promised him dinner, when Archie went missing that day and he found him, remember?"

"Yes. And you kissed him."

"By mistake. And I'm still really embarrassed about that, actually, so thanks for reminding me."

"Darling, I've told you, he could be gorgeous if he got rid of that tragic haircut."

"It's grown a bit since you last saw him."

"Good."

"And he's talking about buying a flat."

"Excellent. The sooner he gets out of Elsie's clutches the better: he's far too old to be living at home with his mother."

"It was only temporary, while the divorce was going through."

"What are you wearing?"

"It's not that kind of dinner. It's just friends."

"You don't need any more friends—you've got me."

"Yes, but you're not quite so handy at putting up shelves. Anyway, I've told you, I practically grew up with him; we were here every summer for our holidays, don't forget. He's like a cousin or something."

"A kissing cousin, obviously."

"Stop it. Anyway, look what happened the last time I tried a bit of romance."

"I assume we're talking Daniel Fitzgerald now?"

"Yes."

"That was just bad luck. And you had a nice wanton moment in Venice. What more do you want?"

"Maybe for him not to get back together with his ex-girlfriend?"

"You can't let one little setback put you off, darling. Take Martin out of his box and give him a twirl. You never know, he might surprise you."

"Yes, and it'll be a nice surprise for Elsie too. She'll go into a massive sulk with me in the shop, which is all I need."

"She's sulking for most of the time anyway, so how will you know?"

"Trust me, if I'm giving her Martin anything remotely resembling a twirl, I'll know."

"Go for it, darling. You deserve a bit of fun."

"I don't think Martin would be just a bit of fun—he's too nice. And he's still getting over his wife."

"Trust me, wear something tight, and he'll get over it."

"Everything's tight at the moment, so that won't be hard. I've told you, Elsie keeps feeding me custard creams in the shop."

"It's probably a plot to turn you into a porker so her Martin won't fancy you."

"Well, it's working."

"Just promise me you won't wear a baggy sweater."

"Well, it's either that or my nightie."

"Not very subtle, darling, but I like your thinking."

"Night, Ellen."

"Night, darling."

Damn; I wasn't feeling that nervous about Friday, but I am now. Ellen's always trying to turn things into something they're not, although she was right about Daniel, briefly. But Martin's totally different: he's not at all cosmopolitan like Daniel; famous photographers can cope with low-level affairs with no harm done, it's almost part of the job, but Martin's just not the type. And anyway, Ellen's only imagining things, as usual; it'll be a nice friendly supper, and it won't matter at all what I'm wearing. But still. Damn.

I'm sitting in the kitchen having a cup of tea after making the packed lunches ready for school in the morning, feeling

very pleased with myself for being a proper organized mother for once, even if I still don't know where Jack's PE kit is. I'm finishing knitting the pink rabbit while I try to work out how I'm going to hide the horrible peach matinee jacket Elsie's made for the shop window that will ruin my color scheme; I've gone for nutmeg and caramel and buttermilk cotton, little cardigans and a striped blanket, and some tiny socks, which I'll hang on a washing line strung across the window with some little wooden pegs. Gran's knitted some baby ducks in pale primrose too, so if I can finish off the pink rabbit I'll have a few toys to put in; I've already knitted a penguin and a pale blue elephant, and a doll with clothes you can take off, which will hopefully attract a few mother-and-small-daughter combos into the shop. Things have been fairly quiet since Christmas, so I'd like to boost sales before the new summer stock starts to arrive.

I'm about to go up to bed when Mum calls.

Damn.

"I've just been talking to your grandmother about the wedding."

"Isn't it lovely?"

"Lovely? It's ridiculous, and I might have known you'd take her side. Who is this Reg, anyway?"

"He's very nice. He used to be captain of the bowls team. She's known him for ages."

"Getting married at her age is ridiculous."

"She's very happy, Mum. Isn't that all that matters?"

"It's so suburban. Nobody gets married anymore."

"You're married to Dad."

"Don't be deliberately stupid, Josephine—it's so unattractive. Is he after her money, do you think?"

"What money?"

"That ghastly bungalow's got to be worth a small fortune by now."

"He's got his own house, Mum."

"Well, I think it's very suspect, and I'm not sure your father and I can get away. We're so busy here, and just think of the expense. I've got a new commission; there are some beautiful panels in a local church, the one I showed you with the marvelous altar, and they've said I'm the only person they trust them with. They practically begged me. It was very touching."

"It would only be for a few days, Mum."

"I suppose we could stay with you, but as for Vincent agreeing to give her away, I've never heard of anything so silly in all my life. If anyone is going to give her away, it should be me. Or your father, although he's bound to make a hash of it. No, I suppose it will have to be me. Tell her, would you?"

"Tell her what?"

"That I'll give her away."

"I think that's up to her, Mum, don't you?"

"I might have known I could count on you to be completely hopeless, as usual."

I'm counting to ten now.

"Are you still there, Josephine?"

I'm tempted to say no, I'm in the bath, please leave a message.

"Yes, Mum."

"I'll get your father to talk to her."

"Is his knee better?"

"He's absolutely fine—he was just being dramatic. You know what he's like. The doctors have given him some tablets, and the stitches come out soon. I really don't know what all the fuss was about."

Actually, Dad never makes a fuss about anything, not even falling off a ladder and gashing his knee, but never mind.

"My wrist is still total agony. In case you were wondering."

Mum always invents a mystery ailment if anyone in the family has anything medical going on: when I was having Jack she had an appendix drama, and with Archie it was an invisible neck injury that required one of those plastic braces. Which she kept taking off when she thought nobody was looking.

"Oh, dear."

"I'm sure I've fractured it. I don't trust the doctors here, but I'm going to a nice man now who does herbal healing, and he says he can't believe how I've managed to cope with such pain. He's very expensive, of course, but worth it. I'll call you later in the week then, so you have time to talk some sense into her. Night, darling."

Bloody hell.

I'll call Vin tomorrow, and we can try to work out how to handle this; he's usually much better at dealing with Mum than I am, mainly because he tends to completely ignore her. But I'm determined she won't end up spoiling things for

Gran. Perhaps her new herbalist could make up a special Don't Ruin Your Mother's Wedding potion: a bit of chamomile, maybe, with a spot of arsenic. Or perhaps she might not make it over in time; I wonder how much you'd have to pay easyJet to divert to somewhere unusual: Reykjavík maybe, or a disused airbase somewhere, with no telephones.

I'm locking the back door and having a last round of Hunt the PE Kit when Jack appears at the bottom of the stairs.

"I can't get back to sleep. I was asleep but then I woke up, and now I'm stuck."

I walk him back upstairs, whispering so we don't wake Archie.

"Come on, let's snuggle you in. You'll be back to sleep in no time."

"Is Dad in heaven, Mum?"

Oh, God. I'm too tired for this now.

"Well, if there is a heaven, then I'm sure he's there, sweetheart. And he knows how much you love him, and that's the important thing."

"Absolutely definite?"

"Absolutely."

"And he can always be in my heart, can't he, Mum?"

"Yes, love."

"People you love are always in your heart, aren't they?"

"Yes, love, forever and ever."

"Yes. And I've got lots of love in my heart, haven't I? And my best things are Trevor, and you and Gran and Archie."

Excellent: beaten to top place by a sodding dog.

"Into bed now."

"And if we got our own dog, he could be in my heart too, couldn't he, Mum?"

"Nice try, love."

He smiles. "It would be so nice to have my very own dog. It would be my best thing ever."

"And my worst."

He giggles. "I'm going to wish for it with all my heart, and then it'll come true."

"Night, love."

"I'm scared I'll have my bad dream. If I still can't get to sleep in ten minutes, can I come in your bed?"

"Twenty?"

"Fifteen?"

"Okay."

He grins.

Damn.

the thin
blue line

February

Monday morning isn't going very well so far, and it's only half past eight.

"You're a big fat grumpypotamus."

"Archie, get your socks on and stop being rude."

"Well, he is. And so are you. And I don't want cheese for my packed lunch. I hate cheese. I really do."

"Shoes and socks, Archie, and come on, Jack, or we'll be late for school."

Jack sighs.

"Alicia has prawns in her sandwich sometimes. And she has pasta salad."

Archie nods.

"And Tyrone has cheese dippers. Which is much better."

"I thought you hated cheese."

"Yes, but not dippers."

"I'll be counting to ten soon, and the last person in the car is a squashed tomato."

They both pretend to ignore this, but I know they'll do anything to avoid being the tomato, squashed or otherwise. Not that it involves anything special, although stickers might be good. I could do a whole set of them: I Eat Very Slowly, I'm Very Annoying in the Mornings—they'd be a great alternative to the I'm a Good Helper stickers they get at school. I'd probably make a fortune.

"Shoes, Archie, come on. Four. Four and a half."

Jack's racing for the front door now, closely followed by Archie, holding a shoe and hopping. Excellent.

I'm halfway to school when I realize I've forgotten to do the Project Knitting notes for Annabel Morgan. Bugger.

Archie's humming tunelessly, still clearly enjoying the fact that since I was the last person to reach the car I am now officially the squashed tomato.

"What are we having for tea, Mum? We could have tomato pasta."

They both giggle.

"Very funny, Archie."

"Or we could have sausages?"

"Maybe, if I get time to go to the butcher's."

"Then we could have toad-in-the-holes."

"Maybe."

"Promise."

"Archie, I said maybe. Let's just see, shall we?"

"No, let's just promise."

Damn: if I try to back out of a solemn promise now he'll get agitated, and I'm not really up for another tearful march across the playground, especially given last week's Oscar-winning performance when I told him I was making chicken casserole for tea.

"All right, I promise."

There's a round of applause from the backseat.

Connie's already waiting for us in the playground with Marco and Nelly, and Annabel Morgan, who's clutching her PTA clipboard. Oh, dear.

"Good morning, Jack and Archie. Are we all ready for a lovely day at school?"

Archie nods, while Jack just looks nervous. Annabel's in Talking to Small Children mode, which involves a cheery smile and a very loud voice.

Archie rallies. "I got a gold sticker for my painting from yesterday. It was leaves, and a tiger. But not a very big one because Jason Lenning wouldn't let me have the orange enough. But Mrs. Berry said it was a very good tiger. It was like the tiger who came to tea, but with no tea. We're having toad-in-the-holes for our tea."

Annabel's not looking quite so happy now. Her son, Horrible Harry, who goes in for a fair bit of sly nipping and name-calling, is in Archie's class, and any mention of gold stickers is bound to prompt a competitive parenting moment.

"Gold stickers are so nice, aren't they? Harry's always so pleased when he gets them. We stick them up on our notice board at home. We've got such a lot of them, we'll need a new notice board soon."

She trills out a little laugh and turns to make sure we've all heard that she has a record-breaking collection of gold stickers.

"Oh, here's Mrs. Berry. Time to line up now, dear."

She taps her clipboard with her pen as we watch them walk toward their lines: Jack and Marco are running while Archie and Nelly saunter. Horrible Harry's already toward the front of the line and appears to be pushing a smaller boy out of the way so he can be first, but Annabel doesn't seem to notice.

"Now then, let me see . . . there are so many things to organize. Still, there's no point in being president if you're not willing to work, is there? Now, let me just check my list. Oh yes, the Summer Fayre. Have you had any thoughts about your stall?"

"Our what?"

She smiles at me as if I'm mentally defective.

"Your stall, for the fayre. I did assume you'd want to do something together, so if you could just let me know what you're planning, that would be super. Since both of you are in trade locally, I'm sure you're full of marvelous ideas."

The way she says "trade" makes it sound like we spend a fair bit of time standing on street corners after dark. And she's still tapping her bloody clipboard.

"I haven't really thought about it, Annabel, but—"

"I've assigned the majority of the stalls, of course, but

you could do face painting, or the tombola. Or funny fish—
that's always popular."

Connie looks confused. "Why are the fish funny?"

"Oh, it's all rather super. You just need to fill the paddling
pool, and Mrs. Palmer has done a marvelous job painting all
the little fish, although the fishing rods are in a bit of a tangle,
but I'm sure you'll manage. Orange fish for prizes, and if you
catch any other color you just get a little sweet. She'll also go
to the cash-and-carry with you. She has our card, and it saves
us so much money. And there's a hose pipe in the schoolkeeper's shed. Shall I put you down for that?"

Bloody hell, we'll get completely soaked.

"I'm sorry, Annabel; I'm not sure. Summer is so busy in
the shop. Isn't there something a bit simpler we could do?"

Actually, last summer was pretty quiet, but I'm hoping
to do better this year with summer knitting kits, if I ever
get time to make them up; I'm thinking cotton beach bags
and lightweight wraps. And Connie will be frantic in the
pub—they were booked solid at the weekends last year.

Annabel's smiling. I think I may have just fallen into a
cleverly laid trap.

"Well, there's always the white elephant, I suppose. We
always get lots of bags of jumble. Yes, let me put you down
for that. You can sort through things on the day, and I'll
give you your notes and your target sheet in the next few
weeks, and there'll be a preliminary planning meeting soon.
It's so important that everyone knows what's expected of
them or it's total chaos. Good. Now, have you done the
notes on your little knitting project? I do like to keep my
files up to date."

Bloody hell: a white-elephant stall with a target, and now she's hassling me about the bloody notes. Actually, sod this.

"No, I haven't had time, Annabel. Maybe you should ask Mrs. Chambers if you want more details for the files; she did give me the impression that she's got it all under control, and since it's really her project, I think it comes under the school curriculum rather than the PTA. But I'm sure she'll be happy to talk you through it. And on the white elephant, I'm sure Connie and I can manage on the day, but neither of us can do planning meetings, I'm afraid. We simply don't have the time. What with being in local trade. I'm sure you understand."

She's gone rather pale. Fury, I expect.

Connie's looking like she's trying not to laugh.

"Maybe we can make some changes. Connie might be able to persuade Mark to make us some of his amazing cakes; people can have a free slice if they buy a bag of jumble. That way we should sell out in ten minutes flat."

"Oh, I'm not sure the ladies on our cake stall will like that. It could get rather confusing."

"Well, let's not tell them then. I'm sure people will be able to spot the difference between a cake stall and a load of jumble. Anyway, thanks, Annabel, but we must get on."

We walk back across the playground toward the gates, leaving Annabel standing slack-jawed with her clipboard clutched tightly to her chest.

"I really shouldn't have done that."

Connie giggles. "I think it will be fun, I like elephants."

"There's no elephant, Con, just a load of tatty old jumble."

"And cake?"

"Not usually, no."

"Well, it can be an Italian elephant then. Little glasses of Prosecco, and some cake, maybe apricot tarts, and Tom will be your uncle."

"Bob."

"Bob is your uncle?"

"Yes, sort of, but are you sure Mark won't mind making cakes? I shouldn't have volunteered him like that. Sorry."

She raises her eyebrows. "If we ask him the right way he'll be happy, and you can knit some little white elephants and it will be perfect. Annabel will be surprised, I think?"

"Yes. And bloody livid. She'll be on our case big time now."

"Porca Madonna."

"Oh yes. Double porca, I'd say, and very little Madonna."

Gran's already arrived when I get to the shop; I think she's rather enjoyed being free of it since I took over, but today is clearly an exception with news of the wedding breaking on the High Street. She's holding court with her friend Betty, and Elsie's in attendance, and she's already been to see the vicar about the church, and now they're talking about flowers while I'm wedged in the window trying to get a small knitted penguin to stop falling over. A fairly steady stream of old ladies wheel their trolleys in during the morning, desperate for snippets, and there's a great

deal of lobbying for carnations and freesias before they all go next door to see Mrs. Davis, who's run the florist's shop for years and does all the local weddings.

I'm rearranging the Scottish tweeds, which Elsie has put into unfortunate color combinations, so I'm separating the sage greens from the heather purples with a buffer zone of slate gray and oatmeal, while Elsie watches. She's not that keen on me Moving Stock; but we've negotiated an uneasy truce over the past few months, which involves me trying to stop the shop looking like a color-blind nutter has thrown balls of wool into random heaps, while she stands with her arms folded and watches me, in between putting the kettle on and making cups of tea and eating custard creams. I'm trying to make sure we've always got biscuits in the tin, and it's costing me a fortune, but they're a key part of my staff-training plan.

Elsie can be incredibly domineering when she wants to be, but she's very kind underneath it all, and completely reliable, so I can't afford to lose her. She knows everybody, and since she only lives two streets away, she's always around to nip in if I can't open up or I need her to do an extra shift. But I know all her bossing and sulking really got to Gran over the years, so I'm trying not to let her do the same to me, and the biscuits are definitely helping.

Gran comes back from the florist's humming. "You wouldn't believe the price of some of those bouquets." Betty nods. "It's terrible, you'd never think a few roses and

a few ferns would add up to nearly fifty pounds, would you? They should be ashamed of themselves."

"Yes, but she says she'll do me something special. Isn't that kind of her? I've got the brochure in my bag. Shall I show you?"

"Lovely, Gran. Just let me finish this."

Elsie leans forward slightly, desperate to be involved.

"Shall I put the kettle on, Mary? There's such a lot to organize, isn't there? I know what it was like with my Martin, not that she would let me do it properly, insisted on the church near her parents, which wasn't a patch on ours. Horrible concrete thing. And the flowers were terrible. I tried to tell him, you know. I could see what she was like right from the start—only out for what she could get. Still, he's learned his lesson the hard way, and he can't say I didn't try to warn him."

Gran and Betty nod sympathetically. Although why it still matters what Martin's wife, Patricia, chose for their wedding is beyond me, particularly since they're divorced and she's moved in with the area sales manager at the company where Martin used to work. Apparently she's insisting on being called Patsy now, and wearing a gold ankle chain.

"Will you be doing lunch or tea for the reception, Mary? I always think a tea's nice, and that way you don't have to provide a big meal. Some people will eat you out of house and home if you let them."

If there's anyone in Broadgate who knows how to snork their way through a wedding buffet better than Elsie, I'd like to meet them.

"I thought we'd have a tea, and then maybe a quiet dinner for the family."

"Lovely." Elsie's smiling, but there's a steely glint in her eye, and I think we're all fairly clear that there'll be hell to pay if she's not invited to the dinner.

The bell above the door jingles, and we turn to see Mrs. Marwell getting her trolley stuck on the mat, with Mrs. Davis bringing up the rear. Excellent. More bouquet snippets.

"I just thought, Mary, what about some lily of the valley? I know how much you like it."

Elsie moves behind the counter, frowning; she's caught between maintaining her long-running feud with Mrs. Davis over change for ten-pound notes and making sure she doesn't miss out on lily-of-the-valley details.

Mrs. Marwell has finally wrestled her trolley over the doormat.

"I always think freesias are nice at a wedding."

Everyone agrees that freesias are nice at weddings, and Elsie goes into Superior Shop Assistant mode, bustling about behind the counter being Busy.

"Did that pink wool knit up all right, Mrs. Marwell?"

"Oh yes, lovely, thanks, Elsie, but I need some navy now, for my Stewart's boy. I'm doing him a sweater, with a train on the front, like the one I made for him when he was little. They all love trains at that age, don't they?"

Elsie nods.

"He must be getting quite big. How old is he now?"

"Eleven, nearly twelve. Now where did I put that pattern? It's here somewhere."

I'm not sure about knitting a sweater with a train on

the front for someone who's nearly twelve; Jack would throw a fit if I tried to get him to wear anything so babyish, and he's only seven. I think I'd better suggest something else before she finds her pattern and spends ages knitting something her grandson is pretty much guaranteed to hate on sight.

She's rootling through her basket, putting things on the counter while she searches: a thermos, some string, an assortment of shopping bags, and for some reason best known to herself a very rusty old tin opener. It's like a Twilight Zone version of *The Generation Game*.

"Maybe something a bit more grown-up might be better, Mrs. Marwell. They get so picky at that age, don't they? I've got a lovely cable pattern, and I know how good you are at cable. Why don't you go upstairs with Gran and I'll sort you out something nice?"

Gran nods. "We were just going up for a cup of tea, if you fancy one."

"Oh, well, if you think so . . . that would be lovely."

Gran winks at me as they walk through into the back of the shop toward the door to the stairs. I lit the fire in the workroom when I got in, so it'll be nice and warm up there, and more important, it'll get them out of my way, because I don't think I can cope with much more of the freesias-versus-carnations debate.

I sort out some dark gray flecked double knitting for Mrs. Marwell and put in a few stock orders with a steady hum of chatter and clinking teacups from upstairs, and I'm just about to go up and retrieve Elsie so I can go to the butcher's when Lady Denby sweeps in, with Algie

and Clarkson, her Labradors. Brilliant: perfect timing, as usual.

Elsie, who's got hearing like a bat's, belts down the stairs as soon as she hears Lady Denby telling Algie to sit. This is shaping up to be a top day for her: first Gran's wedding and now our local mad aristocrat.

"Just come from the committee, and I thought you'd like to know we've decided to splash out on new bunting for the High Street this summer. We need to pull out all the stops if we're going for gold this year. Counting on you for one of your special window displays, my dear. Some places have won more than once, you know—faint whiff of money changing hands, if you ask me—so let's pull out all the stops, shall we? Jolly good. Gather congratulations are in order, your grandmother. I must say I do approve of getting hitched. Never too late. . . . Do pass on my best wishes."

"She's upstairs, Lady Denby, if you'd like to pop up and say hello." Elsie's practically curtsying.

"Is she? Right, well, I might just do that."

She hands Elsie two ancient-looking dog leads, and Algie and Clarkson stand up. They're both quite keen on licking people's feet, particularly Clarkson, and I'm fairly sure Algie has just farted.

Elsie's looking very nervous, and I don't blame her, so I take the dog leads from her and head toward the shop door.

"I'll just take them outside, Lady Denby, if you don't mind. A few of our customers aren't that keen on dogs, and I'm sure they'll be happier in the fresh air. I'll tie them to the railings, shall I? You go on up; Elsie will show you the way."

Elsie gives me a look of undying devotion, which is rather similar to the one Clarkson is currently giving to my new boots as I tug on the lead and try to keep out of licking distance.

"I'm off in a minute, Elsie. If Mr. Prewitt rings, tell him I'll bring the cashbooks round later on, would you?"

"Right you are, dear. This way, Lady Denby. Have you heard we're doing special knitting classes at the infants' school? I'll be helping out too—I'm really looking forward to it."

Lady Denby looks impressed. "Marvelous, used to teach all the girls to knit in my day."

"The boys will be learning too, Lady Denby."

"Oh yes, quite right. Got to be multisexual nowadays, haven't we?"

Elsie hesitates at the mention of the S-word but manages to rally as they head toward the stairs. "Might I offer you a cup of tea, Lady Denby?"

Bloody hell; sometimes I think I should just open a tea shop.

It's starting to rain as I drive toward Graceland, but at least I'm away from the wedding fest. I've got some balls of cashmere and silk mix in raspberry, with a few balls of dark chocolate too. Maxine, Grace's PA, rang yesterday to tell me Grace wants to make another blanket for Lily, although how she gets the time or the energy to knit with a three-week-old baby is anybody's guess. But having a nanny, a cook, and a driver as well as a full-time PA and

security in the shape of Bruno probably helps, and I suppose I count as staff too, since I'm officially on the payroll as knitting coach to Ms. Harrison. Which is a good thing too really, because the 400 pounds a month they pay me has been a lifesaver. Sometimes it's more than I make in a whole week in the shop if it's quiet. Although the new stock is starting to pay off, and we do have days like we did at the weekend, when we got a couple of people in who bought bags full of the more expensive yarns and bamboo needles.

The house looks damp and chilly in the drizzle, and much less like a gorgeous stately home than usual. God knows how they managed in muslin frocks and silk slippers when they built the place—they must have been half frozen most of the time. No wonder they kept fainting: it was probably hypothermia.

I'm waiting by the gates for Bruno to recognize me on the security monitors and buzz me in when PC Mike comes over for a chat; he's our neighborhood policeman, wearing his fluorescent jacket today and looking very pleased with himself. "Pretty quiet this morning. It was bedlam here yesterday. I had to call for backup."

Grace hasn't released any photographs of Baby Lily yet, so the press have been down here in force, climbing up ladders, trying to get over the walls, and generally annoying everyone within a five-mile radius.

"Oh, dear, what happened?"

"There were stacks of them, obstructing the public high-

way, but I soon put paid to that. They might get away with it in London, but not down here they won't. Not while I'm on duty."

The gates are starting to open, very slowly.

"I'll see you in, shall I? Make sure none of them follow you?"

"Thanks."

He's having a lovely time being on patrol at the gates. There are two Jeeps and a green VW Golf parked farther up the lane, with various men inside with cameras slung round their necks, talking on mobiles and looking very bored, who've shown a brief flicker of interest in my arrival, but since my name doesn't appear on any kind of A list, except for Annabel Morgan's A for Annoying one, they just take a few halfhearted snaps and then go back to talking on their phones.

PC Mike stands slightly to one side, with his arms outstretched to hold back the invisible hordes, as I drive forward.

"Thanks, Mike."

He salutes.

Bless.

I park at the side of the house, as far away as possible from the enormous new silver Jeep that makes my car look even more sordid than the gleaming black one does, and I'm just about to get out when two huge dogs come racing over. Jesus, they must be Great Danes or something. I close my door and lock it: they probably can't open car doors, but

I'm not taking any chances. It's like I'm suddenly appearing in *The Hound of the Baskervilles*, only there's two of the sods. One of them leaps up on the bonnet and starts slavering all over my windscreen. Bloody hell.

Bruno comes jogging round the corner blowing a whistle, but it doesn't seem to be having much of an effect on the Baskerville boys.

He grabs collars and starts pulling, laughing, as I open my window.

"Sorry about that, Jo. They're only playing."

"You could have fooled me."

"I'm training them, but they haven't really got the hang of it yet."

"Right."

We both look at my windscreen, which is now opaque.

"I'll sort that out for you, love. I don't think he's scratched the paintwork, but we'll pay for any damage, of course. Do you want to have a look?"

"Bruno, it's covered in dents and scratches—don't worry about it. It was just a bit of a shock."

I get out of the car and have my hands licked while Bruno tries to get them both to sit.

"They're only babies."

"Jesus."

"That's the whole idea, put those bastards off coming through the woods."

"What are they called?"

I'm expecting Titan and Trojan.

"Tom and Jerry."

"Good names."

"Grace wanted names she could remember. Look, I'll sort your car out for you, give it a wash, don't you worry. And if you wouldn't mention it to Her Highness I'd be grateful, only it took me ages to persuade her we needed them."

"Okay."

"They're as soft as butter, when you get to know them."

"Like I can't believe it's not butter, only with dogs?"

He's chuckling and yanking on collars when Maxine comes out of a side door and walks toward us across the gravel.

"Hi, Jo. I see you've met Bruno's babies then?"

"Yes."

"I meant to warn you—sorry."

Bruno stiffens. "They're an important part of our security."

"And what about last night then? What were they barking at? An intruder?"

Bruno looks at his feet.

"A member of the press hoping for an unscheduled interview?"

Bruno mumbles something, and Maxine winks at me.

"Sorry, Bruno, I didn't quite catch that."

"They're still learning."

"It was a squirrel. Right?"

"Yes. But it shows they're alert."

"We were all pretty alert, Bruno. It was just a shame it was half past two in the bloody morning."

"Has she said anything?"

"Grace? Oh yes. She said quite a lot, but I don't want to repeat it in front of Jo."

Bruno's looking a bit worried now.

"You're all right, you can keep them for now, but you'd better fit them with silencers if they're going to be chasing squirrels again. The floodlights came on and everything."

He nods. "I'm going to give Jo's car a quick clean for her. Do you want yours done too?"

She softens slightly. "Yes, please, and Ed's due soon, so chain Tom and Jerry to something solid, will you, because he'll have a fit if they jump on his precious Porsche. You know what he's like."

Bruno grins. "They could say hello, though, couldn't they, if I had them on their leads?"

Maxine laughs. "Yes, they could, but make sure I get to watch. Grace is upstairs, in the gray room, Jo, if you want to go on up. Tea?"

"Lovely."

Grace is lying on a gray velvet chaise longue, in skinny jeans and a pale blue T-shirt, with Lily asleep in a basket at her feet.

"Sorry I look such a state—I've just got her off."

She looks amazing, and even though she's a mega film star, it still surprises me how stunning she is, whatever she's wearing. It's like she's made out of something different from the rest of us: something more ethereal and photogenic. She's got her hair pulled back, and she's wearing huge drop earrings, which clink slightly as she reaches for the phone.

Seconds later the nanny appears, in a smart striped uniform, and picks up the Moses basket.

"I'll just pop her into her room, shall I, Miss Harrison?"

"Thanks, Meg, but call me if she wakes up. Okay?"

"Of course."

Meg closes the door behind her, and Grace sits up.

"I can't get her to call me Grace, and it's driving me crazy. She keeps forgetting. It's like I'm suddenly in *Upstairs bloody Downstairs,* and I'm so not into all of that. Is Max bringing tea up?"

"Yes."

"Great. I'm getting so dehydrated with all this breast feeding, but I think I've finally got Meg to get with the program."

"She seems very efficient."

"Oh yes, apart from calling me Miss Harrison all the bloody time, but they're all obsessed with this four-hourly thing. Put Baby down to sleep, all that rubbish."

"What happens if the baby wakes up?"

"You leave it to sob, I think. Christ. As if. Not with my gorgeous girl they bloody don't. What did you do with your boys?"

"Fed them all the time. I tried to get a schedule going, but neither of them was very keen. I think it depends on the baby. Some of them are just hungrier than others."

She smiles. "Lily's like me, always starving. Although I've had years of practice, so I'm used to it."

"Really?"

She gives me a look, like I might be about to cross into the danger zone of personal questions—there's a sort of un-spoken rule to all our conversations, where she can tell you things, but you never ask. But given how many people sell

the tiniest scraps of information, or misinformation, about her, I don't really blame her.

"Sorry, I didn't mean—"

"I've been dieting for years—it's part of the job. Did you think this was all just luck? It takes hours of fucking work to look like this."

"No, sorry, of course. . . . It's just you look so healthy and everything."

"That's because I'm not obsessive about it. Well, I am, but in a healthy way. I don't do pills. Or surgery. Yet. But I can still tell you the fat content of every substance on earth. I've done GI, combining, and colors. You name it, I've done it."

"Colors?"

"Only eat green. A bit of purple, very little white. None, actually."

"That sounds good. So would damson crumble count as purple?"

She smiles. "Sadly, no."

Maxine comes in with tea.

"Thanks, Max. Is Bruno still playing with those fucking dogs?"

"Yes, and washing Jo's car. They got a bit carried away saying hello to Jo."

Grace grins. "I'm hoping they'll slow Jimmy down if he decides to put in an appearance."

Jimmy Madden is Grace's rock star ex-boyfriend, and father of Lily, and he's definitely persona non gratis round here, as Gran would say. He was in the papers when Lily was born, whining about how he wants to see his baby, but so far I don't think he's actually tried.

"Is he likely to turn up then?"

"You never know with Jimmy."

"But he hasn't been in touch?"

She hesitates. Damn, I've done it again, strayed into tab-loid territory.

"Not directly, but give him time. He'll get round to it, once he's got his exclusive lined up. Has Ed arrived yet, Max?"

"He's due any minute."

"Well, bring him straight up, would you. Now then, wool. Show me, Jo, and I hope the pink isn't Pepto-Bismol puke pink."

"Raspberry and dark chocolate?"

"Perfect."

I'm casting on two hundred stitches for her when Ed ar-rives, with paw prints all over the front of his trousers. "Fucking dogs, whose bright idea was that? And where have all the police pissed off to? There's only one of them out there now. Christ, talk about a thin blue line."

"Morning, Ed. Lovely to see you too. What's the latest on the photos?"

"*Vanity Fair* suit you, madam?"

"Sure. Who with?"

"They're sorting that out now. Daniel Fitzgerald, pos-sibly, if they can get him."

I try to seem nonchalant at the mention of Daniel's name, but I think Grace has noticed. She's giving me a rather care-ful look as Ed sits down on one of the gray sofas.

"Do you remember Daniel, Jo? He was the one who did that shoot in the summer. With the rowing boat."

"Oh yes, vaguely."

I'm still trying for nonchalant, but I'm not sure it's working.

Bugger.

"The only thing is, they want an interview."

"Tell them to fuck off."

"I'd never have thought of that."

"They can have what we give them and work with that. Or we'll go with someone else."

"No we bloody won't. Leave it with me, babe, and I'll get back to you. Yes?"

"Babe?"

"Fuck. Sorry."

"Off you go."

"Jesus. Not again."

"Ed."

"All right, I'm going."

Ed stands, looking rather fed up.

"If he calls me babe he has to do three circuits of the house. Is Bruno still out there?"

"I think so, why?"

"Then you'll have Tom and Jerry for company, won't you?"

"Fucking hell."

There's a sound of barking and shouting, and then we stand at the window and watch Ed racing past the cars at full pelt with Tom and Jerry chasing him.

Grace turns to me and gives me a very searching look. "So. Daniel Fitzgerald? Tell me."

"Tell you what?"

"There's no point trying to kid me—I know every trick in the book. Come on, tell me."

"I don't know what you mean, Grace. There isn't anything to tell."

"Either you've had a fling or you came close. I need details. How was he, out of ten? I've always wondered. Tell me, or you're fired." She's smiling, but I'm not entirely sure she's joking.

Oh, God.

"There really isn't anything to tell."

"I mean it."

Christ.

"Ten."

She laughs and claps her hands.

"I knew it, although nobody's a ten, except me, of course. When?"

"Grace, it was just a one-off."

"Of course. When?"

"In Venice."

"Good for you. Found a way to make Christmas with your mother that little bit more bearable, did you? Clever."

"Yes, but it really wasn't serious or anything, and he's back with his girlfriend now."

"Liv, yes, I heard. Who's a total bitch, by the way, kept trying to steal shots off me when we did the girls in space film."

"Oh, right."

"I won all the awards, though. Still, she's a piece of work. He'll have a job keeping up with her, and serve him right. So you're over it then?"

"Oh yes. It was nice, lovely actually, but it wasn't real."

She looks at me and gives me one of her Megastar Smiles, and I feel like I've just won some sort of prize.

"Good for you, darling, and you're spot-on: it's never real with men like him. They want to be swept off their feet, overcome by beauty; creative types like him always do. She's perfect for him, she's always posing. But she'll totally fuck him over in the end."

"Why?"

"She'll get bored. Trust me. Been there, done that, got the diamonds. And pearls."

She moves her head slightly, and her earrings jingle.

"Oh."

"They arrived this morning. I think he was just checking I'm not about to hit him with the daddy of all paternity suits. And before you ask, no, I'm not talking about Jimmy. And that's all I'm going to say on the subject."

"Right."

"Nice, though, aren't they?"

"Beautiful."

"You've got to keep them guessing. And know when to move on. Timing is everything, right?"

"Yes."

"So if he's here doing snaps, you'll be okay with that?"

"Of course."

"Good. Now then, what do you think of moss stitch

for my blanket? I'm getting bored with just plain stocki-
nette stitch."

"Lovely. Or maybe a moss-stitch border and then
squares? You could do plain ones, and some with bobbles.
You said you wanted to do bobbles, didn't you?"

"Yes, and that other one. What was it called? The one
you showed me on that little hat."

"Seed stitch. You can try out some of the other ones we
were looking at too if you like, do little squares in different
stitches."

"Sounds perfect."

It's pouring with rain on Friday morning, and I feel like
I'm wearing a very tight invisible hat, which is particularly unfair since I didn't drink anything last night at the
Stitch and Bitch group because I was too busy. Everyone
was agog about Gran's wedding, and how Grace is doing
and how beautiful the baby is. Apparently one of the photographers tried to push past PC Mike yesterday afternoon, so
he arrested him, and now the thin blue line has some extra
reinforcement and PC Mike is in bliss. They're doing a
piece on it for the local paper, according to Tina, and they
took his photograph, only he's a bit worried about what his
sergeant will say, because he likes to be center front in any
photographs.

We spent most of the evening talking about our top
wedding moments, and Tina Davis told us all about her
honeymoon with Fireman Graham—his watch from the fire
station filled their honeymoon caravan with foam, which

must have been nice. Linda told us about her hen night too, which culminated in her being handcuffed to a lamppost in a basque and suspenders, although I can't see Gran going in for that kind of thing, so all in all it was a really good evening.

The group feels relaxed now, which is just what I wanted; like friends meeting, catching up on the latest news, with no need to make direct eye contact if you're sharing anything a bit embarrassing or the conversation moves on to freesias versus bloody carnations again. That's the great thing about knitting: you can look at your stitches if you're bored, or someone needs a bit of space, like last week when Maggie started talking about her mother, who sounds like a total cow, and we just let her talk until she'd finished, and then Linda got her a tissue while Connie cut her another slice of cake.

Last night it was fabulous almond tarts, which Connie says Mark is experimenting with for the restaurant, where they'll be served with homemade apricot sorbet; it's no wonder they're getting booked up at weekends really. The pudding menu alone should have people queuing down the street.

I sorted out Tina's poncho for her, which was going a bit rectangular, and we chose the wool for Linda's new cardigan, and Tina had us all in fits about her recent run-ins with Annabel Morgan, who keeps sending her increasingly rude notes about getting Graham to bring his fire engine into school. He's not that keen on assorted mixed infants swarming all over it pressing buttons and trying to climb up the ladder, and I don't really blame him.

Maggie's started on a complicated cable pattern on a sweater, but she'd gone wrong on the first repeat, which had put the second one out of kilter, so I showed her how to fix it while Connie made a start on the cardigan she's knitting for Mark's birthday. She's chosen a lovely flecked felted tweed, with dark green for the neckband and cuffs, and I've promised to do the sleeves for her since they're so busy in the pub. Mark's celebration-cakes sideline is really taking off, and he's cooking seven days a week now, so Connie's trying to get some more help in; she found him fast asleep by the big mixer last week, with marzipan stuck to his forehead.

Archie's relaunching his campaign for the kind of breakfast cereal that makes the milk go an unusual color, although why he thinks I need a five-year-old with a massive sugar high on the school run is anybody's guess.

"It's not fair. We never have proper cereal. We always have rubbish ones."

"Shreddies are proper, Archie, and please stop shouting, I've got a headache."

"Yes, stop screeching like a baby. It's just ridiculous."

Archie glares at Jack; they'll be nudging and shoving each other any minute. Sometimes I think I should just buy a whistle and a set of red cards.

"Jack, go up and do your teeth, and Archie, stop fussing and finish your Shreddies."

He tuts but starts eating, albeit in slow motion.

"Hurry up, love, I think you've got music this morning."

"Damn."

"Archie."

"I hate music. And I hate Mrs. Nelson, she's so stupid. She makes you sit with your arms crossed all the blimming time, and I can't sing in my proper voice with my arms crossed."

"I bet you can. You've got a lovely voice."

He starts belting out "If You're Happy and You Know It, Clap Your Hands." Lovely.

A pparently we're still Happy and We Know It while we're in the car on the way to school, but we've substituted clapping for stamping our feet and jabbing our brother, so I have to reluctantly launch a "Ten Green Bottles" countermaneuver. We're down to two green bottles by the time we reach the safety of the playground, and my invisible hat feels significantly tighter than it did half an hour ago.

Connie's standing by the fence, with a selection of bags slung round her neck, while the kids run round for a final five minutes of yelling before the bell goes. There's some sort of tag game going on, and Nelly appears to be It. She's racing round looking frantic, trying to catch Marco and his friends, who are much faster than she is.

"He knows she can't run so fast. She'll be crying soon. Marco, vieni qui."

He ignores her, and just as Connie predicted, Nelly starts to cry. Archie trots over to her and whispers something, and they both grin.

"Oh, dear, this isn't going to be good."

Connie laughs. "She'll be fine now with Archie on her team."

"Yes, but will Marco?"

Sure enough, Archie appears to have come up with some cunning pincer-movement plan where they both circle Marco and Jack and there's a flurry of darting and shoving until Marco and Jack are It and Nelly belts straight back to her mother for a quick cuddle, with Archie puffing along behind her looking triumphant.

"We got him, we got him."

"Yes, you did. Well done, love, but that's enough now. Time to calm down. The bell will be going in a minute."

"But, Mum . . ."

He looks past me toward Jack and Marco, who are now standing a few feet away from the safety of the mummy zone, looking menacing while they wait to tag Nelly and Archie back.

"Jack, come here a minute, love."

He saunters over but can't resist giving Archie a filthy look as he passes him.

"What?"

"I just need a hug before school, that's all."

"Right now?"

"Yes."

He sighs.

Connie smiles and beckons Marco over.

"We can do a group hugging."

The kids look horrified.

"Or you can play, but no more games with the big ones chasing the little ones, yes?"

They nod, clearly relieved to be escaping a group hug. "Brava."

They race off to the other side of the playground, no doubt to commiserate with each other about the horrors of having mothers who go in for public hugging, as Mrs. Chambers comes out with the bell and everyone starts to line up. Excellent: nobody going into school in tears or vowing revenge at morning break.

We've just reached the gates when Horrible Harry arrives with Annabel, looking flustered. She's usually been here bustling about with her clipboard for ages before us, so she must have had a Domestic Moment. I'm hoping for a dodgy washing machine, because there's nothing like gallons of water sloshing all over your terra-cotta tiling to start you off with a bang on a Friday morning. But whatever it was, Harry's definitely sulking as he walks to the front of the line and tries to push in. The kids all close ranks, and as he reaches Archie and Nelly he takes a sudden and dramatic dive and hurls himself to the ground, just like an Italian footballer only with less convincing hand gestures.

Mrs. Berry comes out of the classroom as he starts rolling around yelling, but she's obviously been watching because she doesn't fall for any of it. He's standing at the back of the line in no time and seems fine. Unlike Annabel, who marches straight over to Mrs. Berry, who Stands Firm, which is rather brave of her, and before we know it Annabel's barreling across the playground toward us, looking very

thin-lipped. Christ. Quite a few parents are lingering now, and she's in full presidential mode.

"I hope you saw that, Mrs. Mackenzie. Your son just pushed poor Harry to the ground. I really do think you need to speak to him. It's not the sort of behavior we want to encourage in school. I'm sure you agree."

Bloody hell. I'm trying to work out what to say that doesn't involve the words *off* and *fuck* when Connie steps forward, looking pretty thin-lipped herself. "Archie did not push, he wasn't even near him. So how can he be apologized for something he didn't do?"

Annabel gives her a particularly condescending look. "Perhaps you didn't see the incident quite as clearly as I did, Mrs. Maxwell."

Connie mutters something in Italian, and there's an intake of breath from some of the other parents. They'll be chanting "Fight Fight Fight" in a minute if we're not careful.

I try to smile, to calm things down, but I'm not sure it's working. "I was watching them too, Annabel, and I don't think Archie did push Harry. I know they've had their differences in the past, but I think they're over that now. So perhaps you need to have a word with Harry. I think he tripped when he tried to get to the front of the line."

Tina Davis is now standing next to us, nodding. "He's always pushing in. Actually."

Annabel glares at her.

"My Travis was just the same, but you've got to tell them, haven't you? They can't always be first, can they?"

Annabel is looking Tense now; a playground mutiny was probably the last thing she expected, and quite a few of

the parents are smiling. I think it's starting to dawn on her that she may have misjudged things a tiny bit.

She seems to falter for a moment and then rallies. "Well, I'm so glad we had this little chat. So important to nip things in the bud, and we all need to do our best to keep our school a happy place, I'm sure you agree. Now I really must get on, so much to do, as usual, but thank you for raising it with me; that's what I'm here for, to keep things running smoothly. Always happy to help. Good morning."

She nods at the other parents and turns sharply on her medium-heeled court shoes and marches toward the main doors.

Connie mutters something under her breath, and Tina laughs.

"What was that, Connie?"

"I can't translate, it's too rude."

"Oh, go on, whisper, I used to collect rude words when I was little. Drove my mum mad."

I do like Tina, she's a real trooper, and her Travis is a sweetheart too, only he's the kind of sweetheart you're very glad isn't one of yours. Last time he was in the shop he was telling me all about electricity and circuits, and even though he's only seven and three-quarters he's going to make a motor in the garden shed that will power a light so bright it can burn paper. So having a fireman dad will probably be coming in very handy any day now.

"Do you want a lift, Tina? I'm dropping Connie off, and then I'm due in the shop."

"Yes, please, love. It looks like it'll be chucking it down again any minute. I think I might nip in the baker's and get

myself a bun to celebrate. I've been wanting to tell that Annabel where to get off for ages."

We cross the road and walk toward the car.

"Well, we'd better keep an eye on those PTA letters, or we'll be down for holding the sick bucket on every coach trip from now until the end of time."

"Don't you worry, I've got her number. We do her hair in the salon, so if she pushes it I can always do her a poodle perm, and she won't need her velvet hair band for quite a while after that. Stuck-up cow. Anyway, that's enough about her. What are you wearing tonight?"

"Sorry?"

"For your dinner with Martin. A little bird told me."

I look at Connie, who shakes her head.

"Which little bird was that then, Tina?"

"Quite a big one actually, Betty. She was in the salon yesterday, and between you and me, I don't think Elsie's that keen."

"Oh, right."

I did notice Elsie seemed extra stroppy yesterday: it's quite hard to bang balls of wool down onto shelves, but she was definitely giving it her best shot.

"It's not really a dinner dinner. It's just to say thank you for making the shelves in the shop."

Tina raises her eyebrows. "Right."

"I've known him for years, Tina, ever since we were kids. It's just a friendly supper."

"Shame. He could put my shelves up any day."

Connie laughs. "And me. Mark is hopeless."

"So's my Graham. He's put up two rolls of wallpaper

upside down in our lounge, honestly he has. All the birds look like they're diving toward the floor. Every time I look at them it upsets me. Silly sod."

Connie's planning to paper her spare bedroom in honor of her mum and dad coming over at Easter from Italy, so she's keen on getting wallpaper tips from Tina, and the subject of my supper with Martin is fortunately dropped.

When I get to the shop, Elsie is even more narky than yesterday. She's dusting, and she only ever dusts when she wants to make a point.

"Morning, Elsie, I'm just putting the kettle on. Do you want a cup of tea?"

"No thanks, I want to get this done, and then there's more stock to get out."

"Oh, good, it's arrived. We were running low on the tweed and the chunky mix at the weekend."

"Yes, well, I wish you'd tell me when you put new orders in."

"It was in the book, Elsie."

"Well, that's as may be, but I used to do all the ordering for your gran, you know."

Yes, and that's why the shop was stuffed full of horrible pastel four-ply.

"I know how busy you are, Elsie, and anyway I like doing it—it helps me keep track of things. I'll give you a hand in a minute. Are you sure you don't want anything? I got some more biscuits yesterday, Hobnobs and digestives."

She hesitates. "Oh, go on then. I need something to give

me a bit of a boost, I've been at it since six. I did all my nets before I came out. It feels like I've done a full day already."

I know just how she feels.

After a busy day in the shop, with Elsie niggling away and a dribble of customers including Mrs. Dent, who brings in her tangled knitting for us to sort out, again, and a group of women from Tonbridge who look at a huge range of colors before they all buy mohair for shawls and chunky tweeds for sweaters, I'm back at home, standing in front of my wardrobe and hoping for inspiration when Ellen rings.

"How are you doing, darling? Found your killer outfit yet?"

"Not really. My black jeans are pretty lethal, though: if I do the zip up I can't breathe."

"Totally not breathe, or just have to sit up very straight to breathe?"

"Passing out, face-down-in-your-soup not breathe."

"Go for the velvet skirt then, but wear a tight top."

"That won't be a problem, trust me."

"You're meeting him at the pub, and Connie's fully briefed, right?"

"She knows we're having supper, if that's what you mean. I haven't booked under a false name or anything. It's no big deal, Ellen."

"Unless you kiss him again."

"Look, I've told you, it wasn't a *kiss* kiss. He'd just found Archie—that was different. It was a Thank God kiss."

"Whatever. Just ring me later with a full debrief."

"Okay."

"And darling—"

"Yes?"

"If you feel like not kissing him again, just go for it."

Great. That's made me feel so much calmer.

G ran's reading stories when I leave and promises not to get conned into reading past eight-thirty, although we both know she'll cave. It's a ten-minute walk to the pub, and I'm feeling rather grown-up being out in the evening without the boys. I can't remember the last time I had supper without a small person in tow, keeping an eye on my chips for any extra-crispy ones.

Martin's wearing a dark gray suit when I arrive, looking unusually smart. Bugger. Now I feel underdressed in just my skirt and sweater; and I should at least have gone for high heels instead of my boots. He's sitting at the table with a bottle of wine, and Connie winks at me as she takes my coat.

He stands up as I walk across the restaurant. "You look lovely. I'm sorry I'm dressed like this, but it was either this or jeans, and most of them are covered in paint at the moment."

"You look great, Martin."

He blushes. "No, I look like I'm off to a sales conference, but Mum had ironed a shirt, not that I ask her to do my ironing or anything, far from it, but she won't have it."

"She's the same in the shop. Oh, sorry, I didn't mean—"

"No, it's fine. I know what she's like."

There's an awkward silence. Bloody hell: I've managed to make him feel uncomfortable in his suit *and* made fun of his mother, and I've only just sat down. I wonder what I'll come up with for an encore.

"Would you like a glass of wine? Connie brought this over; she said it was one of your favorites."

"Lovely."

"Do you know a lot about wine?"

"Not really, but Connie usually brings a bottle when we have our Stitch and Bitch group."

"That's your knitting group, isn't it?"

"Yes, knitting and cake. Mark makes them. I think they're the real attraction."

He smiles. "And how's it going, with the shop, I mean?"

"Pretty well. I'm never going to make my fortune, but as long as it pays the bills I'm happy, and now the upstairs is opened up with your new shelves and everything, there's so much more room for stock, which has really made a difference. I've been thinking about starting another group on Saturdays, for beginners. Unless you already knit, buying wool isn't really something you do on impulse, but once you get going it's really addictive."

"Have you thought about a website?"

"Sort of. It's on my list, but I'm not that good with computers. I'm fine with the orders and e-mails, but that's about it."

"I could help, if you like. It wouldn't need to be anything complicated, but you really should have one. Everyone's got them now."

"Not in Broadgate they haven't."

"Well, you can be the first then."

By the time our food arrives, he's drawn all over three paper napkins, and I seem to have agreed that I need a website, with online shopping capabilities and a customer database.

"Have you got a digital camera?"

"I did have, until Archie dropped it in the sea taking pictures of a crab."

"You'll need one so you can put things up on your site."

"Okay. . . . This fish is delicious. Is yours good?"

"Lovely. What laptop have you got?"

"A blue one."

He smiles and shakes his head.

"What's your budget?"

"About twenty quid."

"Am I sensing a bit of resistance here?"

"Sorry, no. It would be great, I'm sure it would. It's just, well, imagine how you'd feel if I handed you a ball of wool and some needles and asked you to knit a sweater."

He puts his fork down. "Wouldn't it be quite a small sweater, with only one ball of wool?"

"Very clever. A glove then. Wouldn't you be a tiny bit daunted?"

"I'd be more than daunted, particularly if it was an emergency."

"An emergency glove?"

"If we were in the Arctic." He's smiling. "Look, I know what you're saying, but honestly, once I've set it up a monkey could do it. And it could double your business in no

time, maybe even triple, with no real effort. You should think about it, you know."

"I will, I promise."

"Do you think Grace Harrison would let you put her picture up? That would be great—you could do a VIP customers page."

"She might, as long as they got to approve the picture. I could ask her, I suppose. But honestly, Martin, I'm having enough trouble just keeping up with the shop and the kids without going interactive. I'd want to start really slowly, nothing too complicated, and anyway, I don't want to take up too much of your time."

"I've got an ulterior motive, actually."

"Oh?"

"I need your help with Mum."

"Help with what?"

"You know I told you my divorce was through and I wanted to start looking for somewhere to live round here?"

"Yes."

"Well, I've found something. Only it's not really a house, it's more of a barn."

"Barn conversions can be lovely."

"Yes, but this is definitely more like a preconversion barn."

"Has it got a roof?"

"In places."

"Oh."

"It's got so much potential, and I can live there while I do it up, and it'll be great for all my wood and everything, and that's what I really want to do. I don't mind computers,

particularly now I'm freelance, as long as I'm not stuck in an office all day, but it's not what I really care about. And it's important, isn't it, to care about what you do all day?"

"Definitely."

"I want to go into cabinetmaking, general carpentry. I'll probably have to do all sorts until I get established, but that's the plan. So will you help me explain it to her? Dad's all behind it, but you know what she's like. I don't want her to worry."

"Or be popping round every five minutes with a hot pot."

He laughs. "There is that too. I know she'll fuss, and I hate it when she fusses. She comes over so bossy, but she's as soft as anything underneath, you know, she really is. But she worries. And then she gets bossy, and I want to kill her. Which isn't good."

"Of course I'll help, if I can. How bad is this barn? Has it got electricity?"

"Oh yes, all mod cons. Well, not gas, but there's water. Quite a lot of water, actually. Mostly in puddles all over the floor."

Elsie's going to throw a fit.

"But there's a tap, and a loo?"

"Not exactly."

She's going to freak out. Big time.

"So it'll be more like camping then, for a while?"

"Yup. I knew being marched along to Scouts every week would come in handy one day. I can toast marshmallows round the fire while I try to work out how to stop the whole place falling down."

Four napkins later I know exactly where he's going to put the new biodegradable cesspit, because the barn's not on mains drainage, and where the solar panels will go, and the woodburner, and how beautiful the old beams will be once he's cleaned them, apart from the rotten ones, which he'll replace with some green oak he's been saving. And why ash is such a great wood, and what design he's going to use on his chair legs.

Connie brings the coffee over, and he shows her his drawings too, and then he starts telling me about yew, and how pliable it is, which is why they used to make longbows from it, which requires another napkin for illustrations.

He's telling me about the two-hundred-year-old yew tree in the churchyard, which apparently is practically a teenager in yew terms, as we walk back to the house.

"There's one in Ireland that's over a thousand years old. I've only seen pictures, but I'd like to get over there to see it. Not that I'm obsessed or anything. I wouldn't want you to think I was like a train spotter. I haven't been boring you, have I?"

"Not at all."

Actually, this is strangely true; not that I knew I wanted to know quite so much about Wood, but he's so passionate about it I've really enjoyed listening to him.

"Thanks again for the meal, although I still think we should have gone halves with the bill."

"It was my treat, Martin, to say thank you."

"Well, let me know if you need any more shelves. I'd be more than happy. I like having a project on the go."

"It sounds like the barn might be keeping you busy."

"If I get it, yes. But that's a big if."

"I've been thinking about some more shelves downstairs by the shop door, if you're sure, but only if you'll let me pay you this time, especially if you're going into business. You can give me a proper quote. Would that work?"

"That would be great. You can be my first official customer. But I enjoyed doing the last lot, I really did. It took my mind off things. Divorce can be a tricky old business."

"I was so sorry when I heard, Martin. It must have been very difficult for you."

"Me too . . . I mean about your husband. Not that it's the same."

There's a silence.

"Sorry."

"It's fine, Martin. In some ways I think it was probably easier: when something like that happens you get lots of sympathy, but with a divorce everyone takes sides. And it's not always that simple, is it?"

"No. It was a bit humiliating at first, what with him being my boss and everything. But now, to be honest, it's all a huge relief. We should never have got married; I was never the right sort of husband for her. I'm too fond of wandering off to my workshop, and she really hated all that—she wanted everything chrome and glass. We had to have a glass dining room table, you know. God, I hated it. It was mainly my fault. She was so keen to get married, and I wanted to leave home and get away from Mum, have my own place, so I let myself get rushed into it. Anyway, I'm sure she's much happier now."

"And what about you?"

"Me? Oh, a hundred times. A thousand, if I can get my offer in on the barn before anyone else spots it. I've already talked to the agent, and I'm trying to sort out a mortgage. I just hope nobody beats me to it."

"Well, I'll cross my fingers for you."

He seems very pleased with this and starts whistling, just as we turn in to our road, which unfortunately attracts the attention of Trevor, who's bringing Mr. Pallfrey home after their evening promenade. There's a brief tangle of dog leads and legs, and lots of hand licking, and Mr. Pallfrey tells us about his latest plans for the Seaside in Bloom competition as we reach my gate, and there's an awkward pause while Mr. Pallfrey wrestles with Trevor, who seems intent on nipping into my garden to see if he can wake the boys up.

"Good night then, dear. Come on, Trevor, my lad, let's get you indoors—it's getting a bit parky."

"Night, Mr. Pallfrey."

Martin is hesitating by the gate. "Thanks again for supper, Jo. I'll try to get into the shop tomorrow to measure up, shall I?"

"That would be great."

"Night then."

"Night."

He leans forward to kiss me good night. I think he's going for a peck on the cheek, but he ends up kissing my ear. It's quite nice, actually, but he's mortified.

"Oh, God, sorry. I'm a bit out of practice. Sorry."

"It's fine, Martin. It was quite nice."

Even though it's dark, I can see he's blushing.

"So I'll see you tomorrow then, at the shop?"

"Great. And I'll keep my fingers crossed for the barn."

I turn to kiss him good night, but while I'm aiming for something light and friendly, it all goes a bit mouth-to-mouth. Christ, I've done it again.

"Crikey."

His voice has gone all gruff.

"Sorry, Martin. Maybe we should practice on mirrors."

"Sorry?"

"Didn't you do that, practice kissing on the bathroom mirror?"

"No."

"Oh."

"Sounds like fun, though."

"You feel like a bit of a twit, actually."

He laughs. "We must do this again sometime, supper, I mean. We must have supper, or lunch. Or tea. No, not tea. Sorry. Supper. We must have supper."

"I'd like that."

"Would you? Really?"

"Yes."

"Crikey."

"I'll look forward to it. Only, there is one thing."

"Yes. I know. I'll give the mirror thing a go if you think it will help."

"Actually, I meant your mother."

"Oh, right. Well, just ignore that. I really don't care."

"That might be because you don't have to work in a shop with her all day."

"Point taken. Righty-ho, let's keep this secret squirrel, shall we?"

"Secret squirrel?"

"Yes. Low-profile, for now, don't you think? No need for her to be going into one."

"Absolutely."

Secret-squirrel suppers, with potential kissing practice. Who'd have guessed? I'm so pleased I could skip.

"Night, Jo."

"Night, Martin."

He hesitates, and then very slowly and deliberately kisses me on the cheek before he walks back up the road, whistling. Crikey.

Gran's got the front door open before I'm halfway up the path.

"I thought you might ask him in. I've had a little tidy-up in the living room, just in case. Not that I meant any funny business, only I thought you might want a coffee or something."

"Funny business?"

She goes pink. "You know what I mean, nice-looking man like him. Nobody would blame you if you wanted a little fling, you know, pet. Only natural, after all."

Dear God. Now my gran's telling me to go for it.

"Gran, it's very early days, and it was only supper. I've got quite enough on my plate without starting on flings."

She smiles. "You're a good girl, but there's no harm in having a bit of fun, you know."

"I'm having lots of fun, Gran."

"Are you, dear? Well, that's all right then. Life's too short,

that's what I say. Now then, I'll just ring Reg and he'll be here in five minutes. He's watching snooker tonight. Boring game if you ask me, but he seems to like it. Now where did I put my glasses?"

I ring Ellen for a debrief as soon as Reg has collected Gran.
"God, what will his mother say?"

"I'd rather not think about it. I didn't do it on purpose, Ellen. Still, it's rather nice."

"Rather nice? For Christ's sake, darling, it's fucking brilliant. Exactly what you need, a man who's good with his hands."

"Well, let's see how it goes. I'm not going to rush into anything. And neither is he. Which is perfect."

"I love a man who knows how to take his time."

"Stop it."

"When are you seeing him again?"

"Tomorrow at some point, in the shop. He's coming to measure up."

She makes a rude noise. "Try not to snog him in front of his mother, darling, or she'll probably stab you with a knitting needle."

"I know. Actually, we've already agreed to keep a low profile on that front."

"Sounds like a plan. So you're still on for tomorrow night then?"

"Of course."

"Sure? No Saturday-night plans with Dovetail?"

"No. And stop calling him that."

"Well, if you change your mind, ask him round and we can all play strip poker. That always sorts the men from the boys. And Harry's great at male bonding. He'll home in on any secrets."

"I don't think Martin has secrets, Ellen."

"Well, he has now."

I'm driving to Sainsbury's on Saturday morning to stock up on food for the weekend while Gran keeps an eye on the boys at home. I'm trying to decide on roast chicken or lamb for tonight's supper with Ellen and Harry, scribbling on my list every time I get to a traffic light, and a woman comes on the radio and starts talking about her husband, who died last year, in a car crash that sounds weirdly similar to Nick's. There's something about the way she's talking, very quietly, and with fairly long pauses, like she's completely exhausted, that really gets to me, and suddenly I'm crying. And I can't seem to stop. I'm in the car park at Sainsbury's, sobbing, and I can't stop. Bloody hell, this is getting ridiculous. And it doesn't feel like this is really about Nick at all; it's more like something else, like when I was pregnant with Archie and I kept bursting into tears all the time for no reason. And there's no way I can be pregnant, so it can't be that. Unless. Oh. My. God.

Oh. My. God.

My hands are shaking now. Bloody hell. I can't be. I'm just panicking. It must be some kind of hormonal echo because I've been seeing Lily over the past few weeks. It must be some sort of newborn bounce back. I can't be

pregnant—it's too ridiculous. I'll go in and get a test, and it'll be fine. I'll get a trolleyful of shopping and do the test and it'll be negative. And everything will be fine. No surprises from a Christmas moment in Venice, definitely. Christ.

I'm sitting in a Formica cubicle in the loo in Sainsbury's, looking at a plastic stick, and even though I know it's going to be negative, I'm still feeling like I'm dangling off a bit of rope from a very tall building, and I daren't look down. Or up. It's exactly the same make of test that I bought when I was pregnant with Archie. Only last time it was positive, and this time it's going to be negative and I'll feel like a total fool. Actually, I'm going to feel like a total fool whatever the result. Jesus. I'm holding my breath, which probably isn't a very good idea since I really don't want to be discovered by the customer services team passed out on the floor still clutching my plastic wand. Maybe I should try breathing into a paper bag or something. But I've only got a shopping bag, and I'm not sure that would have quite the same effect.

There's a blue cross in the window.

Fuck. It's positive. I read the leaflet again.

Fuck.

I call Ellen.

"What's the matter? You sound really weird. Where are you?"

"In the loo in Sainsbury's. And I need to see you."

"Sorry, what did you say? I can't hear you properly."

"Ellen."

"Yes?"

"I need to see you."

"I'll be there by five, darling. What's the matter?"

"I think I might be pregnant."

"What?"

"Venice."

"Fucking hell."

"I know."

There's a silence.

"Have you done a test?"

"Yes."

There's another silence.

"So it wasn't the custard creams then."

"Sorry?"

"Why you can't fit into your jeans."

"Apparently not."

"Fucking hell."

Oh, God, I'm crying again.

"Sweetheart, please don't cry. Look, I'll come down early; we'll be there as soon as possible, yes?"

"Yes."

"God, darling, just when you thought it was safe to go back in the water. I can't believe it."

"I know."

"I'll be there as soon as I can."

By the time I've got back home and unpacked the shopping, I'm due at the shop. Gran's taken the boys for a walk on the beach with Reg, and Trevor, and I've almost

managed to calm down, mainly by trying not to think about it.

I'm sorting through the mohair and silks, and trying to pretend everything's normal, when Martin arrives and starts trailing a tape measure about, whistling.

"Two sets, or one?"

"Sorry?"

"By the door. Do you want a set either side, or just the one?"

"I'm not sure. Both sides, I think."

"Okay. That shouldn't be too tricky. Great meal last night. But it's my treat, next time."

"Sure."

"So, whenever you're free?"

"Sorry?"

"If you'd like to . . . Look, are you all right? You seem a bit strange. If you've changed your mind or anything, I completely understand." He's looking worried now.

"No, it's not that. It's just, well . . ."

"What?"

"I think I might be pregnant."

Christ, why on earth did I say that?

He takes a step backward.

"But you can't be. It was only a kiss." He sounds panicky now.

The poor man must think I've gone into some kind of nutter meltdown; one kiss and now I'm announcing I'm pregnant.

"I know, Martin. Sorry, I shouldn't have said anything—

this is none of your business. I've only just found out, that's all."

"Oh, right, for a minute there . . . Sorry. So who— I mean, God, sorry, just ignore me. It's none of my business."

"Do you remember that photographer who came into the shop, when Ellen was down a few months ago? The one who was doing the pictures of Grace for the magazine? Well, we met up, in Venice. Anyway, I've only just found out, I haven't really had time to . . . Well, anyway, sorry. I shouldn't be telling you all this. Please don't say anything."

There's a silence.

"Of course. Right. Sorry."

"Please stop saying sorry, Martin."

He moves forward, and then he hesitates. "I should probably go."

"Okay."

"We can sort the shelves out any time—just let me know. I've got all the measurements I need."

"Great."

"But call me, if you need anything. Not that I'll be much use, but still, sorry . . . Look, I'd better be off."

"Thanks, Martin."

Damn. It looks like that's all over, before it even began, whatever it was.

By the time Ellen and Harry arrive, I'm exhausted. I've rearranged most of the stock in the shop in between serving customers and helping Tina pick up the stitches for

the front border of her cardigan—all excellent diversionary tac-
tics, but pretty knackering. The boys are building train track
all over the living room floor. Harry's helping them, while
Ellen and I sit in the kitchen.

"So how are you feeling, darling? A bit less freaked out
now you've had time to think?"

I nod, and then burst into tears, as quietly as I can, so
there's a fair bit of shoulder heaving and smothered gulping.

"It might not be definite, you know. How many tests
have you done?"

"Three."

"Oh."

"Yes. And anyway, I know it is. I can't believe I've been
so stupid—it's just like I was with the boys. Christ, you'd
think I'd have realized sooner. And what if something goes
wrong? What if I die? What'll happen to the boys then?"

"Nothing's going to happen."

"But what if it did?"

"Then me and your gran would take care of them, and
Vin and Lulu, but nothing's going to happen, please. Christ,
you'll have me in tears in a minute."

"I don't know what's the matter with me."

"Yes, you do. Don't you remember how obsessed you got
when you were pregnant with Archie? You made us all
show you our life-insurance policies, and you made Nick go
on that first aid course."

"Yes, and I bloody wish I'd gone on it myself now. I
can't do artificial respiration or anything."

"Neither could Nick. He just did splints and bandages,

remember? He put that bandage on my arm so tight I couldn't hold my glass."

"Yes, but I don't even know how to do splints. Christ, I really don't think I can do this, Ellen."

"You mean not go ahead with it? That would be all right, you know, darling. It's a lot to take on."

"No, I couldn't, not after having the boys. It would feel like tempting fate."

"Sorry?"

"Turning down the chance of another baby, it would feel selfish when I've been so lucky with the boys. The gods would punish me or something. I've looked at too many scan pictures for too long. Christ, what if it's a girl? I can't do girls. I can barely do boys."

She smiles. "Of course you can."

"I'm nearly forty, for Christ's sake. I thought I'd be moving toward hot flushing, not having another baby."

"Forty's not old, darling."

"I know it's not, but I've had my babies, and anyway we were sensible, we used condoms, we really did. It's so embarrassing, I feel like a complete idiot."

"Is it a mistake then?"

"Well, I didn't bloody plan it, that's for sure."

"I know, but I was thinking about it on the drive down, and maybe it's a kind of payback for all the crap you had last year. It's something positive and new, like fate has stepped in. Maybe it's all just part of life's wonderful journey."

She tries to keep a straight face but then snorts with laughter, which makes me laugh too.

"Christ. It's just one thing after another with you, isn't it?"

"Thanks."

"I used to be so jealous of you."

"But not anymore though, right?"

She smiles. "No. I still am, actually."

"Then you must be mad."

"Darling, think about it: you meet Nick and get married and have two lovely boys, and it was all so perfect, I could hardly bear it sometimes. Not that I was in love with Nick or anything like that."

We both smile.

"But still, it was all so grown-up and real, I used to feel like your silly teenage sister sometimes, never really getting to do any of the proper stuff."

"And that's another thing I can't get my head round, the idea that it's not Nick's baby, you know. I want to ring him up in Jerusalem and say number three is on the way, and hear him say, 'Oh, Christ, we just got rid of the cot,' like he did with Archie. And then he'd get tearful when we went for the scan, and pretend he wasn't, and flirt with the midwife."

She puts her hand on my arm.

"Stop it."

"Okay."

"This is your baby. And Daniel's. At least I assume it's Daniel's, unless you've got any more surprises up your sleeve. God, I need a drink."

"So do I, but I think I'd better stick to tea. There's still some of that vodka you brought down last time in the pantry, if you fancy that?"

"Hallelujah."

She fills a tumbler with ice, pours herself what must be a quadruple vodka, and takes a more modest one in for Harry.

"They're having a fabulous time in there—they've got trains everywhere. So, have you thought about what you're going to do, about Daniel?"

"I think I'll wait, until I'm sure everything's all right."

"Good plan."

"And then, I don't know. I'll have to tell him, but I don't think he'll want to be part of it, not now he's back with Liv. And that's fine."

"Is it?"

"Yes. Absolutely. He didn't sign up for this."

"Neither did you."

"No, but I've got a choice. So if I go for it, and I will, then I don't want him guilt-tripped into anything, mucking us all about. I really don't want that. It'd be crap for everyone, but most important of all it'd be crap for the boys."

"Or boys and girl."

"Please."

"Well, good for you. I'd leave it until you've had the baby, if I was you. That way, if he wants a DNA test it'll be simple."

"I don't think it'll come to that, Ellen."

"He's loaded, darling—he'll think you're after his money. Which you bloody should be. Why should this be down to you?"

"Because it's me that's having it. I haven't asked him to decide, and I'm not going to. This is my choice, and there's

no point pretending there's anything else going on. I'll tell him, of course I will, and then it'll be down to what he wants to do about visits or whatever, but it'll be nothing more than that. We're not a couple, Ellen, we never were. Christ, if you'd told me this time last year that all this would be happening, I'd never have believed you."

"No, but at least you're making hay while the sun shines."

"I don't like hay—it brings me out in a rash."

"I'm trying to be helpful here. Work with me, would you? When you think about it, all the really big stuff just happens, you know, the really major stuff, like having babies. And dying. Not that the two are connected. But we think we're in control, although all we can really do is faff about around the edges."

"Have you been reading one of your Who Moved My Chicken Soup from Venus books again?"

"No. But it's true, you can only play the cards you're dealt, right?"

"Well, I think I'll fold on this hand, if nobody minds. I'll just sit this one out and eat crisps."

She smiles.

"But you're definitely having it, right? For better or worse?"

"Yes. And definitely bloody poorer."

"Well then, so am I. I'm going to go for it."

"Go for what?"

"A baby. There, I've said it. I really want one. And if I may just say, I think it's absolutely typical of you to get pregnant at the exact moment I realize it's what I really want. I'm going to be so jealous, all over again."

"Oh, sweetheart, I thought you'd already decided."

"Can't a girl change her mind?"

"Have you talked to Harry?"

"He's up for it, if I am. But he's not desperate. So it's fine either way. Just think, if I get a move on, we could be pregnant together. Wouldn't that be fabulous? I can be a bigger bride than I was planning on, and we can sit knitting and looking at our big fat stomachs."

"I can already do that, thank you very much."

"Yes, but at least you've got a good excuse now."

"It's very early days, you know, Ellen. Anything might happen. Things go wrong all the time."

"I know. But I can see you with another baby."

"Can you?"

"Yes."

"How am I doing?"

"Great. And the boys are too."

"Thank God for that. If I survived last year, I can survive this one, right?"

"Exactly. And if you have a girl and I have a boy, we can always do a swap, can't we? Boys aren't really into shopping, are they?"

"Not so you'd notice; not unless it involves buying plastic swords."

She laughs. "I'm starving. What have you got in the fridge?"

"God knows. What do you fancy?"

"Lamb chops with celeriac mash, and a passion-fruit pavlova."

"Spaghetti carbonara? I meant to buy a chicken, but I

forgot. But I've got two packs of Kit Kats, and a jumbo assortment of chocolate mini-rolls."

"Sounds good to me."

"Go and sell it to the boys, would you?"

"Sorry?"

"Sign them up for carbonara, and don't mention the Kit Kats, or they'll want them now. And don't let Jack start obsessing about the bacon. He thinks he doesn't like it, but he does. And Archie's not keen on Parmesan—he'll ask you if there's cheese. Just say no. He likes it when it's melted, so I don't tell him."

"So no bacon, invisible cheese, and no mention of Kit Kats to soften the blow. And if I fail?"

"They'll both whine and refuse to eat anything, and Archie will get very stroppy—he always does when he's hungry—and throw a fit."

"Bloody hell. So no pressure at all then?"

"Welcome to my world."

now we
are six

April

"What time's your hospital appointment?"

"Ten, but that could mean lunchtime if they're anything like they were in London."

"And you're sure you don't want me to come, darling?"

"I'll be fine, Ellen. Jack, go up and find your socks, and tell Archie to do his teeth, love. We need to leave for school soon."

"Are you still feeling sick?"

"A bit."

"Isn't that supposed to wear off after the first twelve weeks, or something?"

Ellen's been doing her research; she's still talking about

having a baby, and she always likes to be thoroughly prepared when she's about to embark on a big story.

"I polished off two chocolate Easter eggs last night, so I think that might have something to do with it. I was trying to finish them up so the boys would stop bickering."

"Isn't that cheating?"

"I do it every year, otherwise I've got bowls of half-eaten chocolate in the fridge for weeks. Jack can make a small piece of chocolate last longer than anyone I know."

"But that's only to upset Archie, right?"

"Mainly, but he's always been the same—he loves saving things."

"He'll probably grow up to be a bank manager."

"Well, that'll come in handy. Oh, hang on a minute."

There's thudding and shouting coming from upstairs, and with the help of my maternal X-ray vision, I know that Jack isn't letting Archie get any toothpaste.

"Stop it, Jack, and come down and get your shoes on."

There's a silence, which means there'll be Quiet Seething going on, but at least we won't end up with toothpaste all over the bathroom floor again.

"All quiet on the Western Front?"

"Temporarily."

"How's the shop going?"

"Fine. I'm sure I can build it up more, and Martin's starting on the shelves at the weekend so I can have more stock out."

"So he's got over you being up the duff then?"

"Sort of. We didn't really mention it last time I saw him. He seemed a bit distracted; I think he's concentrating on his

offer for the barn. But he was talking about the website again, and that's bound to help sales. What's that thing they say, Work smarter, not harder?"

"Now you're talking. Sell up and come back to town and I'll get you back into news. You'll be earning a fortune in no time, and we can have lunch, like we used to. It'll be great."

"And do I tell them I'm pregnant at the interview, or what? Actually, I probably won't need to tell them—you can already tell."

"Well, after the baby then. It's a brilliant plan, and we could do a nanny share."

"Maybe we should wait until you're actually pregnant before we start talking about nannies."

"It's on my list."

"I know, sweetheart, but sometimes it takes a while."

"It didn't for you."

"Yes, it did, with Jack."

"Oh yes, I'd forgotten about that."

"I'm sure it'll be fine."

"A nanny share would save us a fortune, right?"

"Yes, but I like it here, Ellen, you know that, and so do the boys, and I need Gran as my backup. I don't think I can do this without her, I really don't. She makes me feel safe, and I can use as much of that as I can get at the moment."

"I suppose so."

"And anyway, I can't afford to live in London. Whatever I was earning would just go on the mortgage and child care, and I'd be no further forward—and a lot more stressed out. And so would the boys."

Archie comes downstairs, looking furious. "He spitted on my arm, on purpose."

"Look, I'd better go. There's spitting going on down here. But I'll call you later."

"The minute you've finished at the hospital."

"Promise."

"Good luck, darling."

"He did it on purpose. He did, Mum. Tell him."

"I'm sure it wasn't on purpose, was it, Jack?"

Jack's standing in the kitchen looking sheepish while I de-toothpaste his brother.

"Sorry, Arch."

"No, you're not. I don't accept. You can say that when somebody says sorry and you don't believe them. Mrs. Berry said you can."

"Right."

"Yes, because Harry pushed me when I was doing painting, and he said sorry, but he didn't mean it because he was smiling, and he did it on purpose because I was doing such good painting. So I pushed him right back, and he made such a fuss. Like this." Archie starts yelling and clutching his arm. "Stupid baby, like I'd really hurt him. But I will do, if he does it again."

"Hurting people never works, Archie, you know that. It only makes things worse. What did Mrs. Berry say?"

"She said we were both wrong because pushing is never the answer. But it is, with Harry it is."

"No, it isn't, Archie. If everyone went round pushing, think how horrible it would be."

"It wouldn't be horrible for people who were good at pushing."

"But sooner or later they'd meet someone who was bigger than them, and then everyone would get pushed."

He glares at me. "Don't say it, I know. You have to be nice and kind and la la la. It's so stupid."

"Archie."

"All right, keep your hair on."

"I've told you not to say that, Archie. It's very rude. And if Harry does it again, just find Mrs. Berry and ask her to help you. Promise?"

"Yes, because I'm one of her favorites."

Jack tuts.

"I am, I asked her. And she said all her children are her favorites, so I said she was my favorite, in the whole world, of all the teachers, even Mr. O'Brien, and he has sweets. And she was very pleased, I could tell."

"Into the car now, love."

"Mum, can Mrs. Berry come to my birthday party?"

"Yes, but she might be busy."

I've noticed that teachers tend to steer well clear of birthday parties. Not that I blame them: turning up at a series of thirty birthday parties to pass the parcel in the course of an academic year has got to be way beyond the call of duty, even if you have signed up for one of the caring professions.

"But we can still give her a party bag if she can't come?"

"Yes, of course. Now find your book bag, love."

Damn, that's something else I've forgotten to put on my list for his birthday party: bloody going-home bags. Although

at least round here you can get away with a packet of Smarties and a slice of cake, unlike the London versions, which used to get more elaborate every year. Archie wants the same sort of bonfire party that we had for Jack last year, when we'd only been here a few months. Only with Superheroes fancy dress. But at least he's forgotten about the fireworks.

"Mummy."

"Yes, Archie."

"I want fireworks at my party too, like Jack, only I want more sparkers and I don't want Elsie to be in charge of them because she's too bossy."

"It's sparklers, Archie, and I'm not sure you can get them this time of year."

"If you try hard I bet you can."

Bugger.

"Just pop yourself on the bed and we'll have a look, shall we?"

The ultrasound woman is wearing too much lipstick and has one of those special Health Professional smiles. Actually, I'm feeling sick, so I wonder if she'll still be smiling when I throw up all over her sensible shoes.

"It might take me a moment or two to find Baby once we get started, so don't worry."

Don't worry? Why would I be worrying? This is only the vital moment of truth when I get the final proof that this is really happening. I've been half pretending to myself that this is some kind of phantom pregnancy dreamt up by my

hormones, and half obsessing about where to put a cot and how the boys will react. But after this moment there'll be no going back. If there's a baby on this monitor screen in a minute or two, I'll have to say good-bye to my phantom get-out-of-jail-free card. I sneaked a look at one of my old pregnancy books when I was in the bath last night, and the baby should be around three inches long now, and have fingers and toes. It might even be learning how to suck its thumb. Oh, God.

"Just lift up your T-shirt, dear. The gel is a bit chilly, I'm afraid. Have you been feeling any movements?"

"I think so."

Tiny flutterings, which I remember from Archie, like I've drunk too much fizzy water too quickly. Although I've been trying to cut down on tea and coffee by drinking bottles of San Pellegrino, which I seem to have developed a passion for, so it might be that. Still, at least I'll be hydrated, even if I'm not actually pregnant.

I'm looking at a flickering screen, and there's nothing. No baby, no flutterings, nothing. Oh, God.

"Now you might feel a slight pressure, and— Oh, sorry, I haven't switched the monitor on. Now then, let's have a look, shall we? This might take a minute . . . Oh, there you are."

There's a baby. On the monitor. Who appears to be waving at me.

Christ. A real baby.

I half want to wave back; actually, what I really want is to touch the screen to say hello. There's a tiny little waving person, just like I remember with Jack and Archie. And it

feels like it's nothing to do with me, like the baby has just been getting on with it, despite having a mother who's so daft she didn't even know she was pregnant. Perhaps the waving thing is an attempt to make sure I've finally got the message. Hello. I'm here.

I'm crying now, fairly modest, quiet weeping rather than donkey-noises sobbing.

"Sorry."

"No need to apologize, dear."

She hands me a tissue, and I lie looking at the screen while she clicks buttons, taking measurements.

"You must have one of the best jobs in the world."

"Most days, yes. Sometimes it can be difficult."

There's a silence, and suddenly I feel a wave of guilt: there are so many women out there who long for this moment, just to get to this stage, and I've been trying to pretend it's not really happening. But not anymore.

"I had twins in before you, and that's always lovely."

Bloody hell. Twins.

"There's no sign of twins, though, is there?"

She smiles. "Not as far as I can see."

"And everything looks okay?"

"Perfectly fine."

Perfectly fine. The baby is perfectly fine.

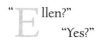"llen?"

"Yes?"

"It's a baby, all perfectly fine, the right size and everything, and they've done all the tests and the GP will get the

results, but it all looks fine, a bit on the large side for my dates, but all healthy. And my blood pressure and everything else is totally normal, except I keep crying. Isn't that wonderful?"

"Well, thank fuck for that. I've been feeling pretty tearful myself, all bloody morning."

"I got to see the consultant, which is more than I ever did in London. He was quite nice, actually, no amusing bow ties or anything, and he didn't treat me like I was an idiot. They think I should go for a C-section, like with Archie, but I can have a trial labor if I want one."

"Trial labor, Christ. Couldn't they come up with something more depressing-sounding?"

"They all talk like that. Anyway, I said I'd think about it, but I'm pretty sure I'll go for the C-section. That way I can choose the date and get things organized for the boys. And it's safer for the baby too, especially with an ancient mother like me."

"Hello?"

"Anything over nineteen is ancient in the wonderful world of pregnancy, don't worry about it. And under nineteen you're a teenager breeder and they make you go to special classes, so you can't win."

"Fuckers."

"There was one bad moment, when I was booking in with the midwife. She asked me for my husband's name, so I gave it to her, and it was only when she asked me for his work number that I remembered. How daft is that?"

"Sweetheart."

"She had to get a new form out and start all over again,

so I felt like a complete idiot. But at least it meant she didn't ask me for the father's name. She did ask me if I was going to have a birth partner, though."

Ellen's desperate to be the official birth partner, and she's been dropping increasingly unsubtle hints about it.

"And?"

"I told them I'd call Mum tonight, see if she's up for it."

"Oh, right."

"Ellen, I'm pregnant, not insane. Of course I want you, if you're up for it. Although if a big story breaks and you're on a flight somewhere, I'll understand. I'll ask Gran too, as backup."

"Tell her I'm the official birth partner: I don't want her muscling in. I'm going to put it on my CV."

"Britain's Favorite Broadcaster and part-time birth partner?"

"Yes."

B y the time I get to the shop, it's nearly half past twelve, and Elsie races off home to get her washing in because it looks like rain.

"I think Martin might be home, so I'll probably stop and make him a bit of lunch."

"Of course. I'll be here until three, there's no need to rush."

Actually, a couple of hours in the shop is just what I need. I can't help thinking everyone must have guessed that I'm pregnant, so it'll be nice to have a bit of peace.

I'm standing behind the counter looking at my scan picture when Martin comes in, whistling.

"I got it."

"Sorry?"

"The barn."

"Oh, Martin, that's brilliant."

"I've got the papers from the agent's, if you'd like to see?"

"I'd love to."

The papers are creased and folded, with splatters of mud on the back, so I think he's probably been out there measuring things. It looks a lot more like a large field with the remnants of a barn collapsing in it than I was expecting, but I'm sure it'll be stunning when he gets it finished.

"It's beautiful."

"I know, I still can't quite believe it. Normally when I want something, it's a pretty safe bet that it won't happen."

"But not this time."

"No." He's beaming.

"Well, I'm really pleased for you, and if there's anything I can do, just let me know. Have you told Elsie yet?"

"No, I'm building up to it."

"Well, let me know if you need backup. Shall I start talking about barns being brilliant investments?"

"Please, that would be great."

He leans over the counter and kisses me on the cheek, and I hand him back the papers as Elsie opens the shop door.

Bugger.

I don't think she saw anything, because I'm pretty sure she'd have slapped me by now if she had, but still.

"There you are, Martin. I got you a bit of ham for your lunch. I thought you'd be back."

"I did say I'd be out, Mum."

She gives me a furious look.

"Martin was just talking to me about the website, Elsie. I think it'll be great for business."

If she finds out he's told me about the barn before her, I'll never hear the end of it.

"Can't see the point of it myself. Not many of our customers have got computers, you know."

"Yes, but that's the point, Mum. It'll help you get new ones. Anyway, I'd better be off, Jo. I'll put a few more ideas down on paper for you, and then show you."

"Lovely."

He leans forward and kisses me again, like it's something he does to everybody, which he doesn't. People don't really go in for social kissing round here. But still, you've got to admire his nerve. He winks at me.

"I'll see you later, Mum. What time will you be back? Only I've got something I want to talk to you about."

"Oh yes, what's that then?"

"It's private, Mum. Nothing to worry about, just an idea I've had I want to talk through with you."

She smiles, clearly mollified by the idea that it's not something he wants to talk about in front of me.

"Well, I'll be back by quarter to six. I've got some lamb chops in for tea."

He goes off whistling, and Elsie smiles. "I'll just pop the kettle on, shall I, dear?"

"Lovely."

Clever old Martin.

I'm sitting in the car outside school looking at my scan picture again. I'm a few minutes early, and I don't want to risk standing in the playground without backup in case Annabel collars me and sticks me on another one of her bloody lists. Connie's at home with Mark, wallpapering their spare bedroom, so I'm picking up Nelly and Marco today. She's really excited about her mum and dad coming over from Italy, and she wants everything perfect for them, so we've battled with Gran's sewing machine and made new curtains in the shop, which took us nearly a whole afternoon with Elsie nipping up with handy hints, and now she's papering and painting. God, I suppose I'll have to start on some of that too now, and turn the spare room into a bedroom for the baby. Still, first things first; I'll have to work out how I'm going to tell the boys before I start worrying about bedrooms.

There's a knock on the car window that makes me jump, and of course it's bloody Annabel.

"Hello, you were looking very thoughtful."

I walk across the road with her.

"Just running through a few ideas for the shop, Annabel."

"It must be such a strain, running your little shop. I don't know how you do it, you working mums, I really don't. I never seem to have enough hours in the day as it is.

Of course, I do have very high standards, I accept that. But still."

I try a smile, which she ignores, and now I'm panicking that she saw me looking at the scan picture; I'm trying to remember if I'd put it back into my diary before she knocked on the window, and I'm fairly sure I did, but still.

"Well, I must get on, PTA business calls. Mr. O'Brien has asked me to look into more sports equipment, so I've got brochures arriving I need to check on. So important, proper equipment. We take Harry to a marvelous gym, private, of course, but well worth it; he's doing so well in his martial arts class, they want to move him up a group. You should take your boys, although the classes are mainly on Saturday, so I suppose that might be a problem for you, being in the shop. Anyway, must dash."

Bloody hell, so now I've got to feel guilty we don't belong to a gym, on top of everything else. Although I'm not sure I'd really want them learning martial arts in any case; bedtime is tricky enough already without finding myself overpowered by two small people in baggy white pajamas.

After sausages and chips for tea, which I've chosen in the hopes of building up some goodwill, even though the oven chips always weld themselves to the baking tray, they're both sitting watching cartoons relatively peacefully when Gran arrives to show me her latest batch of cruise brochures. Actually, maybe now would be a good time to show her my scan picture—it'd certainly take her mind off cabin sizes. And if bloody Annabel Morgan did catch a

glimpse in the car, there'll probably be an emergency PTA communiqué circulating tomorrow, so it might be handy if Gran already knew.

"You're looking peaky. Are you sure you're not coming down with anything, pet?"

"No, I'm fine, Gran."

"Good."

Here goes.

"There was something I wanted to tell you, though."

"I knew it."

"Knew what?"

"There's something wrong, isn't there? I knew it. Mrs. Marwell saw you at the doctor's a couple of weeks ago, and again last week. She told Betty, and she said you looked ever so pale. What is it?"

Bloody hell, they're like the secret service. Thank God none of them have really got the hang of mobile phones or they'd be group-texting video snippets backward and forward.

"I'm fine, Gran, honestly."

"But?"

"There's no but."

"Josephine, this is your gran you're talking to. I can see it on your face."

Bugger, I'm really mucking this up.

"I'm not ill, Gran. It's just, well, I'm pregnant."

There's a pause, and then she smiles. "Well, thank heavens for that. I've been that worried. But are you sure, pet? It could be the change, you know. We start very early in our family."

I reach for my diary and hand her the scan picture.

"Well, bless my soul. And how did that happen then? You don't have to say if you don't want to. He's not anyone local, is he?"

"No, Gran."

"Well, that'll make things easier. You know what people are like round here, putting two and two together and coming up with six. So will he be moving down here then?"

"I don't think so, Gran. He's just someone I met, nothing long-term . . . God, this is embarrassing. I'm not in the habit of doing this sort of thing, you know. In fact, never."

"I know you're not, pet. Now don't you go upsetting yourself. What's done is done, and we'll manage. Let me see the picture again. Isn't that lovely? Look at those tiny fingers, like little pearls. Actually, I think he looks a bit like our Archie."

"So you think it's a boy then?"

"Oh yes, you're carrying like you did with the boys. But it's what you think that matters, pet."

"Well, it was a bit of a shock at first, but now I've got used to the idea I'm pleased. I really am. And I feel very lucky. I never thought I'd have another baby, but now, well, I'm very pleased."

I haven't realized how true this is until I've actually said it out loud. Nick and I never talked about having another baby. I knew he wouldn't be keen, so we never discussed it, and I sort of shelved the idea without ever realizing that I'd wanted one.

"Well, isn't that grand? And how are the boys taking it?"

"I haven't told them yet. I wanted you to be here."

She smiles. "Well, there's no time like the present."

"Yes, but what if they're upset? They've had so much to cope with, Gran, and I don't want them worrying. Maybe I should wait a bit."

"You don't want secrets, pet. They're terrible things, secrets are."

"I know, and it probably won't seem real to them, not until there's actually a baby. Okay, let's tell them. I've got strawberry ice cream in the fridge—I thought it might help."

"Good idea, pet."

The strawberry ice cream goes down very well, and the boys are both remarkably calm about the idea. In fact, they're much more interested in getting back to their cartoons, although they are unanimous that under no circumstances am I to have a girl. Apart from that, they seem fine about it. But I'm still bracing myself for Questions later.

Gran shows me her cruise brochures and goes off to tell Reg the good news, and it's nearly half past eight by the time I'm getting them into bed.

"Night, Archie."

"Night, Mum. And, Mum?"

"Yes?"

"If you have a baby, will we get presents? When Seth Johnson's mum had their baby, he got a present. He got a bike."

"Did he? Well, we'll have to see about that."

He claps his hands.

"And I won't be the baby so Jack can't call me a baby

anymore, can he? Ever. And I already know what I want for my present."

"Oh yes, what's that?"

"A dog. Just like Trevor."

"Night, Archie."

"Night, Mum. And will I get my fish for my birthday, do you think?"

"I don't know, Archie. We'll have to wait and see."

I've already got him two goldfish in a small tank, which Gran's keeping in her kitchen. I've been telling him one of the reasons we can't have a dog is that we need to practice on smaller pets first, so he added goldfish to his birthday-wish list after I vetoed a snake or anything with fur. I've bought him a starter tank, and a little pirate's chest that bubbles air through the water, so I'm hoping the fish will survive at least a few weeks.

"I really want them, more than anything, I do, and then you can see how sensible I am and we can have a dog."

"Night, Archie."

Jack's fussing with the knitted blanket I made for him when we first moved here as I'm tucking him in. He likes it folded over his duvet, but only a couple of inches.

"Put it on again properly, how you do it, please, Mum."

"Better?"

"Yes."

"Night, love."

"Mum?"

Here we go again.

"Yes, Jack."

"You know the new baby?"

"Yes."

"Well, is it left over, from when Dad was alive?"

Christ, I wasn't expecting that one.

"No, darling."

"So it'll have a different dad then?"

"Yes."

"But not living with us. Not like Dad?"

"No."

He's very quiet.

"I'm sorry, love. Does it all feel a bit confusing?"

He starts to cry, silently like he does, as I kneel down by his pillow and put my arms round him. "What's the matter, sweetheart?"

"It's just I thought he might be coming back. Not really. You know. Just. Well, a bit."

I hold him and stroke his back.

"But he's not, is he?"

"No, love. If I could fix it, I would. You know that. But some things can't get fixed."

"I know. It's a bloody bugger."

"Jack!"

"That's very rude, isn't it?"

"Yes. But you can say it one more time if you like. Just once, though, and then never again."

"Bloody bugger." He giggles. "If Archie knew it, he'd probably say it at school. But I never say it at school because I'm your best boy, aren't I, Mum?"

"My best big boy."

"And I always will be. Forever and ever?"

"Yes."

"Will you stay here, until I'm asleep, and do my arm, in circles? Please. Very please." He snuggles into his pillow and drapes his arm over his blanket so I can stroke the back of it, in circles.

"Okay, but not for hours or my knees will go numb."

"I'll be as quick as I can, but promise to stay until I'm proper asleep."

"I promise."

I tidy up the bathroom and go downstairs, but I can't settle; I keep thinking about Daniel, and how it feels wrong that I've got a scan picture and he doesn't know anything about it. Maybe I should call him, but then again perhaps I should wait. I don't really need him to know, not for me. And I could definitely do without any more stress right now. I'm going through my Filofax writing in all my hospital appointments, but I keep looking at his number. Right. I'll have a cup of tea and make a decision. Perhaps biscuits might help. I'll write myself a script and see how it feels; that always helps when you've got a tricky call to make. And then I'll decide.

Christ.

The biscuits haven't really helped, but if I want to call him I'll have to get on with it before it gets much later. I dial the number, feeling sick. But that might be the biscuits.

"Hello, Daniel, it's Jo."

There's a pause.

"Jo? Oh, Jo, great. How's it going, angel?"

"Fine, thanks."

"Boys all right?"

"They're great."

"I was thinking about you the other day. Liv was knitting and it reminded me of your shop. How's business?"

"Pretty good, thanks."

Oh, God, this is much harder than I thought it would be. And we've already gone off my script. I glance down at my piece of paper.

"Daniel, is this a good time to talk?"

"Sure."

"There's something I need to tell you."

There's a silence.

"It's, well, it's . . . I'm going to have a baby."

"Are you? Well, congratulations, angel. That's great, if you're pleased. Which I guess you are or you wouldn't be telling— Oh, fuck."

"Yes, but I really don't want you to feel—"

"You mean?"

"Yes."

"Fucking hell."

"I know, and I'm sorry. Well, not sorry exactly, I'm really pleased, of course, but—" Now I'm sounding like a nutter. I look down at my paper again. "Even though this wasn't planned and I'm perfectly happy to go it alone. I want you to understand that, perfectly happy. But I thought you should know, so you can be as involved as you want to be, or not at all. Either way, the baby has to be the important one in all this, but I wanted you to know."

"When's it due?"

"October."

"So is it too late not to go through with it?"

Christ.

"Yes. And anyway, I'm sure I've made the right choice."

"For you, maybe."

"Look, I know this is a shock, Daniel, but once you've had a chance to think about it, I'm sure we can sort something out that works for everyone."

"There's no we."

"Sorry?"

He's sounding much more hostile now. "The only we in this is me and Liv. We're talking about getting married. So the last thing I need is something like this fucking dumped on me. You're a hundred percent sure, right, that it's mine?"

"Of course I'm sure."

"Well, I don't want Liv to know, okay? Not until I've had a chance to think about this."

"That's up to you, Daniel."

"What do you mean by that? Is that some sort of threat?"

Damn, I don't think I'm handling this very well.

"No, of course not, for heaven's sake. I only meant that it's your business. I'm only telling you because I thought you had a right to know. I don't want anything from you, Daniel—we'll be fine, all of us. The boys are quite excited. I just wanted you to know, that's all. I thought you should have a choice."

"Well, it doesn't feel like much of a fucking choice."

"I meant a choice about how you want to handle it."

"I don't. Christ, if Liv finds out, she'll throw me out, for sure. Jesus fucking Christ. Look, I'll have to call you back."

"Of course."

The line goes dead, and I feel strangely calm.

Christ, what a relief. I'm not keeping anything secret anymore. And talking to him again has reassured me that somewhere deep down I'm not secretly hoping for a hearts and flowers moment. I was worried that when I spoke to him I'd mind if he wasn't pleased. But I don't, not really. Hopefully he'll call back and want to visit when the baby's here or something, but if he doesn't then that'll be fine too. Actually, I feel a bit sorry for him; I think I've got a good idea of how his relationship with Liv is working out, and it's just like it used to be with me and Nick, where everything is filtered through them and what they'll think. But I've told Daniel now, so I can get on with it, and not feel like I'm somehow cheating not telling him.

Great. I call Ellen.

"How did it go?"

"You were right. Gran's thrilled, and the boys are fine about it."

"Told you."

"I'm not sure Daniel's going to be rushing to Mothercare, though."

"Christ. You called him."

"Yes."

"And?"

"He wasn't pleased. Pretty hostile, actually. I think it's all about Liv, and what she'll think. Which I can understand."

"Tough. He'll just have to get over it. It's not like you planned this."

"I know, I said that."

"You never know, he might discover some hidden paternal instinct. Give him time."

"I doubt it. But that's fine. I can do this on my own. I always knew I would really. I'm sure I can make it work, if I'm careful."

"You're not still worrying about money, are you?"

"Ellen, I'm pregnant with two chocoholics to support. It's a tad worrying, yes."

"I know, but Daniel can cover some of it, and at least you haven't got a mortgage to support as well."

"They'd probably have repossessed the house by now if I did. I barely make enough to keep us going as it is, without adding a baby into the mix. And I don't want Daniel's money."

"But—"

"We've had this conversation, Ellen. Either he's around or he's not, but it can't be about money. I'll manage."

"Use Nick's life insurance."

"That's my rainy-day money."

"Surely this counts as a spot or two of rain, darling?"

"Not yet it doesn't, and I've still got a bit left over from selling up in London, so if I'm careful I must be able to manage. The shop's starting to do quite well, you know. I just need to make it do better."

"Darling, you can't double your business and do the mum thing and be pregnant with number three all at the same time."

"Why not?"

"Because you'll be completely knackered."

"Well, that'll make a nice change then."

I'm in the shop the next morning, trying to pluck up the courage to ring Mum. I couldn't face it last night, although I did call Vin, after I spoke to Ellen, and he was lovely, and Lulu came on the phone and got very excited, which was nice. But I'm pretty sure Mum's going to be less enthusiastic. She was distinctly underwhelmed when I told her I was pregnant with Jack, and with Archie she gave me a lecture about wasting my life changing nappies. So I'm not holding out much hope for this time.

I'm changing the till roll as a diversionary tactic when Tina comes in, looking very excited.

"Maggie's just been in to tell us we've won—the library's staying open. They had a meeting last night, and it's official."

"That's brilliant."

"I bet our knit-in helped, and the petition."

"I'm sure it did."

Actually, I think Grace arriving and giving a megastar interview to Ellen about how local libraries are vital, with us all sitting knitting in the background, is probably what swung it, but never mind.

"We'll have to celebrate at Stitch and Bitch tonight."

"Good idea."

She smiles. "And we'll have something else to celebrate, by all accounts?"

"Oh?"

"Betty was in the salon this morning. She was so excited she couldn't help herself, and your Gran's tickled pink, apparently. But of course we won't talk about it, if you don't want everyone to know."

"So who knows then?"

"Everyone."

"Right."

"And your gran says you'll be on your own. Is that right?"

"Yes."

"Well, good for you. But if he's from round here, we'll make sure he does the right thing, don't you worry. My Graham can be very persuasive when he wants to be."

"Thanks, Tina, but it's fine, honestly."

"You know how people talk. They'll be trying to guess who he is if you don't put them straight."

Christ, it'll be like a guess-the-weight-of-the-cake competition.

"Maybe we could do a raffle for our white-elephant stall at the Summer Fayre. I'll probably be looking like an elephant by then anyway."

"Good idea."

"Or I could put a notice in the shop window. Do you think that would stop them?"

"It might do. Or you could just tell Betty and leave it for an hour or two; she'll make sure word gets round. Anyway, I just wanted to tell you about the library, and say congratulations, I think it's lovely. I'll see you later."

"Thanks, Tina. And he's not a local, okay?"

"Right you are. Leave it with me."

Betty and Gran are in next. Gran looks flushed, and Betty looks sheepish.

"I'm ever so sorry, Jo. Mary made me promise not to say anything, but I was that excited, only I shouldn't have spoken out of turn. And I'm very sorry." She looks really upset; actually, I think she may have been crying. Gran can be very forthright when she wants to be.

"People were going to find out sooner or later, Betty. Don't worry about it."

Gran tuts. "Yes, but it could have been later, couldn't it, if someone had been able to keep a secret."

"It's not like it was a proper secret, Gran, not with the boys knowing; you know what Archie's like. He's probably making an announcement in assembly."

She laughs as Betty hands me an envelope. "It's only those snaps I was telling you about. I've been meaning to bring them in for ages. I got some copies done for you."

There are two black-and-white photographs of Betty and Gran in the war, one of them sitting knitting on the seafront, and another of Betty looking rather glamorous in a summer frock and sandals, standing in front of the shop with a soldier.

"And I just want to say I think it's marvelous, and I'd have done the same thing, if I was you. Well, I nearly did. I expect your Gran's told you."

"No."

"It was a long time ago, and things were different then, of course. He was American; he was killed before I knew I'd fallen for a baby, but I was that happy I didn't care. Only it wasn't to be." She's close to tears now.

"I'm so sorry, Betty."

"It was a long time ago now, love, and I married my Ted a year later, and then we had our Simon, so it all worked out in the end. Although I do wonder sometimes. I'd have loved another one. Anyway, I keep telling my Simon he needs to get a move on and have some grandchildren for me, because I'm not going to last forever."

Gran pats her on the arm. "You'll see us all out, Betty. Come on, we'll be late if we don't get to that bus. Bye, pet."

"Bye, and thanks for the photographs, Betty. They're lovely."

"I'm due at the Lifeboats this afternoon, but I'll probably pop in later."

"Thanks, Gran."

She's got a long-standing feud with Mrs. Oakley over who gets to operate the till in the Lifeboat tearoom, and Betty tends to go in with her when she's on duty, for moral support.

"Don't you worry, Mary, I'll soon put her right. I'm not in the mood for her today, I'm really not."

I've got quite a collection of photographs in the shop now. Maggie took some black-and-white ones of us at the Stitch and Bitch group, and there's one of the magazine ones that Daniel took of Grace sitting knitting in a rowing boat wearing a ball gown. And a lovely one of Gran, with

me aged about eight, sitting next to her on the settee knitting a doll's blanket with pink sparkly wool I remember
loving. I'll put these ones from Betty in frames too, and they
can go up behind the till with the others.

I'm knitting a sleeve for Connie's sweater when Elsie
bustles in, looking pretty narky. She doesn't even wait to
take her coat off.

"I gather we're to expect a happy event." She's standing
with her arms folded, looking furious.

Maybe I should put that notice in the shop window
after all.

"Yes, sorry, Elsie. I was hoping to tell you myself, but—"

"You should have told me first."

"Sorry?"

"I already know all about it, you know."

"All about what, Elsie?"

"You and my Martin, having supper. I suppose the barn
will have to go on hold now."

"I think you should talk to Martin about that."

"Well, he can't go wasting his money on a dirty old barn
with a baby on the way, can he? And before you say anything, just you let me finish. I can't say I'm pleased about the
way it's all been handled. Not at all. I should have been told
first, properly, and I'll be having words with him, you can
count on that. But what's done is done."

Bloody hell.

"Elsie, you don't think the baby has got anything to do
with Martin, do you?"

"I'm sure I don't know what to think."

"Well, it hasn't."

"Are you sure?"

I give her what I hope is a firm look. "Absolutely."

She looks rather deflated, and a tiny bit sad. "Oh. Right. Well, I'm sorry I spoke then."

There's a silence.

"It's just, well, I've always wanted grandchildren."

Christ, now I'm feeling guilty that this baby isn't going to be her first grandchild.

"So what were you whispering about when I came back from lunch the other day then?"

"He was showing me the papers for the barn."

"Oh. Right. Well, good, because I don't want him mixed up in any unpleasantness, not that I mean, well, that didn't come out right, but he's had enough to cope with over the past year with Madam. Would you like a cup of tea, dear, or a biscuit? I might as well stop now I'm here. I could pop out and get some ginger ones—they're meant to be just the job if you're feeling a bit sick. Are you feeling sick? I was terrible with Martin. Couldn't keep anything down for weeks."

"I'm fine, Elsie, thanks, but I'd love a cup of tea. There's some new tea bags in the cupboard under the sink, decaf ones."

"Isn't that just coffee?"

"No, tea has a fair bit of caffeine in it too."

"Fancy. Well, I'll nip up and put the kettle on then, shall I?"

"Please."

She pats my arm as she goes past. "And then you can tell me all about it."

Christ. Between her and Betty, and Tina in the salon, I think we can safely say the whole town will now be in the picture, so there'll be no need for a notice after all. So much for trying to keep a low profile.

It's Friday morning, and I'm having a last-minute dash round Sainsbury's, trying to get everything ready for Archie's party tomorrow, before I'm due at school for knitting with the reception class. And my jeans keep sliding downward because I can't do the zip up anymore: I've rigged up a bit of elastic as a temporary measure, but it's not really working. I'll have to get changed when I drop the food off. Unstable trousers are the last thing you need when you're in with mixed infants.

Things have started to calm down on the baby breaking-news front, though, thank God, now that everyone within a five-mile radius seems to have popped into the shop to congratulate me, or smiled at me in the playground. Apart from Annabel, of course, who's been perfecting her superior and disapproving look. It does feel like I've been entered into some sort of competition, and I'm now representing the Pregnant and Not a Man in Sight category, but the excitement is definitely on the wane: not least because Mrs. Taylor from the chemist's has finally run off with the man who sells the multivitamins. Mr. Taylor has retaliated by throwing most of his stock out in the street, so everyone's been stocking up on evening primrose and picking up

snippets of who said what to whom, which has knocked me off the lead item and into the And Finally slot, thank God.

Even Mum was all right about it, which I'm pretty sure is because Vin had already called her and told her to be nice. She did say she thinks I'm far too old and why on earth I want another one is beyond her, but then she moved on to trying to winkle out the name of the father. She knows I met Daniel in Venice at Christmas, and since she also knows he's a famous international photographer, she'd go into overdrive if I let her think he might be involved. So I've put her off the scent by hinting that we were talking about someone local, who has now disappeared, and she completely lost interest and put Dad on the line. And then she came back on again to tell me she'd bought a marvelous outfit for the wedding in shades of orange, so that's something to look forward to. I spent far too long traipsing round after her while she was wearing clogs and artistic outfits when I was growing up and everyone else's mum was wearing proper skirts and court shoes, so I should be used to it by now. But I can't help hoping that it's not too bright orange or she'll look like one of those adverts for Tango.

I'm pushing my trolley round, with fairly frequent waistband adjustments, while I call Connie on the mobile to find out if Mark really wants to make mini-pizzas as well as the cake for Archie's party, or if she was just volunteering him to be kind. She keeps trying to do things for me, and she's been so sweet about the baby.

Her mum came with her to Stitch and Bitch last night, and she's everything I knew she would be: lovely, with lots

of arm waving and hugging, sort of the opposite of mine really. She kissed everyone good-bye and gave me an extra-long hug, so I can see why Connie misses her so much.

Her dad, Salvatore, was at home with Mark teaching him the secret family recipe for some special kind of fish soup that takes days to make, after spending hours at the fish market in Whitstable poking things and walking off in feigned horror at the prices. Connie was telling us Mark got so embarrassed he ended up sitting in the car while Salvatore continued negotiating. They're such a sweet couple, and they arrived with so many presents they had to bring an extra suitcase.

By the time I'm home and trying to wedge stuff into the fridge, I'm starting to panic. Mark might be heroically doing the cake and the pizzas, but there's no getting away from the fact that I've got ten small boys coming for a birthday tea, followed by hordes of adults for the bonfire, and I haven't even started on tidying up the house yet. I've changed into my black stretchy skirt, which is at least likely to stay up throughout this afternoon in school, but I'm no further forward on the clean-kitchen front when the phone rings.

Bugger.

"How's it going?"

"Fine, thanks, Maxine."

"It's the birthday party this weekend, right?"

"Yes."

"Grace wants to book a time for you to come over."

"Lovely, only can it be next week? I'm a bit tied up to-day."

"Sure. I gather you've been pretty busy all round. Congratulations."

"Thanks, I was going to tell you when I saw you."

"Bruno beat you to it. He and PC Mike are new best friends. Yes, I'm on the line to her now . . . yes, I was just going to—"

"Jo, it's Grace. Congratulations. Get me a juice, would you, Max, and not that mango crap, I hate that. Thanks. There, she's gone. So this is a late Christmas present from Venice, yes?"

"Yes."

"Brilliant. Have you told him?"

"Yes, and I don't think he was exactly thrilled."

"Don't worry, give it a few months. Liv will probably have finished with him by then, and who knows what might happen."

"I think I know, Grace."

"And do you mind?"

"Not at all, I thought I might, before I rang him, but no, not really."

She laughs. "Good. Max is sorting out dates for Paris."

"Paris?"

"We're doing the Simone de Beauvoir thing, and it looks like the *Bedknobs and Broomsticks* is on too, only that'll be the UK. So I'll want you around for that, however pregnant you are."

"I'd love to. How exciting. What would I do exactly?"

"Be my knitting coach. You can help me knit my way through the endless bloody hours of hanging about. Although neither of them are costume, which will also help."

"Are costume things tricky then?"

"They're a total nightmare. All that corset stuff really gets to me after a while, and I'm nowhere near back to my normal size yet."

"You looked amazing last time I saw you."

"Yes, but my arse wasn't up on a big screen then, darling. Trust me. It's still huge. I'm seriously thinking about Botox."

"For your bottom?"

"Sure. Best place for it. I don't want one of those dead faces. I'm thinking of doing Bruno too; he's been looking very weather-beaten lately. It's probably all the time he spends outside with those bloody dogs."

"Won't he mind?"

"Not if we jab him while he's asleep. Now, the birthday party. It's this weekend, right? And I know we said we couldn't make it, but it looks like we can now."

Bugger.

"Oh, right, well, that's brilliant."

"I'll get Max to sort out a present. Tell her what he wants, and we'll see you tomorrow. It'll be Lily's first party. I can't wait."

Double bugger.

Maxine comes back on the line.

"We thought four-thirty, if that's okay?"

"Lovely. You do know it's only local kids and cake, and then a bonfire party with a few people from the shop, though, don't you? Nothing remotely glamorous. And it'll be chaos."

"Sure. It'll just be me and Bruno with her, and I shouldn't think there'll be much press."

"Press?"

"We released the official photograph of Lily on Monday."

"I saw, she looked beautiful."

"So now we're just being a normal mum, going to birth-day parties with local friends, part of the local community. Yes? Not at all the superstar hiding her baby from the world."

"Oh. I see."

"So if there's a few snappers at your gate, you'll be okay with that?"

"Sure, but the house is a bit of a tip."

"I'm sure it isn't, and anyway Our Gracie has normal friends, not just people with big houses."

"Right, of course."

"Good. We're not handling it, so they'll probably only run a few pictures. Jimmy's about to do his piece on how Grace has turned into a recluse and won't let him see the baby. Not that he's ever tried, of course. Bastard."

"How awful."

"Don't worry. Ed's got the lawyers onto it. Now, presents, what does Archie want?"

"A dog, but if you bring him one, I'll kill you with my bare hands."

She laughs. "Something I can wrap up?"

"Lego, anything from the Star Wars range, or the knights, but small so Jack's not too jealous, or paints and paper, that kind of thing. He loves painting."

"I'll sort that now and we'll see you tomorrow."

"Lovely."

"And don't worry about food. She won't eat. Bruno will,

if you let him. Actually, I can bring extra for Bruno; I'll get Sam to bring some patisserie over, or jellies? He does great vodka jellies."

"Thanks, but I'm not sure getting them drunk is going to help. But thanks for offering."

Christ. A Superheroes fancy-dress tea party, with bonfire, and God knows how many adults, and a megastar with snappers and her own pastry chef. So no pressure at all then. And now I'm late for knitting with reception class.

Excellent.

M r. O'Brien is walking across the playground with a small boy when I get to school. "We're just going for a walk. Stephen and I find it helps when we're getting cross."

Stephen nods, with rigid little shoulders and clenched fists.

"Stephen is one of my best boys. I shouldn't really have favorites, but I have to admit I do. And Stephen is one of them." Mr. O'Brien winks at me, and there's a flicker of a smile on Stephen's face.

"Do go in, we won't be long. Mrs. Chambers is in the staff room, I think."

"Great."

I walk down the corridor looking at the wall displays.

I've done mini-training sessions with most of the staff, and lots of them already knew how to knit, which is a bonus, and they've all been really enthusiastic, apart from Mrs. King, who's been at the school for centuries and isn't keen on anything that involves staying after three-thirty. And

Mrs. Nelson, who's a friend of Annabel's so she doesn't really count. Their husbands play golf together and will bore you rigid about it if you stand too close to them at school barbecues. She's only in part-time to do music, but it's surprising how many children you can upset even if you're only in two days a week, especially if their dads don't play golf.

The top class have already started their knitting project—recycling plastic shopping bags by cutting them into strips and then knitting them into mats and bags—and they've all done lovely notes for their project folders, writing about the van Gogh *Sunflowers* sweater I brought back from Venice and coming up with alternative pictures they'd like to knit for sample squares. Mrs. Chambers is going to start the squares with them today, I think, while I'm in with reception, so I've definitely drawn the short straw on that one.

The staff room is full of boxes of wool alongside the usual piles of papers and half-drunk cups of coffee. Mrs. Chambers wrote off to all the wool manufacturers, and I asked a few of the reps, and now we've got all the wool we could possibly need, and lots of sets of small plastic knitting needles in bright colors.

She's sorting through the wool and looking very chirpy.

"Coffee?"

"Please."

Mr. O'Brien comes in, smiling.

"He's such a nice boy, that Stephen. He's just been telling me the best way to deal with drunks. His dad drives the night buses in Margate, and by all accounts it can get

pretty nasty out there with fights and all sorts, but the crucial thing is to have a laugh with them. I must remember never to catch a night bus in Margate. I'm terrible in fights, I tend to faint."

Mrs. Chambers giggles. "I do, and it's a very good tactic. In my old school in London, if a particularly threatening parent arrived promising to sort me out, I'd go all dizzy and do my slow-motion crumple. It worked every time."

"I must remember that."

"Do, but I wouldn't do it with the children. They tend to just climb all over you, particularly the smaller ones. Now then, Mrs. Mackenzie, how's Operation Knitting going? I've seen the recycling one, such a brilliant idea, and the project folders, fascinating—I never knew Egyptians invented knitting—and the photographs from the war that Mrs. Chambers was showing me are wonderful. Are socks tricky to knit?"

"They can be if you want heels. But scarves are easy."

"My grandmother was telling us at the weekend about knitting scarves for aircrews in the war. She said the pilots had to have silk ones, though, because the only way you survived was if you kept turning your head looking for fighters, and wool used to rub their necks raw. Can you imagine? It must have been so terrifying. There was a base round here somewhere, I think."

"Yes, my gran remembers it too."

"We must look into that. It could link into history and geography. We could do maps, and a field trip. I liked all the ideas about textures too, string and raffia—so useful to

key maths skills, how different materials make different widths. Anyway, well done on all the planning. I'll give you one of my sweets for excellent work if you like."

"Mrs. Chambers has done most of the work. But thank you."

"And I hear congratulations are in order. Another name for our registers on the way—marvelous. We'll look forward to welcoming him or her into our reception class in due course." He's beaming now, as is Mrs. Chambers. "You must let us know if you need to take a rest or anything. Feel free to pop into my room if you need to. Or the staff room." He hands me a box of biscuits.

"Thanks."

"Yuck."

We both turn to Mrs. Chambers, who's looking through one of the knitting magazines I've brought in.

"There's an article here about how you can spin hair from your pets and knit it into hats."

"I know, I saw that too. Probably not one for us, though?"

Mr. O'Brien grins. "God no; not unless we want to get blamed for a lot of bald hamsters."

Mrs. Chambers puts the magazine down. "True, and I don't think Sooty would be that keen either. He's our school cat, Jo. Well, he belongs to our schoolkeeper, but he lets us stroke him. Sometimes. Although I'm sure that would change if we were trying to make Sooty hats."

"I'm sure it would."

Mr. O'Brien sits down. "So tell me more about this new school banner. Won't a picture of the school be quite difficult to knit?"

"We're only planning on everyone knitting a small shape, brown squares for the school building, white for the windows, different greens for the trees, that kind of thing. And then we'll sew on little matchstick children."

"Like a woolly Lowry?"

"Exactly."

"Well, I'd better get cracking then. If I can cope with rock climbing, I'm willing to give it a go."

"Rock climbing?"

"On our school trip, with the leavers, last year. Absolutely appalling. But they loved it, and the center were very good: they winched me back down when they realized I wasn't joking, which the children enjoyed a great deal. In fact, I think it was the highlight of the day for some of them. Anyway, let's not dwell on that. How do I start?"

Mrs. Chambers hands him a pair of pink plastic needles.

"Here you go, Jim. Jo will start you off. It's ever so easy once you get going."

"Oh, Lord, me and my big mouth."

By the time I'm heading down the corridor toward Mrs. Tindall's reception class, Mr. O'Brien has knitted a small green square, which I've promised to turn into some sort of bush for the banner, and he's in his office with three rows of silver sparkly wool on his needles. Mrs. Pickering, everyone's favorite dinner lady, is helping him with increasing so they can make a bell shape for the top of the clock tower.

I've been into the hall and briefly seen Archie not eating his packed lunch, and had a beaker of water spilled over my feet, and a quick hug from Jack on his way back to his

classroom, but I'm still not feeling anywhere near ready for reception.

M rs. Tindall's got her painting apron on, and a small boy holding on to her hem.

"We're just getting into our groups, Mrs. Mackenzie. Michael, I think you can probably let go now, dear, and Trent Carter, we never run with paint pots. Walk slowly, there's a good boy, or you'll get paint everywhere, yes, just like that. Go and wash your hands, dear. Now then, let's have fingers on lips, shall we?"

The class seems to ignore her.

"Fingers on lips, everybody."

Everyone clamps a finger, and in some cases a whole hand, over their mouth, including Trent Carter, who now has an orange chin. The noise level reduces to muted scufflings.

"Well done, everyone. Matthew, please sit down and get a tissue if you must do that. Now here's Mrs. Mackenzie, come to help us make lovely pom-poms for our Sammy Snake. And then we're all going to knit things for our new school banner. We talked about it this morning, remember?"

Some of them nod, but quite a few look blank, or mildly panicky.

"Let's all sit nicely on our chairs and show her how sensible we can be, shall we? Ellie, is that being sensible?"

Before I know it I'm trying to fit on a tiny chair, with six children at my table, pom-pomming like my life depends on it while Mrs. Tindall sorts out the paint and the

glue, and the classroom assistant, Mrs. Channing, makes a start on knitting small brown squares with her group. We've already worked out that if we cast on for them, and take it slowly, most of them can cope. But that was with the older ones, so who knows what'll happen with the littlest ones. I've shown my lot how to wind their wool around the plastic semicircles we got in the pom-pom kits, and Finlay and Connor are busy winding away, while Natasha and Laura watch my every move as I start Kyle and James off with some thick blue cotton.

"My mum says I can have a dog for my birthday."

"That's nice. When's your birthday, Kyle?"

"In two years. Or four. And when it's my party I'm having a disco, only not with girls."

Natasha tuts. "You can't have a disco with no girls."

"I might have some. Just not you."

Natasha doesn't seem particularly worried by this. "When it's my party I'm having a magician, and swimming. And a disco."

Kyle looks rather crestfallen and starts kicking the table leg while he carries on winding his wool.

Finlay puts his hand up. Bless.

"I don't want to do knitting. It's crap."

The rest of the group giggle.

I think I'll just pretend I haven't heard: I'm pretty sure we don't say *crap* in school, however much we might be tempted.

"Boys don't do knitting. Only girls do."

He puts his pom-pom down and fixes me with a very determined look.

"Well, clever boys do, Kyle. A long time ago the men

used to do all the knitting, in special groups called guilds, and you had to be very good to join them." I'm quite pleased with my vaguely educational answer, but he carries on looking at me. "And all the sailors in the navy used to learn how to knit, so they could fix their sails, and the soldiers in the army did too, so they could make socks and mend their uniforms. It's no good being in the middle of a big battle with no socks on."

He picks up his pom-pom just as Mrs. Tindall comes over to congratulate them on their progress, and then we're tying off and cutting and trimming, with very blunt scissors, and then I've got a whole new group of expectant faces, and my skirt is covered in tufts of wool.

"Could you help Mrs. Channing if she brings her group over to join you? She's having a bit of trouble."

Like I didn't see that one coming.

"Sure."

Mrs. Channing brings her group over, and the children all squash round the table.

"How does it go again, miss?"

They're learning a rhyme to help them remember how to knit a stitch:

In through the front door,
Around the back,
Out through the window,
And off jumps Jack.

Unfortunately one of the smaller boys turns out to be called Jack, so he's showing us how good he is at jumping until

Mrs. Channing rallies and starts on a quick bit of number work, and we all begin counting our stitches, with answers ranging from three to nine, holding up our fingers and counting together and checking our needles, by which time half of us have dropped them on the floor.

"One two four six."

I'm not sure if Michael, who's sitting next to me, is doing some special kind of binary maths or he's just not that good at number bonds, so I put my needles down and count on my fingers slowly.

"One two three four five six."

He grins.

"I miss out five, because I don't like it. I like four. And seven. That's my favorite."

"Oh, right. What about three?"

"Sometimes I quite like it."

I think he's either a budding maths genius or one of life's Challenging Learners.

He looks down at his needles and sighs. "In through the front door. And off jumps Jack."

We finally get six vaguely square shapes and I help them cast off, and then it's playtime, thank God, followed by another round of pom-poms and then story time, during which I almost nod off. So it's quite a shock to find myself standing in the playground waiting for the boys to come out, and I'm wondering if I can have a nice little sleep when we get home, before I start on the ironing, which is reaching epic proportions in the cupboard under the stairs.

Jack's had a good day, but Archie's not pleased when he

eventually comes out, trailing his packed-lunch bag along behind him.

"We had to do stupid knittin'. And it was meant to be choosing time."

"I bet you'll be very proud when you see your knitting on the banner."

"No, I won't. I wanted to do cars in the home corner."

He swings his packed-lunch bag around and then releases it, just in time to narrowly miss Horrible Harry, who is throwing some sort of fit with Annabel.

"Go and pick that up, Archie."

"No."

Jack sighs and goes over to pick up the bag.

Harry is now clinging on to the railings while Annabel tries to pull him off and keep a smile on her face. Thank God she's too distracted to make a formal complaint about flying lunch bags.

Connie's laughing. "Harry has extra maths today perhaps, or French? The lessons he loves so much?"

Annabel was boasting about his prowess at French classes and some kind of special boffin maths last week, but it doesn't look like Harry's too keen.

Archie's decided to be penitent. "Sorry, Mum."

"Say sorry to Jack. He had to pick it up."

"Sorry, Jack."

"It's all right, Arch. I used to do that, when I was only five."

"But I'm nearly six now."

Jack ignores this.

"What's for tea, Mum?"

"Cheese omelets?"

They both pretend to vomit.

"Or fish fingers, for people who aren't being annoying."

By the time the first guests arrive for Archie's party, I'm perilously close to complete hysteria. I hate the bit just before parties, when there's still time to produce some dazzlingly stylish backdrop, if only you knew how. But once we get going I feel much calmer, which is strange since I'm trying to help Connie pass the parcel while simultaneously discussing sausage rolls with Gran and the timing of the bonfire with Martin.

Reg has tracked down a few fireworks and a boxful of packets of sparklers, and he and Mr. Pallfrey have been in the garden for most of the day filling buckets with sand and burying rockets in the flower bed by the back wall, with Trevor helping with the digging. Mr. Pallfrey's been busy making a start on the garden for the Seaside in Bloom competition, so at least it's looking tidier now, even if it's all gone a bit bare now all the weeds have gone. The Diva's due any minute, and there are already a couple of photographers by our front gate, much to the amusement of Jane Johnson, who posed for them when she dropped Seth off.

Martin's wearing the bobble hat Elsie knitted for him, which makes him look like he's out on day release, but she's still having a major sulk about the barn, so I think he's trying to be as conciliatory as he can, without actually promising to stay living at home for all eternity. So far he seems to

be meeting with a fair amount of tutting and pursed lips, but you've got to give him marks for persistence.

"Shall I light the fire now then, so it's got going by the time they've had their tea?"

"Please."

"It's just possible this bloody hat might fall into the flames by mistake."

"Good plan. Only make sure the kids don't see. I really don't need Archie getting the idea that fire is the solution for clothes you're not keen on."

He laughs. "I'll bear that in mind. Actually, it's not so much the hat that I mind, it's the bobble." He shakes his head, and the bobble moves.

"I see what you mean. Still, she means well."

He gives me a Look.

"Anyway, thanks for helping, Martin. I'm sure there are better things you could be doing with your Saturday."

"Oh no, I loved bonfires when I was little. Still do, actually. I'm having quite a few at the barn—you must bring the boys out. I think they'd enjoy it."

"We'd love to."

Actually, I'm not sure bringing them to a building site with bonfires is exactly top of my list of things to be doing in the near future.

"How are you feeling?"

"Fine. Oh, you mean . . . fine. Great."

He's blushing.

"Is that her arriving then? There's quite a lot of flashing going on in your front garden, if you get my drift."

Elsie's opening the front door as we walk into the hall,

to see Ellen posing for snappers before sweeping up the path. I notice Martin quickly takes his hat off, which leaves his hair standing up in little tufts, and I'm tempted to lick my fingers and flatten them down, like I do with Archie, but fortunately I manage to resist.

"Hello, darling; hi, Martin."

She looks amazing, in very high-heeled boots and a tiny tweed skirt with a fabulous leather coat.

I'm still in my stretchy black skirt, which is now much shorter than it used to be, with black woolly tights that I used to wear when I was pregnant with Archie. I thought I'd thrown them out, but they reappeared in the back of my sock drawer, like magic, which was a lucky break; otherwise I'd be in socks. The local shops don't seem to sell giant tights, so they're on my list for the next trip into Canterbury. And my green sweater's a bit tighter than I meant it to be, but I can't quite keep up with my ever-expanding chest.

"Great sweater, darling." She kisses Martin, which makes him retreat into the garden pretty sharpish.

"Here, let me hang your coat up."

"You're right about his hair, much better. I think we should definitely keep him on your list for later."

"I haven't got a list for later, and I'm having a hard enough time with his mother as it is, so stop it. Do you want a drink, or something to eat? Mark's in the kitchen with a fabulous fish soup, and Antonella and Salvatore are here, Connie's mum and dad, and they're lovely. And Gran's making sausage rolls. So take your pick."

"God, the noise is amazing. It reminds me of that football thing I did last year."

"They'll quieten down when they have tea. Well, a bit."

"So what can I do to help?"

Ellen doesn't normally do birthday parties, unless they're the private-members'-club-with-champagne-and-Michelin-starred-canapés sort, but she couldn't pass up the chance for a bonding moment with Grace, even though I've made her promise not to go into interview mode.

"Go and help Connie—she's doing party games. And remember, you promised you'll leave Grace alone."

"Yes to the first, possibly to the second. She might fancy a quick heart-to-heart."

"She won't. And Bruno will stick you in a hedge if you push it. And Mr. Pallfrey's just finished pruning it. So pretend you're not Britain's Favorite Broadcaster, just for today, yes?"

"Relax, darling. You know me. Subtle charm. Have you got any oranges? I know a great pass-the-orange game for later, great for grown-ups too, especially after a few vodkas."

Oh, God.

I'm in the kitchen trying to fit all the food onto paper plates and hiding the oranges while Elsie takes things into the dining room.

Gran's putting jellies in little shiny gold plastic cups on a tray.

"Aren't these jellies lovely? She sent them, that Grace Morrison, she sent a young man round. Fruit jellies with strawberries, look, and little cakes. Aren't they pretty? I didn't know you could do icing in those colors, and the little gold sweeties look very smart, don't they? Out of the blue

when I was here this morning, he arrived with trays and everything, such a nice young man. Lovely manners."

Elsie's very impressed; in fact, she's so overexcited she almost drops a plate of sausages on sticks when the door-bell rings.

It's Grace, with a background of flashing lights, with Lily fast asleep in her car seat, the hood up so you can't quite see her face. Maxine is holding two huge shopping bags, and so is Bruno. Christ.

"Can we come in?"

"Yes, of course, sorry."

"Where's the birthday boy then? Oh, how lovely, bal-loons. I love balloons." Grace is doing her Megastar Smile, and we're all rather dazzled.

Elsie steps forward. "Good afternoon, Miss Harrison. Isn't she beautiful? We all saw the pictures in the papers, but they didn't do her justice." Elsie is practically curtsying.

"Thank you."

"Would you like a sausage?"

"I think maybe we should let Grace get her coat off, Elsie, but if you could put them on the table, that would be great."

"Oh yes, of course, well, just let me know when you want anything, Miss Harrison, and I'll make you up a plate. Anything at all." She walks backward toward the door to the dining room, which she misses with a small thud.

Christ.

By the time we've played Musical Statues, and passed two more parcels and played a lively round of Musical

Chairs to the *Batman* theme tune, which on balance was probably a mistake, the birthday tea goes very well, with the adults milling about in the kitchen complimenting Mark and Salvatore on the soup.

I think everyone's enjoyed themselves, although I notice that whenever Ellen gets anywhere near Grace, Maxine is somehow standing in between them, in a subtle but effective way, which is quite impressive. Gran gets to cuddle Lily, and Elsie gets an autograph from Grace, which is a tad mortifying, but apart from that everyone behaves as if Grace is just another local mum.

Archie's thrilled with his presents from Grace, which turn out to be a Lego castle, with one for Jack too, and pretty much every kind of knight and horse and extra soldier that they make, with swords and pointy sticks, and enough art supplies to keep us going until he's a teenager. And it's all posh stuff, with thick paper and fabulous colors in little pots that look suspiciously nonwashable, so they might be going onto the top shelf of my wardrobe until he's slightly less likely to be wearing them all over his sweatshirt.

He's so excited he even kissed Bruno to say thank you, and he loved his goldfish so much there was a huge debate about what to call them until he finally settled on Nemo and Bruce.

We're all outside in the garden, watching the bonfire, with the doors open to the dining room so people can help themselves to more food. Elsie's finally given up on her mission to get Grace to eat something and is now bringing plates of food to Bruno, who's very impressed by the way

Trevor keeps chasing round the front garden barking at the photographers.

"He could teach Tom and Jerry a thing or two, you know. I might bring them round one day. Nice for them to get to know other dogs."

Maxine shakes her head. "They're enough trouble already without picking up new tricks, Bruno. Great party, Jo, but I think we're going to be off soon."

"Oh, right, well, thank you for coming. And for the presents. He's thrilled."

"I gathered." She smiles: she got a sticky thank-you kiss too.

Grace comes toward us, holding Lily, who's starting to get fed up. "I think we'd better make a move, but I can't wait until I'm doing her first party. Are all these kids from his school?"

"Yes."

"Is it only boys at his school?"

"No, but he banned girls this year, apart from Nelly."

She smiles. "So we'll see you next week. Ready, Bruno?" Bruno stuffs another sausage roll into his mouth. "Jesus, don't you ever stop eating? Go and get the car."

We walk back into the house, and Maxine gets her mobile out and stands by the front door as I hand her a *Batman* party bag and a balloon; God knows what they'll make of a bottle of bubbles, a jelly snake, and a packet of Smarties, but I'm thinking Bruno will be pleased.

"There's cake too, if you want a slice for later."

Grace smiles. "We're okay, thanks."

Maxine's phone beeps. "Bruno's outside."

"Great."

There's another round of flashing as she gets into the car, just as Tina arrives to collect Travis, and then I'm in the back garden trying to make sure the sparklers don't lead to any emergency dashes to A&E. Martin's being stalwart with a bucket of water, and Archie's on his third pair of gloves because he keeps plunging them into the bucket to make sure everything is properly extinguished, but Gran and Reg are keeping an eye on him, while Connie ladles out more bowls of fish soup for everyone.

Salvatore is sitting at the table in the kitchen flirting with Elsie and Betty as parents start arriving to take small people home, thank God. Gran and I put slices of cake into party bags. Mark's really outdone himself on the cake: I was worried the Superheroes theme might be tricky, but he's made a circular Batcave, with a Batmobile on top, and black candles and black-and-gray icing over a chocolate sponge, with cherry jam. It's so delicious I've already had two slices, and I'm hoping for a third. Or possibly some more soup, and then more cake. I'm seriously getting into this eating-for-two thing.

Ellen's pouring herself a drink as I go back into the kitchen. "Great party, darling. This is just the kind of thing I want for my wedding."

"A Batcake and balloons? I bet Harry will be thrilled."

"No, but everyone relaxed, nothing too formal. Did I tell you I think we've found the hotel?"

"Great, where? Hang on, Seth. Don't run with that, love; you might trip and hurt yourself."

"It's my stick, for later. I found it in the garden. Can I keep it?"

"Yes, but let's put it over here until your mum comes, shall we?"

"Okay."

He runs back out into the garden.

"Sorry, so where's this hotel?"

"Scotland. It's more of a castle, but very postmodern, fabulous spa, and acres of private land so the snappers will be easy to control. Rebecca found it; she's talking rates with them now. They're not open yet, so this will be one of their launch events, which should save us a few quid."

"Sounds perfect."

"I always thought wedding planners were crap, but I've got to admit she's turned out to be incredibly useful, although with what she's charging she bloody should be."

"It'll be handy for Harry's family too."

"Yes, that's the only drawback. They'll all be belting over from Glasgow, and there's millions of them."

"I'm sure it'll be fine."

"So we're still thinking kilts, for the boys."

"Jack, possibly."

"I thought I'd try a spot of bribery with Archie?"

"Good luck."

"I've got a dress fitting next week and she's starting on yours. What size do you think you'll be by June?"

"Huge."

"Can you be a tiny bit more specific, darling? She really needs to know. There'll be room to spare, though. We're going for an empire line."

"It'll have to be a bloody big empire then."

She laughs. "How big did you get with Archie? I can't remember."

"Enormous. Nick used to call me Big Bertha by the end. Don't you remember?"

"Oh yes, he called you BB for short, didn't he?"

"Yes."

There's a silence.

"I really wish he was here on days like this."

"I know, but look on the bright side, darling. At least nobody will be calling you Big Bertha."

"Or laughing when I get stuck in wicker chairs."

"That was a kid's chair, though, wasn't it?"

"Not really."

"I'll tell them to make it extra floaty, and then we can adjust it, if it's too big."

"Trust me, too big is not going to be an issue."

"Will Vin and Lulu be back by then?"

"Looks like it. Gran's is only a week before yours, so I'm sure they'll be around."

"Great, I'll put them on my invitation list."

"How many are you up to now?"

"Six hundred. And the castle ballroom holds three hundred, max, so we're talking about a marquee."

"I thought you said you hated marquees."

"I do. But not as much as I hate the idea of being pressed up against the walls at my own wedding reception by hordes of pissed Glaswegians. It's a fucking nightmare."

"Mummy, Aunty Ellen said the F-word." Archie's thrilled.

"Did she? Well, never mind. . . . Where are your gloves?"

"They got wet. And, Mum?"

"Yes?"

"There'll be six people in our family, when the new baby comes, you and me and Jack, and Bruce and Nemo, and the baby, and I'm six too. Gran was telling me. That's very clever, isn't it?"

"Yes, love."

"And if we had a dog, we'd be seven. Which is even better. Can we do our castles now, Mum? We've done all the sparkers and Martin says he'll help me, so I can beat Jack and get my castle done first. Marco's going to help Jack build his, but I bet me and Martin will beat them."

"Okay, but hang on a minute. There's something Aunty Ellen needs to ask you. About kilts."

Ellen's giving him one of her Big Smiles as I retreat into the garden to check all the sparklers are really out and there are no children lurking by the bonfire. Ellen can be very persuasive when she wants to be, but I've got a funny feeling she might have met her match with our birthday boy.

FOUR

wedding belles

June

Flaming June has begun with a heat wave. I'm wearing baggy shorts around the house, which are far too Morecambe and Wise to wear outside so Gran's made me a couple of voluminous pinafore dresses on her sewing machine; I've got one with pink flowers and one with lavender, and they both make me look like I'm auditioning for a part in *Little House on the Prairie*. All I need is a bloody bonnet. But at least they're cool, and that's all I really care about at the moment.

I'm opening the post on Tuesday morning, and there are a few catalogs, so I'm looking forward to a mini-Boden moment, not that I buy anything from them anymore; there's something faintly depressing about all those amusing patterns

in stretchy cotton, soon to be seen on all the Tabithas and Olivers of every middle-class family with a Volvo Estate and private health insurance. And anyway, they're far too expensive for me now. But I like a quick perusal of the catalog to see what we'd be wearing if we lived in Fulham.

There's a letter on posh cream paper, which I'm opening while I put the kettle on. Christ, it's from Daniel. Or rather his lawyers. I recognize the firm; they're one of the ones who issued injunctions on behalf of big names when we were in the middle of researching stories at work. Very expensive, and very aggressive. God.

"Without prejudice." This isn't going to be good.

Their client has informed them of a potential claim, and a test at an approved laboratory would seem to be best way forward in the circumstances as outlined above. Bloody hell.

I call Ellen.

"I'm not surprised, darling. I told you he'd do something like this."

"They're practically calling me a liar."

"That's just lawyer bollocks; they're all like that. Get your own fuck-off-and-die firm—they'll sort it. Do you want me to talk to James?"

"No."

"You'll win, darling, so he won't charge you. I'll square him with an interview or something. He loves being on telly."

"Win what?"

"Don't start all that again, sweetheart. You've told him the good news, and now he's saying prove it. So prove it."

"I don't have to. If he doesn't believe me, then that's his problem."

"Not if you want child support, it isn't."

"But I don't. You know I don't."

"That's because you've gone all hormonal."

"No it isn't, Ellen. If he wants to do something for the baby, he can, but not via me. It would make me feel like I was beholden to him, and anyway, as soon as money comes into it everything always changes. He can start a savings fund or something for the baby, if he wants to. I've still got Nick's money for Jack and Archie, in accounts for them, so they'll all have a little bit put by."

"Stop calling it Nick's money—it's your money, for Christ's sake. And what about you? Who's starting a savings fund for you?"

"I'm fine."

"Yes, but Daniel's worth an absolute fortune, darling. Why not make it easier on yourself?"

"Because it wouldn't be easier, not really, and I can do this, Ellen. I didn't know I could, not when Nick died; I thought I'd go under on my own. But now I think I can. And it's peaceful; I don't feel like I've been hijacked anymore, that what someone else wants always comes first. Which I really like. Well, apart from the kids, but I don't mind that. We won't have to go on parish relief or anything, you know. I can manage, if I'm careful, I know I can."

"Christ, is this some postfeminist thing?"

"There's nothing post about it. Sisters are definitely doing it for themselves round here, have been since the war in Gran's case. And look at Grace: nobody thinks she's being a postfeminist, whatever that is."

"That's because she's incredibly rich. Rich people and

aristocrats have always been able to write their own rules."

"Well, so can the rest of us. I mean if it's really working, like with you and Harry, or Connie and Mark, then great, but the average version, like me and Nick, where the mortgage is what really keeps you going more than anything else, well, no thanks. Been there, done that. Almost stopped feeling crap about it. Of course that could be because I haven't actually got a mortgage anymore. But still, I like the idea that I can take care of us, all of us. And I don't want to rush into changing that, not just for the sake of money."

"Yes, but why not have lovely clothes at the same time, the occasional gorgeous handbag? Would that be so terrible?"

"Yes, I think it might. I've had enough of compromising; I'll compromise for the kids, but not for a handbag. And it's amazing how little you can get by on when you stop buying stuff you don't need, you know."

"Oh, God, you're starting to scare me now. You're not going to start knitting your own shoes, are you?"

"No, but you know what I mean."

"Not really, but then my definition of need has always been different from yours, darling."

"I just don't know what to do about the letter."

"Ignore it, if you're determined to be poor forever. Make the bastard sweat, and then he'll realize that he's got it wrong and you're probably one of the only women in Europe who doesn't want to help herself to his assets."

"Sounds like a plan. Great. I'll do that."

"What?"

"Ignore it."

"So what are you up to today then? Got a consciousness-raising session in the shop, have you, reclaiming the night?"

"We do that on Thursday at Stitch and Bitch."

"With the fabulous cakes. That's definitely my kind of women's group, excellent patisserie and knitting on-trend items. Germaine Greer, eat your heart out."

"Or not. I bet she knits."

"I bet she bloody doesn't. How is the gorgeous Mark, by the way? Connie still got him locked in the kitchen?"

"Yes, but he loves it, although he works too hard."

"Unlike my future husband, who was out on a bender last night, so God knows what time I'll see him. One of his freelance mates celebrating not getting shot, or getting shot but coming home with all his bits, I forget which."

"Sounds like a good reason to celebrate."

"They don't need a reason, trust me; freelance camera-men are a law unto themselves. They should get special jackets. They're always in and out of bloody hospital, pretending it was in pursuit of a breaking story, but usually they've just got pissed and fallen off something. They should open a private press ward somewhere, make the sods pay."

"How was the meeting with Rebecca about the guest list?"

"A total nightmare. Harry keeps adding names, including all his ex-girlfriends."

"Sweet."

"Sorry?"

"He's obviously so proud of you, he wants to show you off."

"I hadn't thought of it like that. Maybe. But what if I look

like an idiot in my dress? Some brides do, you know. It's a hard look to get right, and you can end up looking like the dress is wearing you."

"You won't. And you'll have a giant person behind you, as a useful contrast."

"True. Thanks, darling. And you're right, fuck it—throw it in the bin and go for it. You don't need him or his money. I'll always help out, if you get stuck. You know that, don't you?"

"Thanks, Ellen."

"And then I'll sue the bastard."

I'm in the shop on Wednesday morning with Gran and Lulu. She and Vin arrived yesterday, jet-lagged and exhausted, but they've both perked up after a big breakfast, and Vin's doing his helpful-big-brother act and moving beds around at home. We're borrowing a double mattress from Connie for him and Lulu, so Mum and Dad can have the spare bed when they arrive tomorrow, which I'm still dreading. She was on the phone last night complaining again about the wedding, so I'm knitting the last triangle for the bunting to hang across the shop window and trying not to think about it.

Gran's handing Lulu shells, and we've already draped dark blue net over some pale blue to suggest waves. And I've stapled silver velvet to the partition and covered it with more net, so it's all looking very nautical. And we've got real rocks at each side, which we'll put back on the beach when we're done: they'll be perfect to sit the little knitted

teddies on for a mini Teddy Bears' Picnic alongside the little bathing ladies I've knitted, with their striped towels and beach bags. They're slightly more Beryl Cook than I intended, and look surprisingly lascivious for woolly people, but I'm hoping they'll inspire people to buy the beach-bag kits I've put into our McKnits shopping bags: four balls of cotton in jaunty colors, with a simple pattern and a pair of wooden needles and a stick of rock, all for fifteen quid. They're starting to sell quite well, which is great, especially since I'm making nearly seven quid profit on each one. Old Mr. Prewitt, who does the books, says last month's takings were the highest he can remember—which is basically since the dawn of time, so that's encouraging; even if a hefty proportion of it did come from Grace's big cashmere order.

Gran's giving the shells a quick squirt of Pledge before she hands them to Lulu; there's pretty much nothing she can't polish, or wipe down with a damp cloth.

"Did you see Jo's scan picture of the baby, Lulu? Doesn't he look like our Archie?"

Gran came with me to the second scan at the hospital and has decided the baby's definitely a boy because the nurse kept saying "he."

"It's wonderful what they can do now, isn't it? In my day it was only trumpets."

Lulu looks confused. "What did they do with trumpets?"

"Listened to the baby, but you never got to hear, only the nurse. Those microphone things they've got now are much better, and his little heart was beating so fast, I was telling Reg."

She gives me a sideways glance: she took a great deal of

persuading in the hospital that the baby's heartbeat was meant to be that fast and we didn't need to get the doctor in.

"And he passed his nuclear test too, didn't he, clever thing."

Lulu turns to me. "Nuclear test?"

"Nuchal fold. It gives you the odds of the baby having Down's. The older you get the higher the odds are, but I got the results last week and they're better than Archie's."

"Oh, right. Well, that's good."

Gran nods.

"And he's the spitting image of our Archie, and Reg agrees with me. And so does Betty."

I got a copy of the scan picture for Gran too this time, and by the sound of it there aren't many people in Broadgate who haven't seen it; she's got it in a special little plastic frame in her handbag.

Lulu clambers back through the hatch and starts tucking knitted fish in among the net. "I think Moby's a lovely name for a boy."

Gran peers over the partition. "Do you, dear? Fancy that. I like family names. I've always liked Tom, or Albert. I had an uncle Albert, and he was ever so nice. Always had sweets."

"Tom's a nice name, but Archie and Albert sounds a bit like one of those old music hall acts, don't you think?"

Gran hands her more fish. "True."

"And what about if it's a girl? Flower names are pretty, like Daisy and Rose. Or Ocean—that's a great name for a girl."

Lulu's obviously been giving the name thing a fair bit of

thought; in fact, quite a few people seem to have been pondering names; Elsie was lobbying for Neville yesterday, for some reason best known to herself.

Gran hands Lulu another knitted fish.

"Rose is pretty, and I had an aunty Ruby, she was nice; and there's Mary, of course, for family names, but we've got far too many of those already, and Pearl, my grandmother was a Pearl, lovely woman, she was; and my mother had a sister called Nancy, I think, only she never talked about her. Took up with a bad lot and used to drink. We should ask the boys, you know. It would make them feel involved."

"I don't think that's a good idea, Gran, unless you want a grandchild called Gandalf."

Lulu and I arrange the dangling fish, which I've put onto nylon thread, and then Lulu positions the fat ladies on their rock and puts the finishing touches to the Teddy Bears' Picnic, while I hang a couple of the beach bags and a bucket and spade from the hooks in the corner of the ceiling.

"Thanks, Lulu. I don't know how I'd have done this without you."

"I think it looks brilliant."

"Well, good, because they'll all be in complaining if it's not up to scratch."

Broadgate won the silver medal in the Seaside in Bloom thing last year, and the shop window got a mention from one of the judges, so practically everyone on the Parish Council has been in reminding me how vital it is that I pull out all the stops.

"I bet you'll win gold."

"I doubt it. Whitstable is in our group this year, and they win everything. Lady Denby's furious about it; she reckons money's been changing hands."

Lulu heroically offers to go next door with Gran to have another floral moment with Mrs. Davis, while I worry about what Mum's going to say when she sees the wallpaper in the spare bedroom. I'm trying to take my mind off it by putting in another order for the cheap cotton when Lord Denby wanders in, looking even more vague than usual.

"Morning, my dear. Haven't seen my wife, have you? Meant to be meeting her somewhere, only I'm damned if I know where, and there'll be hell to pay if I don't track her down. Could I wait here? Think she said something about wool."

"Of course. Would you like a cup of tea while you're waiting?"

"Delightful."

I'm handing him a Rich Tea biscuit while he tells me about his battles with the greenfly on his roses when Lady Denby comes in, looking flustered, dragging Algie and Clarkson in her wake.

"George. I thought we agreed you'd wait in the car."

"Did we, my dear? Completely slipped my mind. Been having a lovely chat with Moira here."

Lord Denby calls everybody Moira. Nobody really knows why.

Lady Denby gives me an apologetic look.

"Would you like some tea, Lady Denby?"

"No thank you, very kind, but we must get on. George,

you're worse than the dogs, always begging for food. I do hope he hasn't put you to any trouble."

"Not at all, we've been talking about roses."

Lord Denby puts his cup down. "Charming girl offered me a cup that cheers as soon as I set foot in the place. No begging involved, Pru. Absolutely delightful."

Lady Denby smiles at me. "Now there was something I wanted to say to you. What was it? Oh yes. I hear congratulations are in order. Lot of that sort of thing in the war, you know."

"Sorry?"

"Unmarried mothers. Hordes of them. Still, times have changed—nobody's business but your own now. As long as you can support yourself, can't see any problem with it myself, so don't let anyone tell you otherwise. Far too much gossip in this town, in my opinion. Hope you're feeling well. Felt ghastly with all of mine."

"Yes, fine, thank you."

"Good. Excellent. Noticed the new display in the window—glad to see you're keeping up to your usual standards. We'll give them a run for their money. That's the spirit. We'll fight them on the beaches, what?"

Clarkson is now edging forward trying to lick my flip-flops until he's yanked backward.

Lord Denby stands up. "Thank you so much for the tea, Moira. Must remember to pop in here more often, and remember, soapy water, that's the thing for greenfly. The buggers hate it. Good afternoon."

He winks at me as he opens the door, and there's a tangle

of dog leads and they end up wedged in the doorway for a moment until Lady Denby manages to release them. "Blasted dogs, you'll stay in the car if this is how you're going to behave."

I get another wink from Lord Denby and a wave from Lady Denby as she shepherds them all back toward her ancient Volvo; I must remember to tell Elsie he might be popping in for a cup of tea and calling her Moira: she'll be absolutely thrilled. Maybe we can teach him to knit, and then he can sit upstairs making dog blankets while Lady Denby goes shopping. He did have a reputation for pinching people's bottoms, according to Betty, but I think he's well past that now. At least I hope so.

Vin and Lulu have gone to collect Mum and Dad from the airport while I get the boys from school. Actually, what I really need now is a nice little lie-down, with someone else being in charge of supper, rather than Mum and her Comments.

"Oh, great, here comes Annabel."

I'm treated to another disapproving sideways look at my stomach as she hands us the latest communiqué about the Summer Fayre. Connie smiles at her, which Annabel ignores as she trots off in search of other people stupid enough to have got themselves landed with doing a stall. The latest missive from mission control has decreed that we all have to appear in Victorian costume behind our respective stalls, and today's proclamation informs us that a subcommittee is meeting to coordinate outfits.

Houston, we may have a problem.

"I bet she'll have told them to put us down as chimney sweeps."

"We shall ignore them, yes? I will be Queen Victoria. I've got a long black dress, and Mark says he will make me a crown. She will hate that, I think?"

"Brilliant. And I can be Albert. She'll hate that even more. A heavily pregnant Albert."

"Or we could make beautiful dresses like Anna in *The King and I?*"

"I don't think they make crinolines that big, Con. And anyway, I don't know how to waltz."

"I will show you."

We're having a quick practice as the kids come out.

Jack and Marco are shaking their heads.

"Can we go home now, Mum? I want to see Mariella." Mum insists the boys don't call her Gran and has adopted Mariella as her name since they've been living in Italy.

Trust Jack to bring me back down to earth with a jolt.

I'm putting a vase of tulips on the chest of drawers in the spare bedroom when Jack thunders upstairs yelling, "They're here, they're here."

I'm trying to take deep calming breaths, but it doesn't seem to be working. Brace, brace, brace.

"Good journey, Mum?"

Vin's standing behind her rolling his eyes and shaking his head. "They lost Mum's suitcase." He's trying not to laugh.

"Oh, dear."

"Oh, dear? It's much worse than that, Josephine. My wedding outfit was in that case, and if they think they're going to get away with this, then they're very much mistaken. I do have connections, you know."

Vin sniggers. "With who, Mum? The Mafia won't cut much ice with British Airways."

She gives him a furious look. "Thank you, Vincent, so helpful as usual. Josephine, I need you to make some calls. Start with your friend Ellen."

"Ellen?"

"Once they know the press are involved, they'll soon buck their ideas up. And could someone please make me an infusion—I've got some herbal mixtures my little man has given me. He says my stress levels are extraordinary and this is hardly going to help. Derek, where did you put my Rescue Remedy?"

By the time I've persuaded her that Ellen isn't likely to run a story about her lost suitcase on the six o'clock news, and I've called the lost-luggage number what seems like hundreds of times and listened to the annoying music only to be told that they're still trying to locate the bag and will call us back when they have an update, Mum is in a major sulk. The boys have tried to introduce her to Trevor the Loony Lurcher, but she wasn't terribly impressed, so I'm helping her unpack while everyone else is outside in the back garden playing football. Luckily all her herbal sachets appear to be in Dad's case, so at least I won't need to be tracking down an emergency herbalist.

"So what do you think of the house, Mum?"

As soon as I've asked her this I wish I hadn't; she's doing one of her Tactful Faces. "It's got potential, but it needs
lots of work. Why on earth did you paint the hall that terrible color?"

"It's only magnolia, Mum. I had lots of tins left over
from all the decorating I did in London, but it's a start. I'd
love you to tell me what colors would work best."

"I'm far too exhausted to start decorating, Josephine."

"I didn't mean—"

"And if you don't mind me saying so, that dress is terribly unflattering."

"Gran made it for me. It's been really hot."

"Hot? It's barely warm. You should try a summer in
Venezia if you want heat. Actually, are you feeling all right,
darling? You do look rather bloated."

Bloated. Great. Just the look I was going for.

"A bit tired, that's all. The boys are very excited, though,
about the baby."

"Well, I'm pleased for you, you know that, darling, if
you're sure this is what you want. But perhaps this might
be a good time to take stock."

"Of what?"

"You can't stay stuck in that dreadful shop forever, and
now might be a good time to move back to civilization. I'm
sure you could afford it if you tried. Get a job in television
again, a proper career. So much more suitable."

In other words, much more suitable for showing off to
her friends about her daughter who works in television.

"I know, but I like it here, Mum. I know you didn't like
growing up here, but it really works for me and the boys."

"Well, I can't imagine why. Don't you find it terribly stifling? That's one of the lovely things about Venezia—so much freedom, and artistic spirit. Surely you don't want to stay stuck here forever?"

"I don't know, but for now I do. The boys are really happy; they love their school and being near Gran."

As soon as I've said this, I realize it's exactly the wrong thing to say. She stiffens and refolds a T-shirt. "Yes, well, of course, as far as she's concerned, Broadgate is the center of the universe."

"Where shall I put this, Mum?" I'm holding up a long green caftan, with what look like parrots appliquéd onto the sleeves in purple. Dear God, I hope she won't be wearing it at breakfast or I'll have to gag Archie.

"On the chair, please."

"I really want you to see the shop. I've made quite a few changes, you know. Gran's bringing Reg round for tea later, and then we've got our Stitch and Bitch group tonight, so if you fancy coming along to that, everyone would really love to meet you."

"Perhaps tomorrow. I'm far too stressed today. Are there any more hangers? Wooden ones, please—I want to hang your father's suit up. Why you use these dreadful wire ones is beyond me. Nobody in Italy would dream of using them."

"Sorry."

"I think I've got one of my heads starting."

I know exactly how she feels.

"Oh, dear. Is there anything you need?"

"Draw the curtains, please. If I lie perfectly still, I might

stave it off. Perhaps you could bring me up something light. Have you got any broth?"

Broth? Dear God, she'll be asking for calves-foot jelly next.

"I've got some tins of soup, if that's any good. I'll go and have a look."

"Never mind."

Vin and Dad are at home waiting on Mum, who's consumed a tin of Scotch broth and two slices of toasted cheese and was agitating for cake as Lulu and I were leaving for the shop. She managed to come downstairs briefly to meet Reg before retiring back to her bed; Reg didn't seem to mind and was very solicitous, making a huge fuss of her, which went down well, but I could see that Gran was annoyed, and a little bit hurt.

Lulu's putting the cups and saucers out on the workroom table while Connie arranges biscuits on a plate; Mark's been experimenting with biscuits over the past few weeks, and they've all been delicious. Tonight we've got chocolate shortbreads and almond macaroons, so things are definitely starting to look up.

"So, your mother, is she coming later?"

"No, Con, she's at home sulking. She thinks she's got jet lag."

"From a two-hour flight?"

"Gran brought Reg round, and I think the strain of having to be nice for more than five minutes finished her off."

"But you are all still coming for supper tomorrow night, yes?"

"Please."

"Mark is making something special. He says it will be a prewedding banquet. And the wedding cake is nearly finished. Your gran had a picture of one with three layers, but Mark thinks she was worried it would be too difficult for him, so she chose a smaller one. But he has made one with four layers, as a surprise, and the people on top, they dance."

"That sounds brilliant."

"Have you tried on your dress yet?"

Connie's definitely more excited about my bridesmaid's dress than I am.

"Not yet. I'm saving it for the big day."

Actually, I'm trying to ignore the fact that I'll be appearing in public in a large pink tent with a matching jacket because deep down I know I'm going to look like a very big blancmange.

"It is pink, yes?"

"Yes."

"Lovely."

Oh, God.

By the time everyone's arrived and we've made the teas and coffees and poured wine for anyone who wants it, I'm starting to feel calmer. Angela's showing us the latest pictures of Baby Stanley, with her daughter, Penny, and her partner, Sally, looking on proudly; Stanley's developing a very impressive quiff for a nine-month-old and seems a particularly smiley baby.

Tina hands her back the packet of photographs. "He's lovely, Ange. Isn't he getting big?"

"He's nearly walking too. He pulls himself up on their coffee table, and Sally's been so clever, she's padded all the corners with foam so he can't hurt himself. She's such a nice girl."

Angela's been transformed over the past few months; when she first came to the group, she was so timid she practically quivered when anyone spoke to her, but becoming a grandmother has changed all that. Her husband, Peter, who takes his role as our local estate agent and pillar of the community very seriously, and is the kind of man who doesn't like women wearing trousers except for gardening, wasn't exactly thrilled to find himself with a pregnant daughter with a partner called Sally who's good at DIY. But Angela has simply ignored him and goes to visit them all the time.

Cath smiles. "Olivia was the same when she was a toddler, always banging into things."

"Where is she tonight?"

"At home not speaking to anyone because we won't let her go hitchhiking in the summer."

Linda puts her glass down. "Where does she want to hitchhike to?"

"I don't think they know. Her and her friend Polly have just picked the thing they know will upset us the most. They're such a handful at this age; I thought toddlers were hard work, but teenagers are lethal."

Tina helps herself to another biscuit. "I don't know how

I'll manage if my Travis gets to be any more of a handful. He locked me in our conservatory last week, you know. He wanted to watch some film and I wouldn't let him, and I was watering the plants when he slid the doors shut and clicked the catch up. And that glass is ever so thick, you know. My Graham was on night shift, and he gets so stroppy if I call him at work."

We're all trying not to smile at the thought of Tina trapped in her own conservatory by her eight-year-old, although I'm sure Archie would be perfectly willing to lock me in ours, if we had one.

"I thought about ringing the police on the extension, but Graham's always going on about people calling them out for daft things and I bet the police are the same. So I sat down and went all quiet, and he hates it when I do that. And then I told him I loved him. Well, I had to shout it through the glass, but I made my face go all sad and everything. And then he opened the doors and I could see he just wanted a cuddle. So I gave him one. What do you think? He gets himself in such a state, and he's promised never to do it again. Graham says I'm too soft on him, but he's even worse than me—he gives in to him all the time."

Connie nods. "Mark is the same. Nelly has him wrapped round her fingers. She cries and he is finished."

Cath pours herself some more tea. "Yes, but everyone needs someone who always caves in when they cry, don't they? Imagine how awful it would be if nobody minded. Damn, I've gone wrong again."

She hands me her knitting, which now has rather more holes in it than it should have: she's making a cream silk-

mix cardigan with a tricky cable pattern on the sleeves, and by the time I've taken it back a few rows and helped her sort out the cable, Linda needs help with picking up the stitches for the border on her poncho, and then Lulu wants me to help her choose some wool for a sweater for Vin.

I love evenings like this, when everyone's busy chatting and planning. Angela buys some navy cotton for a jacket for Stanley while Lulu makes some more tea.

"Does anyone want this last macaroon?"

"No, you have it, love—got to keep your strength up. How are you feeling?" Tina's looking at my tummy, which always makes me feel a bit weird, not least because I keep forgetting I'm pregnant so I just feel like a bit of a piglet.

"Fine, thanks."

"That's good."

"Lady Denby was in the shop today, congratulating me."

Linda makes a huffing noise and then tries to pretend she didn't, but Tina's noticed. "We're all very pleased for you, aren't we, Linda?"

"Yes, of course. It's just . . . Oh, never mind."

Angela coughs. "If you've got something to say, perhaps you should say it, Linda." Angela's gone pink. Blimey: she's really getting the hang of her new assertiveness; maybe she's been on a course, or she's been reading some of the books Penny's given her.

"It's just I don't want my Lauren thinking it's all right to have a baby on your own, that's all. What with Grace bloody Harrison, and now Jo, well, it's like it's gone all glamorous or something, and it's not, not for girls like my Lauren. I'm sorry, but it's not."

Everyone looks uncomfortable, particularly Linda.

Bugger.

"So you think you must be married to have babies, yes?" Connie's sounding quite sharp, and her eyes look darker than usual, which is never a good sign.

"No, of course not, not if you've got few quid behind you, but for girls like my Lauren it's a total disaster. She hasn't got the sense to come in out of the rain as it is, and the last thing she needs is a baby. She couldn't even look after that hamster we got her. It spent half its time under our settee before the bloody dog got it." She's looking really upset now, and Tina puts her arm around her.

"I don't want her thinking she's got a choice, not at her age. When I was sixteen you had to be married if you wanted a baby, and that was that. And I know we're divorced now, me and her dad, but all the same I don't want her thinking a baby might be a laugh. That's what she said to me, you know, at the weekend, it might be a laugh, and she wasn't going to waste her time getting married to some wanker just so she could have a baby."

"Well, she's got a point there, Lind. But I'm sure she was only winding you up."

"Well, it bloody worked."

Cath puts her knitting down. "But we don't want to go back to the bad old days of back streets, or going into a home, do we?"

"No, of course not."

"Then I think it all comes down to education, and talking to them. They need to know how much work babies

are, that kind of thing. I want Olivia to have choices, but I want her to have all the facts too. I'm sure your Lauren is far more sensible than you think, Linda, and you talk to her all the time."

"I know. Much good it does me."

Angela's collecting up plates. "Personally, I don't think there's anything wrong with women deciding to have babies on their own, not anymore. I used to, but I think that was just a way of keeping women in their place. Penny's been explaining it to me."

Tina smiles and nods. "And the same goes for getting married, doesn't it? Marrying too young can be a life sentence too."

Linda sighs. "Tell me about it. God, when I think of the years I wasted, it makes me sick. And I'm sorry, Jo. I didn't mean I wasn't pleased for you or anything. You know that, don't you?"

"Of course I do. Look, why don't you bring Lauren round for a few hours of nappy-changing when I have the baby, maybe midnight to six in the morning? Do you think that would help? Let her see the less glamorous side of it."

"Oh, would you, really? I'd be ever so grateful."

Tina puts her arm around her again. "Your Lauren's a lot smarter than you think."

"Well, I bloody hope so, because I'm nowhere near ready to be a granny yet. Sorry, Ange, but I'm really not."

After commiserating with me and Connie about the impending Summer Fayre in Victorian Costumes Disaster,

we move on to talking about Gran's wedding and what everyone will be wearing, and the mood's much lighter as they're all leaving. Linda gives me a long hug, so I think she's okay, which is a relief. That's one of the drawbacks of small-town life, I suppose: everything you do becomes public property. Used by teenagers to taunt their mothers. Christ. I'm so not ready for teenagers.

I'm feeling extra tired when I'm washing up the cups with Connie and Lulu.

"You should go home and sleep. And don't let your mother upset you. Promise?"

"She's not, Con. It's fine."

"No, it is not. With the baby and the shop, sometimes I think it is too much. Some people you cannot please. So you stop trying."

"Okay."

"*Brava.*"

"God, I've just remembered, I've got to take her shopping tomorrow if her bloody case doesn't turn up."

"No, Lulu will take her, or I will, not you. You will be in resting before the wedding."

"Will I? Has someone told the boys?"

Lulu brings the last of the plates in. "I'm happy to go shopping with her."

She's so sweet sometimes, Lulu; naïve, but sweet.

"I should probably warn you, she tells shop assistants off, all the time. And throws stuff on the floor if it doesn't fit. Actually, she's a total nightmare in shops."

"Sounds like fun."

"You're on."

Vin's watching telly when we get home, surrounded by train track. "Nice time knitting, girls?"

Lulu sits on him. "Shut up, Vin. Nice time playing trains?"

"I've told you before, real men don't play trains, they facilitate their nephews' enjoyment."

She kisses him. "You're such a wanker, Vin. You know that, don't you?"

"Get off me, you big lump. I can't breathe."

"Charmed, I'm sure."

"Oh, I get it, you've had your woolly women's group and now you're all fired up and ready to pick on me. Great. Well, you'd better keep it down because Mum and Dad are asleep, and she was in a foul mood last time I saw her, still in a strop about her outfit. Apparently it's orange. Can you wear orange to a wedding?"

"If you want to look like a nutter, yes. What time did the boys conk out?"

"Around eight-thirty."

"Vin."

"Just before ten."

"Well, at least we might get a lie-in. Lulu's volunteered to take Mum shopping tomorrow if the case hasn't turned up. Talk about mission impossible. Try to prepare her, would you, so she knows what she's in for."

Lulu smiles. "I like the way she dresses—it's unusual."

Vin kisses her. "I worry about you sometimes, Lou. You

wait until Saturday—she'll probably have a tiara on with flashing lights."

"When can we see your outfit, Jo? I'm dying to see it."

Vin sniggers. "Me too."

"Stop it, both of you. It's pink, that's all I'm saying. Head-to-toe pink, and lots of it. Right, I'm off up to bed, and try not to make any noise when you come up, because if Archie wakes up you're on your own. Help yourselves to anything you fancy in the kitchen. There's Jammie Dodger biscuits in the cupboard by the washer, and cocoa if you want some."

Lulu claps her hands, and Vin winks at me: Jammie Dodgers and cocoa are Lulu's favorites, and I've got an extra pint of milk in the fridge specially.

"Shall we bring you some cocoa up?"

"No thanks, I'll be asleep as soon as I get into bed. I'm totally knackered."

It's 2:00 A.M., and I can't get to sleep, so I'm having one of my slow-motion panic attacks instead, which is bloody annoying. I think the combination of Mum and the baby is really starting to get to me. And the prospect of having to dress up as a blancmange in front of my nearest and dearest isn't really helping, and then we'll be in Scotland with Ellen and she's still talking about kilts, and I'm uncomfortable and hot and I can't get to sleep so I'm going to look like a sodding pastel panda in all the wedding photographs.

If everything could stop for a minute, I might be able to get my breath back. Actually, a few weeks would be good;

being a tragic bloody widow was bad enough, with everyone thinking I'd lost the love of my bloody life and me
knowing he wanted a divorce. But this is far more complicated, and Linda's right, babies are a big deal, and I'm really
not sure I can do this on my own.

Christ. It's all so ridiculous. I hardly even know Daniel;
how can I be having his baby? Except it's not really his, not
like the boys were Nick's. And anyway, I thought I knew
Nick pretty well, and look how that turned out. And I'm
pretty sure Mimi the bloody teenager nymphet UN worker
wasn't the first person he'd had a fling with either. I was
thinking about that the other day, and it suddenly dawned
on me how disconnected he'd been from us, for ages. He'd
been gone for years really, when I think about it. But I'm
not having this baby by myself, I've got to remember that;
I've got the boys, and Gran and everyone else popping in
on a daily basis. So the only difference will be missing out
the middle bit, where you marry him and then he leaves
you, or drives his car into a bloody tree. So at least this baby
won't have to go through what Jack and Archie have had to
cope with, feeling lost and frightened and worrying that losing their dad was something to do with them, like Jack did,
and still does a bit, I think. If Daniel's going to be around at
all, then we all know right from the start that he's not part
of our family, which has got to be better for the baby. But
still, Christ knows how I'm going to do it all and keep the
shop going and everything.

What I really need is a nanny, not another bloody husband. Actually, two nannies: one for the baby and one for
me. And then someone else can be in charge for a while;

someone else can sort out the boiler, which is now only heating the water when it feels like it, and the cold tap in the bath, which has started dripping. All of it. I'm completely bloody fed up of being strong and getting on with it. I don't want to get on with it, I want some other poor sod to be getting on with it while I run away with my boys and lie down somewhere quiet.

I've got no idea what's bloody going on and how it's going to turn out. And my knees hurt. And my back. And I'm too tired to go downstairs for tea and biscuits. There should be a bell I could press for emergency assistance, and someone would arrive in a clean uniform and sort it all out for me: a cross between Mary Poppins and a brilliant PA with a splash of Nigella thrown in for good luck. I could be off on a spa break deciding what color I want my nails.

Actually, that's another thing I've got to add to my bloody list: Gran's spent ages finding the perfect shade of pink polish to match the blancmange dress, so I need to paint my bloody nails in the next twenty-four hours. Maybe I should haul myself downstairs and do it now.

Someone gets up to go to the loo, and then flushes. Great: that'll be Archie awake any minute.

"Mummy."

"No, Archie. Back to bed."

He stands in the doorway, swaying slightly.

Bugger. I'll have to get up if I want to put him back into his own bed without him having hysterics and waking up Jack.

"All right. But be as quiet as a mouse."

He shuffles across the floor and gets into bed, wrapping himself in most of the sheet and the duvet.

I tug hard and retrieve myself a bit of sheet.

"Lie still, Archie."

He makes a squeaking noise. "I'm being a mouse."

"Well, be a mouse who's asleep then."

I can feel him smiling in the dark.

The baby moves.

"And you can stop that right now. I'm not in the mood."

"I'm not doing anything."

"I'm talking to the baby."

"Night-night, Mum, night, Baby." He pats my back, and the baby shifts again, with a small jab toward my left hip.

Excellent. Another child that doesn't take a blind bit of notice of anything I say. What a surprise.

It's nearly ten on Saturday morning, and total chaos. For some reason best known to herself, Gran has decided to get married from my house, so we've got Linda upstairs doing her hair, while Vin is round at Reg's helping him get ready. Elsie's tying white ribbon onto everything, including Trevor, who's now sporting a big white bow round his neck, which Mr. Pallfrey's trying to persuade him not to eat while he has a final tweak of the border of white geraniums and lavender that he's planted on either side of the front path.

Martin's been volunteered as our parking valet by Elsie and is busy rearranging all the cars in the street so there can be a line of wedding cars outside the house, while Mum is

busy putting the final touches to her outfit in the bathroom. Her suitcase arrived yesterday, thank God, although I almost wish it hadn't now I've seen the full extent of the orange outfit, with hallucinogenic scarf and matching hat. She looks like a Pearly Queen on acid.

Lulu's giving her nails a final coat of my tea rose pink while I try to do my sandals up; the bloody things fitted perfectly three weeks ago, but now I can't get the straps done up so I'm trying to make an extra hole with a darning needle. I'd forgotten about the pregnancy ankle-puffing thing, but I need to keep a low profile about it or Gran will have me on the sofa for half an hour with a flannel over my face.

I'm having a quiet five minutes with a packet of digestives when Mum comes in, looking narky.

"That mirror in your bathroom is absolutely dreadful, darling. I can't imagine why you don't get a proper one."

"I haven't got round to it yet, Mum. Is Gran ready?"

"No, and that woman wouldn't let me into the room, said she didn't want to spoil the surprise. She was quite rude, actually."

Good for Linda.

"Would you like a cup of tea?"

"No thank you, and don't keep eating biscuits, unless you want to get fat."

"I think it might be a bit late to start worrying about getting fat, Mum. What do you think of the outfit?" I parade up and down the kitchen.

"Very nice, only do try to stand up straight; you don't want to waddle down the aisle. Pink's never really been one of your colors, but never mind. I still think it's a mistake having a bridesmaid at her age, but my opinion obviously counts for nothing, as usual. Where's your father?"

Dad's very good at disappearing during times of crisis: usually by doing a bit of urgent DIY. He was threatening to take one of the living room windows off its hinges earlier; it keeps sticking and he wanted to sand it, but I diverted him onto small-boy patrol, with the promise of a nice bit of sanding later on.

"In the living room keeping an eye on the boys."

"Trust him to be sitting down somewhere while I do all the work." She stands in the doorway. "Derek, have you done your tie properly? Actually, perhaps a cup of tea would be nice. Could you bring one in, darling?"

I'm putting the kettle on when Lulu comes in with Martin.

"The cars are here."

"Thanks, Martin."

"They're vintage, really beautiful, but just so you know, Mum's desperate to go in one. I've tried telling her. I mean it's not as if we're family or anything, but you know what she's like."

"It's fine, Martin. Everyone can squish up, and you are, practically family, I mean. Could you go up and tell Gran the cars are here, Lulu? And don't let Mum hear you or she'll try to get in to see Gran before she's ready."

"Sure, no problem."

Martin's wearing what I'm guessing is his best suit, and looking rather handsome.

"Great suit."

"Thanks, you look great too."

"Martin, there's no need to be kind. I look like a large blancmange."

"I like blancmange. I'll go and tell Mum the good news then, shall I? And then I'd better get off to the church."

"Please, and thanks for sorting out the cars."

"No problem."

"God, I'm nervous. I've never been a bridesmaid before, and Mum says I'm starting to waddle. So that's a good start."

"Ignore her. That's what I do with mine."

"Good tip. But it doesn't really matter as long as Gran enjoys it, and the boys don't start shoving each other by the altar. Or bickering."

"I'm sure they'll be fine."

"I hope so."

"Mummy, Jack keeps pushing me. Tell him."

Martin grins. "Or maybe not. I'll see you later."

A t ten past eleven everything suddenly speeds up, and the crowd departs, leaving me and Gran at the house. Elsie makes it into the second car, and Martin takes Betty, who's arrived in her wedding outfit complete with a massive hat.

"She's ready."

Linda stands at the bottom of the stairs as Gran starts to

come down, very slowly, holding her bouquet of pink roses and being very careful in her new shoes.

"Oh, Gran, you look beautiful."

"You don't think this hat is silly?"

"No, it's perfect."

She's got a cream silk hat to match her suit, with pale cream dots on it and a tiny veil.

"Aren't the flowers pretty?"

"Lovely. It's all lovely, Gran."

I'm beginning to feel tearful as Linda pats me on the shoulder. "Don't you start, love, or we'll all be at it. Right, I'm off to the church. See you there, Mary, and you look a picture. Reg won't know what's hit him."

"Thanks, Linda. What time is it?"

"Ten to, so take your time. Have a gin or something. Always does the trick for me."

We're sitting sipping tea with clean tea towels over our frocks, just in case, when Gran delves into her handbag and hands me a small box, wrapped in pink tissue paper.

"They're from me and Reg, to say thank you for being our bridesmaid. And they're real diamonds, only little ones, mind. But still. I hope you like them."

"Oh, Gran, they're gorgeous. Here, help me put them on."

I put the silver heart earrings I wore when I married Nick onto the dresser. Actually, I'm glad I'll be wearing something new today—it seems more fitting. Which reminds me.

"So what's your something blue, Gran?"

"My pants. I couldn't think of what else I could wear that wouldn't show, and I've got my old pearl necklace on, and Betty's lent me her earrings, and they nearly match, look. Isn't that lucky? And my new is the watch Reg got for me for Christmas. I've only worn it once, but that still counts, doesn't it?"

"I'm sure it does."

"Takes me back to marrying your grandad."

"Gran."

"I know, but I can't help thinking, pet. He was such a handsome boy. Of course he'd be an old man now, but still. I was talking to Betty about it, and we reckon he wouldn't mind, not after all these years."

"I'm sure he wouldn't, Gran."

"And I'll tell you something else: I wish your Nick was here, even if he hadn't come to his senses and he'd gone ahead with the divorce and everything. I wanted you to know that. I know he made mistakes, and it would be better all round if his mother knew it, and then maybe she'd be a bit nicer to you, but what's done is done and it's a shame, that's all. I can still see him in his wedding suit on the day you got married. So young. Like my Tom. Life can be very cruel."

Bloody hell. If she carries on like this, we'll be sobbing all the way to the church.

"Yes, but not today, Gran."

"No, but it's on days like this that you remember. I know you'll have been thinking about it, pet, but it does get easier as the years go by, that's all I can say. And I'm so

proud of you. I wanted to say that too. If it wasn't for you taking over the shop, I doubt me and Reg would be getting married. It means the world to me having you here. You know that, don't you?"

"Yes, Gran."

"Good. Well, we'd better be off then. I don't want to keep Reg waiting. He'll be getting nervous, and his stomach plays him up something terrible when he gets nervous. Come on, hold my hand and walk your gran to the car, pet. I'm still not feeling right in these shoes."

The church is packed when we arrive, and Mrs. Davis has put flowers everywhere, so it smells of roses and hymnbooks with a hint of freesias. "For Those in Peril on the Sea" is playing, and the Lifeboat people are attempting something tricky with the chorus; I didn't know they were meant to be singing, but I'm guessing they've been practicing because they're all standing in a bunch at the back wearing smart suits and their Lifeboat badges.

The wedding march starts, and Gran begins to shake as we walk up the aisle; I'm meant to be behind her, but she grips my arm so tight I end up walking next to her, with Jack and Archie sprinkling petals in front of us in slow motion. By the time we reach the vicar, Archie's basket is empty, so he turns and hands it to Mum with a beaming smile, and then bows to Gran before sitting down next to Dad, and Jack does the same, and then we're into "Dearly beloved, we are gathered here today . . ."

Vin winks at me when Reg nearly drops the ring, and

it's all very touching, so most of us are sniffing by the end, including Lady Denby, who's wearing a giant hat and blows her nose with a very loud trumpet as we're processing back up the aisle, which makes Jack giggle.

Reg is looking less pale as we pose outside the church for photographs, with me and Vin waiting in the wings; we're sitting on the wooden seat in the churchyard while Lulu takes the boys for a wander round before they get too fidgety.

"They look so happy, don't they, Vin?"

"You're not going to start crying again, are you, because I've run out of tissues."

"You're such a romantic, and anyway, I saw you."

"Saw me what?"

"Dabbing back the tears."

"Tears of relief, trust me. And men don't dab. Christ, I thought he was going to have a stroke or something this morning. He was so shaky I even had to do the buttons up on his shirt for him. And that old codger Alf was no use. I thought the best man was meant to calm everyone down, but he was as bad as Reg. That bloody tie took us about six shots before they were both happy."

Reg chose his oldest friend, Alfred, as his best man; they were at school together, I think.

"Well, you all looked lovely. Morning dress really suits you."

"I feel like a total idiot."

"Lulu looks great, doesn't she?"

"I hadn't noticed."

"Vin."

"She always looks all right to me."

"That's because you love her."

"Steady on."

"Go on, say it."

"No."

"I'll tell Mum it was you that burnt the hole in the living room carpet. And you can't give me a Chinese burn, because it's illegal."

"Since when is it illegal to give your sister a Chinese burn?"

"When she's pregnant and you're sitting outside a church. Go on, I want to hear you say it."

"I quite like her."

"Vin."

"If she wasn't around, it would feel like the world had shrunk. Forever. Will that do you?"

"That'll do nicely, thank you."

Oh, dear, I think I'm going to cry again.

Vin coughs.

"Mum's managed to behave herself pretty well so far, hasn't she? Those herbal things must be stronger than we thought. I wonder if she'll be calling Reg Dad?"

"I doubt it. But it must be a bit weird for her. Imagine how you'd feel."

"What, if she dumped Dad and married someone else, you mean? I wouldn't go."

"Everything's so simple in boy world, isn't it?"

"Yes, if you don't let girls complicate it for you."

"It must be strange for her, Vin. She never knew Grandad Tom, don't forget, but I bet she still feels a bit torn."

He puts his hand over mine. "Are we talking about Mum, or the baby? She's always been fine about it, you know that."

"Yes, but there was a war on; not having a dad because he was blown up in the Atlantic during the war is one thing, but if he's not around because he's not up for it, that's something else. And I'd really hate that, if the baby felt like it was second best or something."

"It won't. No kid of yours is ever going to feel like that."

"Thanks, Vin."

"Times have changed, sweetheart. Families come in all shapes and sizes. We don't all have to fit into little suffocating boxes anymore, thank God."

"Well, that's a relief, because I don't think I'll be fitting into anything little for quite a while."

He squeezes my hand. "Come on then, Big Bertha, let's get you up. I think it's our turn for the happy snaps."

Connie and Mark have hung white ribbon all over the pub when we arrive, unless Elsie nipped round earlier, and Nelly's by the door in her ballerina outfit, carrying a basket full of sugared almonds tied up in little net bundles with white ribbon. There's champagne for everyone, and plates of sandwiches on all the tables, with tartlets and Mark's special cakes and biscuits, so there's a great deal of milling backward and forward, and people drift out into the garden, until Connie claps her hands and shushes everyone and Mark wheels the wedding cake in.

The figures on the top tier are revolving slowly to the sound of a waltz playing on a tiny white musical box. Everyone claps and cheers. Gran's decided she doesn't want any speeches, mainly because we were both worried what Mum might say, so Reg proposes a toast to his beautiful bride and they cut the cake, and Elsie bursts into tears and waves her hankie. It's all perfect, and Gran seems to have gone into a blissed-out daze.

The cake is some sort of magical combination of chestnut and praline, and I'm trying to work out how I can have another slice before I rescue Mum from one of Reg's relatives who's been calling her Felicity for most of the afternoon when Connie comes over.

"Is everything good?"

"It's amazing. Thanks, Con, you've both made it perfect for her."

"She looks so happy."

"If she was any more happy she'd burst."

Connie smiles and sits down. "Two people have already asked us if we can do the same sort of thing for them, and Mark told them a silly price, because he's so tired, and they said yes. Can you believe it? If we continue like this, we can be paying one of the loans early."

"Well, you deserve it, sweetheart—you've worked miracles here. And Alison and Peggy have done well today too, don't you think?"

She nods; finding reliable waitresses who have the same high standards as Connie and Mark hasn't been easy, but

they're gradually building up a list of staff they can rely on, including Dave, the new barman, who's turned out to be a real treasure despite the occasional spectacular drinking session. He's very handsome and is busy making Linda and Tina some special wedding cocktail he's invented, which seems to be going down very well.

"Now I feel like we belong here. A wedding makes you feel like you belong. Like Italy isn't my only home."

I lean forward and kiss her as Vin comes over.

"Not interrupting anything, am I?" He's looking rather flushed.

"How much champagne have you had, Vin?"

"I've lost count. I'd forgotten how much I like champagning. You should have knitted her wedding dress, you know, Jo; surprised you missed that one. Now what was I meant to be telling you? Oh yes, Archie. Up a tree. Can't get down. But if you find me a ladder I can get him down, no problem, so don't start going into one. So, have you? Got a ladder I mean."

"Not on me, no, and you're not climbing up it when we do find one. Con, ladder?"

"We've got a stepping ladder."

"Perfect."

"I'll find Mark."

After we've all gathered round the bottom of an apple tree and watched Mark get Archie down, much to his annoyance since he's now maintaining he wasn't actually stuck at all, it's time for Gran and Reg to leave for their cruise.

The Bowls Club people all line up to form a guard of honor, which is slightly disconcerting, and I'm really hoping they're not going to be chucking bowling balls around and giving someone concussion, but they do some special bowling salute instead, and Gran starts to get tearful.

"Now you're sure you'll be all right, pet? Three weeks is a long time, you know. Promise me you'll call if you need me."

"Of course I will, Gran, but we'll all be fine."

"They can get me off the ship in a helicopter in one of those little basket things if you need me. Reg has found out all about it." She's holding his hand. Bless.

"Nothing's going to happen, Gran. You go and have a lovely honeymoon and we'll be waiting for you when you get back. Have a lovely time, Reg."

He puts his hand out, and then hesitates and leans forward and kisses me on the cheek.

"I've been meaning to ask you, Reg. When you come home, would you mind if the boys called you Grandad? Only they were asking me earlier. They'd like to, if you wouldn't mind. Would you?"

I've been saving this as my final wedding present, since I know they'll both love it.

"I'd be honored."

I get a hug from Gran, and then we help them into the car. Even Mum's looking mildly touched, and she's wearing the amethyst brooch Reg gave her yesterday as we stand waving them off.

"Let's get back inside, shall we, Mum? Say our good-byes and then we can make a move, don't you think? I want to

find Mark and thank him. Would you like to come with me?"

"Yes, please, dear. You can tell he trained in Italy. Those biscotti were delicious."

I kiss her.

"What was that for?"

"Nothing. Can't a girl kiss her mum without a reason?"

"I've changed my mind about you and pink—I think it might be one of your colors after all. Maybe a shade or two darker, but you looked very pretty in the church."

Wonders will never cease: a compliment from Mum.

"You looked lovely too."

Vin winks at me as we go back inside.

I'm in the shop on Wednesday texting Ellen, who's gone into prewedding meltdown and is causing havoc at work. She pushed her coanchor right off his chair yesterday twelve seconds before the six o'clock news and has been given an official warning, which she tore up into small pieces in front of senior management.

HAVE RAISED KILT ISSUE WITH BOYS. SUGGEST
STANDBY TROUSERS, JUST IN CASE.

The phone rings.

"What the fuck are standby trousers?"

"Morning, Ellen. How are we feeling today?"

"Quite close to the fucking edge, since you ask. Technically I think I'm teetering."

"Sweetheart, you've got to calm down."

"No, I don't. Trust me. We're flying up this afternoon, and Rebecca's having some sort of dispute with the florist about white roses, so we've got to tour fucking Glasgow looking for alternatives and then I've got a rehearsal dinner with my mother. So calming down isn't really an option."

"How can a florist not be able to get white roses? I'll ask Mrs. Davis for you if you like. We can bring them up in the car."

"They're some special scented ones she's put on her list, and if it's on her list there's hell to pay if it doesn't happen. But she's got it under control, I think. Actually, can you text her about the standby trousers thing, and don't blame me if she throws a complete fruit loop."

"Sure."

"Am I sounding like a nutter?"

"Mildly."

"Good."

"How's your mum doing?"

"About to find herself under sedation."

"That doesn't sound good."

"I'm getting a few syringes so I can jab her in the leg every time she annoys me."

"What's her latest crime?"

"How long have you got? She rang me at seven this morning to talk about chocolate mousse."

"Are we having chocolate mousse?"

"No."

"Right. So what can I do to help?"

"Buy some poison."

"Ellen. Count to ten. Slowly."

"Just get up there as soon as you can."

"Vin's renting a big car on their way back from seeing Lulu's mum. We'll leave as soon as the boys finish school tomorrow. Is that okay? Vin loves driving at night, so Lulu and me will do the first bit and then he'll take over. We should be with you by Friday morning. Soon enough?"

"No. Tell him to put his fucking foot down."

Oh, dear; after packing Mum and Dad off yesterday, I was hoping for a calm couple of days to get my breath back. We got a text from Reg saying they were having a lovely time; I'm guessing he got their steward to do it since it was full of un-Reg-like *we r* ☺ abbreviations, but apparently there were flowers in their cabin ☺ and a note from the captain. But I can't help thinking that keeping Ellen happy over the next few days is going to make Gran's wedding look like a piece of cake.

I t's 8:00 A.M. on Friday, and Lulu and I are having a map-reading crisis while Vin snoozes in the back with the boys. He did most of the driving last night, so I'm feeling fine; there's something about cars at night that lulls me straight off to sleep, and Vin's rented the biggest people carrier he could find, so it's all been remarkably painless, and much cheaper than flying us all up. Even if Vin does think he's taking part in a new world-record attempt for the number of times a pregnant person can need a loo break on one journey.

"There should be a lake soon."

"How soon?"

We appear to be driving through the middle of a forest.

"About ten minutes ago."

Oh, God. Ellen will kill me if we get lost.

My phone beeps.

"Don't read it—it'll be a text from the bride, and she's getting a bit fraught."

"It just says *Help*. Look, there's a signpost."

I slow down beside a Forestry Commission notice telling us we're welcome to have a picnic but if we could try not to burn the forest down as we're leaving they'd be very grateful. Damn. Lighting a fire may be the only way we'll be able to attract the attention of someone who knows where the hell we are.

"Let's carry on up this road for a bit. It's bound to end up somewhere."

"You're definitely one of life's optimists, aren't you, Lulu?"

She smiles.

Please let there be a lake soon.

"Is this some kind of girlie shortcut?"

Excellent. Vin's awake.

"Yes."

The road starts to bend to the right.

"Liar. You've got no idea where we are, have you? I hope you packed some flares in one of those seven hundred bags you've got in the boot."

Lulu turns round to look at him. "No. We thought we'd set fire to your hat."

He's wearing a tartan fleece hat that he bought in a motorway service station at some point during the night when we were all asleep.

"How long before we get there then?"

"Not long."

Lulu and I exchange anxious glances as the road takes a sharp left turn and we emerge from the forest to find ourselves driving along the side of a lake with what looks like a large castle-shaped building in the distance.

Hurrah.

"There, you see. Pretty nifty shortcut."

Please let this be the hotel, and not some stately home where trespassers will be prosecuted, because we appear to be motoring up what looks like their front drive. We pass a very discreet navy blue sign. It's the hotel. Double hurrah.

A young man comes out to help us with the bags, and it's all going rather well until Ellen sweeps into reception. "Thank Christ you've arrived. Welcome to Loch Loon."

The young man retreats behind the reception desk.

Oh, dear.

Our rooms are beautiful; the boys are in a little bedroom off mine, with a huge telly and a stack of age-appropriate DVDs, and the bathroom is bigger than our living room, with a power shower that's so enormous it nearly knocked me over when I had a quick shower to try to wake up. Everything is in slate and chrome with piles of white towels

and every kind of lotion you could possibly want, so we're all squeaky clean and we've just had breakfast in our room, which was fabulous, particularly the kippers.

The boys are watching *The Incredibles* while Vin and Lulu keep an eye on them; they're just down the corridor from us, and while their room isn't quite as palatial as ours, they've got a sunken bath, which the boys are desperate to try out, after the swimming pool in the spa. So it's all looking rather good.

I'm in Ellen's suite, and the perfect white roses have been tracked down, but the rehearsal dinner wasn't a complete success, particularly after Harry had a drinking competition with his brother Jimmy.

"Where is Harry, by the way?"

"Fuck knows. Last time I saw him he was heading off fishing."

"I didn't know he was into fishing."

"He's not. His mates have organized it, so he'll probably come back superglued to his waders."

"That'll be nice for the photographs."

She pours herself some more coffee. "And my mother wants to see you at some point, to lobby you about the table-cloths."

"What's the matter with them?"

"She doesn't like the color. We're doing the tables in different shades of butterscotch and cream. Something like that. Ask Rebecca. Anyway, she wants pink or something,

for the top table. I wasn't really listening. Christ, it's starting already. I'm turning into one of those women who talk about fucking tablecloths, and I'm not even married yet."

"Ellen."

"Let's do a runner."

"And go where?"

"I don't care." She starts to cry.

"Sweetheart." I kneel by her chair and put my arms round her. "It'll all be fine. You love Harry, and it's all going to be perfect."

"I love him like he is now, but what if I don't still love him when he's my husband? Jesus Christ, even saying it makes me feel like I'm one of those women who settle for total losers just so they can say 'me and my husband.'"

"Harry's not like that."

"I know, but let's face it, he's never going to earn any decent money, so it'll be down to me to keep everything going, and I'm fine with that, at least I think I am. But then I look at other women working full-time so some fucker can sponge off them and be a house husband, and it's always total bollocks."

"I can't see Harry doing that."

"I know. But he might. Freelance work can dry up, particularly if you can't be arsed to get out there and hustle, and then what would I do? And I hate the way everyone keeps saying, 'you'll be having babies next,' like you're not a real woman unless you've got puke on one shoulder and a handbag full of Wipe Wets."

"Wet Wipes."

"Those too. It's total bollocks."

"I know, but you want children, you said you did, so what do you care?"

"I don't want people expecting me to have them. Didn't you feel like that?"

"No, mainly because Mum was never that keen. She'd have preferred it if I'd stayed at work and concentrated on my glittering career."

She smiles. "I keep getting the occasional glimpse of something, like when you see the perfect shoes in a window when you're in a taxi, but when you go back they're not there, or they haven't got them in your size. Do you know what I mean?"

"Sort of."

"What if I hate it? Being married and having babies and everything. What will I do?"

"Have a panic and get on with it, like the rest of us?"

"What if it's not enough?"

"Of course it won't be enough, not for every second of the day. Nothing ever is. But if you love him, and he loves you, it's a bloody good start."

"But you and Nick were like that once; you were so perfect together."

"I'm not so sure about that, not really. I think I always loved him more than he loved me. When I look back on it, I can see that now. He was the beloved. And I was so bloody grateful."

She smiles. "You're selling yourself short, as usual."

"No, I'm not, Ellen, and anyway, you and Harry are different. He adores you. And Nick and I wanted such different things."

"Like?"

"I wanted the boys to be happy, and he wanted to be a famous reporter and sleep with younger women."

She laughs. "Bastard. But promise me, if I fuck it up, you'll help me bail out."

"Of course."

"I can come and live with you by the seaside and knit?"

"Any time."

"Good. That's my emergency exit sorted. Right, let's get down to the spa. Rebecca's booked us in for the full works; they're doing some sort of pregnancy version for you, with special stuff."

"Oh, God. I haven't got the right kind of pants on for a spa."

"Please. You're pregnant. They won't be expecting Agent Provocateur."

I'm pretty sure they won't be expecting vintage M & S, with unreliable elastic in a fetching shade of frequent-wash gray either, but never mind. I suppose it'll make a nice change for them.

The combination of the spa and copious amounts of champagne managed to transform Ellen's mood last night, and she was threatening to start a round of strip poker when I went up to bed. Harry's Glaswegian relatives have turned out to be a real treat, particularly his auntie Nell, who's a total star, although she's very bossy, like Gran; she made me sit with my feet up on a chair at one point, which amused Vin no end.

It was nearly twelve by the time I got the boys into bed; they'd gone past the slow-motion stage like bunnies in the ads, and straight into Tired and Tragic. But at least they're both still asleep when I wake up at ten past nine, which is the longest lie-in I've had since I can't remember when.

I even manage a quick bath before Archie wakes up, in one of his I'm a Little Sunbeam moods, which is encouraging, particularly since I've got to try to get him into a kilt. The wedding's not till two, so all the media types will have a chance to get here from their various smart hotels in Glasgow and Edinburgh. So I think I'll build up to the kilt thing as slowly as I can.

"Are you hungry, darling?"

"Yes, but not for porridge."

"Okay. You didn't have to try it yesterday, you know."

"Jack dared me."

"Well, today you can have pancakes, if you like."

"And sausage?"

"Yes."

"And can we go swimming again?"

Possibly not after pancakes and sausage, unless we want to see if Uncle Vin can remember how to do mouth-to-mouth.

"Let's see, but we could go for a walk. We might see a deer."

"Can I have cartoons first?"

"Yes, but quietly. Let's not wake Jack up."

I give him a glass of juice from the minibar. I've moved the booze and pricey peanuts to a high shelf in the wardrobe, and restocked with juice and water and emergency

Smarties, which I brought with us in a cool bag; I know arriving at smart hotels with your own supplies isn't overwhelmingly stylish behavior, but paying for the room for two nights and renting the car has already blown my budget for the next couple of months, so I'm trying to keep our bill down as much as I can.

I'm making myself a cup of tea when Jack wanders in, with his kilt on over his pajamas.

"Look, Mum, you can wear it over your trousers."

Archie shrieks with laughter. "You're wearing a skirt like a girl."

"Shut up, you've got to wear one too. Tell him, Mum."

Actually, now might be a good time to break out those Smarties.

We're standing outside the doors to the ballroom, almost ready for the off, with Ellen looking breathtaking in Vera Wang. Her hair is up and she's wearing a diamond tiara with matching earrings, so she looks incredibly glamorous yet somehow understated and elegant at the same time. I'm in a violet silk brocade smock with a matching coat and shoes, just like the two mini-bridesmaids; Ellen's mum finally triumphed on the small-relations front, and the dressmaker managed to produce two simple shift dresses for them in record time.

Ellen's cousins are thrilled that their girls are playing

such a pivotal role, and Miranda, the mother of the smaller one, has been driving us crazy with requests for extra rehearsals and suggestions about flowers, but Rebecca's keeping a very beady eye on her. Archie and Jack are both in their kilts, only Archie's insisted on wearing his swimming trunks under his, so there's a fair amount of rustling going on.

Ellen's smiling and holding her dad's hand while Rebecca has one last tweak of her dress and talks quietly into her radio mike as a moment of calm finally descends. And then the door opens to the sound of trumpets and the Wedding March. Ellen's told Harry she'll be walking up the aisle to the theme song from *Titanic*, on bagpipes, so I'm guessing he's pretty relieved, and Archie and Jack start to walk slowly holding their posies of roses, keeping as far away from the bridesmaids as possible without actually breaking into a run, and I manage not to tread on the dress or drop the bouquet when Ellen hands it to me. So far, so good.

They're putting on their rings and Harry can't seem to speak and has three shots at saying his name, while I try to find a tissue and Archie starts to fidget, with more rustling noises. And then they're married, and everyone's kissing and posing for photographs and trying to get their bridesmaid daughters into pride of place in the group photographs.

Ellen's as high as a kite and gives me a long hug in between photographs when she whispers that she's never felt

happier, which makes me reach for the tissues again. And Harry gives me a kiss and thanks me for keeping Ellen from killing anyone, particularly him, in the past few days. So I feel I've passed the bridesmaid test with flying colors, which is a huge relief, and then Ellen insists on some photographs of just her and Harry and me and the boys, which doesn't go down very well with Miranda, but we manage to get into lunch without anyone throwing a fit.

The toasts are mercifully short and not too libelous, and then it all turns into a weird mixture of a networking event for the media types, many of whom have arrived in helicopters, and a family wedding with reminiscences about who said what to whom at the last wedding. The media brigade are all looking very pleased with themselves, and it's strange how alien they seem; I recognize quite a few faces, people I worked with ages ago who are now senior news producers or in the upper echelons of management, and they're all looking like they're at a smart London wedding, but they don't seem to be able to talk about anything but work.

There's a great deal of looking over your shoulder when they're talking to you, in case someone more important might be on the horizon, but being pregnant certainly helps, especially with the men, who seem relieved they no longer have to be Sympathetic About Nick. And the women aren't much better; there's a lot of effusive kissing, and one or two of them think running a wool shop is an excellent joke, until they realize I'm serious, but then we run out of things to say and I'm obviously being boring. But whereas this used to make me feel like a failure with faulty networking skills, now I really don't care.

Once we've waved Ellen and Harry off in their helicopter, bound for seven-star luxury in Morocco via Heathrow, and I've fortunately managed to divert Archie from his secret plan to sneak onboard the helicopter, we go back into the hotel and I'm ready for an early night. Vin and Lulu want to stay in the bar and enjoy observing the Glaswegian relatives making fun of the media lot, but I think I'll pass. If Nick was here I'd be feeling lumpen and second-rate; he'd want to spend all night reminiscing about breaking stories and emergency dashes across foreign capitals in between rocket attacks, and I'd want to get the boys into bed. But now I can suit myself, and it's all rather relaxing.

It's weird, but two weddings seem to have made me realize just how happy I am not being married anymore, thank you very much. And while it's true that some people do seem to think everyone has to go around in pairs like we're all about to board Noah's bloody Ark, I'm just relieved I can sort the boys out without worrying what He will want to do.

Seeing Ellen so happy has been lovely, but it hasn't made me feel nostalgic or lonely or any of the things I thought I might feel. Which is a surprise, but I'm actually far less lonely than I used to be when we lived in London. Because there's nothing quite like the nerve-racking, ego-deflating, gibbering-wreck type of loneliness that you feel when you're married to someone who doesn't really want to be married to you anymore. And you're pretty sure it's all your own fault, for being so boring. Blimey. And on top of all that I've got a

fabulous violet outfit I can wear, if I ever go anywhere smart again. So it's been a good day all round.

V in's in a conga line as I take the boys up to bed, and Lulu's dancing with Harry's uncle Alan, who's very energetic for an eighty-two-year-old.

"Mum."

"Yes, Jack?"

"Can we have cartoons, when we're in bed?"

"No, it's very late. Press the lift button, love."

"But as a treat, for being so good, with our flowers?"

"Maybe for five minutes, quietly."

"Mum?"

"Yes, Archie."

"When I get married I'm not having boys in skirts."

"Okay. Press the button again, Jack."

"And I'm not having stupid flowers either."

"Right."

"But you can be my bridesmaid."

"Thanks, Archie."

Excellent. Another wedding to look forward to.

"And, Mum?"

"Yes, Archie."

"When I get married I'm not sharing my cake. Everyone can just have sandwiches. The cake will be only for us."

More cake on the horizon, albeit a rather distant one.

This just gets better and better.

white elephants
and pink
flamingos

July

It's nearly the last week of the summer term and we've got the Summer Fayre on Saturday, so I'm in the shop knitting white elephants, using up oddments of wool from the charity basket and praying for rain. It's been getting hotter for the past few weeks, and standing behind a stall in the baking sunshine is going to be a nightmare. Connie and I have finally decided on our outfits, after rejecting scullery maids, which we think Annabel is secretly hoping for. Connie's come up with Victorian milkmaids, like the ones she's been watching in the film *Oliver!*, which she and Nelly love, only without the pails of milk slung across our shoulders. We're thinking Annabel will approve of something

with peasant origins, and our cheesecloth blouses with long cotton skirts will be cool—even if mine does involve rather more cleavage than I'm accustomed to, thanks to my newly acquired pregnancy bosom, which I haven't really got the hang of yet. I look like I'm channeling Pamela Anderson.

Connie and I went shopping in Canterbury last week to get the skirts, and I found a couple of pairs of giant wide-leg linen trousers with drawstring waists, so at least I won't have to spend every day in my floral-tent dresses. And we bought some pretty cotton caftan tops in the market too, and Connie got some new T-shirts for Mark.

"I'm putting the kettle on. Do you want one of your teas?"

"Please, Elsie."

I'm getting heavily into peppermint now, which is weird since I hated it a few weeks ago.

"You should be sitting down, you know—you'll get terrible veins. Mine were dreadful with Martin."

It's pretty vital I don't encourage her into another one of her When I Was Pregnant reminiscences, not least because they're never very encouraging. But at least she's stopped telling me gory stories about forceps after I threw a mini-fit about it last week.

"I'll check the computer in a minute and see if we've got any more orders, and then I'm due round at Grace's at eleven."

"I thought you were looking smart today. That color suits you, and I think they'll sell really well, you know, if I say so myself."

I'm wearing one of Elsie's new cotton shawls, from a pattern she's made up. In lilac, over a white shirt and my

new black linen trousers; I even managed to paint my toenails last night after a fair bit of puffing and stretching, so I'm
feeling as ready as I'll ever be for a session with the Diva. In
fact I'm feeling pretty chirpy all round: Gran and Reg loved
their honeymoon, as did Ellen and Harry, and the shop's doing well too, with summer day-trippers really starting to
boost sales. And I got top marks on my latest trip to the
clinic, both for my blood pressure and for the baby's weight
gain. So if it could just stop being so bloody hot, everything
would be perfect.

Elsie comes back down with the tea. "Martin says if
you let him know when it's convenient, he'll come in to do
those photos."

"Tell him any time, Elsie. He's putting your shawl on
the website, so we'd better make up some more of the kits.
Olivia sold two on Saturday, and look, she's written them
down in the book ever so neatly."

Elsie's not happy about Olivia working in the shop as a
Saturday girl, although Cath's delighted. We were talking
about it last week at our Stitch and Bitch group, and she
says Olivia's loving it, and even offered to help tidy up after
supper when Cath told her I had a Saturday job for her.

"The till was in ever such a state when I got in on Saturday afternoon. Five-pound notes in with the tens, and no
pound coins at all."

"That's probably my fault. I told her to leave the change to
you, as the senior member of staff. I think you need to be in
charge of all that, don't you?"

She hesitates. "I suppose that's true enough, and I will
say this for her, she worked ever so hard getting the new

stock out—she'd nearly finished when I got in. I like to be fair."

Excellent; maybe we'll have an uneasy truce on our hands.

"She's good with the computer too."

"Martin's showing me how to use it, so she won't need to be bothering about any of that. But she'll be handy in the school holidays, I suppose. You'll have to start to take it easy soon, you know. The last couple of months can be the trickiest. My ankles were so swollen I could only wear my slippers for my last six weeks."

"I've been fine so far, Elsie. Anyway, if you could tell Martin any time for the photos, that would be great."

Martin's finally got our website up and running, after a series of technical hitches, none of which I understand. We've had half a dozen orders so far, and an e-mail from a nutter who can't do buttonholes and wonders if we'll do them for her, in among the usual deluge of offers for loans and a larger willy. But getting our first order was a real thrill, and Elsie's appointed herself Orders Manager, so she can catch up on the gossip with Mrs. Parrish behind the counter in the post office when she takes the parcels in.

"What colors do you want for the shawl kits?"

"Black, definitely, and the new caramel color, the pale one, and white. And maybe that new eau de nil; people will like that, I think. And the lilac too. And maybe the silvery gray?"

"Lovely."

"I've been looking at some of the new autumn colors, too. I thought we'd do some more of the mohair shawls.

They sold so well last year, and there are some lovely new tweeds. Has that order come in for Mrs. Forrest yet?"

"No. I'll give them a call, shall I?"

"Please. And tell them we'll cancel if they don't hurry up. That usually does the trick."

"Right you are, dear."

It's already uncomfortably hot when I arrive at Graceland, and my shirt's gone all wrinkled. There seem to be a few more snappers than usual lurking as I drive in, but thankfully Tom and Jerry are otherwise engaged, so I get into the house without being covered in dog slaver. Maxine sends me straight up to Lily's playroom, where Grace is surrounded by all the brightly colored plastic toys that Lily loves, and all the expensive wooden ones, which she ignores.

"Hi, Jo. I won't be a minute. Meg's downstairs getting her lunch ready. We had an early start this morning. Madam seems to like waking up early at the moment."

Lily's standing up on Grace's lap, looking very pleased with herself.

"I can't believe how much she's changed every time I see her."

Grace kisses the top of her head. "Standing up is her new favorite thing."

I'd forgotten the way they like to stand up all the time when they're around this age, and not really strong enough. I used to have a row of tiny bruises on my thighs from where Archie dug his toes in when he was that age.

Meg appears and takes Lily downstairs, and we're

looking at patterns for cashmere baby cardigans when Maxine comes in, looking flustered. "I'm sorry to interrupt, Grace, but it's Jimmy."

"What's he done now?"

"He's here, outside at the gates, and he's got press with him. He's saying he wants to see Lily and he's not leaving until he does."

"Fucking hell."

"What do you want us to do?"

"I don't know. Give me a minute. Have you called Ed?"

"Yes, he's talking about helicopters. He's on line three."

Grace picks up the phone. "For fuck's sake, Ed, that'll only encourage him. Look, talk to the lawyers and call me back. See if we can get some sort of injunction." She puts the phone down and turns to Maxine. "How many cameras?"

"A full lineup, I'd say."

"Jesus."

Actually, I'm starting to feel a bit sorry for Jimmy, even though I'm sure it's down to rampant pregnancy hormones. I was in tears yesterday watching a baby penguin on one of Jack's wildlife-in-peril programs. But the idea of leaving Jimmy standing by the gates does seem a bit hard.

"Surely it wouldn't be that awful if he saw her?"

Christ. I *so* didn't mean to say that out loud.

Grace looks annoyed. "Yes. It would."

"But it might not be that bad. I mean—"

"Look, perhaps we should reschedule the knitting for another time."

"Oh, right . . . Well, yes, of course."

"If you leave now, the press will stop you at the gates, so

if you could wait downstairs for a while until we sort this out, that would be great. Maxine will show you where. Thanks, Jo."

Bugger. I think I've been dismissed.

"I'm sorry, Grace. I didn't mean to speak out of turn."

She gives me an odd sort of look, a mixture of annoyance and something else too, a hint of vulnerability in among all the steel. Damn, I've been clumsy, and this is bound to be upsetting for her.

"I know you're trying to protect her, Grace, of course you are. And I know it's hard. You know I do. But won't you have to let him see her at some point, if he's bothering to turn up? Otherwise when she asks you about him, what will you say?"

Maxine nods. "That's true, Grace."

Grace looks at Maxine, who blushes and turns to me.

"And I know how difficult this is, Grace, trust me. I'd hate it if Daniel did anything like this, I really would. Not that it looks likely, but we'd all be here with you. If you need us. And if you let him in, then the press won't have a story, will they?"

She smiles. "Okay, okay, I get it. You might be right."

Maxine looks surprised. "Shall I call Ed back then?"

"Yes."

"Maybe we should release a statement as soon as we let him in. Something about how you're glad he's finally showing an interest, and you hope to work things out amicably?"

"Good plan, Max. Get Ed to sort it out. I wonder why he's turned up now; has he got a new album out this week or something?"

Maxine nods and starts scribbling on her pad.

"Well, why the fuck didn't you tell me? We should have known he'd pull something like this. Christ. Okay, say I'm glad he's here and we're sure it's got nothing to do with the album being out this week. My only concern is Lily. And if he wants to build a proper relationship with her, then fine."

"*Bond* is better."

"Yes, *bond*. But I want him to take a drugs test first, just to make sure he hasn't slipped back into his old habits. Brilliant. That should do it. Jo, can you hang on? He knows Max, so it'll only make him worse if she's around, and I want a witness."

"Sorry?"

"When we let him in."

"Of course, if you're sure. I mean there's a chance he might be reasonable, isn't there?"

"Not really, no. Max, has he brought some babe with him?"

"Yes."

"What's she doing?"

"Posing with a giant pink teddy bear."

"Wearing?"

"Not very much."

"So this is her coming-out party then. Clever. Right, tell Bruno to let Jimmy in, but not the girl, once you're sorted with the statement. I'm going to get changed."

Twenty minutes later we're sitting downstairs in the posh living room with the emerald green velvet sofas

and Grace has changed into a beautiful wrap dress and appears to have gone into some sort of breathing-exercise trance. She looks staggeringly beautiful and is clearly in full Diva mode as the door opens and Bruno escorts Jimmy in.

Christ, it's really Jimmy Madden. He's looking fidgety and very thin but still unmistakably every inch the Rock Star. Bruno positions himself by the door, as if Jimmy might be about to steal a painting.

"Hi, babe, nice place."

Grace smiles, one of her full megawatt smiles. "What do you want, Jimmy?"

"Who knows, darling? I'm fucked if I do."

Grace sighs. "I haven't got time for this."

"Got your attention, though, didn't it?" He grins. "And I've got a right to see my daughter."

She stiffens, and then seems to remember something as she breathes out slowly. "Your what?"

"I only want to see her. What harm could there be in that?"

"And will there be cameras at this touching moment?"

"Fuck off."

"Jimmy, this is me you're talking to."

"I'd like to get to know her. I think it'd be cool."

"What about your other children? Aren't they cool too?"

I've forgotten that he has other children; two, I think, or possibly three, from his first marriage, or maybe the second. I've lost count, and I suspect he has too. They must be teenagers now.

"I know I've made some mistakes, but I'd like this one to be different."

"I bet you would. How's the new album selling?"

"Don't be a bitch. It's very bad karma, babe." He turns to me and does one of his slow-motion, crooked-teeth smiles, and my stomach lurches. Blimey. "Who the fuck are you?"

"She's a friend of mine, Jimmy. Leave her alone."

"Oh, you've got a friend now, have you? How much are you paying her?" He smiles again. "Whatever she's paying you, darling, trust me, it's not enough."

Before I can stop myself I'm blurting, "I don't think this is helping anyone," and going bright red as he looks at me and laughs.

"Oh, don't you? Well, it's definitely helping me."

Grace stands up. "Well, it's been lovely seeing you again, Jimmy. So sweet of you to drop in; do let us know next time you're in the area."

"Where is she?"

"Upstairs. Asleep."

"Babes, I know you're only looking out for her, and I can respect that. Totally. But if I could spend a little time with her and get to know her . . . I'd hate her to think her dad didn't care about her. That's all."

Grace smiles, a sad sort of smile; I think part of her really wants to believe him.

"Okay. Come next weekend sometime, Sunday maybe. Half an hour. No media. And you sign a confidentiality agreement. No interviews, no photos."

"Come on, be fair. All I want is a couple of snaps for my mum."

"Your mum's dead, Jimmy. We went to the funeral, re-member? It was just before my mum got ill. And if you

want photographs I'll get Max to give you copies. She'll even put them in frames for you. Oh, and we've released a statement, saying we'd like you to take a drugs test before you see Lily. The lawyers insisted."

"You're a fucking piece of work, do you know that?"

"Well, as my mum used to say, it takes one to know one. Bye, Jimmy."

Bruno steps forward and opens the door.

"See he doesn't take any detours, Bruno. And Jimmy, next time, pick up the fucking telephone."

He hesitates and then walks out.

Christ. My hands are shaking, so God knows how Grace is being so calm.

She sits back down. "So. Not interested in my gorgeous girl after all, then."

"I'm so sorry, Grace."

"It's fine."

"No, it's not. And I'm sorry I sat there like a dummy. I should have said something. Apart from that stupid thing about how this isn't helping."

"I liked that. He probably thinks you're my lawyer anyway, don't worry about it. You were great."

"You never know, maybe when Lily's older he'll have mellowed a bit."

"Settled down to grow organic veg and play the fucking lute? Not likely, he wants to go out in a blaze of glory, very rock and roll. It's amazing he's lasted this long, actually. There's a hotel room somewhere with his name on it, trust me."

"Well, you gave him a chance."

She smiles. "Next weekend is like next year in Jimmy world. Forty-eight hours is about the most he can cope with. I didn't give him any chance at all. I can't afford to. He'd blow it. There'd be pictures of her in all the papers, and I don't want that for her."

"Of course you don't."

"No more news from Daniel, I take it?"

"No, not since the DNA letter."

"God, men can be so useless."

"Some of them."

"All of them. What man do you know who you'd really trust with your kids?"

"My brother, Vin."

"I'd forgotten about him. Okay, apart from him?"

"There are some nice men out there, Grace, I'm sure there are."

"Names?"

"My friend Connie's husband, Mark, he's lovely, and Martin, he's helping me do the website for the shop, and Reg, he's nice."

"He married your gran, right?"

"Yes."

"I've always had terrible taste in men. I always go for the bad boys. But I think I might try something a bit less complicated next time."

"Next time?"

"I'm holding auditions, cast to be announced."

"How lovely."

Maxine comes back in. "He did a quick interview at the

gates and then got back into his car. He said he's respecting his daughter's privacy, so he won't be discussing anything. He looked pretty pissed off, though."

"I bet he did. Right, I'm starving. What about you, Jo? I think Sam has made cake, if you're interested. And I want to look at those patterns. Have we got those studio dates sorted yet, Max? I want to get them into Jo's diary."

"They're still confirming."

"Well, let her have them as soon as we know. We're off to Paris tomorrow, for meetings about the Simone de Beauvoir film. Come with us, if you like."

"I'd love to, but I've got the school Summer Fayre on Saturday. I'm doing the white-elephant stall. Appropriate, don't you think?"

Maxine smiles. "I'll sort out a couple of bags for you. We get loads of requests for stuff for charity auctions, so I've got a cupboard full of things Grace has signed off. Come and have a look."

"That would be great. If you're sure?"

Grace nods.

"I'll meet you in the kitchen. I need food."

A fter standing and marveling in front of the charity cupboard outside Maxine's office, and recognizing some of the costumes from Grace's films, I realize Maxine hasn't really understood just how low-key our white-elephant stall is likely to be. There's no way we could sell any of these things for anything like the money they'd get at a

proper charity event, so we end up agreeing that I'll take a beautiful beaded shawl, which we can have as some sort of top-prize incentive, and then I sit knitting with Grace for half an hour, while she picks at a salad and I try to resist a second slice of fruitcake.

She hugs me as I'm leaving, which isn't something she's done before. "Thanks, Jo."

"My pleasure. Well, not pleasure, but you know. Any time."

"So you'd come, even if you weren't on the payroll?"

"Of course I would, if only for the cake."

She laughs. "Great. And you signed a confidentiality thing, didn't you, the one Max sent you?"

"Of course I did, Grace."

"Sorry. I shouldn't have mentioned it. You never ask for stuff, and I like that. Everyone always wants something."

"Well, now you mention it—"

"What?"

"I'm joking, but a few top tips on how I'm going to carry off being dressed as a Victorian milkmaid while we're on our white-elephant stall would be good."

She smiles as Maxine appears with a large shopping bag. "Grace asked me to put a couple of extra things in for you and your friend. But not for the stall, though, okay?"

"Thank you so much. That's really kind."

Maxine walks me to my car. "Thanks for today, Jo. It really helped having you here. She was pretty rattled."

"I don't blame her."

"If they try to stop you at the gates, just say you don't know what they're talking about, okay?"

"Sure."

"Most of them have left, so you should be fine. Bruno will see you out. And I'll call you later with those dates."

"Thanks, for the shawl and everything. It'll be the star of our stall."

As soon as I'm out of sight of the house, I stop the car to look in the bag; there's a beautiful pale blue kimono that I remember Grace wearing when she was heavily pregnant, and it's so enormous I'm pretty sure I'll be able to fit into it, even if it won't wrap round quite as much as it did on her. And there's a gold evening bag that I'm sure Connie will love. We'll put some money in the pot for the stall, and get to feel like film stars at the same time. Brilliant.

I'm ten minutes early for school, so I nip into the hall to see how the new school banner is coming along. Mrs. Chambers is sitting sewing on a border of the knitted picture squares the top class made, interspersed with brightly colored squares in different fabrics. Satin and velvet mostly, from the oddments that parents have brought in. She's dyed a large flannel sheet pale gray, and we've made up the letters for BROADGATE SCHOOL from the different strips of knitting Mrs. Callender's class made. The sea looks particularly good in lots of different shades of blue knitted squares,

courtesy of Archie's class, and the school building is looking much clearer now Mrs. Pickering has hemmed round
the gray and brown squares in black wool.

"We're going to start sewing on the trees tomorrow. The
children are so excited. They keep coming over to have a
look and see where their work is going. Even Mrs. Morgan
was having a look earlier on too."

We exchange glances.

"Will you still be in on Friday so we can start on the
people? Mr. O'Brien's doing history with my lot for the afternoon, so I'll be free until three."

"Yes, Friday should be fine. How many squares have we
got now?"

Mrs. Chambers has solved the problem of how to turn an
assortment of woolen shapes into little stick people by sewing them onto pieces of gray flannel and giving them out in
batches to all the sewing volunteers to add arms and legs and
faces. Jane Johnson and Mrs. Pickering have done quite a
few, and Mrs. Williams who runs the Brownies should definitely get a gold sewing badge for her brilliant range of
different-colored faces and hair, all neatly embroidered in
silks and wools.

"I thought we could sew Mr. O'Brien's bell on top of the
clock tower on Friday. He's very keen we don't forget."

"Great."

"And I thought I should warn you, he's mentioned you
in his end-of-term letter. Saying thank you for coming in to
do the knitting."

"That was kind of him. I hope he thanked you too."

"Oh yes, but you get a special mention." She winks, and

I know exactly what she's thinking: Annabel Morgan is going to love that.

Connie's thrilled with the gold bag, and we arrange to sort through all the jumble tomorrow after school; we've already diverted two full bin bags to the recycling skips outside Sainsbury's, and I've got a feeling there'll be more when we start on the next load of shopping bags waiting for us in the school secretary's office.

Connie's taking Nelly to ballet, which she's recently started, mainly because she likes the outfits, so I bring Marco home with us, and Archie throws a strop when he and Jack won't let him join in their Lego game.

I'm knackered by bedtime, but I've tried on the kimono and it fits, so I'm slinking about wearing it after my bath, when it finally starts to rain and everything cools down.

Jimmy's performance today has rattled me; it's reminded me that there's probably still more to come from Daniel at some point. More lawyers' letters, who knows? The baby's moving a lot tonight, like it's trying to get comfortable. Oh, God, I wish this was Nick's baby. I really do. It would be so much simpler. I know, I'll write a list; that always helps. A list and some tea, and I can lie and listen to the rain and try to get some sleep.

I'm in the shop on Wednesday morning making up an order for a beach-bag kit and trying to find where Elsie's

put the scissors when she rushes in looking flushed and breathless.

"You'd better come, it's Mr. Pallfrey. That silly dog's had him over, in the middle of the road. It's a miracle he wasn't killed. I'll stop here. He's outside the baker's, and he's asking for you."

"Is he all right?"

"Well, he's a funny color, but I think so. They've called an ambulance, to be on the safe side, and he was sitting up, but you never know."

The ambulance has arrived, and there's a small crowd, including Betty and Mrs. Davis, both looking worried.

"Here she is, Arnold. Now don't you fret."

He's lying on a stretcher, with an ambulance man putting a needle in his arm and Trevor lying beside him, being unusually quiet.

"Hello, Mr. Pallfrey." I don't think I'll call him Arnold. It seems a bit cheeky somehow.

He smiles, very faintly. "Hello, dear. Sorry about this. Silly fuss about nothing, I'm sure. I only took a little tumble."

I kneel down, which takes a bit of doing, and I notice the ambulance man glancing at my stomach.

"No need to upset yourself, love. He's a tough old bird, aren't you, Arnie?"

Mr. Pallfrey looks faintly embarrassed and nods.

"Broken his elbow and his wrist, if I'm not mistaken. Must have gone down quite hard. Banged his hip too, and they can be tricky. We're taking him to the General."

"Is there anything you need, Mr. Pallfrey? Would you like me to go home and pick up a few things for you?"

"Would you, dear, and could you ring my Christine? She's in Spain, but I've got her mobile number in the book by the telephone. I'll give you the key." He winces as he tries to reach for his pocket, and the ambulance man puts a rubber-gloved hand in and retrieves the keys for him.

"Here you go, love. Need a hand back up? Don't want to end up taking both of you in, do we? Not feeling any twinges, are you?"

"No, I'm fine, thanks."

"Shock can be dangerous, you know. Long time since we delivered a baby—be handy to get some practice in. Usually get in the papers if there's a baby putting in an appearance." He's grinning, and I think this is all part of his upbeat banter. But it doesn't seem to be doing a great deal for Mr. Pallfrey.

"I'm fine. I've got ages to go yet."

"Well, you can't be too careful."

The other ambulance man has wandered over now, holding a nylon bag.

"You don't want to listen to Dave. He likes to tout for extra business when we're out and about. Now then, Arnold, that's you sorted. Let's get you off to the hospital. I'll put the sirens on if you like. No need, of course, but if you fancy it, I'm game. What do you think?"

Mr. Pallfrey smiles.

"So what are we doing with the dog then?" He looks at me.

Bugger.

"Shall I take him home with me?"

"Would you, dear? Only until I get home. I couldn't think who else to ask, and he's so fond of you and your lads."

"Of course, no problem. I'll see you later, and try not to worry, I'm sure it'll be okay."

"I'm sure they won't keep me in."

I bet they bloody will.

"Try to relax, and I'll see you in a little bit."

Betty walks back to the shop with me, with Trevor trotting along quite sedately, only making the occasional lunge.

"Silly thing will pull you over in a minute as well."

"Don't worry, Betty. We've got an understanding, haven't we, Trevor?" I yank on the lead. "Walk, Trevor, or I'll sit on you, like last time, and I'm a lot heavier than I was then. Okay. Walk."

He turns and licks my hand, which makes Betty laugh. "Well, he does seem fond of you, I can see that. And I bet your boys will be pleased."

"Pleased? They'll be bloody euphoric."

It's nearly eleven by the time I've gone to the house with Betty, who's insisted on coming too so she can hold Trevor, but really so she can have a quick look round. She's very impressed by how clean everything is, and apparently Mr. Pallfrey has got the same washing-up brush as hers.

Elsie's agog back at the shop. I'm hoping she might dog-

sit while I go to the hospital to see Mr. Pallfrey, but she's not exactly volunteering, and Trevor's already half terrified Mrs. Marwell when she came in for some more peach four-ply and he got up from his newly designated space behind the counter.

"I'll put the kettle on, dear. You look like you could do with a cup. Does he like biscuits, do you think?"

"That's a good idea. I'll take him some biscuits and fruit when I go in."

"No, dear, I meant Trevor."

"I don't know, but don't give him any. The last thing I need is something that size with a sugar high."

We both look at Trevor, who's now lying prone on the floor, having edged himself out from behind the counter. He yawns, showing a row of rather big teeth, and Elsie takes a step backward.

"Well, he can't stay in here, you know—some of our ladies won't like it. I'd take him home myself, you know I would, but my Jeffrey's never liked dogs. I'll go and make that tea, shall I?"

I stand behind the counter with Trevor giving my ankles the occasional lick while I try to work out how much damage he could do to our back garden if I left him out there while I go to the hospital. I could tie him to something solid, I suppose, but I'm not sure if that's allowed and I really don't need the RSPCA turning up to report me on top of everything else. Bloody dog.

I'm really starting to panic when Gran arrives. Hurrah. Finally, the cavalry have turned up.

"There you are. What a terrible thing. Betty's just come

and told me at the Lifeboats. So I've swapped with Mrs. Tanner and I'm here to help."

"Thanks, Gran."

"I've called Reg, and he's on his way."

"Great. Look, could you go up to the hospital for me, take him in his things, so I can get His Lordship out of here before he frightens any more customers?"

"Of course I can, pet."

"And tell him Trevor's fine, would you? He'll be worried."

Trevor sits up, and Gran tuts.

"You go home and have a bit of a lie-down. Shut him in the kitchen. And I'll be round later."

Shut him in the kitchen? Is she mad?

loody bugger and damn it.

Trevor's in the back garden lolloping about while I'm trying to work out where on earth he's going to sleep. Definitely not upstairs. Definitely. Even if I have to lie across the landing all night.

I call Ellen at work. "You'll never guess what."

"It's twins."

"No. And that's not funny. I've got Trevor to stay. Mr. Pallfrey's had an accident."

"Christ. Is he going to snuff it?"

"Ellen!"

"Sorry. But is he?"

"No, but I think he'll be in for a while."

"Fuck."

"You're telling me."

"The boys will so love it."

"You think?"

"I'll bike Harry down to help out, if you like. He's been really annoying me lately."

"Why?"

"General boy stuff. He left some dry cleaning out for me yesterday, like I'm suddenly in charge of his clothes. Christ. The honeymoon's definitely over."

"And?"

"And I'm still not pregnant."

"Sweetheart, you've only just started trying. Give it time."

"No. Now I've decided I want it, I've started looking at pregnant women in the fucking street."

"Come down for the weekend. You sound like you could do with a break."

"Maybe. I might try to get down for your fete, see you dressed up as a white elephant."

"Milkmaid."

"Trust me, darling, with that much muslin, it'll come to the same thing."

"Thanks a lot."

"Any time."

"Good luck with the dog." She's laughing.

"Ellen?"

"Yes, darling?"

"Piss off."

I'm lying on the sofa while Trevor digs a hole in the garden. Mr. Pallfrey's been digging over the flower beds

recently, and I think Trevor wants to carry on the good work. I'm watching a bossy woman on telly showing everyone how to customize their picnic tables with stenciled napkin rings. If only. Since I'm not in the shop, I should probably be making a start on the epic ironing pile, but I just can't face it. Maybe a light doze would be good; a snooze and then a snack. Perfect.

I've just got comfy on the sofa with strategically placed cushions when the bloody phone rings. It's Martin, which is ideal because obviously what I really need now is another discussion about the bloody website, or Wood.

"Sorry, Martin, I haven't had a chance to catch up with Gran, but I'm sure she'll do it at some point." I'm meant to be getting her to write down her pattern for the frilly tea cozy.

"Oh, right, well, good, but actually I was calling about something else. I gather there's a dog going spare?"

"Sorry? Oh, you mean Trevor?"

"Yes, and well, the thing is, I'd love to have him, if you wouldn't mind."

"Don't tell fibs, Martin. Has Elsie been on the phone to you?"

"I've always wanted a dog, honestly, and this would be a good way to try it out, owning one I mean, but the thing is I've got a bit of freelance work on at the moment, to help with the finances for the barn, so could we share? Until Mr. Pallfrey's back in action. His daughter works in Spain now, doesn't she?"

"Yes, she's on her way back, but she can't stay for long, she says, or she'll lose her job."

"And your gran says they think he'll need an operation

on his hip, and his arm too. Apparently they've got to put a pin in or something. So it might be weeks rather than days."

"So when did you talk to Gran?"

"Bugger. I wasn't supposed to say that bit."

"Martin."

"I really do want him. I was thinking of getting a puppy—I thought maybe a Labrador. I've always had a soft spot for them. But having Trevor would be great practice, as long as he can stay with you when I'm working. I don't think it would be fair to leave him at the barn by himself, would it?"

"Not unless you've got a lot more demolishing you want doing."

"Could you have him when I'm away working?"

"Are you really sure about this, Martin?"

"Definitely."

"Well, yes, that would be great."

"Right, I'll pick him up later this evening then, shall I? I'm in London at the moment, but I'll be back around ten. I thought I'd get him a present, maybe one of those chew things, so he's happy to come with me. What do you think?"

"Bless your heart. The saint of pregnant people will smile on you forever."

"Good. You never know when that sort of thing's going to come in handy."

Gran arrives as I'm starting on the ironing and pretends to be surprised that Martin has offered to dog-share Trevor.

"That was nice of him."

"When did you call him to tell him to volunteer?"

"From the hospital, and I didn't tell him anything, but I remembered Elsie never let him have pets, wouldn't even let him have a rabbit, poor little thing."

"Did he want a rabbit then?"

"Not as far as I know, but I know he wanted a dog, Jeffrey did too, but Elsie wouldn't hear of it."

"I don't blame her."

"Well, at least you won't have a great big dog cluttering up the place for weeks."

"I know, Gran, and thanks. How was he? Do you think he'll be in the hospital for long?"

"I wouldn't be surprised. He'll be quite poorly when they do his hip, you know, and with his arm out of action, I don't think they'll let him home until they're sure he can manage. When's his Christine arriving?"

"Later tonight. She's going straight to the hospital and then I've invited her here for supper. If I'm still at Stitch and Bitch, there's quiche and salad in the fridge."

"Right you are. I'll get some cake in case she's eaten and only wants a cup of tea."

"Thanks, Gran."

Trevor's inevitably the star attraction when I collect the boys from school, although I keep a tight hold of the lead so he can't bowl any toddlers over. He's pretty good with small people, and tends to lie down so they can tickle him, but he sits up attentively as Annabel walks past, and

I'm pretty sure I hear a tut. The kids take turns holding the lead as we walk back home, with Marco and Nelly badgering Connie to buy the largest dog she can find, immediately.

"Mummy?"

"Yes, Archie."

"This is my best day ever. Ever."

"Well, it's not been poor Mr. Pallfrey's best day."

Or mine, come to that.

"I know, but it'll be nice for him knowing Trevor is with us. Because he loves us, Mum, doesn't he?"

"Yes, but he's not staying with us all the time, Archie. It wouldn't be fair on him when I'm in the shop working. He'll be with Martin for some of the time."

Actually, most of the time, hopefully.

"But he's staying with us some nights, isn't he?"

"Yes. Some."

Archie beams.

"It's marvelous, isn't it, Mum?"

"Yes, love."

Christ, I wonder what'll be next; now I seem to have landed myself with a semidetached dog, maybe Bruno would like a weekend retreat for Tom and bloody Jerry. I'll end up on the beach looking like those nutters trying to take packs of dogs for a walk, tangled up in leads with dribble all over my coat.

It's the morning of the Summer Fayre, and I'm stuffing kapok into the last of the white knitted elephants before I sew them up while simultaneously trying to persuade

Archie not to eat his breakfast in the Cath Kidston dog basket Ellen has sent, as a surprise present to make up for canceling coming down this weekend. She's on some story, so it arrived in a courier van, and Archie slept in the bloody thing last night, which gave me a hell of a fright when I got up for one of my increasingly frequent trips to the loo. There's nothing quite like patrolling a house in total darkness looking for a small boy who's meant to be in his bed to make you completely wake up and contemplate dialing 999, until you find him curled up in a dog basket in the kitchen.

"Come on, Archie, please, and sit up at the table."

"It's not fair. You said we'd have Trevor for some of the time, and we haven't. Hardly any. And that's a lie."

"We had him on Thursday, Archie, and Martin's working again next week, so we'll probably have him then as well."

I think Mr. Pallfrey will be in hospital for quite a while yet: I went in to see him yesterday, and he was marooned inside vast pajamas, which Christine bought for him before she had to go back to Spain, trying to be brave but wincing every time he moved.

She's coming back for him when they let him out, and taking him to Spain to convalesce. So it looks like we're going to be dog sitting for a bit longer. Talk about the thin end of the bloody wedge.

"It's not fair. Martin's greeding him off us, and he was our dog first."

"He's Mr. Pallfrey's dog, Archie, and he loves all the space at Martin's house, you know he does."

"We should get him some toys at our house like Martin has. I can use my pocket money."

We collected Trevor from Martin before school on Thursday and found him having a brilliant time with an obstacle course of planks and a growing collection of partially mauled squeaky toys.

"Okay. How much have you got saved up?"

"Nearly fifty p."

"Right."

Excellent. Not enough for anything too squeaky then.

"Mum?"

"Yes, Jack?"

"I might buy Trevor a toy too. How much do you think they'd be?"

This is getting serious; if Jack's considering parting with some of his carefully saved funds, then I'm really in trouble, especially when Trevor finally goes home and we've got the toys but no sodding dog. Damn.

"I don't know, sweetheart. A lot of money, I think. I'm going up to get ready now. Finish your breakfast, Archie."

Victorian milkmaid, here we come.

Oh, God.

Connie and I are standing behind our stall at ten to two, and I'm still fretting about burgeoning cleavage issues and my inability to keep my blouse from slipping off my shoulders in the manner of a Victorian streetwalker. I'm doing my best with a black cotton shawl, but Mr. Nelson's already been over twice, offering to help us unpack.

"Hand me a safety pin, Con. I think I've just had a brilliant idea."

We've got a Tupperware box full of safety pins for attaching price tickets to things, which we haven't actually used because we've decided everything is going to be two pounds. After I've reunited my bra strap with the shoulder seam inside my blouse, Connie asks me to fix hers for her, and I'm delving down her front when Mr. Nelson comes over again, with an old ice-cream tub full of change. He stands watching us, leaning forward slightly with an unpleasant leer on his face. This is probably going to be the highlight of his week.

"Sorry to interrupt, ladies. Annabel asked me to remind you that your target for the day is ninety-five pounds, and here's your float. Quite a tall order, I'd say, but I'm sure you'll manage. Two lovely ladies like you."

It's a pretty hefty target for a load of old tat, so it's a good job we've got a cunning plan.

He puts his hands in his trouser pockets and jingles his change; at least I think that's what he's doing. He's in Victorian costume too; all the PTA people are, although the teachers are sensibly pretending they didn't realize Annabel meant they had to dress up as well. She's livid about it, according to Jane Johnson. Mr. Nelson's wearing a suit with a cravat and a top hat and appears to be channeling Leslie Phillips. Annabel is in pink ruffled splendor with a bustle and matching parasol, and there's a definite swish when she walks past, which I think she's loving, although Mrs. Nelson seems to have drawn the short straw in a rather sickly green, and she appears to be having trouble with her bustle, which has gone rather lopsided.

Everyone else seems to have gone for variations on the long-dresses theme, with a few cotton pinnies, and Jane

Johnson and Tina Davis have joined us with long floral skirts, but they've sensibly chosen white pin-tucked blouses rather than milkmaid décolletage. And then there's Mrs. Denning, who's also Annabel's friend, wearing her Victorian bathing costume, which is particularly brave of her given the size of her bottom; horizontal stripes are terribly unforgiving.

Annabel has kitted herself out with a megaphone and looks very pleased with the size of the crowd as she opens the gates.

Mark and the kids make straight for the bouncy castle.

"Hello, Mrs. Marwell."

"Hello, dear. How much are these flamencos?" She holds up a pair of pink plastic flamingos.

"Everything's two pounds, but you get a go on our lucky dip, and you can win the shawl, or a box of cakes."

Mark's made us cakes, which are waiting for the lucky winner in a white cardboard box under the table in the shade, and we've put Grace's shawl up on a box in the middle of our table, covered in gold tissue paper. The combination of sheer chiffon and beautiful silver beading looks dazzling in the sunshine.

"What sort of cakes are they, dear?"

"Hazelnut and white chocolate ones, and meringues."

"I'm not that keen on nuts—they get under my teeth—but go on then, since it's for a good cause."

She hands me a fiver, and I hand her back four pounds in her change; she's always knitting for charity and I know

her pension doesn't leave her much spare, and she won't notice the bonus in her change, she never does.

"Did I win then?"

"You have to unfold a ticket from the glass bowl."

She doesn't win, but she's very happy with the flamingos, which are destined to stand next to the gnomes by her pond. She thinks they'll scare off the herons.

"Are there lots of herons round here then?"

"Yes, and they're right little Bs, excuse my French—have all your goldfish if you let them. I tell them every morning when I'm feeding them, keep down at the bottom, but I lost two last week."

"Oh, dear."

"I'm looking forward to seeing the new school banner, dear. Mrs. Pickering was telling me all about it. Lovely to get the kiddies knitting—we all did it in my day. Well, the girls, of course. There'd have been a big fuss if you'd asked the boys to join in. Not like nowadays. Anyway, see you later."

We're unpacking more bric-a-brac and trying to arrange it attractively, which isn't easy, as the crowd builds up. Connie's been telling everyone Grace wore the shawl to a film premiere, which for all I know she may have done, and we're running out of our stock of old shopping bags as people buy two or three things in an effort to win it.

The big china bowl where we've put the folded-up raffle tickets is getting emptier by the minute when Jane Johnson wins the box of cakes. She's thrilled, and says it's the first

time she's won anything in five years of working at the school in the office, and I'm really pleased for her, but if the shawl goes soon we'll be stuck trying to flog a load of old tat with no bonus items. Damn; we should have thought of that.

Gran arrives with Reg and Betty and brings us over a cup of tea. Mark's on the field behind the playground playing an impromptu game of football, and hordes of children seem to have attached themselves to him for the afternoon, including Trent Carter and Kyle, who are in goal between piles of sweaters. He waves at us, looking rather panicky, which makes Connie laugh.

"Should we get someone to rescue him, Con?"

"No, he likes it."

Mr. O'Brien comes over and compliments us on the woolly elephants, which are selling really well, before heading off to the playing field with his whistle to join in the fun as Martin turns up with Elsie and Trevor and the football game gets two more players, one of whom runs off with the ball and has to be chased right across the field.

Mr. Nelson comes over to look at a wooden box with a broken lid again and stares at Connie's chest very hard until she does a little jiggle that makes him retire rather speedily, sweating profusely. I get the last of the bags in from the car. Cracked-glass butter dish, anybody?

I'm selling the last knitted elephant to a small girl from Archie's class who he insists on calling Nettle, which can't be right so I'm trying to hear what her mum calls her, as

Mrs. Pickering, everyone's favorite school-dinner lady, unfolds her ticket and wins the shawl.

"But I never win things."

Connie smiles. "Let me put it on for you."

Mrs. Pickering drapes the shawl around her shoulders as she wanders off in a daze to show her husband.

Connie starts putting the last few things on the table back into one of the big cardboard boxes.

"I think we are finished now, yes?"

"Pretty much."

"What shall we do with these?"

"Stick them in my car, and I'll put them into recycling next time I'm at Sainsbury's."

"Brava."

"It was so great that Mrs. Pickering got the shawl."

"Yes."

"Connie?"

"I helped a little bit."

Ten minutes later we've stashed the leftover boxes of tat in my car and I'm standing on the stage next to Annabel, who's edging forward as Mr. O'Brien draws the raffles and hands out bottles of wine and boxes of chocolates. Mrs. Nelson comes up the steps and hands him a slip of paper, looking rather grim-faced, and he announces that the total raised for school funds today looks like being nearly nine hundred pounds, which is a record, and everyone claps.

"And we must all give a special round of applause to Mrs. Mackenzie and Mrs. Maxwell for raising two hundred

and seventeen pounds on their white-elephant stall, which is another record."

Everyone claps, and Mark kisses Connie.

Annabel looks furious.

"Now, before we go we'd like to unveil our new school banner. Over to you, Mrs. Chambers."

She helps two of the bigger boys from the top class wheel in a display board and lift it up the steps to the stage, and there's a hush as she stands in front of it.

"Thank you, Mr. O'Brien. I think most of you know that we've been learning about knitting this term, and everyone has made something for our new banner. So before we admire their work, I'd like to thank Mrs. Mackenzie and everyone who's been helping in our classrooms."

There's applause as the boys lift the sheet off the partition to reveal the new banner in all its glory. God, she must have spent hours sewing on more people and trees because there are no blank spaces anymore, and someone, probably Mrs. Pickering, has embroidered gold thread around the letters of the school name, and sewn little glinting silver shapes onto the sea and what look like green beads into the trees. It looks brilliant, and Mr. O'Brien seems almost overwhelmed, and kisses us both.

Annabel's got a face like thunder when we climb down from the stage, but Mrs. Chambers is beaming. "Isn't it marvelous, something we can really be proud of, and everyone took part. Could you come to the staff room for a minute, only I forgot your flowers. I meant to give them to you to say thank you."

"You didn't need to, honestly, I really enjoyed it."

"Well, good, because Mrs. Pickering says she's happy to help with the knitting as part of art on Wednesday afternoons, and we were both hoping you'd let us have some simple patterns she can use with the ones who'd like to knit."

"Of course I will."

She's showing me a book she's bought on knitting with kids in the staff room when we hear Annabel and Mrs. Nelson going into the secretary's office next door.

"They look like total sluts in those ridiculous outfits."

There's a thrilled gasp from Mrs. Nelson. "I know. Isn't it dreadful?"

"I'm not surprised. That wool-shop woman's always thought she's better than the rest of us with her fancy friends. Of course illegitimate babies are obviously all the rage, so normal standards of decent behavior don't apply to her, apparently."

Christ. Mrs. Chambers looks terribly embarrassed as I stand up and walk toward the doorway carrying my bouquet of flowers.

Actually, as Ellen would say, fuck this.

"Hello, Annabel. I thought it was you."

Mrs. Chambers is standing behind me as Annabel falters; I think she's desperately trying to work out if I've heard her, or more important, if Mrs. Chambers has.

"I bet you're pleased with how well everything's gone today. You must remember to thank Connie."

"Sorry?"

"Thank Mrs. Maxwell. She did most of the work on our

stall, and her husband made the brilliant cakes. Such an important part of being the president of the PTA, thanking people for all their hard work. Don't you think?"

Mrs. Nelson looks positively frightened now as Annabel tries to rally. "Yes, of course. I always thank my team."

"Do you? I must have missed that bit. Anyway, I'd better go and find the kids. Oh, and by the way, Annabel, nobody says *illegitimate* anymore, unless they're a total bigot, of course. Great outfit, although you do look a bit hot. That's one advantage of dressing like a slut; it's wonderfully cool."

I walk back along the corridor toward the hall, feeling very, very pleased with myself. I'm feeling shaken but not really stirred, and for once in my life I've managed actually to say what I wanted to say, instead of thinking of it ten minutes later. And serve her right.

Mrs. Chambers is smiling. "That was wonderful. Well done, you."

"Cow."

"Precisely. I can't wait to tell Mr. O'Brien. It's made my day."

"Mine too."

We're laughing as Annabel storms past us, looking livid, with Mrs. Nelson trotting along behind her.

Shame.

Mark has to head back to the pub to get ready for the evening rush, so Martin and Reg walk home with the kids and Trevor, and I drive back with Connie and Gran. She's made a summer pudding, and I've got cold chicken in

the fridge, so I've only got to make salads and boil some potatoes and we'll be set.

"Shall we eat in the garden?"

"Lovely, pet. It'll be nice and cool under the big tree."

The boys are having a lovely time in the garden while Nelly plays in the tent and we drink tea in the kitchen and make the salads.

I've rinsed out the cool bag we had at school and I'm putting it back in the boot of the car when I notice Martin is tied to a tree in the front garden, with what looks like Trevor's extendable dog lead.

"Having fun?"

"I'm a hostage."

"Right."

"Only I can't actually move my hands, and I think they've sort of forgotten I'm the hostage. You couldn't untie me?"

"Why didn't you shout?"

"They were only playing."

"Martin."

"I was too embarrassed. I thought I'd undo it and slope back into the house, but I've only made the knot tighter."

The little swines have wrapped the lead round his legs and the tree trunk, and then round his hands before knotting it.

Archie comes thundering through the side gate.

"Mum, don't let him free—he's our prisoner."

I carry on unraveling dog lead. "Don't be silly, Archie. You can't leave people tied to trees."

Trevor's running round us now, barking.

"We'll tie you up next."

"Oh no you won't, not if you want any pudding tonight."

He tuts.

"Tea, Martin?"

"Please. Or possibly something stronger."

"What, like for shock? Being taken hostage must have taken its toll."

"I think I'd prefer it if we never mentioned this again, if you don't mind."

"I'll think about it. What's it worth?"

"Sorry?"

"For me not to tell your mum horrible big boys tied you to a tree?"

He shakes his head. "I'm never going to live this down, am I?"

"All right, I promise, subject closed."

"Great."

"Come on, Houdini. You can help me lay the table."

He sighs.

Supper is a triumph. We carry an odd assortment of chairs out into the garden, or rather Connie and Martin do while Reg supervises. I've even found some candles, which we've stuck in plant pots, and Connie's sprinkled rose petals on the tablecloth.

There's an impromptu game of football after we eat, and I'm having a quiet five minutes on the sofa before I make coffee; two helpings of summer pudding have put paid to there being any chance of me even managing to stand in goal.

When I wake up, Gran's sitting knitting, and it's nearly dark.

"The boys are in bed, pet—we didn't like to wake you. Reg has gone back with Martin to see the barn. Sounds like it's coming on a treat, doesn't it? And Connie says she'll call you tomorrow. I gave the boys a quick bath. Our Archie had ever so much ice cream in his hair. I don't know how he does it."

"Thanks, Gran."

"Do you want a drink, pet?"

"Please. What are you knitting?"

"A blanket for the baby."

"Who's had a baby?"

She looks at me.

"Oh, right. Great."

"I'm making a few little things, so I can get ahead of myself."

"That sounds good."

That's what I need to be doing, getting ahead of myself instead of falling asleep on sofas when I've got people round for supper.

"Tea?"

"Lovely. I'll do it. You stay there."

Tea, at the end of a perfect day, when I finally got to tell Annabel Morgan to piss off without actually using the words *piss off.* How perfect is that?

# of shoes and ships and sealing wax

August

The first week of the school holidays heralds the end of the heat wave, so I've been trying to think of things to do in the rain that don't involve spending money or watching twelve hours of television every day. Olivia's doing more days in the shop, and Betty's standing in for Elsie when she has her week in Spain, so it's all getting pretty complicated; and proper mothers have action-packed itineraries all worked out, with trips to museums with bloody work sheets prepared in advance, and all I've got is a new straw hat and some jelly shoes for the boys to wear in the sea. Still, we've made bread, and a rather disastrous fruitcake, and taken Trevor for damp walks on the beach, and by yesterday I was so desperate I even

agreed to a treasure hunt, and had to spend ages writing out clues, which I'm crap at, followed by a mammoth post-treasure-hunt-putting-things-back-in-drawers session after Archie got a bit overenthusiastic. But at least all the towels are now neatly folded in the airing cupboard and Jack's favorite Batman pajamas have resurfaced.

Today is almost sunny, so we've got high hopes. Archie's already wearing his snorkel: one of the great things about having a beach hut, or rather Gran having one, is that you can head off for a picnic without having half a hundred-weight of assorted bags slung round your neck while you try to carry fishing nets and buckets and spades without poking anybody's eye out. Jack's filling a shopping bag with plastic soldiers, but everything else we need is already in the hut, apart from lunch, which I'm about to make: polenta and sun-dried tomatoes in a balsamic dressing, anybody? Or possibly Babybels and Kit Kats.

Ellen calls while I'm buttering rolls.

"How's it going, darling?"

"It's the school holidays—how do you think it's going?"

"On a scale of one to ten?"

"A hundred and forty-eight."

"What are you doing for your birthday? Shall I come down?"

"I thought a picnic on the beach and a barbecue."

"In Broadgate?"

"Don't sound so shocked."

"What if it rains?"

"Then it'll be a picnic and barbecue in my kitchen."

"I can't wait. Okay, count me in. I'll bring Harry, if he's around. He's feeling pretty pleased with himself at the moment, now he's passed all his tests."

"What tests?"

"Didn't I say? We had our appointment with the fertility guru, and everything's fine."

"That's brilliant."

"He says we should give it a year, relax, and he's sure we'll get pregnant. God, I hate the way they say that, 'we're pregnant.' It's total bollocks. Or we can start treatment now, and he'll relieve me of the ten grand and we can buy one instead."

"That sounds hopeful."

"I know, but a year, they've got to be joking. And now I don't know if I want one because I can't have one, if you know what I mean. What if I get pregnant and have it and then realize I'm not really up for it? Christ, I don't want to turn into a breeder just because I can. And trying to talk to Harry's a complete waste of time. He just says he wants what I want. As if I knew. I'm so busy at work there's never time to think properly about anything. They're talking about me doing thirty-minute specials now."

"That's great, Ellen."

"Yes, but not if I'm in a fucking smock, it won't be."

"Why don't you think about it when you're on your sailing week?"

"Luxury yachting, darling, please. I'm not climbing ropes; at least I hope I'm not."

"Well, you'll have plenty of peace and quiet then."

"I hate peace and quiet, but maybe. I'll have to do something—it's driving me crazy. Oh, and see if you can get the Diva along to your birthday thing, and I can get an exclusive on Jean-Luc, would you?"

"Okay."

"Really?"

"No."

She laughs.

"Talk later, darling."

The chances of Grace appearing on Broadgate Beach at my birthday picnic with the man she's brought back from Paris, according to all the papers, who I haven't even clapped eyes on yet, are pretty slim, but I'll tell Maxine about the party when I see them next week; they were so sweet about Archie's birthday, and I wouldn't want to offend her or anything. But I hope they won't be able to make it, because apart from the prospect of us all being filmed in our non-A-list beachwear, and trying to restrain Ellen, who's not very good at backing off and leaving people alone when there's a big story at stake, I wouldn't know what to do about food. I was thinking mixed salads, and maybe some homemade potato salad, but if we're entertaining people with their own chefs, then it will probably involve tricky stuff like quinoa, whatever that is. I bet it's a bugger to cook. Mark will probably know. Actually, maybe I won't mention anything to Maxine after all.

We're finally ready to leave for the beach, now Jack has rounded up all his soldiers.

"Can we go swimming, Mum?"

"Probably. Let's see how warm it is."

"But have you got your swimming costume on, Mum? Because last time you forgot it."

"It's in my bag, Archie. And take your snorkel off, darling—I can't hear you properly."

He starts to skip.

Bugger. I was hoping to avoid appearing in public in my new pregnant-person's swimsuit, which is seriously voluminous. I quite liked the look of the silver one with the little skirt, but I was worried it might float upward and cover my face midswim, so I've gone for giant black Lycra with extra-wide shoulder straps, which manages to be baggy and yet not quite long enough at the same time, so I have to hunch slightly when I stand up. Please let there not be anyone from school on the beach. Or anyone from Whale Rescue, or I'll be in danger of ending up covered in wet towels while they try to refloat me.

"I want to get some rolls at the baker's on the way to the shop."

They both groan.

"Only for a minute."

I need to check how Olivia's doing and pick up some more cotton for another shawl; they're selling really well at weekends now, so I'm knitting fairly speedily to keep up.

When we arrive, Olivia's in the middle of serving Mrs. Bishop, who's doing her usual thing of dithering and fussing but in a particularly snooty kind of way.

I take the boys upstairs for a carton of juice and a quick check through the post: the new stock's in for the beach-bag kits, and Olivia's made a start on unpacking it, so the table in the workroom is covered in half-assembled McKnits shopping bags, each neatly arranged with a pattern and a pair of needles.

I'm looking at the new autumn-shade cards for chunky wool and trying to decide which will be the most popular when Olivia comes upstairs. "She's finally gone. Six balls of that horrible fuzzy stuff. I'm sorry about the mess."

"No, it looks like you've got a good system going here. Don't let me interrupt. I just wanted to make sure you're okay."

"Actually, I wanted to ask you something, about Saturday afternoons, only some of my friends would like to come into the shop, for a group, like the one you do on Thursdays, only not with our mums. We want our own. I could show them how to cast on and stuff, and it'd be great. Could you help with the first one, though? We'd be ever so quiet."

"I was thinking of starting a Saturday group after the baby, actually. Can it wait until then? Only I'm not really sure I can manage it now, with the boys being on holiday and everything."

She looks very disappointed. "I suppose, only it's so boring round here."

"How many of your friends would come, do you think?"

"About five or six. Sophie and Lauren definitely, and Gemma, and probably Anna Maddox too and Polly. They're all really nice, and we'd be really quiet. Please."

Since they're my future customers, I should probably try to make this work.

"How about we try for a week and see how it goes? If they like it, Elsie might be willing to help out, if you get stuck or anything. She'll be downstairs anyway if we go for Saturday afternoon."

"That would be great. Thanks, Jo. And it'll be brilliant. Usually there's nothing going on round here—it's so crap."

Archie's heard the word *crap* and is now trying it out for size by mumbling inside his snorkel.

"Archie, stop being silly."

There's a muffled sigh, and then he breathes out quickly into the tube, making a series of very satisfactorily rude-sounding noises that make Jack giggle.

Olivia's trying not to laugh; it's amazing how rude-sounding snorkel noises appeal to all age-groups.

"You wouldn't have to pay me or anything, Jo."

"Of course I'll pay you, love, you'll be working. But let me talk to Elsie, and then I'll ring you, shall I? I'm sure she won't mind, but let me ask her, she likes to be asked. Jack, put that in the bin if you've finished, sweetheart, don't leave it there. Is there enough change in the till?"

Olivia nods. "I think so, and Mum's coming in later and she gets me change if I need it. Oh, and the credit card thingy has got stripes on the paper. Shall I change it?"

"Please."

Elsie must have left it knowing Olivia was in this morning; she's much quicker at technical stuff like changing the till rolls, or the cartridges on the printer.

"Come on then. Let's go the beach."

Jack puts his sandals back on. "Can I bring my book?"

I've brought some new books and pads of paper with a pack of colored pencils so they have something to do when we're here, but Jack always wants to take them home.

"They're for the shop, remember?"

He sighs.

Archie's already halfway down the stairs as the shop bell rings, and there's the unmistakable sound of Trevor barking. Bugger.

Double bugger. Martin's holding a folder.

"I thought I might find you here. I wanted to show you the latest pictures for the website, if you've got a minute. Sit, Trevor. Sit."

"We're just off to the beach, actually, Martin. Can we do it later?"

"We're going for a picknicker, and you can come too if you like—Trevor loves picnickers."

Great. Trust Archie, although the local council have rather brilliantly banned dogs from the beach from 8:00 A.M. until 6:00 P.M., so while Martin explains this to Archie, I edge us all out of the shop and onto the pavement. I've been trying to avoid the Trevor Dilemma, and I'm not really up for sorting it now. Christine's taken Mr. Pallfrey off to Spain to recuperate, and he was supposed to be coming back in a few weeks' time, but when Gran last spoke to her, Christine said she'd almost persuaded him to rent his house in Broadgate and buy a flat next to hers, with a pool and everything. Apparently he's joining the local expats' club and having a lovely time, which is great, obviously, but does leave a rather big Trevor-size issue looming.

"I spoke to Mr. Pallfrey last night."

Damn, here we go.

"Did you? How was he?"

"Much better. He hardly needs his stick at all now, he says, and he's decided to buy an apartment over there."

"Really? That sounds like a good idea."

"I know, but he's been worrying about His Nibs here, so I've told him I'm more than happy to have him. I've got quite fond of him over the past few weeks, and look, he's getting much more obedient. Lie down, Trevor."

Trevor stands up, just so we know he's not trained, and then lies down.

Martin beams.

"I thought I'd build him a kennel, but until it's ready I was hoping you'd still have him, before the baby, of course. I'd be finished well before then, but I don't like leaving him too long—he tends to dig big holes."

"I know, he does it with us too. We've got two separate ones in our garden at the minute, and as fast as we fill them in he digs them again."

"I think it's only because he gets anxious."

"Not half as anxious as I do when I'm hanging out the washing and wondering if I'm about to disappear into a crevasse."

Martin laughs.

"If you could just have him for another week or two? It'll be two nights next week, but so far I'm on local jobs the week after. I'll be as quick as I can with the kennel. I do realize you can't have a dog with the baby."

Archie throws his snorkel to the ground. "It's not fair.

He should be our dog, not Martin's. It'd be much better to have Trevor than a stupid baby." He bursts into tears.

Great.

Martin looks mortified, and Jack puts his arm on Archie's shoulder. "It's okay, Arch, it's only while it's little. We can have a proper dog when the baby's bigger, can't we, Mum?"

Christ.

"It's not really about the baby, love. It's more about him being in the house all day while you're at school and I'm in the shop. It wouldn't be fair. And you can see Trevor any time you like, and go for walks with him. Can't they, Martin?"

"Of course, and I've found that boat I was telling you about, Archie, in my shed. I'll bring it round later, if you like."

Archie stops sniffing. "The wooden one with the proper sails?"

Martin nods. "Would you like that?"

"Yes, please. And Mum, can we have doughnuts for lunch? Please, Mum, please?"

With a promised walk with Trevor and a wooden boat in the offing, a doughnut will crown his day with glory.

"Yes, Archie, we can."

He's skipping again as we walk toward the baker's shop, and Martin goes off whistling.

Damn.

I think I've just lost another round in the ongoing Canine Campaign. And they're both trying to bloody whistle

again. Martin goes in for a fair bit of whistling when he's in the shop waxing the shelves with his special cloth, but also when Elsie's attempting to boss him about, which I think has particularly impressed Jack. Luckily neither of them can actually whistle yet, but there's a fair bit of puffing and blowing going on as we get to the beach.

A few of the local families are out as we walk down the steps, but it's still fairly quiet. Luckily there's rain forecast for later, which will have put the day-trippers off; I'm starting to develop a rather proprietorial attitude to our beach, so it's nice having a bit more of it to ourselves for a change.

Gran and Reg are sitting outside the beach hut reading their papers, and Reg seems to have invested in a new navy blue sun umbrella.

Gran's got the buckets and spades out ready for the boys. "Here you are, pet. Look, we've got new loungers, from that big new center outside Margate; they were such a bargain we couldn't resist. We thought it would be more comfy for you than the deck chairs. They've got them in all sorts of patterns. Look, mine's ever so pretty." She stands up to reveal the kind of multicolored floral fabric that's never going to feature in a Cath Kidston catalog. "Yours is orange. Look."

Reg staggers out from inside the hut with a sun lounger covered in a riot of red and pink flowers, with orange parrots. God in heaven, what is it with the women in my

family and parrots? First we have Mum and her mad caftan, and now we've got Gran and her amazing Technicolor chair.

"It's lovely, Gran, thanks."

"We knew you'd like it, pet. They're like the ones we saw on our cruise, the parrots, only they had red beaks. Reg has got bluebirds on his one, look."

So he has.

"They're ever so comfy; sit down and try it."

I'll say this for Gran, we might not share a taste for what does, or does not, constitute a lovely pattern on a chair, but she definitely knows how to pick a comfy one: it seems to have extra padding, and Reg is busy adjusting the back and clicking up the bottom bit until it's almost as comfortable as my bed. Actually, possibly more. I wonder if I can take it home.

"That's perfect, Reg, thanks."

"There's a little sunshade too. I'll put it up for you. You just pull it over the top like this." A riot of orange parrots hovers above my head, with a dark orange fringe. "Isn't that clever?"

"Brilliant."

They both flip their sunshades over the backs of their chairs and sit down again.

"Makes you feel like a film star, doesn't it?"

"Definitely."

Actually, all I need now is a tartan blanket and I'll look like I'm recuperating from something tragic. Please let Annabel Morgan not decide to venture onto the beach today. She doesn't usually; I don't think it's exclusive enough

for her, but this would be the perfect day for her to change her mind.

I'm in the shop on Tuesday, having a peaceful, boy-free day: Connie's taken them both to the local zoo for Nelly's birthday treat, with a special birthday picnic prepared by me including pink fairy cakes from a packet with rice-paper ballerinas on top. Mark's making a proper cake for later, but he refused even to contemplate the pink-packet ones she wanted for her picnic, so I stepped into the breach before Connie hit him with his own spatula.

Gourmet tastes are all very well, particularly when they involve making delicious things for your wife to bring to her knitting group every week, but when it comes to fairy cakes, everyone knows neon pink ones win hands down, every time. They'll be gone until teatime, and I briefly considered going along too, but traipsing round miles of Kentish countryside trying to catch a glimpse of a lion is pretty low on my list of fun things to do at the best of times, let alone when you're the wrong side of seven months pregnant.

I'm looking through the wicker baskets on the shelves upstairs in the workroom, trying to put together a new window display. I think we'll be fine with the knitted fish for the rest of August, but I want to change over to tea cozies and knitted fairy cakes in September, with the glass cake stands I got in Venice last year, if I can find them. I'm thinking about knitted hot-water-bottle covers too. They sold really well last year in the run-up to Christmas, and I

want to do more lavender bags as well. They're so simple to knit, and they make the shop smell lovely, and we've got loads of lavender in the garden now. Elsie's already started on some fancy ones in Fair Isle, and I'm thinking about a few simple animal shapes—birds and rabbits, I think—in soft cashmere with ribbons to hang them up. I saw some in a magazine at nearly thirty quid a go, and I'm sure I can do something similar for half the price and still make a hefty profit. They'll make perfect presents and nice, easy projects for autumn evenings when I'm likely to have my lap full of someone who needs another feed before they conk out.

I still can't really believe there's going to be a baby at the end of all this. It seems completely unreal, even though I've been here twice before. A whole new person invisibly getting on with growing, ready for D-Day. It's extraordinary. The midwife says we're already on the top bit of the chart for growth, and all my tests so far have been fine. But it still doesn't seem real.

I'm standing with my hand across my tummy when Elsie comes upstairs. "I'm putting the kettle on. Do you want tea?"

She's been pretty sniffy about Olivia's idea for a Saturday group so far, so any hint of an olive branch needs to be firmly grasped.

"Lovely. Thanks, Elsie. You haven't seen those cake stands we had in the window last year, have you?"

"I put them in the back of the cupboard under the sink, wrapped up in plastic for safekeeping. Dangerous having

glass on those shelves. They could fall off and hurt someone."

"Oh, right. Great."

I wish she'd tell me when she squirrels stuff away in the
kitchen.

"How many teenagers do you think will be coming?
Because you know what they're like—they'll be up to all
sorts, you mark my words."

"Olivia's very sensible, though, don't you think?"

"That's as may be, but put them all together and they'll
be drinking spirits before you know it."

Boozing upstairs in a wool shop with Elsie downstairs?
I'd like to see them pull that one off.

"I'll keep an eye on them this week and we'll see how it
goes, shall we? And if you don't think you can manage,
then Gran says she's happy to come in for the next few Saturday afternoons."

This is my trump card, and now I've played it, I'm
really hoping it's going to work.

"Oh, I'm sure I can manage. There's no need for Mary
to bother herself; I was only saying we need to be careful.
We don't want to attract the wrong element. Some of them
are terrible, you know, stealing cars and all sorts."

"They don't usually want to learn to knit, though, do
they, the ones stealing cars? And I think they're a lot rarer
than you think, Elsie. Not much of a story for the papers,
is it? Nice kids getting on with growing up and annoying
their parents. The ones who nick cars make much better
headlines."

She sniffs. "That Maxine just rang for you, by the way,

said could you make it two-thirty today instead of two. I said you'd call her back."

"Great."

"I'll put the kettle on."

I'm really looking forward to seeing Grace, and possibly Jean-Luc, although I didn't like to ask Maxine about it when we spoke. But Jane Johnson said there were crowds of press outside the gates again when she drove past yesterday, so they must be pretty sure he's there.

"And the sink in the kitchen isn't draining properly again."

"Okay, I'll have another go with the plunger."

How nice. A spot of DIY plumbing before I'm off to Graceland.

There are cars parked all along the shoulder of the road on either side of the gates, and lots of bored-looking men with cameras, but fortunately Tom and Jerry have obviously been off to naughty-dog school and trot three paces behind Bruno as I get out of the car, responding to a series of clicks on a special plastic clicker. I wonder if I should get one for Martin to try on Trevor.

Maxine comes out of one of the side doors and takes me round to Grace. "She's in the garden. Isn't the weather great? It's like being in the South of France. I bet you're taking your kids to the beach every day, aren't you?"

"Pretty much. Actually, we're having a birthday picnic on the beach this Sunday. From around six, if you fancy it."

"Can I let you know?"

"Of course."

"Maybe Bruno and I could come, if that would be okay. I think Grace will probably be busy."

"I'd love that."

"At least you won't have press climbing down the cliffs trying to get shots of Jean-Luc."

"Oh, right. He's here then?"

"Oh yes, he's definitely here."

The kitchen garden is helpfully surrounded by an old wall that shields people from long lenses. It's immaculate, with beds of flowers and vegetables mixed in with fruit canes, and what look like bunches of fledgling grapes hanging down from the vines over the huge wooden table. I've got no idea how many gardeners work here. They've got a contract with some big firm, I think, but there must be hordes of them to keep it looking this stunning.

Lily's having a lovely time in her paddling pool under a cream linen awning, with Meg sprinkling water onto her from a baby watering can. Grace is lounging on a wooden steamer chair with cream cushions, wearing jeans and a tiny white T-shirt.

"Water or juice, Jo?"

"Water, thanks, Grace."

"We're learning to ride for the film, so we've got horses in the stables now. Very *Country Life*, don't you think?"

"Very."

Maxine hands me a glass of water and nods toward the gate at the far end of the garden, where a vision in a billowing

white shirt and jodhpurs is walking toward us. Dear God, I'm glad I'm sitting down. He's absolutely gorgeous. And he's even managing to look good in jodhpurs, which isn't easy.

"Did Sartre do a lot of horse riding then?"

"Sorry?"

He's getting nearer. Good God, if Jean-Paul Sartre had looked like that, we'd all be existentialists.

Maxine smiles.

"No, Jean-Luc's doing Professor Emelius Browne in *Bedknobs,* Jo. They're looking for a big American name for Sartre."

"Oh, right. I don't remember them riding horses in *Bedknobs and Broomsticks.*"

Grace smiles, one of her Diva smiles. "They didn't. But there's all sorts of new stuff in the script. And trust me, when you see him on a horse, you'll be glad there is."

Maxine pours Jean-Luc a glass of water as he leans down and kisses Grace on the cheek and brushes a curl of hair from her face.

"Good ride, darling?"

"Yes, but it is so hot, I must change. I think I will swim. Do you need anything?"

His accent is divine. Do you need anyzing? Oh yes, I think we probably do.

"No thanks. I might join you later. Ask Sam for anything you want."

He kisses her again and wanders back across the path toward the house.

Maxine sighs, which makes Grace laugh.

"The read-throughs have been great so far, brilliant for chemistry. Angela Lansbury, eat your heart out. Although they're getting him a voice coach, so he'll probably end up sounding like bloody Hugh Grant."

Maxine's collecting up plates and putting them on a tray. "Somehow I don't think that's going to matter."

"Probably not. Is she getting fed up, Meg?"

Lily is busy throwing plastic boats out of her paddling pool.

"A bit. Shall I take her in now?"

"Please. And Max, ask Sam to bring us out some more juice, and ice, would you?"

"Sure."

Sam arrives with a jug of juice and a plate of fruit.

"Thanks, Sam. Is he in the pool?"

"Yes. And he wants a coffee. Shall I go for decaf?"

"Please."

He smiles and walks back toward the house.

"I'm cutting down on his caffeine, slows him down; otherwise it's just too exhausting. So, what do you think of the garden?"

"It's fabulous. You're a very lucky woman."

"Lucky? I worked bloody hard for all of this."

"Sorry."

"I was joking. Jesus, why doesn't anyone ever think I'm joking? Although getting them to cast Jean-Luc was lucky, I'll admit that. Stroke of genius, actually."

"So is he French, in the film, I mean?"

"Kind of. He's more heroic than in the old version, ex-Army, half-French, evacuated from Dunkirk. And then I meet him and he forgets all about the Resistance."

"I bet."

"We start shooting in a couple of weeks. Has Maxine given you the dates?"

"Yes. I'm really looking forward to it."

"They want me to knit, in the film. Did she say? So we've said you'll come up with something suitably wartime. They all knitted socks, didn't they?"

"Yes, or balaclavas. My gran's got loads of vintage patterns. I'll bring some over if you like."

"Sure. They'll pay you, for research. Max has already sorted it."

"Really? That would be great, if you're sure."

"Talk to Max, she's got the details. Fuck, who's that?"

The phone is ringing on the table.

"Fine, put him through. Hi, Ed . . . Because I don't want to. I'm having a quiet English summer. If I wanted to be in fucking L.A., that's where I'd be. Okay, but bring them down here. Sam can do a lunch or something."

She puts the phone down. "They're up to serious money now."

"What for?"

"A picture of me and Jean-Luc. Triple if we're shagging. Bastards. Ed's on the case, so we'll do a dinner in London, or Paris maybe. Max is sorting it out now."

"Don't you mind?"

"Part of the job, darling."

"I suppose so, but—"

"There's no but. It's the job—you do it, or you don't. But you can't whine about it. You can sue them if they cross the line, but the rest of it is how you earn your money."

"Cross the line?"

"If they go after your family."

"Right."

"I finished Lily's cardigan, by the way, the wrapover one, and she loves it. I thought I'd make her another one, in that olive green you were showing me. Was that cashmere?"

"Cashmere and silk."

"Okay, and I want to make something for Max, for her birthday. There's a cardigan in that book you left me that's perfect for her. I've marked the page. Tell me the colors and you can get that for me as well. I want to customize it, though—the sleeves are awful. . . . Fuck, it's hot out here. Let's go in."

"When's her birthday? I'd like to get her something too."

"Next month sometime. But don't knit her anything. I want mine to be the star gift."

"Of course."

She smiles. "You could get her a jigsaw. She loves them."

"Really?"

"When Sam and I want to annoy her, we hide a couple of pieces. It drives her crazy. She's quite obsessional; has to be, doing her job. She's always putting things in straight lines and rearranging flowers. If you ever need another assistant in your shop, go for someone who's bossy and likes everything neat."

"I've already got one of those, thanks. I don't think I could handle two."

"Do you fancy a swim?"

"No, thanks. I haven't brought my costume."

And even if I had, I'd pay serious money rather than appear in front of her and Jean-Luc wearing it.

"Sure?"

"Yes, but thanks."

"Pick up the book before you go, and call me about the colors. Thanks, Jo. Lovely to see you." She heads toward the pool.

I'm looking through Gran's collection of vintage knitting patterns on Saturday, waiting for her to arrive to look after the boys so I can go into the shop for Olivia's first knitting group. There seem to be lots of wartime patterns for balaclavas and gloves, and a rather fetching child's vest with matching body belt, presumably for keeping your pocket money safe. Gran says wool was rationed for ages, and used to come in skeins rather than balls, so we'll have to get that right for the film, and she remembers making Aran socks for sailors as well as scarves and gloves, and she and Betty knitted themselves swimming costumes, only they tended to sag rather dramatically the minute you got in the sea, which must have been a worry. Although since most of the beach was covered in barbed wire, with the Home Guard marching up and down and shouting at anyone who tried to have a paddle, it probably didn't really matter how baggy your costume went.

Lots of the pattern booklets seem to have been given out free when you bought the wool, although there are some

baby-clothes ones that cost three pence, and a few American ones for glamorous dresses and sweaters; since wool wasn't rationed there, the colors are much more varied, and I'm rather drawn to a bed jacket with ruffles. I wonder what the boys would say if I appeared at the breakfast table wearing a jacket with white lace frills over my nightie: nothing terribly polite, probably. I think the perfect choice for Grace in the film will be air force blue wool for a scarf, or maybe a balaclava.

I'm sorting out a few possible colors when Gran arrives, with a cake for tea. "You look tired, pet. I'll just go and say hello to the boys, shall I? Put the kettle on."

I'm feeling completely knackered, actually: I didn't sleep very well due to a combination of the baby twirling about for half the night and a rather rude dream involving Jean-Luc, who somehow morphed into Nick at a crucial moment, which had me waking up with quite a start, and then staring into the darkness for ages having a panic attack about exactly how I'm going to do everything. And then just as I got back to sleep, Jack came in all shaky because he'd had his dream where he can't find me and he's in a boat that's slowly sinking. He hasn't had it for months, but I think Gran going on about the baby's room yesterday unsettled him.

Reg arrives while we're drinking our tea, with some wallpaper samples: Gran's sent him to B&Q with strict instructions to bring back a nice range of colors and patterns. Oh, God.

"We need to get a move on, pet. You want everything sorted before the baby arrives."

"Yes, but we've got until October. There's no need to worry about it right now."

"I've got one of those mobile things, by the way. I meant to tell you."

"I thought you used Reg's."

She tuts.

"For over the cot. It plays a tune, with little rabbits. It's ever so sweet, isn't it, Reg?"

He nods. Actually, I think he's quietly excited too.

"Amazing what they can do now. You just press a button and it plays a tune, and Martin says he'll help me with the floor. Messy job that, but he's got a sander, so it won't take us long. We thought we'd sand and then seal it, and then we thought a white wax, soften them down a bit, if you're sure you don't want a carpet?"

"That sounds lovely, Reg, but—"

Gran puts her cup down. "And Tina from the hairdresser's was telling me about those baby showering things they have now, so she's organizing one with Elsie. They were thinking about one of your Thursday nights. Isn't that nice? Only I think they want to surprise you, but I know what you're like with surprises, so I thought I'd better warn you."

Right, so that's floorboards, painting and wallpapering, and a surprise baby shower: nice and low-key then, just how I want it.

"I don't want a fuss, Gran—it only makes me nervous."

"No, pet, what'll make you nervous is when you come

to your senses in a few weeks' time and realize you've got nothing ready."

"I've knitted a blanket."

"I know, pet, and it's lovely."

"I'm not in denial or anything, Gran, but I've done this before, you know, and they never go in their cots for the first few weeks anyway. All you really need is a Moses basket and a car seat."

She looks stricken.

"Car seat. I never thought of that."

"Gran, it'll be fine. Please. I'd love it if you want to do the room, but it'll be okay if we haven't got every single thing ready."

Reg puts his arm on Gran's shoulder. "She's probably right, Mary."

"And, Gran?"

"Yes, pet?"

"If you could help me sort out the boys' rooms too, particularly Jack's, maybe we could do a bit of painting for them as well so they don't feel left out."

"That's a lovely idea."

She's off, getting the boys in. "Me and your mum and your grandad Reg are talking about painting your bedrooms. What colors would you like?"

Jack looks worried. "I don't know. Mum, what color should I have?"

"What about blue and silver like Marco's?"

"Yes, please. Can I have moons and stars on my ceiling too?"

Gran nods.

"And before you start, madam, you're not climbing up any ladders."

"All right, Gran."

Archie's hopping. "And I can have Superheroes, can't I, Mum? Or sharks. I quite like sharks."

Shark wallpaper. How relaxing.

Reg is making a list. Me and my big mouth.

O livia's tidying upstairs and putting out glasses when I get to the shop. "Everyone's bringing a drink."

Oh, God, maybe Elsie was right.

"We couldn't decide on water or Cokes and stuff, so everyone's bringing their own. Are there any more spare needles?"

"In that box on the top shelf."

"Elsie was quite cross when she arrived."

"She'll be fine."

"And Lady Denby's been in. She says she'll be back later."

"Okay."

"Oliver Benson and Matt Lewis might come too, only I've told them they've got to knit. It's all right if boys come too, isn't it?"

Teenage boys. I wasn't really counting on that. Some of them are huge, at least the ones I see getting off the bus, with their ties off and their shirts untucked, busy flirting or having mock fights with their massive backpacks slung over one shoulder.

"Sure."

"Oliver really fancies Polly, like there's any hope we'd go

out with boys in our year. That's so not going to happen. But he's all right, and Matt's quite nice."

"I'll look forward to meeting them."

I only hope they're medium-size boys, because I'm not sure the chairs will stand up to any large teenager activity. If they're anything like Jack and Archie, they'll be leaning backward and rocking shortly before the chair legs snap.

A n hour later, Polly and Sophie are busy knitting while Lauren and Gemma are still trying to cast on, and Olivia's showing a girl called Clare how to purl. Oliver and Matt are sitting at the far side of the table, struggling to remember which way to put their wool for a knit stitch. They've given up trying to cast on after Sophie took pity on them and did it for them, and now Oliver's giving Polly the occasional longing look, but she seems oblivious. Poor thing, he's trying ever so hard; when she put some lip gloss on earlier, I thought he was going to pass out.

"Excuse me, Mrs. Mackenzie."

"Please call me Jo, Sophie."

She seems quite pleased with this. "Is there a loo here, Jo?"

"Straight down the stairs on the landing."

"Thanks."

"How's it going, Gemma? Need a hand?"

"Yes, please."

Oliver puts his knitting down. "Me too. Jo."

Polly glances at him, and he reddens.

I help Gemma pick up a dropped stitch and then move round to Oliver.

"You're getting the hang of this really quickly."

He smiles. "It's quite good, when you get going. I might make something for my mum, for her birthday, a scarf or something. Do you think she'd like that?"

Everyone smiles.

"I'm sure she would."

Polly takes a sip from her bottle of water. "I'll help you choose the right colors and stuff if you like."

"Great."

What a triumph. He's thrilled, and looks so pleased I'm tempted to give him a hug. It must be tricky being a boy surrounded by such sophisticated girls, with their shiny hair and lip gloss. They seem much more confident than I remember being at that age, and I'm not sure many of the boys I knew would have been able to handle spending the afternoon knitting.

Matt looks at Gemma and grins, which seems to fluster her.

"Would you help me get something for my mum too?"

"Course. What do you want to make?"

He looks at his knitting. "Something very small."

L ady Denby arrives when I'm looking at patterns for weird cape things that Polly has brought in from her sister, who's studying fashion somewhere in London. They're rather impressive, in bright colors with wide ribbon threaded through as fasteners, or huge safety pins. I can't see them

catching on in Broadgate, but they're undeniably stylish. And warm too, no doubt. Maybe I'll make myself one just to see Elsie's face.

"Hello, my dear. Busy as usual, I see. Dogs are down-stairs, so I won't stop."

So that'll be Elsie wrestling with dog leads again. Oh, dear.

"Wanted to let you know we won silver again, Seaside in Bloom. Absolute scandal."

Oliver picks up his can of Coke. "My dad reckons the judges need a backhander if you want the gold."

"Wouldn't be surprised, young man. Disgraceful. But a silver is not to be sneezed at, I suppose, especially two years running. Gold next year, even if we have to bang them."

Oliver chokes on his Coke as I put the cape patterns down on the table.

"I think you might mean bung, Lady Denby."

"Do I? Quite. Still, I'm sure your window display helped again, so well done. Thought you'd like to know."

"Thank you, that was kind of you."

"No trouble at all. Nice to meet you all. Good to see young people learning something useful. Excellent skill to have, knitting; never know when it will come in useful. Good afternoon."

I follow her downstairs to find Elsie trying to keep Al-gie and Clarkson at arm's length by keeping the counter between her and them. Clarkson's edging round the corner as Lady Denby takes over and yanks him back.

"Thank you, Enid."

"It's Elsie, actually, Lady Denby."

"Is it? Are you sure?"

Elsie looks momentarily confused.

"Always had you down as an Enid. Must dash—left George in the car. Lord alone knows where he'll have got to by now. He will get out and go for wanders. So annoying. Still, the boys usually track him down."

She yanks the leads again, and off they trot.

"You'll have to tell her."

"Sorry?"

"She can't keep bringing those dogs in; it's not nice."

"Any ideas how I'm going to pull that one off, Elsie?"

She smiles. "Are they behaving themselves up there?"

"Beautifully. One of the boys wants to knit something for his mum."

"Does he? Well, bless his heart. I always loved the things my Martin made for me. We still use the little table he made me in woodwork, you know, and they did seem very polite, I will say that for them."

"They are, they all seem really nice."

"Well, I'll give it a chance, I'm all for giving people a chance, you know that. But if there's any funny business I'll call you, shall I?"

"Sure."

"I used to see one of them when he was little. Always in with his mum, he was. He was mad on Thomas the Tank Engine, and she used to knit him sweaters. She made him a dressing gown too, I think."

"Well, for heaven's sake don't ask him about it now—

he's trying to impress the girls. God, I've got all that to come, haven't I? With the boys."

She smiles. "Your Jack will be fine; it'll be your Archie who'll need watching, he's such a charmer. Shall I go up and see if they'd like a biscuit? I saw you'd got a new tin of shortbread, and they're always starving at that age, aren't they? I could make a cup of tea, if you fancy one."

Excellent.

I knew the tin of shortbread would lure her up there sooner or later.

By lunchtime on Sunday I'm exhausted. An emergency supermarket sweep after I realized our summer-holiday routine of soporific days on the beach with picnics, in between sessions in the shop and trying to get the salt out of the boys' hair at bath time, is all very well, but it does tend to mean that things like what we're actually going to eat at my birthday picnic slip right off my list.

Ellen and Harry are due later, and most of the Stitch and Bitch group are meeting us on the beach, along with Connie and Mark, who are coming with the kids once Mark's finished the lunches in the pub. They're closing the restaurant this evening. Sunday night's always pretty quiet, and there'll be bar snacks for anyone who's desperate.

I've told Mark not to worry about making anything for the picnic, which I'm really starting to regret now. I've made vast quantities of potato salad with chopped chives, and I'm marinating salmon steaks in honey and ginger and a splash of soy, actually a bit more than a splash since the

nozzle on the bottle wasn't quite as small as I thought. The chicken can be plain for the people who like to pick chives out of their mother's potato salad, but after I've got all the food in Tupperware boxes, there still doesn't look like enough, and I'm running out of plastic boxes. I could ring Gran, who has an epic collection of useful containers, all with matching lids, but then she'd Help, and I wanted to do most of the food myself, even though she's insisted on making the cake.

"Mum."

"Yes, Archie."

"It should be fancy dress, your party."

"It's a beach party, love."

"Yes, but we could all be fishes. Can I have a fish costume for the party, please?"

"No."

"Or I could be a cowboy with my potato gun. Where is my potato gun?"

"I don't know."

And even if I did I wouldn't tell him.

"I think fishes would be better. And, Mum?"

"Yes?"

"When's lunch? I'm starving."

Bugger. I'd forgotten about lunch.

"Have some cereal."

"For lunch?"

"Yes."

He looks at me, and finally starts to recognize the signs of a mother close to crisis.

"I don't want Shreddies."

"Don't have them then, have Weetabix."

There's a fair amount of tutting and sighing, but I'm too busy banging saucepans and trying to stop the rice from going into sticky clumps while I get the skin off the roasted peppers and the peas come to the boil to bother about tutting.

Jack wanders in. "What's for lunch?"

"We've got to have cereal."

"What?"

Archie gives him a Look.

"I don't want Weetabix."

"Have Shreddies, Jack, and then you can both help me get all this into the car."

"Have you got balloons, Mum?"

"No, Jack, I haven't."

He tuts. "It's not a proper party without balloons."

"Well, don't come then."

They both sigh.

If anyone starts trying to whistle again, I think I might start throwing sticky clumps of rice.

Ellen arrives at three, with Harry, who's in disgrace after arriving home with a traffic cone on his head at half past five this morning. He's lying on the sofa "helping" the boys with their Legos while Ellen and I retreat to the kitchen.

"Jesus, how many people are coming?"

"I don't know, stacks."

"Well, they won't go hungry, darling."

"That's the plan."

"Have you made your potato salad?"

"Yes, but don't tell Archie it's mayonnaise or he won't eat it. It's salad cream; he thinks it's like ice cream."

"Sure. I'm starving. Bloody Errol had me on that running machine for hours yesterday. I'd sack him, only I'd be the size of a house if he didn't bully me so much."

She's wearing a tiny white sundress with pink polka dots and looks like an advert for something slimming. Even her hair looks slim.

"You look great."

"Thanks, darling. So what are you wearing?"

"This?"

"No, you're not. Those trousers are terrible. It's your party. Wear something nice."

"They're cool."

"Not from where I'm standing, they're not. Please. Wear the dress you had on at the wedding. That looked great on you."

"At your wedding, you mean, the violet silk one? No, I'm saving it."

"What on earth for?"

"Good point."

B y five it's starting to cool down, and the light's gone all soft on the beach when we arrive. There are still quite a few people sitting inside their windbreak encampments, but you can hear the sea in among the noise of people chatting or packing up for the long drive home; it's my

favorite time on the beach, especially when the tide's out, like it is today.

"Here, give me the big bag. It's down these steps, right? Where's the beach hut?"

"About halfway along. Oh."

Gran and Reg are here already and have covered the hut in streamers and balloons, much to the boys' delight.

"Hello, pet, hello, Ellen. What do you think? We thought we'd make a bit of an effort. What are you doing carrying those bags? Reg, get them off her before she does herself a mischief. Sit down and have a cup of tea."

"There's more in the car."

"We'll get it in a minute. You've got to pace yourself— I keep telling you. Sit down, Ellen, love. I'll go and fill the kettle. All mod cons we are here. Cup of tea coming up."

Ellen smiles and hesitates by one of the parrot sun loungers.

"Christ, where on earth did you get the chairs?"

"Gran and Reg."

"I'm glad I've got my sunglasses on."

"They're very comfy."

"They'd have to be."

By six the beach is lovely, still warm but without the chilly breeze that sometimes blows in at the end of the day. I'm wearing my gray mohair shawl with the silver beads around the edge, and everyone's complimenting me on my dress. Ellen's even painted my toenails for me, which I've pretty much given up on until I'm less spherical, and

she's making her special punch, which is usually lethal so I've been adding lemonade when she's not looking. Not that I'm going to be drinking any, but I'm not sure any of us are quite ready for a completely plastered Elsie.

"God, this is perfect. Fuck spending hours in departures and then twelve hours on a bloody plane when you get a view like this."

The tide's gone right out now, and the kids are building sand castles and army bases to some complicated plan of their own devising, running backward and forward to the sea with buckets of water. Everyone seems to be enjoying themselves, and I've got more birthday cards than I've had since I was little. They all seem to have brought a present, which is sweet; Maggie from the library has given me a lovely old copy of *Mrs. Beeton*, after we were talking about how much we love reading recipe books at last week's Stitch and Bitch, and Tina and Linda have brought me posh-looking bath stuff for pregnant people and are busy admiring my fabulous new cream leather handbag from Ellen. Olivia and Polly are giving it very longing looks in between trying to sneak glasses of punch when their mothers aren't watching.

The food has worked beautifully, mainly because Mark arrived early and arranged rosemary twigs on the barbecue and did something clever to the chicken with olive oil and herbs. But the best bit is how relaxed it all is: everyone seems to be having fun, without me feeling like I'm in charge. People are sitting on blankets they've brought with

them, chatting or wandering down for a paddle, or in Tina's case trying to stop Travis from swimming off into the sunset.

Fireman Graham is helping with the barbecue too, and Maxine and Bruno have arrived with a beautifully wrapped bottle of Calèche, which is my favorite perfume, as Maxine cleverly winkled out of me ages ago, and Bruno's sharing dog tips with Martin while Tom and Jerry and Trevor dash in and out of the sea with the kids. It's perfect, and I can't believe we've only been here a year, because it feels like we've lived here forever.

I'm having a paddle when Maxine says she and Bruno have to get back to Grace. "But thanks, Jo. This was great."

"You're welcome, and thanks so much for the perfume."

"No problem. I haven't been to a beach party where people actually eat anything for years. It was great—nice normal people, really relaxing." She turns to smile at Ellen, who's been busy trying to bond with her in the hopes of landing an exclusive with Grace. "Good to meet you again, Ellen, and if she decides to do an interview, you'll be the first to know."

"Really?"

"No."

Ellen laughs. "Fair enough. But I promise I wouldn't do a hatchet job."

"I know, and I'll add you to the list, I promise. Jo, I'll call you."

She kisses me, and we walk up the steps with them and wave as they drive off, with Bruno tooting.

"Nice woman. Always a good sign when the PAs aren't desperate to tell you what bitches their bosses are. And Dovetail seemed to be getting on really well with Bruno."

"They like sharing dog tips, and stop calling him Dovetail. He doesn't talk about wood nearly so much now."

"He does if he's telling you all about his bloody barn conversion. What's it like?"

"Very muddy at the moment, but I think it'll be beautiful."

"You should get a move on. I was watching him earlier. Where did he get that tan?"

"Working on his roof."

"Well, take him out, get him drunk, and see what happens. At least you won't have to worry about getting pregnant."

"Ellen, please."

"Please what? Nice bit of flirting won't do you any harm. I know, let's dump the kids and go out clubbing. What are the choices round here?"

"Bingo."

"Or?"

"Going home and making hot chocolate."

"Dear God. I should have brought my slippers."

"You haven't got any."

"I have. Mules. With feathers on. Harry bought them for me. One of his guilt presents after one of his disappearing acts. Let's bring Dovetail home with us and play strip bingo then."

"Mum, tell Jack to stop bossing me. Boss, boss, boss. That's all he does."

"Ignore him, love. You're not spoiling his game, are you?"

"No, me and Nelly are doing our own boat, in the sand. And it's much better than his. Come and see."

E llen's talking to Gran as I collect up the bowls from the barbecue. She looks very pleased with herself.

"Right, that's all sorted."

"What is?"

"Your gran will take the boys home, and we can go off for a drink. I thought we'd head to a bar in Whitstable. There's bound to be somewhere there."

"I suppose, but—"

"It's fine, the kids are fine. Shut up." She turns to Martin. "Do you fancy joining us?"

"I'd love to, but I've got Trevor. I could ask Dad if he'll take him home for me, though."

"Great."

Ellen winks at me.

Oh, God. Poor Jeffrey.

W hitstable's pretty busy when we arrive, at least the wine bars and restaurants are, but Ellen somehow manages to wangle us an outside table on a terrace overlooking the beach; being Britain's Favorite Broadcaster definitely has its advantages.

She's introducing Martin to a selection of her favorite cocktails while Harry tells me how much he wants to move out of London.

"What are the prices like round here? Maybe we could get a weekend place, something with a view of the sea."

"It would set you back a fair bit in Whitstable, but there are still a few villages nearby that are pretty reasonable."

"I've always wanted to live by the sea. What do you think, darling? Shall we buy a house down here?"

"No, I'm trying to get Jo to move back to London, not the other way round."

"I've told you, Ellen, I like it down here."

"See? She's not moving, so what do you say, light of my life? Fancy a weekend cottage?" He starts kissing her shoulder.

"No way."

"We could get something to do up, like Martin."

"Yes, except DIY isn't exactly your strong point, is it, my darling? Unlike Martin, who knows what he's doing."

"Well, we'll get the experts in then, and I'll have you know I sanded my uncle's boat one summer, and that went all right. And we varnished it as well. It took bloody days."

Martin puts his glass down. "What kind of wood was it?"

They're off, talking about boats and special deck wax as Ellen shakes her head. "Let's order something else."

Ellen turns to look for the waitress as a woman comes over and stands staring at her, swaying slightly. "Are you that one off the telly?"

"No."

"Are you sure?"

"Yes."

The woman goes back to her friends.

"Bloody hell. I definitely need another drink now."

The waitress comes over and returns with something involving vodka in three tall glasses.

"Are you sure you don't want anything? Another juice?"

"Actually, what I'd really like is tea, but I don't suppose—"

"Sure, no problem."

Brilliant. I'm out on a Saturday night in my best frock, being a grown-up, and I can still have a cup of tea.

Ellen's laughing. "Cheers, darling."

"Christ."

"What's the matter, Martin? Is the vodka starting to hit home? Drink it slowly and you'll be fine, darling. Aunty Ellen will take care of you."

"No, it's Patricia."

"Who?"

"My ex-wife. With Phil."

Ellen and I exchange glances and turn toward the doors onto the terrace. There's a tall woman in a minuscule dress, with dark hair. I always thought she'd be blond. She's hesitating, looking for a table, and then she sees him, and so does Phil, in his casual shirt and jeans with slightly too high a waist.

Martin seems to be shrinking into his seat. "Oh no, she's coming over."

Ellen laughs. "Let me handle this, darling. Just follow my lead, okay?"

I give her a warning look. Which she ignores.

"Okay. Bandits at ten o'clock. This is going to be fun. Harry, put your arm around me."

"Why?"

"For fuck's sake, just do it. Christ, you really can't get the help anymore."

He smiles and puts his arm across her shoulders as she moves her chair a bit nearer to his.

"Just watch it, okay? I don't want anything kicking off—I'm too knackered."

She smiles.

Oh, God.

"Martin."

"Hello, Patricia."

"Fancy seeing you here."

Ellen's giving her a long, hard look, the kind of look that would make most women want to rush home to change their outfits. "Aren't you going to introduce us, darling?"

"Sorry, this is Patricia, and Phil."

Phil nods, looking uncomfortable.

"Nice to meet you. Ellen Malone, and this is Harry. You're the first wife, I take it?"

Patricia looks rather shaken. "I've seen you on the telly."

"Possibly. But I'm trying to keep a low profile tonight. People get so overexcited. I'm sure you understand."

Patricia looks impressed but is clearly trying to hide it as she turns to me, giving me a quick glance that suddenly stops at my stomach.

Ellen smiles. "I know, so exciting, isn't it? And not long now, is it, Jo? We were just talking about it, actually, wondering if Martin will get the barn conversion finished in time."

Patricia doesn't look happy.

"What barn?" She looks furious as she turns to Martin. "Christ. You didn't waste much time, did you?"

"It's—"

"So lovely to have met you, Trish. And you, Phil. Have a lovely evening." Ellen gives them one of her Big Smiles and then fixes Patricia with one of her killer you-are-now-dismissed looks.

Phil steps forward. "Come on, Patsy. Just leave it, babes."

But she can't. She's glaring at me, looking as hostile as you can in a skimpy shift dress and high-heeled sandals.

"When's it due?"

Suddenly I get a flash of inspiration and reach across and take hold of Martin's hand. "Not long now."

She turns and walks back toward the doors, with Phil nodding at Martin before following her.

Martin can't stop smiling. "Thanks so much, both of you. That was so brilliant. I know it's petty, but the look on her face. God, it was so brilliant."

"Can I have my hand back now?"

"What? Oh yes, sorry. It was just so great."

He kisses me on the cheek. "Thanks, Jo."

"I don't think she's looking anymore, Martin."

"I didn't do it for her benefit."

Ellen clinks her glass with Martin and winks at me.

The drive home takes ages, mainly because I get lost. And Martin's drunk so much vodka he's barely coherent on the backseat next to Harry, who's fast asleep.

"Are you sure it's down here?"

"Yes. You turned left when I said right. Or it might be the other way round. Anyway it's bound to be down here. Or not."

"Shut up, Martin."

He laughs.

I finally find the barn, mainly by going back into Broadgate and then out again so I don't have to try to follow Martin's daft directions.

"Here we are."

"Who wants to see my barn?"

Harry wakes up. "I do, I want to see it."

Ellen sighs. "Well, hurry up then. . . . Christ, I hope that's your bloody dog or we're in big trouble."

There's a great deal of barking before Trevor appears and goes into a frenzy of jumping and tail wagging, nearly knocking Martin over.

"Night, Martin."

"Night, Ellen. We must do this again sometime."

"What, completely piss off your ex-wife?"

He laughs. "No. Well, yes. But I meant a drink or something. I could make supper, when I've got a kitchen."

"Great. Fix it up with Jo, and we'll be there."

Harry walks up the path with Martin to see the barn, while Ellen and I wait in the car.

"You should have gone in with him, fixed up a second date."

"Ellen, this was hardly a first date. And anyway, I can't be doing dates when I'm seven and a half months pregnant. It's too . . . something. I don't know what exactly, but there

definitely isn't a chapter on it in *What to Expect When You're Bloody Expecting*."

"Well, there should be. Welcome to the real world. Pregnant by one man, out with another, and neither of them your husband. My baby girl has finally grown up. I'm so proud of you, darling."

"Piss off."

"I like him."

"So do I. But I'm so hormonal I can't tell what's really me and what's not."

"Well, he's definitely got potential, that's all I'm saying. Don't cross him off your list."

"What is it with you and lists?"

"You're a fine one to talk."

I'm drifting off to sleep a few hours later feeling tired but happy; it's been my best birthday in ages. Ever, really. Nick was always hopeless at presents. He got me a new ironing board one year, until Ellen found out and took him shopping. But this year has been completely different. The kids are happy, and I've got a fabulous new handbag and enough perfume to last me for years, and Ellen's invented a new recipe for hot chocolate with vodka that she swears is going to make her a multimillionaire. So it's been a top day all round really.

And seeing Martin vanquish the dreaded Patricia was pretty good too. And Ellen's right, I do really like him. But I'm not going to get into a panic about any of that now. I'm

not. I'm going to think about it tomorrow. Or in a few months' time. Not now. I've got too many other things to worry about. Like how to head Gran off Operation Decorate before she goes into overdrive, and how I'm going to sort out the shop and get all the autumn stock in before the baby. My back's starting to ache again, and the baby's moving a lot tonight.

Actually, maybe I'd better make a list.

lights
camera
action

september

The boys are back at school, after a last-minute flurry of new school shoes and trousers, and things are feeling slightly calmer, thank God. Martin's been busy working on some freelance job so he can afford his new kitchen, and we're talking about fixing up supper with Ellen and Harry in a few weeks' time. Ellen is insisting on calling it a double date, because she knows it gets me into a panic. I've decided heavily pregnant people don't do dates, it's unseemly, so I'm thinking of it as supper, and that's fine.

Actually, I can't believe how quickly time is passing; they're even starting to talk about the Christmas play at school, and Archie's landed himself the role of an aubergine, although thankfully not in the Nativity; I don't think

I could cope with Annabel's smugness at wangling a better role for Harry, and let's face it, pretty much every part has got to be better than the aubergine. Each class is singing or acting out a poem, and Archie's class are making giant papier-mâché models to wield onstage. Jack's class are doing "Slinky Malinki," which Archie's already renamed "Stinky Maplinki," and I'm supposed to be knitting him a black chenille cat, which I could do without but Mrs. Chambers was so keen I didn't really have the heart to say no.

"Now, are you sure it's all right? I can always rebook, you know." Elsie's got an appointment at the chiropodist's because her corns are playing her up.

"No, you go, Elsie."

"My Martin might be in. I took him round a bit of fish last night on that new thermal plate I got in my catalog. Ever so good, it is. And he said he might drop it in later."

"Okay."

"He's always been fussy about fish. I had the devil of a job to get him to eat it when he was younger."

"Right."

"I did him a nice bit of cod in parsley sauce—he likes that. Lord, look at the time. I'd better be off."

"Okay."

Dear God. Although cod in parsley sauce sounds quite nice, actually; maybe I could make some tonight. Archie will pick all the parsley out, but cod in parsley-chopped-very-fine sauce might work. Gran and Reg will probably be around. Operation Decorate is well under way, and after an initial

bumpy start when we had to spend all day in the garden while Reg and Martin sanded the floor, closely followed by Gran in a face mask wielding the Hoover and a damp cloth, it's all been fairly painless. And the floor looks fabulous. Jack's room is finished and he loves it, especially the fluorescent glow in the dark moons and stars, and Archie's room just needs the wallpaper border of spaceships and it's done. I might try to stick it up today if Reg doesn't beat me to it.

I've been worried they'd overdo it, and I'd have someone from Age Concern showing me a red card, but they're both much better at pacing themselves than I am. There are lots of cups of tea and little rests, and Gran seems just as chirpy at the end of the day as she did in the morning. We've chosen new material at the market for curtains, so the spare room now has buttermilk walls and white cotton curtains with yellow daisies, with blackout linings to encourage new small people to learn to sleep. And in between painting they've been having trips up to John Lewis at Bluewater so they can haunt the baby department and make the assistants demonstrate all the different prams and cots.

I've promised to go up with them soon for the final decision, but I'm trying to put it off for a bit longer because I've still got a few weeks yet and I'm nowhere near ready for pram rehearsals. I've booked my slot for my C-section, but I'm trying not to think about it. The midwife at the doctor's says everything's fine, so I'd really like a bit more normal life before everything goes into baby mode.

I'm finishing off the teatime window, which Olivia helped me with on Saturday. Polly was in too; she's taken to coming in before the rest of the group arrive and sitting

knitting with Olivia. So far they've knitted themselves short skirts, and now they're knitting bags, which is great because Polly's definitely the trendsetter girl in their year, so a few of the others are bound to follow suit. Even Elsie's been impressed at how well the group is working: it's like we're opening up the shop to a whole new generation, which reminds me, I'd better order in some more of the gray flecked tweed, which seems to be their current favorite.

Martin arrives with the thermal plate and matching lid twenty minutes after Elsie's left.

"You timed that well."

He grins. "She's driving me mad. She'll be doing me boiled eggs and soldiers next if I let her."

"I love boiled eggs and soldiers. I haven't had them for ages."

"I hate parsley sauce, and she knows it. Trevor liked it, though, but he'll eat anything. How's the new floor?"

"Lovely. We've moved the bed up against the wall now, so the room looks much bigger."

"Mum was saying you want a new shower, for the baby."

"Sorry?"

"A new shower."

He must mean the baby shower. Trust Martin to think a baby shower involves plumbing.

"Actually—"

"So I've had a word with Kevin—he's helping me out with the plumbing at the barn—and he'll give me a half day free if I help him with his kitchen cabinets. So I thought I could do it for you, if you like. What sort of shower were you after?"

"I hadn't really thought."

"I noticed the base was cracked when I was in doing the floor, but they're easy to replace. But if you want it ready for the baby, we'd better get a move on."

I can't tell him it's not that sort of shower now or he'll feel like such a twit.

"Well, that would be great, but only if you let me pay."

"Sure. You could teach me to cook. I can't keep living on tins of soup, and I'd like to learn how to do a few simple things."

"Like boiled eggs and soldiers?"

He grins. "Yes. And roast chicken, is that difficult?"

"Not really."

"Great. Well, you give me cooking lessons and I'll sort the shower out. Shall I bring you some brochures in? I've got a few at the barn. Some of them are very pricey, but there are a few good basic ones. You'll probably need a pump, though. What's your water pressure like?"

"Fine, I think."

"Right. Well, I'll bring the brochures in and we can start from there, yes?"

"Great. Thanks, Martin."

"No problem. I'd like to do one actually—give me a clearer idea of what's involved for when I do mine at the barn."

A proper shower that produces more than a tepid trickle wasn't exactly top of my list, but I'm sure it'll come in handy, especially since I'm going to be needing as

much help as I can get in the waking-up-in-time-for-the-school-run department. And there's still a bit of money left over from the curtains, and I've got the money coming from the film people.

Actually, I'd better call Maxine and check what time they want me on Friday. I'm due to visit them on location, which is exciting; Ellen's still trying to come along as my helper, like anyone would fall for that. But the press interest in Jean-Luc hasn't really subsided, even though they've all run photographs of him and Grace kissing in a Paris bistro.

"Maxine?"

"Hi, Jo, how are you? Still baby onboard?"

We were joking about those silly car stickers last time we talked: she's seen a Baby I'm Bored one, which we both think is much better, so she's getting one for Ed, to put in his Porsche.

"So far so good. I wanted to check what time I should get there on Friday."

"Around lunchtime, or earlier if you like."

"Do you need me to bring anything?"

"Not unless you've got any Valium."

It's a three-hour drive to the hotel in Sussex that the film people have taken over as their base, four if you keep having to stop for loo breaks. But it's a treat being away from Broadgate for the day, and I feel rather glamorous, off to meet my film-star client. That's one of the things I miss most about working on the news: feeling like a real grown-up, with a high-pressure job. If I order the wrong wool, no-

body really cares except me, and Mr. Prewitt when he sees the books, and I do miss the pace sometimes, and the drinks after work and all the in-jokes. Not that I'd really change things, but still, it's nice to be out and about for a change.

Everyone's having lunch when I arrive, queuing up at a canteen trailer and sitting at a variety of tables in the car park. Maxine had already warned me it would be a bit shambolic, but I didn't think it would look like something the Women's Royal Voluntary Service might have set up during the war: lots of people seem to be wearing *Dad's Army* costumes, and there are boxes and piles of equipment all over the place. At least with news you only get a cameraman, or a van at most; this is more like an invasion.

I'm supposed to find one of the assistant producers called Rick, who will take me to Grace, but Maxine spots me first.

"Hi, Jo. Do you want some lunch?"

"No, I'm fine, thanks. This is so exciting. How's it going?"

"Okay. The weather's been hopeless, but we're getting there. Let's have some lunch. Grace is a bit busy, rehearsing with Jean-Luc." She raises her eyebrows.

"Oh, right, well, yes, please then. Lunch would be great."

I'm sitting on a plastic chair eating chicken salad while a series of men in black nylon padded jackets check things with Maxine or hand her bits of paper.

"A quarter to five—I'm not telling her a quarter to five."

"Tom wants to get the light."

"Well, he can tell her then."

"Is there a problem?"

A small, slightly disheveled-looking man is smiling at Maxine.

"Jo, this is Tom, our director. This is Jo, Grace's knitting coach."

"Her what?"

"Jo helps Grace source patterns and materials for her knitting, and she runs master classes too."

I must remember that, it sounds so efficient and professional.

Tom smiles. "What a great way to make a living, better than this madness. So, Maxine darling, I gather Grace is having a run-through with Prince Charming. Is she going to be long, do you think?"

"Yesterday was my fault, Tom. I didn't give her the right time. I'm sorry."

"Of course, no problem. Lovely to meet you, Jo. We'll see you later, I expect." He wanders off, trailed by a gaggle of the black-nylon boys and a woman wearing an earpiece.

"Grace was late yesterday, and he's still furious about it."

"He seemed very nice."

"He's a brilliant director, and not such an arse as the rest of them, but he's in his own head most of the time. He emerges occasionally to give everyone a bollocking, apart from Grace, of course. He fired two assistants yesterday, but they were doing a crap job so I don't really blame him. This business is full of assistants who think they're Special. Oh, and we don't call Jean-Luc Prince Charming in front of

Grace. It's a joke the crew have got going, what with him being a Frog. They think it's very witty."

"Right."

"Have you got all the wool and stuff?"

"Yes, it's in the car. Shall I get it?"

"No, have a coffee first. Decaf, right?"

"Please. I've half-knitted a few versions, so she can choose, in air force blue; is that right?"

"Great."

"Where's Lily? I thought she'd be here."

"She is. We've set up a playroom for her next to Grace's suite. She's loving it."

The woman with the earpiece comes over while Maxine gets the coffee. "You're the knitting woman, right?"

"Yes."

"Well, get me the stuff then. I need to take it to where we're setting up. And hurry up, would you, please. I haven't got all day."

"I'll just—"

Maxine has come straight back over, without the coffees.

"Good, you've met Jo, VIP friend of Grace. We'll bring the knitting props over in a minute. We're having a quick drink first. Okay?"

"Right. Sure, of course."

"Actually, could you get us two coffees? There seems to be a queue. Both white, no sugar, decaf for Jo. Got that?"

"Yes. I'll do that right now."

"Thank you. So much."

"Crikey."

"She's been annoying me all week. She's a total cow."

"So shall I get the knitting then?"

"No. When she comes back you can give her the keys and she'll get it. Now she thinks you're a VIP, she'll be all over you like a rash. There's something else I wanted to mention to you, actually."

"Oh, yes?"

"Grace is in London tomorrow afternoon, for a photo session. *Vanity Fair* are sending Daniel Fitzgerald over to do a piece on the film."

"Oh."

"He won't be coming here."

"Right."

"But I thought you'd like to know."

"Thanks, Max."

"Have you sorted things out with him? Sorry, I don't mean to pry, but Grace mentioned the letter. Have you spoken to him since then?"

"No."

"Bastard. Well, just tell me, if you want me to give him a message or anything."

"Thanks, Max, but I'm fine, really."

"Good for you. But let me know if you change your mind. Oh, here she comes with the coffees. Have you got your car keys handy?"

Christ, Daniel, in London. With Grace. It feels a bit weird knowing he'll be in England. I'm used to thinking of him in airports off to exotic locations. But nothing's changed.

He'll get in touch if he wants to, and if not, then that's fine too.

There's a fleet of black people carriers to ferry everyone to the river where they're filming this afternoon. Maxine tells me the scene involves Grace sitting under a tree knitting while the three evacuee children are trying to fish, but since they're not having much luck, she says some magic words and they catch a trout. And then Professor Jean-Luc arrives.

There are people everywhere, and cameras and lights, and a man climbing up the tree to saw one of the branches off because Tom doesn't like the shape of it. Everyone's here except Grace and Jean-Luc, who are still in makeup. We nipped in to see them just before we left, and Grace was wearing a lovely tweed suit and having her hair put up into a bun. But there's no sign of her now.

The woman with the earpiece is giving Maxine a very frosty look, while giving me the occasional hesitant smile until a black car with tinted windows arrives, and Grace gets out, looking amazing. She's in full Diva mode and sits down under the tree looking very relaxed, and breathtakingly beautiful.

"Quiet, everybody, please."

A young man steps forward and raises his hand, and everyone falls silent as he raises an electronic version of a clapper board. There's a beep as he presses the button and the clock starts.

"Scene fourteen, take one. Action."

God, this is so exciting. I'm frightened I'm going to make a noise or trip over something and ruin it, just like when you're buying secondhand furniture at an auction and you're terrified you'll end up buying a set of pottery owls by mistake.

I'm trying to keep completely still while they're filming the children mucking about by the edge of the river. It's weird, because even though you know it's not real, and there are all sorts of lights and big white screens and people standing out of the way of the cameras, for a minute or two all you see are the kids standing with their fishing rods in the sunshine and Grace smiling at them.

We're on what seems like the hundredth take of the kids fishing and not catching anything.

"Right, get the fish in, and can it look as natural as possible, please, no hey presto—we're not making bloody *Bewitched* here. Grace darling, divine, as usual. Love the knitting."

Grace laughs, but she really does look divine. The light through the leaves is falling on her hair, and Tom is kneeling down talking to her, and she's smiling.

Maxine hands me a bottle of water. "This shouldn't take long. She only has to look at the kids again and then Jean-Luc arrives. An hour tops."

An hour. God.

"But let me know if you need a loo break or a rest or anything—there's a car on standby."

Thank God for Maxine being so good at her job.

"Actually, I wouldn't mind a sit-down."

"The car's just at the end of the track. Would you like to go now and then come back?"

"Perfect. You stay here. I'll be fine."

"Sure?"

"Of course. You need to be here, and I won't be long. Shall I bring you back a coffee?"

She looks surprised, and rather pleased. "That would be great. Thanks, Jo."

"So, did you enjoy it?"

"It was great, Grace, fascinating. Thanks so much for inviting me. I can't wait to see it at the cinema."

"I think it'll be okay. He's great, Tom. Genius, actually."

"The bit with Jean-Luc was good. Well, it looked good to me."

We got to watch the close-up bits on the monitor, and there was a lot more sexual tension going on than I remember in the Angela Lansbury version, particularly the moment, after he'd sat down next to her on the blanket, when he touched her arm and she sort of froze, and then looked at him. And even standing thirty foot away, peering at a monitor and desperate for another wee, you could feel it.

"Glad you liked it. We're off to Cornwall next week, I think."

"Maxine told me."

"Bit far for you to come, I guess. Not long until the baby now, is it? Are you all set?"

"No."

She smiles. "Lily adores babies. I can't wait for her to see yours. And rabbits, actually more the rabbits, to be honest. I thought I might knit one for her. Can you get me a pattern?"

"Sure."

"Did Max tell you we're seeing Mr. Fitzgerald tomorrow?"

"Yes."

"Okay?"

"Fine."

"I know nothing, yes?"

"Please."

"No problem. Take care, darling, and we'll see you soon." She stands up and gives me a hug. A real hug. And then she snaps back into film-star mode. "Where's Prince Charming, Max?"

Maxine looks confused. "I thought you didn't know about that."

"I know everything, Max darling. You should know that by now."

"He's having a swim."

"Is he? God, where does he get the energy? Right, I'm going to see Lily, and then can you get Sam to sort me out a salad, and some rice, but not that brown stuff, okay? I hate that now."

"Sure."

Maxine walks me back to my car. "All the research was great, Jo. I'll chase the money for you. They always take ages to pay anything."

"Thanks, Maxine."

"Drive safely, and call me when anything happens, yes? We'll probably see you before, but if not, call me."

"Sure."

"You're trying not to think about it, right?"

"Pretty much."

"Okay. I've sent something from us, for your baby shower."

"How did you know about that?"

"Elsie, the woman from your shop. She was telling me all about it at the beach party."

We're standing by my car now.

"I'd better go and find Bruno. She wants to go out to dinner with Jean-Luc tonight; there must be a Michelin-starred place somewhere round here."

"Good luck. All I saw on the way down was a series of Little Chefs."

"Now that's a front-page picture I'd pay money to see."

I'm having tea with the boys on Thursday night before Stitch and Bitch and the official baby shower, which we're doing tonight because Angela's going to be away next week and then Maggie's got a holiday booked. There's been no news from Daniel, which I sort of knew there wouldn't be. Although Maxine did ring to say he was being more of an arse than usual about being a creative-genius photographer, and he's got two assistants now, and is wearing much trendier clothes, so Liv is obviously having an impact. It was kind of her to call, though, not that I really expected

anything to happen, but it was nice to know they'd finished and there hadn't been any Conversations.

Archie's sulking. "I hate pasta, you know I do. Why do we always have pasta?"

"We had fish pie last night, Archie."

"Yes, and I hate that too. And I don't want sauce on mine."

"Just plain spaghetti?"

"Yes."

"No cheese?"

"A bit."

"You have to have sauce if you want cheese."

He throws his fork on the floor.

Time for a bit of diversionary attention, I think.

"Archie, I've been meaning to ask you, well, both of you, actually— Pick your fork up, love, and put it in the sink; I'll get you a clean one, but please don't be silly like that again. I wanted to ask you about presents, from the baby."

"*From* the baby, not *for* the silly baby?"

"No, definitely from. When you were born, you helped me get Jack a big present."

"What was it?"

"The Playmobil zoo."

"That's only for babies."

"Yes, but Jack was only two when you were born. I thought this time we could choose together."

"Not clothes. Gran says everyone's bringing clothes for the baby at the party tonight."

"It's not a party, Archie. It's only people giving us things for the baby."

"It's called a shower."

"Yes, Jack."

"Which is stupid."

"Well, maybe, but it's nice of people to want to give us presents, don't you think? Only they'll all be quite boring, clothes and things, so why don't you think about what you'd like, and I can see if I can find it ready for when the baby comes."

"I'll go and get my catalogs."

Jack loves looking at toy catalogs and has got quite a collection in his bedroom.

Archie nods. "Yes, and then we can write a list."

Martin brings the cups down from upstairs: he's fitting the shower with Kevin, which hasn't been quite as straightforward as they thought. They've been here all day, and Martin's got the soaking-wet trouser legs to prove it.

"Sorry to interrupt. You haven't got a bucket, have you?"

"In the cupboard under the sink. I'll get it for you. How's it going?"

"We couldn't get the level right, but it's sorted out now. We should be able to turn the water back on soon."

"Great."

"The pump's all fitted."

Reg will do the tiling when they're done, so that'll be him spending hours wandering about with tubs of grout tomorrow. God, I wish I'd never started this.

"Would you like a cup of tea?"

"Please."

"It's two sugars for Kevin, right?"

"Yes, and he says if there's any more biscuits he'd be grateful; they keep him going."

I know the feeling.

"Are we still on for roast-chicken practice on Sunday?"

"Sure."

"Shall I bring anything?"

"Just your pinny."

"My what?" He's grinning.

"Don't worry. You can borrow one of mine."

I 'm late getting to the shop, and Elsie's already arrived and opened up, and is helping Connie put out cups and saucers when Tina and Linda arrive.

Tina's carrying a Tupperware box. "I've done a few sausage rolls. Shall I put them in the kitchen?"

"Please, Tina."

Connie's got a large white cake box. "Don't look. It will be a surprise."

Elsie's got the kettle on. "Why don't you go and sit down and we'll make the tea, dear."

"Okay."

I lit the fire earlier; it's getting chilly in the evenings now, so I'm sitting watching the flames when Cath and Olivia come upstairs with Polly, who's wearing the new gray tweed skirt she knitted, over black leggings with ballet shoes and a stretchy black top. She looks fabulous, and everyone is admiring the skirt when Maggie arrives.

"I remember wearing something like that years ago. Of course there was a lot less of me then."

Linda laughs. "There was a lot less of all of us, Maggie, but me and Tina are on this new diet now, the plate one."

Tina nods. "It's ever so simple. You eat like normal, but on a small plate. I've lost three pounds."

Linda pokes her tongue out at Tina. "And I've put on two. It's amazing how much you can fit on a small plate if you're really trying."

Elsie's busy bustling about. I think she's quite excited; she doesn't usually come to the group, which is probably why they're so relaxed. She's already given Connie a shocked look when she started pouring out glasses of wine.

Cath sits down next to me. "Are we waiting for Angela?"

Linda passes her a glass of wine. "She said to start. She'll be along soon. She's had to go into Maidstone to drop Peter off at some council thing. Open this one first." She hands me a parcel wrapped in shiny silver paper. "It's from me and Tina."

Half an hour later there's wrapping paper all over the table, and all sorts of gorgeous baby kit in a pile in front of me. They've really thought about it all, and Connie's gone out to her car and returned with a Moses basket with a white cotton frill, and two sets of soft flannel sheets, one with ducks on and one with elephants. It's perfect, and she's knitted a sweet little blanket in soft cotton to go on top, in caramel and cream squares. I've got vests and sleep suits and more knitted blankets and cardigans and hats than one baby could possibly need, and Elsie's spent hours on a beautiful shawl, and a peach pram set with satin ribbon rosettes,

which I think we might be saving for our first trip into the shop. Maxine and Grace have sent a very smart blue-and-white-striped changing bag, with the pockets full of little tubes of posh baby cream and wipes and two tiny old-fashioned flannelette baby nightgowns with lambs embroidered on the front.

I'm pretty close to tears by the time we're finished.

"It's all so lovely. Thank you so much, I'm—"

Linda gets up. "Don't start, love, or you'll have us all going. And anyway, I've been waiting for the cake and I don't think I can last much longer. Connie?"

Connie nods and goes into the kitchen as Linda turns the big light off. "We thought we'd start a new tradition, and do you a Happy Nearly Birthday cake. You've got to blow the candles out and make a wish, love."

Everyone leans forward as Connie puts the cake, covered in flickering candles, on the table in front of me.

"Let's all make a wish."

Chocolate and chestnut with bits of meringue, my absolute favorite.

"Tell him thanks for me, Connie. It's lovely."

"He didn't put the amaretto in, so there's something else, only I've forgotten."

We spend a happy ten minutes eating cake and trying to identify the mystery ingredient, until Connie remembers it's homemade quince jam, which sounds like it wouldn't be nice but is absolutely delicious, as the conversation moves toward babies. Cath annoys Olivia by remembering bringing her home from hospital and staying up all night to make sure she was still breathing, and Linda tells us about

the time she left baby Gemma outside the shop when she was a few weeks old.

"I'd got right back home before I realized. It was awful; I'd bought some buttons for a cardigan and I put them on the kitchen table and then, God, I've never run so fast in all my life. And your gran was so nice about it. I was beside myself, and there was your gran walking her up and down inside the shop, standing by the window so she could see me, patting her on the back, and Gemma was loving it, looking round at everything, and your gran just said, 'Thanks, that was kind of you, I've been wanting a cuddle,' and then she handed her back to me like it was the most normal thing in the world. Made me feel like she didn't think I was the worst mother ever. I've never forgotten it."

"I did that with my Travis too. I left him in his car seat in our porch and I was halfway down the road before I remembered. Thank heavens there wasn't anyone behind me. I've never been that good at reversing, but I was back up our drive in about three seconds."

Linda pours Tina some more wine. Actually, the only time I really miss a glass of wine is at our Stitch and Bitch groups.

"I did something similar with Jack once. He was teething and we hadn't had much sleep, and Nick thought I'd put him in his car seat, and I thought Nick had, so we'd got halfway down the road before we realized he was still in his playpen in the living room. And Nick just got out of the car and ran back, down the middle of the road. He left the engine running and everything."

Olivia and Polly seem slightly shocked by our tales of maternal malfunctions.

"Does everyone do it then, forget they've got a baby?" Polly's licking her finger and dabbing it into the cake crumbs on her plate.

Tina smiles. "No, love, not really, but you get so tired you'd forget your own head if it wasn't on your shoulders."

Linda nods. "You were a terror for sleeping—never went more than an hour until she was eighteen months. Oh, sorry, Jo."

"It's fine, Linda. Archie was the same. So if everyone could keep an eye out, outside shops, that would be great."

Gran's thrilled when Connie and I get home and show her all the presents.

"Well, isn't that lovely, and look at Elsie's shawl. It must have taken her hours."

"I know, and look, there's blankets for the Moses basket and a baby bath and everything."

"Well, thank heavens you've got a few bits to start you off. I was beginning to think this baby would be wearing a sheet for the first few days, and sleeping in a drawer. Mind you, your mum slept in the bottom drawer of my big bedroom set and it didn't do her any harm. So I expect we'd have managed."

"Did she? Why?"

"She was early, and I was trying to get old Mrs. Butterworth to let me swap bedrooms. We were in the back one, freezing cold it was, and she was keeping the big front one

for her spare room, miserable woman. I hated her so much by the end, you know. I know you shouldn't speak ill of the dead, but I did. Anyway, by the time I'd got my way and moved my things into the room, there wasn't time to buy a cot. I was moving a wardrobe the day before she was born."

"So you didn't have everything neatly folded in drawers then?"

"I'd made a few things; you made most of it in those days. But no, I wasn't exactly ready, pet. So I suppose we know who you take after."

I'm woken by someone knocking on the front door at a quarter to six in the bloody morning. Christ. The postman's not usually this early, and the milkman doesn't knock. Maybe it's another parcel from Vin and Lou by some special wake-you-up-at-the-crack-of-dawn delivery service.

It's Graham in his fireman's uniform, holding a yellow plastic helmet in his hands, looking exhausted. "I'm sorry, love, but there's been a fire."

"What?"

I turn to look back into the hall, a surge of adrenaline hitting me as I head for the stairs to get the boys. A fire. How could I have missed the house being on fire? Christ. I've got to get the boys.

"No, sorry, not here, love, at the shop, I should have said. You'd better come and see."

"A fire? At the shop?"

"You idiot, Graham—you've half terrified her. Get out of the way. It's only the shop, love, it's not that bad. Well, it is

quite bad, but try not to panic. Graham will show you, and we've called your gran, so I expect she'll be here any minute."

I hadn't noticed Tina standing behind Graham, with Travis looking half asleep with his anorak hood up, wearing his Batman slippers. She's got her hair in giant foam curlers; I always wondered how she got it so curly.

"Come in, I should probably . . ."

Actually, I don't know what I should probably be doing.

Tina puts her arm round me. I'm having flashbacks to the policeman standing on the doorstep at our old house telling me about Nick's crash. Oh, God.

"Let's get the kettle on. You sit down; it'll be fine. Nobody's hurt and that's all that matters. Travis, would you like to watch telly, very quiet, mind?"

He nods.

"Graham, sort him out with some cartoons, would you? Nice cup of tea, that's what we need."

The boys are still asleep when I check on them as I'm getting dressed. I must remember to test the smoke alarm on the upstairs landing; the one in the kitchen is always going off when I make toast, but I haven't checked the one on the upstairs landing for ages.

"How bad is it?"

Tina pours me a cup of tea and looks at Graham.

"It's just the top floor really. The roof's gone in a couple of places, but downstairs is fine."

God, I've just thought, I bet it was the fireplace. We had the fire on last night for the Stitch and Bitch group, and I

was so busy getting all the baby things back into the car I must have forgotten to put the fireguard across properly.

"Mum's shop has the most damage, especially her store-room. I've been telling her for ages to get that wiring sorted. We should have done it for her. Four grown-up sons and one of them in the fire service and not one of us got round to doing it. She's ever so upset."

"Are you sure it was wiring, Graham? It might have been the fireplace in our shop, you know. I usually put the guard up, but maybe I forgot last night."

"No, love. It started above Mum's shop. This is unoffi-cial, of course, there'll be a report, but I can tell you now, it was definitely electrical. When your gran gets here, I'll walk round with you and show you, but it could be worse, honestly, you'll see."

Tina tuts. "Apart from the water."

"Well, yes, Tina, we do have to use water, what with trying to put the fire out."

"I'm only saying. Why they have to go and make every-thing soaking wet is beyond me. It does more damage than the fire half the time."

"I'll make sure to tell that to the boys. Any bright ideas on how we're meant to put the fires out, though, with us not using the water?"

"Shut up, Graham."

Gran's wearing her dressing gown when they arrive; she's dressed, but she's put her dressing gown on in-stead of her coat.

"Oh, pet, what a thing to happen. We came straight round. How bad is it? Have you seen? We drove round the one-way system, so we didn't see."

"I don't know yet, Gran."

"You go and have a look and come back and tell me. I'll stay here with the boys. Reg, you go with her. I don't think I can face it."

"All right, Mary."

Tina stays with Gran, and Reg and I walk down the hill with Graham. As we turn the corner, I can see the fire engine, parked in the entrance to the side road.

Graham's put his helmet back on. "Lucky it's just your two shops really, or it could have been much worse."

Reg takes hold of my hand.

"Yes, I suppose it is."

There's a narrow side road between Mrs. Davis's florist's shop and the rest of the parade, an access road for deliveries. Most of the shops have small backyards; her shop has got one too. In fact the only shop without a back door is ours, since we're right on the corner. The lights from the fire engine are still flashing.

Stan from the greengrocer's is standing on the pavement by our window. "It was me who called them, I'd had pickled onions for my tea and they always play me up, so I woke up around four and that was when I saw the smoke."

Reg is looking in through the window. "Thank heavens you did, Stan. It doesn't look too bad, you know, love."

It looks pretty bad to me: the glass in the door is smashed, and there's water everywhere.

Elsie's standing to one side with Mrs. Davis.

"Isn't it dreadful?" She's obviously rather thrilled with the excitement of it all. "And I've been thinking, we could all have been killed, you know, if it had started while we'd been open. Those stairs would be a death trap."

"We'd have smelled the smoke and been out long before that, Elsie. There's a smoke alarm in the kitchen, don't forget."

"I suppose."

"I'll never forgive myself. I'm so sorry, dear." Poor Mrs. Davis looks very shocked and cold.

"Please, it was an accident. I'm just relieved it wasn't my fireplace that started it."

Elsie looks annoyed; I think she was hoping for a bit more tension.

"I'll pay for any damage, of course."

"Please don't worry about that now. I'm sure the insurance will cover it."

Thank God we're up to date; Mr. Prewitt was only talking about the premiums going up a few months ago, and I remember writing the check. And resenting it hugely, since it had gone up so much.

Graham comes over and puts his arm round his mother. "Mum, you should go. There's nothing to do here until we've finished. I've phoned Pete, and he's on his way over. Why don't I walk you round home?"

"No, I'm fine here. I want to make sure it's definitely out."

"It's out, Mum. Do you want to go in, Jo? You'll need to borrow a helmet, but I can take you in if you'd like a closer look."

I really don't. Actually, I'm feeling rather frightened, but I need to see exactly how bad it is.

"Thanks, Graham."

It's much worse than I thought it would be, and strangely better too. Downstairs is pretty normal, apart from the smell of smoke and wet wool and a few black marks on the walls. There's water on the floor, but everything else seems fine, and the shelves near the front door look completely untouched. The door to the stairs must have been closed, because as soon as you get past it everything's black and soaking wet—the floor, the walls, everything. And you can see daylight through the holes in the roof, and the smell is much worse, so thick and acrid you can almost taste it.

Christ, this is going to take a lot of fixing.

"Next door's worse, love. Lost the floor in places too as well as the roof."

"Right."

"Seen enough?"

"Yes, thanks."

"Let's get you back out in the fresh air then."

"How bad is it?" Elsie's desperate for an update.

"It's a mess, but I'm sure we can sort it out."

Actually, I'm not, but I'm not telling her that on the pavement, particularly with poor Mrs. Davis looking like she'll burst into tears at any minute.

"Let's all go back to my house. It's nearest and Gran's there and she'll want to see you, Mrs. Davis. Come on, you shouldn't be standing here."

"I'm not sure I can face her, not after all these years."

"Don't be silly, Mum. You didn't do it on purpose." Graham takes her hand, and Reg nods.

"Please come, Pat. Mary will want to see you."

We start walking back up the hill, but Mrs. Davis is still standing looking in our window.

"I never knew you could knit pumpkins."

I'd better call Mr. Prewitt and get on to the insurance people. And then I should get the boys ready for school. Actually, maybe Reg could take them this morning. I don't think I can face all the questions.

G ran's made bacon sandwiches for everyone, and the boys are watching cartoons with Travis.

We're sitting round the kitchen table, and everyone's gone quiet as Mrs. Davis puts her cup down. "Well, that's it for me, I'll not reopen. I've spent too many years with my hands in buckets of cold water; it plays havoc with your joints, you know—my hands are terrible some nights. No, I've had enough. There's no money in flowers now anyway, not with the supermarkets all doing them and the computers."

"Don't rush into anything, Pat."

"No, Mary, I've been thinking about retiring for ages now."

Everyone seems to be looking at me. And I realize this is one of those moments when you have to make a decision. I suppose I could claim on the insurance and then decide. But actually, I already know.

"After all your hard work, pet, it's such a shame." Gran's close to tears now too.

"It's all right, Gran, honestly, I've been wanting to re-decorate."

Everyone smiles.

Actually, I think it's going to take more than a few coats of paint to sort that lot out.

"We'll be open again before you know it, you'll see. We'll tidy up and start again. I'm good at starting again."

Elsie blows her nose. "Of course you will, dear, and I'll help. We'll have it sorted out in no time, Mary, probably better than before, what with all the lovely ideas Jo has."

Reg stands up and puts his cup in the sink. "Right, well, what we need now is a plan. I'll get on to the insurance people. We can't start clearing up until they've been round. Elsie, do you think your Jeffrey will know the person the insurance people are likely to send round?"

"I should think so. He used to know everyone before he retired, and he keeps up with a lot of them."

"Right, well, that gives us an advantage. Let's work out our plan of action then."

As news of the fire spreads, more people arrive at the house, and by the time the boys are leaving for school with Reg, it's like Piccadilly Circus.

"Mum."

"Yes, Archie?"

"Can we go and see the fire later?"

"It's all over, I told you, Archie. Everything's fine now. You go off to school and have a lovely day, and I'll see you later. What would you like for tea?"

He tuts. "It's not fair. I wanted to see it, and have a go on the fire engine."

"They were far too busy for boys to be playing on the fire engine, Archie."

"They might not have noticed."

"Go and find your shoes, love."

I can still smell the smoke. I think I'll have a bath and wash my hair.

Reg is putting his coat on. "Come on, boys, we might have time to get sweets if we hurry."

There's a rush for the front door.

I'm in the bath, trying to pretend everything's normal. But it's not. I really don't know if I can do this. I'm too tired. The baby moves, and I start to cry, quietly. It's absolutely bloody typical. As soon as I start to think I've got things sorted, bingo, another crisis comes along to tip everything upside down. Maybe I should think about this. I want to carry on, but this might be one of those moments when you're meant to make a new start. Except where would I go? We like it here, we all do. And the shop's just starting to work, with the website and the groups and everything.

Christ, I hope the insurance people don't try to wriggle out of paying, because there's no way I can afford a new roof. And I'll have to make sure the boys aren't worried; Jack

will be imagining a small pile of charred embers. I'll have to take them round and show them as soon as it's safe. Archie will love it.

"Are you nearly done, pet? Only Reg is back and he wants to talk to you. He's working out a cleaning rota."

"I'll be there in a minute, Gran."

"Are you sure you're all right? You sound funny."

"I'm fine."

"You should go back to bed, you know, pet, have a rest. I don't want you doing too much."

"Don't fuss, Gran, I'm fine."

"Shall I do you another bacon sandwich?"

"No, thanks."

"I could do you a crispy one, with an egg?"

Actually, that might be quite nice.

"Yes, please. I'll be down in a minute."

"I'll put the pan on."

"Thanks, Gran."

A crispy bacon sandwich with a fried egg. It's a start, I suppose.

the twilight zone

September/October

It's Tuesday morning, and I'm walking to the shop with Connie after dropping the kids off at school.

"I've had an idea, Con, and I want to talk to you about it, but I want you to be honest, okay? Tell me what you really think."

Actually, I've been up half the night thinking about it, so I'm really hoping she's going to like it.

"Sure."

"You know Mrs. Davis says she's selling her shop next door to us?"

"Yes."

"Well, if I can sort out the money, I thought maybe I should try to buy it."

"Then you will have a much bigger shop, yes?"

"Yes, but not just for the wool. I was thinking, the knitting groups have worked so well, and Elsie's always making people cups of tea, so I thought maybe we could have a tea shop too."

"Like a café?"

"Yes, something simple, doing teas and coffees and toasted sandwiches, nothing like a restaurant. A cross between Starbucks and an old-fashioned tea shop, that kind of thing. A place for people to meet, of all ages, Olivia and Gemma and Polly too, as well as all our old ladies."

"*Brava*. There's no real café here, not open all year, and the coffee from the fish and chip shop is awful. People will love it, I think."

"The only thing is I don't know anything about catering, so would you and Mark be interested in helping me?"

"We'd love to, but we don't have money, although maybe—"

"No, the money should be fine. I think I can sort out a business loan. The shop's all mine, so I should be able to raise something against that, at least I hope so. No, I meant you could be my café advisers, then you could decide what kind of coffee machine we need, and all that kind of thing, and take a percentage of the profits, if we make any. What do you think?"

She kisses me. "Mark can make all the patisserie?"

"Exactly."

"He will love it; he wants to take on another chef for the kitchen so he has more time for the cakes. It's what he loves

most now, and he's got so many ideas, but there's never enough time."

"Great."

"It'll be perfect for the birthday cakes; people come to see them in the pub, but it's too busy, and I can't take anyone into the kitchen because Mark says it is against hygiene."

I was really hoping she'd see the potential: me selling a few cakes isn't really going to be much of a benefit to the pub, but if we use the café as their base on the High Street for Mark's wedding and birthday cakes, then it'll make much more sense. And it won't need much space; one of those glass-fronted fridges and a few cake boxes should be all we'll need.

"Can I tell him now?"

"Of course."

Connie's babbling on her mobile when we get to the shop to find Gran and Reg are already there.

Gran's got her pinny on. "What did she think?"

"She loves the idea."

I called Gran first thing this morning, and she's really excited. I wanted her to sound out Mrs. Davis to make sure she really wants to sell up; I thought she'd talk to her at some point over the next couple of days, but instead she rang her straightaway, and then rang me back to say she was really pleased.

"We've got all the windows open upstairs."

"Great."

We're launching Operation Cleanup today since the combined efforts of Reg and Jeffrey have got the insurance assessor round in record time and he's said we can write off most of the stock. It looks like they won't be haggling over the claim for the roof either, so Reg has sorted out the electrics with his friend Malcolm, who used to work for the electricity board, and we've got two big dehumidifiers going upstairs and one downstairs. It's amazing how often the plastic containers have to be emptied of thick black water, but it's definitely starting to feel less damp now.

The plan is to clean up as speedily as we can and open again next week, and then close again after Christmas and get the replastering done; the ceilings are all stained and mottled and the plaster is cracking, and the roof needs a complete overhaul, but I think we can manage until then.

Everyone's been so kind, offering to help and coming over in the playground at school to ask how it's going; apart from Annabel Morgan, of course, who looked faintly pleased until she heard me say that we'll be opening up again as soon as we can. I wish I could see her face when she hears Grace has agreed to come and cut the ribbon at the grand reopening ceremony when everything's properly finished. Which reminds me, I must ring Max and ask her what we should get for Lily's birthday. Last time I spoke to her she was balancing her laptop on her knees on location somewhere, trying to track down snow machines and let everyone know the party's been moved to the last week of December because the filming is running late, and Grace

doesn't want to do it in January because she'll be in America. So it didn't seem a good time to ask about birthday presents.

Martin and Jeffrey are busy tacking up plastic sheeting under the holes in the roof, and the rest of us are washing walls and pouring filthy water down the drain outside the shop. It's already starting to smell fresher, and I'm trying to salvage the balls of wool that were still in their plastic packets, or tucked in the backs of shelves, and chucking anything damp into black bin bags. It's rubbish day tomorrow, so I want to get rid of as much as I can, although I'm putting the more expensive yarns to one side because I can't quite bear to throw them out: it'll be a lot of washing and rewinding, but I'm sure I can salvage some of it, even if it's only for me to knit up at home.

I'm completely knackered by lunchtime. My sleeves are soaking wet from washing down shelves, and I'm grimy and cold, although somehow Gran's still managing to look fairly pristine. But even she's starting to look tired, so I should probably be organizing some sandwiches or something.

"Does anyone fancy a cup of tea?"

Elsie's brought the kettle downstairs and we're making tea when Maggie arrives from the library, offering to help during her lunch hour, and then Cath comes in with homemade pea-and-ham soup, followed by Tina and Mrs. Davis with rolls and pasties.

"Linda will be in later; she's finishing off a perm but she said she'll be along and she's happy to help, and you can put stuff in our machine in the salon if you want, and we've got the tumble dryer too, so you can use that as well."

"Thanks, Tina. I've taken the curtains home, but there are a couple of cushions upstairs, if you're sure."

"I'll take them back with me."

Jeffrey finishes his pasty.

"Lovely pastry. Who made them?"

Mrs. Davis smiles. "My boys have always liked my pasties."

Elsie sniffs.

We're eating and chatting when Betty arrives with scones and Angela arrives with homemade mince pies, and it turns into a rather jolly party, albeit with a rather grubby backdrop.

Everyone's very keen on the café idea, especially Betty.

"There used to be an ice-cream parlor along the front, and it was ever so nice."

Ice cream. Brilliant.

"That's a great idea, Betty. If we've got a fridge for the cakes, we could do ice cream too, couldn't we, Con?"

She smiles. "We can do sorbets too; Mark makes an apricot one—one taste and you're addicted. Forever. It's one of the reasons I married him."

Betty pours herself some more tea. "You'll have people queuing down the road, love; make a change from all those lollies from the kiosks. You should do those smoothlies too. I had a lovely banana one last week, from Sainsbury's, I think it was."

Connie nods. "Mark wants a new juicer for the pub, so maybe we buy two?"

"Great."

I'm stacking bin bags of the soaked-beyond-rescue stuff outside on the pavement when a Labrador starts licking my feet.

"Hello, Lady Denby."

"Hear you're opening a tea shop. Excellent news. Hasn't been anywhere to get a decent cup of tea round here for years. Just wanted to say well done, and do let me know if there's anything I can do. Still have a bit of sway with the council, so if there's any problem with permits or anything, you just let me know. Ridiculous nonsense, most of it. Didn't have to wear special hairnets in my day to serve food, and it got us through the Blitz so it can't have been that bad."

She steps into the doorway.

"I see you're all busy. Stop that, Clarkson—you'll have to stay in the car if you can't behave."

Clarkson is going into a frenzy of floor licking, for some reason, and is edging toward Elsie's feet.

"I don't know what gets into him, I really don't. Anyway, I wanted to say well done. Jolly good. Must be off; got to get George some new glasses. Claims he can see for miles, silly man, but he keeps breaking my china. Keep up the good work, everyone. Good afternoon."

Gran's chuckling, and Elsie's recovered from being stuck midcurtsy while trying to avoid having her feet licked.

"That was nice of her."

"Yes."

"She still has a lot of pull with the council, you know."

Great; so now I've got half the town on my side, plus our local aristocrat ready to take on the council on my behalf. And we're doing smoothlies and ice cream too. Sounds like a winner to me.

We've almost sorted the shop by the weekend, and I've had my appointment with the midwife to reassure Gran that my blood pressure hasn't gone up, which it hasn't, so I'm in the shop on Sunday morning, trying to finish the new window display. Martin and Reg are upstairs tacking up more plastic sheeting. It rained last night, so Elsie was round first thing emptying buckets and trays; she's been really brilliant in the past few days, and she seems almost as excited about the café as Connie and I are, which is great.

"There, that's all done. Should last until we get the tiles up now."

"Thanks, Martin."

"I think you should leave the shop counter where it is when you do all the building work for next door. It's such a lovely piece."

Reg nods.

"I can remember old Mrs. Butterworth standing behind that counter. Maybe you could make something similar for the café, Martin?"

"I could try."

They're measuring and scribbling on pads of paper when the shop door opens, and we all turn as a man walks in.

Jesus Christ.

It's Daniel.

"Hello, angel. How's it going?" He's wearing a leather jacket and jeans, and looking tanned and rather glamorous.

Christ.

He walks toward me, and kisses me.

"Hello, Daniel."

My voice sounds strange.

Dear God, what's he doing here?

"Are you redecorating or something?"

"No, there was a fire."

"But everything's all right?"

"Yes, a huge mess, but—"

"I meant with the baby."

"Oh, right, yes. Fine."

"Good." He stands back and looks at me. "You look great, darling. I thought I'd buy you lunch. You haven't eaten yet, have you?"

"No, but I need to get the boys, and—"

"It's fine, love. You go and have lunch. Me and your gran will see to the boys."

"Daniel, this is Reg, and—" I turn and realize Martin's disappeared upstairs.

"Nice to meet you, Reg."

There's an awkward silence.

"Come on then, angel, I'm bloody starving, I've come straight from the airport. In the world's smallest car. A twango something. Totally hideous."

"Oh, right."

"Is there anywhere local, so we can walk?"

"There's the pub, but they get very busy."

"Sounds great."

W e drive to the pub in the end because it's starting to rain. The world's smallest car turns out to be perfectly normal-size, even if it is a rather horrible turquoise color.

"I'm sorry about this; it was the last one they had at the car rental place."

"It's fine."

"I'm on my way to New York for a job. But I thought I should call in, see how you're doing."

"Right."

There's a silence. God, I don't know what to say to him. Apart from please go away, I can't do this now. There's too much going on, I can't cope with anything else.

"Should I have called?"

"Sorry?"

"Before I turned up?"

"No, it's fine."

"Good. Look, I'm sorry, angel. I know I should have called you, but I've been putting it off. Although you could have called me, actually. Why didn't you?"

"I didn't want another letter from the lawyer's."

"Right. Sorry about that. I panicked."

"I know the feeling."

"You look great."

"Thanks."

"I didn't realize you'd be so . . . so . . ."

"Huge?"

He laughs. "Pregnant. So pregnant."

"The baby's big."

"Right. Well, that's good, yes?" He's smiling.

"Yes. Putting on weight and doing all the things they're meant to do."

"Great. So do I park in here?"

"Yes, or there are more spaces round the side."

Connie finds us a table at the back by moving a reserved card. She hands Daniel a menu.

"I'll just be a minute."

"Thanks, Connie."

"No problem."

"Excuse me a minute, Daniel—I won't be long." I walk toward the ladies', and Connie joins me in about thirty seconds flat.

"Is he?"

"Yes. Daniel."

"Porca Madonna."

"With knobs on. He just turned up, at the shop."

"Okay, but this is good, yes?"

"I don't know. I don't know what he wants yet."

"Yes, it's good; he wants to talk about the baby."

"I think so."

"Of course he does. Why else would he be here?"

"I don't know."

"If he upsets you, Mark will hit him. I will tell him."

"Great."

She kisses me.

"It will be okay, but remember, you give me the winking and I will get Mark."

"Great."

Christ, so now I've got to remember not to wink, on top of everything else.

"I think I'll go for the steak and kidney pie; the food's good here, right?"

"Brilliant."

"Great. Look, I'm sorry about just turning up like this. I know I should probably have a plan, but I'm not that hot on planning. I just didn't want you to think I'm not bothered. I have been thinking about it."

"Okay."

Connie comes over to take our orders and makes me have lamb stew when I try to order a salad.

"She's a friend of yours, I take it?"

"Yes."

"She seems nice."

"She is. Her husband does all the cooking."

"Is he Italian too?"

"No, but they met over there."

God, this is strange, sitting chitchatting with him, like we're just old friends meeting up for Sunday lunch.

"So are you okay for money?"

"Fine, thanks."

"Sure?"

"Yes. Definitely."

"We'll have to sort something out about that. It's just, well, I wasn't up for anything like this. Babies haven't really been part of my plans. I'm just not ready. I think that's the problem. And I'm so fucking busy with work you wouldn't believe it."

"I know the feeling."

"Sorry, angel. I do realize this is tough for you."

"This isn't really about me or you, Daniel, is it?"

"No, I suppose not. Only it's difficult for me right now, angel."

"How are things with Liv?"

"Fine. Great, actually. But—"

"You still haven't told her?"

"No. It's never seemed the right time. Her first husband had kids, and it was complicated."

"I didn't realize she'd been married."

"Twice."

"Oh, right."

There's another silence.

"But I don't want you thinking I'm some callous bastard. I want to do the right thing here."

"Only you're not sure what that is?"

"Exactly."

The food arrives, and I can tell he's surprised at how good it is.

"Did Grace say something to you when you saw her?"

"No."

"Really?"

"Nothing specific. She was treating me like I was radioactive, so I asked her what her problem was."

"And?"

"Big mistake."

"Oh."

"Made me think, though."

"What did she say?"

"Not much, just that she didn't think you'd let me anywhere near the baby since I'm such a fucked-up loser."

"Oh."

He grins. "Sweet girl."

"She is, when you get to know her."

"Sure. So will you? Let me see it? The baby, I mean."

"Of course I will."

"Good. I thought maybe I could come down here sometimes . . . actually, maybe London would be better. I could buy a house. What do you think? I love London. I don't suppose you fancy moving?"

"Where to?"

"I could buy a big house, use it as a base when I'm in town."

"What, and we'd live in it? How would Liv feel about that?"

He grins. "She'd go ballistic."

"You've really thought this through, haven't you?"

We both start to laugh.

"Christ, I'm trying to do the right thing here. How am I doing so far?"

"Not great."

"I love her, that's the trouble. If I didn't, I'd dump her

and move in with you, play happy families for a while, see how it goes."

"No, you wouldn't."

"I would. Seriously. Might be just what I need. Would you, if I asked you?"

"Would I what?"

"Give it a go. You, me, and the baby."

"And the boys."

"Sure."

"What do you mean, sure? They're not an optional extra. Look, this is silly."

"I'm just trying it out for size, exploring all the options."

"Well, don't. Don't tell me maybes, tell me what's happening. I'm too pregnant for maybes."

"Sorry, darling."

"It's okay."

"The thing is, I never know what's happening next week, never mind next month."

"I know."

"What about if I was like an uncle, who turns up once in a blue moon?"

"Once in a blue moon doesn't really do it for babies, Daniel. And I don't want anything clandestine; it wouldn't work, and it wouldn't be fair on the baby."

"No, I suppose not. Look, I'm sure we can work something out. I'm due in New York but then I'm back for a few days. Leave it with me and I'll call you, yes? When I've talked to Liv."

"Okay."

He looks at me. "It suits you, being pregnant. I'd love to

take some pictures. Maybe we can go for a walk—the light's great down here. Is there a beach nearby?"

"Yes. But if you think I'm prancing about posing for photographs in this weather, you can think again."

He grins. "Fair enough. Let's order pudding. I'm assuming pregnant girls are into puddings, yes?"

"Now you're talking my language."

After he's dropped me off at home and I've told Gran that nothing's been decided, much to her annoyance, I call Ellen.

"I'm with your gran. What a wanker."

"No, I think it was good; at least he's thinking about it."

"Like how he tells his bloody girlfriend is your problem."

"I know, but he reminded me of how I used to be with Nick; you don't know what you think about anything until it's been filtered through them. I mean obviously I wish he'd stop being so hopeless, but in a way I feel sorry for him."

"For God's sake get a grip, darling."

"He doesn't know how to handle this, and I think deep down he really minds."

"Well, he'd better get over it then, and start being useful. Did you talk about money?"

"He said he wanted to sort something out, but we didn't talk about anything specific."

"Christ, you really haven't got the first idea."

"Ellen, you know how I feel about the money thing: it's not the point."

"Yes, it bloody is. Why should you be worrying about

the bills while he swans round being creative? Bastard.
Next time you talk to him remind him I'm keeping a close
eye on him, okay?"

"Okay."

"Poor old Dovetail. He just disappeared?"

"Yes. And we were meant to be cooking roast chicken,
so the poor thing hadn't had any lunch either. Do you think
I should ring him?"

"And say what?"

"I don't know."

"Probably not then."

"It's all so complicated. I think I need to wait until the
baby's born; that'll uncomplicate things, won't it?"

"I'm sure it will."

"Christ, I've just thought. What if Daniel tells Liv and
they decide they want the baby? Joint custody or something
like that. Liv might want to adopt—that's very fashionable
now, isn't it?—especially if you're a film star with a tiny
waistline to protect."

"Stop it, darling."

"Yes, but they might, and then I'd have to get a lawyer
and have press camped outside the door like Grace, only I
won't have Bruno and electric gates to protect us."

"Sweetheart, there's no way that's going to happen."

"It might. You never know. I should have thought of
that before I told him."

"So what else is worrying you? What was it with Jack
again?"

"That he'd be stolen from his cot in the middle of the
night while I was asleep."

"And you rigged up some mad early-warning system with chairs tied to rope, and Nick nearly broke his neck falling down the stairs."

"He did not. It was only the two steps down to the bathroom. He made such a fuss you'd think he'd fallen down six flights. And anyway, it was wool, not rope."

"He rang me, you know. He was so worried about you going round the twist."

"I was fine after the first few weeks, and anyway he was loopy as I was. He kept going into panics about cot death and waking him up just to make sure he was still breathing. We both did a fair bit of that, actually."

"I know, darling, and this is the same. Nobody's going to try to take your baby away from you."

"Well, they'd better bloody not."

"What was the panic-button moment with Archie, the mad-dingo thing?"

"It wasn't dingoes, it was any dog. Bit bloody ironic really when you think about it, since he's spent the last few years desperate for one."

"But he's stopped sleeping in the dog basket now, right?"

"Yes, mainly because it's in the garage."

"Okay, so you're fine. No mad-dog nightmares, and you can rig up the woolly early-warning thing across the banisters again."

"Stop making fun of me. I've got serious hormones winging about here. I can't help it."

Archie comes in, in a state of high dudgeon because Jack won't let him watch his *Lord of the Rings* DVD.

"I've got to go. They're fighting again."

"No problem. Give Daniel a few days and then I'll send him a lawyer's letter of my own. Hand-delivered. And Dovetail will be fine, I'm sure he will."

"Thanks, Ellen."

Actually, I'm not sure he will. Maybe I should ring him, only I don't want any more tense conversations today. But I could just call and fix up a new time for us to do the roast-chicken thing. Keep it neutral but friendly; that might work.

He doesn't answer his phone, so I leave a message on his voice mail before Mum rings to moan about Dad, and Jack remembers we haven't done his reading book and stands hopping up and down while I try to get her off the phone.

"I've got to do five pages."

"Okay."

"But I might do more."

"Come and sit down then, love, and Archie, turn the telly off, and go and get your book too. Let's have a reading half hour."

"And then a snacker?"

"Maybe."

It's Wednesday morning, and I'm unloading the washing machine before I go to see Grace. They're back at home for a week's break in filming, so I'm going round today at eleven to deliver the wool she's ordered. I've just got time to

hang the washing out before I leave. And then just as I'm getting into the car it starts to rain.

Maxine is waiting as I'm parking the car.

"Sorry I'm late."

"You're fine. How's it going with the shop?"

"Okay, I think. We're open again. Only downstairs, but fine so far."

"Great, and don't forget to let me know when you want Grace to do the grand reopening thing."

"Probably in the new year, when we've got all the work done on the café?"

"Sure, as long as I get a free ice cream."

"It's a deal."

"I should probably warn you: she's in a pretty foul mood."

"Why?"

"Jean-Luc's ex-wife has turned out to be not quite so ex after all. They've been separated for ages and the divorce is still going through, but that hasn't stopped her doing a deal with the papers for a four-page exclusive."

"God, how awful."

"Ed's sorting it; he's down doing damage limitation now. He's loving the car sticker, by the way." She nods toward a navy blue soft-top Porsche, with a rather incongruous Baby I'm Bored sticker stuck in the back window.

"He says the girls love it."

"How annoying."

"Tell me about it; he was even trying to get one of Lily's old car seats in the back of his car last week, said it would improve his chances no end. He says the Divorced Dad thing works every time. Although how the prospect of

hooking up with someone who'd already dumped their kids would be attractive is beyond me."

"Me too, although I'm guessing the Porsche would probably help."

"The way he fusses over the stupid thing it might as well be a baby. We stuck one of those scratches on once. Sam did it, and it looked so realistic, a great big scratch right down the side; it was fabulous. He got into such a state we thought he was going to pass out."

We're both laughing as we walk upstairs, but she goes straight back into professional PA mode as we approach the door to the upstairs sitting room.

"Great, you've arrived. Max, get me a juice and some tea, would you, and can it be hot this time?"

"Yes, of course. Jo, what would you like?"

"Tea, please."

She winks at me as she goes out.

Lily's getting bored and starts throwing pieces of plastic fruit around the room until Grace takes her downstairs for a swim with Meg. I'm looking at all the toys and pondering the advantages of motherhood on a major budget. I wonder how it feels when one of your options with a narky baby is taking them down with the nanny for a swim in your heated pool. Bloody brilliant is my guess.

Maxine comes back in with a tray with a glass of some kind of revolting-looking green juice on it and cups of tea. She hands a shopping bag to Grace and then stands by the door.

"This is from me and Lily. You made such lovely things for her when she was born, so I wanted to do the same."

There's a beautifully wrapped parcel inside, swathed in tissue paper and ribbon; she's knitted a cream cashmere blanket and a rabbit with floppy ears. And there's a check, for a thousand pounds.

"Oh, Grace, thank you, thank you so much, that's amazing. I don't know what to say."

"It's nothing really; it's for your maternity leave."

"I didn't realize I got maternity leave."

"You don't." She smiles.

"Right. Well, thanks so much; it's really generous of you, and the knitting is beautiful."

"My pleasure."

Maxine smiles. "I'll go down and check with Ed, Grace. Is there anything you want me to ask him?"

"Yes, what the fuck is he doing about the magazine thing? I'm not giving them Lily's birthday party, so he'll have to think of something else."

"Sure."

She sips her juice as Maxine closes the door.

"I had a visitor at the weekend."

"Oh yes?"

"Daniel."

"Oh yes?"

"I think your pep talk really hit home."

"Did it? Sorry about that. I know you said not to mention anything, but when I saw him I couldn't resist. What did he say?"

"I'm not really sure."

She smiles. "That sounds like Daniel. His type always like to be enigmatic."

"No, it was good, actually, I think. He was talking about the baby and how he wants to be involved, only he hasn't worked out how yet."

"So he wants you to sort it all out for him?"

"Kind of."

"And are you?"

"No."

"Good. Last thing you need is another child to look after."

"I think he's a bit worried about how Liv will react."

"I don't blame him. She's definitely a girl who likes to be the center of attention. Speaking as one who knows the type."

I put my cup down. "Grace, I know I'm probably being stupid, but you don't think she'd suddenly decide she wants the baby, do you?"

"Not her style, darling; earth mother to the world is far too serious for her. But if there's any hint of it let me know, and I'll sort you out with the right lawyers. By the time they've finished with her, nobody will let her have a budgie, let alone a baby. Okay?"

"Thanks."

"Christ, men are so useless: if they're not forgetting to tell you they've got a baby on the way, they're forgetting to tell you about their ex-fucking-wife, who's not actually an ex. I wonder why we bother sometimes, I really do. More tea?"

"Please. How's the filming going?"

"Taking forever as usual, but looking good so far. And

Jean-Luc is going to be top of everyone's wish list next year, that's for sure. He's in London, seeing his lawyer at the moment."

"Maxine mentioned something about that. I'm sorry, it sounds awful."

"It's his own fault, but I don't want it becoming a story, so it needs sorting. Jesus. I thought the French were supposed to be discreet. Still, that's his problem, not mine. I've got more important things to worry about, like Lily's first birthday."

"You must let me know what she'd like."

"Pretty much anything tacky that makes an annoying noise. She's got terrible taste, like her mother."

"Grace, you've got impeccable taste."

She smiles. "I thought I'd invite a few kids round, for an old-fashioned tea party. What do you think?"

"How many?"

"Fifty-three, so far."

"Fifty-three one-year-olds? Dear God."

She laughs. "Some of them will be older—your boys and a few others—but most of them will be under two. What sort of help will we need?"

"Armed assistance might be good."

"I thought a Winter Wonderland theme. Fairground rides, and a magic show, with rabbits—she's still very into rabbits."

"That sounds lovely, but you'll need to think about allergies. Some of the kids are bound to have a problem with fur."

She picks up the phone. "Max, check out allergies, would you? If too many of them have got them, cancel the rabbits.

And I was thinking earlier, let's find out about snow—she's never seen snow. No, tell him not to leave until I've spoken to him."

She turns to me. "Hang on here a minute, would you, Jo. I've got to go and talk to Ed. Max, tell him I'm coming down, and you come up and talk to Jo about the party. Get all her top tips."

Maxine sits down and pours herself a glass of water. "What's the green stuff Grace was drinking?"

"Vitamins and grass, basically."

"Really?"

"Special grass, you understand. Special film-star skin-boosting grass."

"Does it taste nice?"

"Absolutely disgusting, and if I told you how much it cost you'd probably faint."

"Would ordinary grass do?"

She laughs. "No, or we could make a bloody fortune."

"Where have you got to so far on the party?"

"Pass."

"I'm happy to help."

"She wants a Big Production."

"Okay."

"I mean Epic."

"Right."

"I've got quotes for the fairground, and entertainers, and inflatables for the pool, but I still need to source lifeguards. And now she wants snow."

"Anyone under two will only try to eat it. . . . I might be able to help on the lifeguards front though. We're having a swimming party for Jack's birthday on Saturday. Come, if you like—I think I mentioned it to you ages ago. Lots of screaming and yelling and everyone gets soaked."

"Yes . . . think I'll pass on that one, thanks, but I've got a present for him downstairs."

"Oh, Max, you shouldn't have."

"No problem."

"I'll ask them about renting lifeguards, if you want—"

"Could you? That would be brilliant. And food-wise—Sam and I were thinking a traditional English tea, with canapés for adults and champagne."

"Sounds lovely, but just do the usual stuff. The kids won't eat anything too fancy, and their parents will be too busy trying to make sure the kids don't break anything."

"Most of them will be bringing nannies, so they can circulate. I've already had e-mails asking about arrangements for arriving by helicopter. So apart from the normal ones, like you and the makeup woman from the film—Grace really loves her—they'll all be nightmare high-maintenance types."

"God. Just don't have anything with nuts in."

"I think we're way past the point of no return on that one."

It's Saturday morning, and I haven't heard a peep from Daniel, or Martin, come to that. But it's Jack's birthday party today, and somehow I've managed to land myself with Fiona and James and the girls coming to lunch, so I've

been concentrating on that. I spent most of yesterday getting the house tidy, ready for Fiona, who seems to have appointed herself as some sort of annoying Family Liaison Officer. I think Nick's mother is still sulking about the baby. I'm guessing I was meant to spend the rest of my life wearing black as a testament to her marvelous son, which is fair enough, I suppose, but she's such a terrible old snob I'm sure her real problem is what the snooters at the Golf Club will think of her son's widow being seen with a new baby, and no new wedding ring.

When Fiona rang on Thursday to announce they're popping in with a present for Jack, she hinted something about us visiting Nick's grave, like that's my top way to spend Jack's birthday weekend when he's only just stopped having his bad dreams and the dry skin on his elbows is almost healed up.

I'm calling Ellen for moral support and trying to tidy the living room at the same time.

"What time are they arriving?"

"Around twelve, I think."

"Give them a sandwich, thanks for the gift, bugger off. You can turn them round in an hour tops."

"Ellen, I can't bundle them out of the door that quickly—it's a long drive."

"You didn't invite her. It's her own fault."

"I know, but I don't want her going home saying it was all a shambles."

"So this is about her telling the old bag mother-in-law that you're doing brilliantly then?"

"Kind of."

"Get over it. It's not going to happen."

"I know."

"How's Dovetail?"

"I haven't seen him. Elsie says he's got a big job on, in Birmingham."

"Never mind, darling. I still love you. Try to be cool about it. You're too pregnant now to let things get to you."

"I know, but if one more person tells me I've got a lot on my plate, I think I might slap them."

"I'd love to see you giving Fiona a good slap. Damn, I'm supposed to be in sodding Cardiff later, or I'd be down there like a flash."

"Cardiff?"

"Don't ask. Part of our Isn't Our Country Great bollocks. So tell me more about this plate thing."

"People keep saying you've got a lot on your plate, and smiling, like they're being friendly, which makes me feel like I must look like a total gibbering wreck or they wouldn't keep saying it. Like I don't already know exactly how much I've got on my sodding plate, thank you very much. Actually, it's more of a full dinner service."

"With salad plates?"

"Yes."

"Bastards. Aren't you supposed to be flooded with happiness hormones around now, ready for the birth?"

"Not yet I'm not."

"Tell Fiona to piss off. Say you're not in the mood."

"Or I could heat up the lasagne I've made and play nice."

"Top plan. Lull her into a false sense of security, and

then the first time she says something, pop her one. Is your gran going to be around?"

"Yes, she's coming to lunch with Reg."

"No problem then. Anyone trying to disparage you and yours will be in big trouble."

"That's what I'm hoping."

"It's a dead cert, darling. So you just have a great party with Jack, and I'll look into the hormone thing for you."

"Great."

"Testosterone's supposed to be good. Marina, my friend in New York, her mother's on it, I think. All sorts of old bags are taking it over there. It's mainly for postmenopause, but I bet it works for any age. You grow a slight beard, but it's worth it. Might perk you up?"

"Thanks, but I think I'll pass."

Actually, all I really need right now is to start growing a beard.

Jack's helping me set the table for lunch.

"I'm really helping, aren't I, Mum?"

"Yes, love, you are."

"That's because I'm eight now."

"Is it?"

"Yes. When you're eight you're much more grown-up. And then after lunch it'll nearly be time for my party, won't it?"

"Yes, nearly."

I'm wearing my boots today, which I can't quite zip up, due to extra pregnancy calfage. My long, stretchy black

skirt is still okay, though, with one of Nick's old sweaters that I knitted for him years ago. It went all baggy and I used to wear it when I was pregnant with Archie. I'm really hoping I look like a mother who has Got Things Under Control, and I've rather brilliantly arranged the swimming bit of the party so I won't actually have to appear in my swimming costume, thank God. Polly and Gemma will be in the water with the kids, and I'm paying them ten pounds each as an extra incentive not to let anyone drown.

Fiona's knitted herself a rather lively sweater, which she's clearly very proud of; it's a complicated pattern of fruit and leaves and autumn berries, which must have taken her ages. There are so many different colors it makes you feel dizzy if you look at it for too long. And she's had a problem with the shoulder seams, so she looks like she's midshrug all the time.

"It's lovely, Fiona."

"It did take a while, but I didn't want you to think you were the only one in the family who could get busy with her needles."

Perish the thought.

"Ever so many people have asked me where I got it."

I bet they have.

"Would you like a coffee? Lunch is nearly ready."

"Super. I'll just check on the girls; I don't usually allow television during the day."

No wonder she looks so Tense.

"Gran should be here soon, with Reg."

"Super. I'm so looking forward to meeting him. So sweet, getting married at her age, don't you think? Still, it goes to show, doesn't it? You should never give up hope." She looks rather pointedly at my stomach. "What's the lovely smell?"

"Lasagne."

"I make all our pasta now—so much nicer, don't you think? James got me a marvelous machine for my birthday, for rolling it out."

Christ, when was her birthday?

"And thank you for your lovely card."

Panic over. Something else that's disappeared off my short-term memory radar. I must have sent a card on automatic pilot. Whole days can go by like that now.

"I must give you my recipe before we leave. I've adapted it from the Women's Institute one, but it's very easy."

"Lovely. Let's take our coffee into the living room, shall we? Oh, here's Gran and Reg."

Hurrah. The cavalry have arrived.

"This lasagne is lovely, pet."

"Thanks, Gran."

"Very nice, dear; you're very clever."

"Thanks, Reg."

Reg has been stellar with James, letting him show off about the new satellite navigation system in his car and the best route to take for London, not that Reg ever drives to London.

"Do you use nutmeg in your béchamel?"

Oh, God, Fiona's off again.

"Sometimes." When I remember.

"And do I detect anchovies?"

Archie puts his fork down.

"No, just mince and pancetta. That's just bacon, Archie—eat up, love. You'll need lots of energy for swimming later."

"Mum, do I have to eat all my salad?"

"No, Jack, but don't take so much next time."

"I thought I liked it, but now I've gone off it."

"That's fine, love."

Lottie puts her fork down, looking relieved, as Fiona gives her the evil eye.

"Well, if everyone's finished, there's ice cream for pud, and Gran's apple tart. Lottie, would you like to help me clear the table? Bring your plate out first, love."

I'm sure I can hear a hint of a tut from Fiona.

James passes his plate to me without a word.

"Play much golf, do you, Reginald?"

God, he's annoying.

"Shall I make some coffee, pet?"

"Thanks, Gran."

She winks at me.

"And then Reg thought he'd take the children for a walk to the sweet shop. James, you could go with them—I'm sure you'd like a walk."

Fiona looks horrified. I'm not sure if it's the sweets, or the idea of James going for a walk with the girls without her assistance; I'm guessing he doesn't usually do much with them on his own.

"Leave the mums at home for a rest, that's what I say.

I'm sure you agree. Work too hard, don't they?" Reg is smiling at James, who looks unconvinced.

"What? Oh yes, they do."

"Right you are then, soon as you've finished your ice cream we'll be off. Who wants to come out with us for sweets then?"

Everyone under ten puts their hands up.

We're sitting at the table drinking our coffee, or our decaf tea in my case.

"Are you sure Beth and Lottie don't want to come to Jack's party, Fiona?"

"No, really, we must make a move when they get back. We're buying a pony for Beth, and there's a place that comes highly recommended we'd like to visit on the way home."

Gran puts her cup down. "A pony. Fancy. We'll have to think about that for the boys—they might like it."

Oh no we bloody won't. Anything that requires mucking out is definitely not on my list of new hobbies for us to be trying out.

Fiona smiles. Now we're into *Horse & Hound* territory, I think she feels back on safer ground.

"Beth's terribly keen; she adores riding. Although it does take commitment, of course, and it is terribly expensive, but the competitions are such fun."

"I'm sure. And thanks again for all the presents, Fiona. Jack loves his books."

"I'm so glad you like them. I know they're a tiny bit old-fashioned, but they are classics."

I've always found Beatrix Potter terribly mimsy and moralistic, actually, in a faintly boring kind of way; a bit like Fiona, now I come to think of it. And not an obvious choice for a boxed set for an eight-year-old boy. God, I'm turning into a complete grumper. I must try to be nicer.

"Is Elizabeth over her cold yet?"

"Oh yes, fully recovered. She won the competition at our Ladies' Lunch at the Golf Club this week—it was super. I'm sure she'll be our Senior Ladies Captain next year. It's terribly exciting. She'll do such a marvelous job."

"I'm sure she will. I must remember to congratulate her when we see her at Christmas."

Fiona puts her cup down and looks anxious. "Are you thinking of coming over?"

We took a mini Christmas tree to Nick's grave last year. Jack wanted to make sure he knew it was Christmas.

"I haven't talked to the boys yet, but I think they'll probably want to. Why, is there a problem?"

"No, not at all—oh dear, this is a tiny bit awkward—it's only I think Elizabeth might prefer it if, well, if you didn't visit at the moment."

"Sorry, Fiona, I'm not sure I understand."

"I'm sure she wouldn't want to cause any unpleasantness, but I think she feels it might be a tiny bit awkward; it is her church, after all, and . . ."

Gran's furious.

"*Her* church? How can it be *her* church? For heaven's sake, I've never heard anything so nasty in all my life."

"People are bound to ask her about the baby, and I think she feels—"

"Fiona, why don't you just tell me what she said?"

"It was nothing really; she'd prefer it if only the boys visited by themselves, to avoid any awkward questions, that's all. Just until the New Year. Becoming Captain is such an honor, and I think, well, after that it would be fine, of course, but if you could let her know in advance she can make sure she's got the key. They're having to lock the church now, but there's a rota for the key."

"Fine. I'll call her later."

Gran gives me a Look, but Fiona's delighted.

"Oh, good, I'm so glad you understand. I realize you've got a lot on your plate, but I do think—"

"I'll call her and explain that I'll be visiting Nick's grave, my husband's grave, whenever I choose, pregnant or with the baby, whenever the boys want to go. If the church is locked, that's fine. We don't need to go in. And if she doesn't like it she can . . . well . . . she can bugger off."

"That's right, pet. About time you stood up to her, dreadful woman. You've got nothing to be ashamed of. Not like some people I could mention."

"Gran."

"Well, I think someone should tell her."

"What does she mean?" Fiona's looking rather desperate now she's caught a hint of a missing entry in her little book of family secrets.

"Nothing."

"Oh yes I do. I'm an old woman and I can speak my mind, it's one of the advantages of getting older. Left with

two little boys and hardly a kind word from his family. Shocking, I call it, and he was no better than he ought to be, let me tell you; and I'm sure you do your best, Fiona, but to be honest I think you should spend a bit less time going to all your fancy charity things at that silly Golf Club and a bit more taking care of people in your family. Because she's done this house up all by herself, you know, and the shop, worked wonders, she has, and you can tell Elizabeth from me, since you seem to be the messenger, grandmother to grandmother, if she upsets any of them, the boys or Jo or the baby when it's here, well, she'll have me to answer to. And that's all I'm saying. It's about time someone told her to get off her high horse. Now then, shall we make a start on the washing up? We'll need to be off to Jack's party soon. And if there's an atmosphere when they get back, they'll know; our Jack is very sensitive like that."

She hands Fiona a tea towel. "I'll wash, you can dry. Jo needs a rest."

Gran stands up.

Somehow I don't think Fiona will be making her usual comment about how super her dishwasher is today.

"Good plan, Gran. I'll finish clearing the table."

"Oh no, you won't. We'll do that. Won't we, Fiona?"

"Yes, of course."

Reg knows something's up as soon as they get back from their walk; we've finished the washing up and Fiona's busy telling us her recipe for lemon curd for some

reason best known to herself, but I think he's guessed we've had words, as Gran would say.

We're standing waving them off when he puts his arm round me. "Did she tell her then? I knew she would. She said she'd try to keep the peace, but Mary's a woman who likes to speak her mind."

"She did, she really told her. She was pretty scary, actually."

"The best women always are, love; you don't get to my age without realizing that. You're not upset, are you?"

"Not at all."

I am a bit, actually; I hate the idea that there are people out there who think the baby is somehow less than the boys just because I'm not married. I really hate it, even though I know it's total rubbish.

"That's the spirit. There's always people who spend their time trying to pretend they're better than the rest of us, love, but they always end up lonely in the end. Miss out on all the precious things. And I'll tell you something else for free, with the route he was planning on taking, they'll be lucky to get home before midnight. There's roadworks on the M2, I heard it on the local radio this morning, and the bypass is shut too, and I'd like to see his satellite get him out of that one. Unless he can beam himself up with it. Now that I'd pay money to see."

It's raining when we arrive at the swimming pool, and there's a teenager in a sweatshirt and jogging bottoms holding a bunch of balloons by the entrance, who turns out

to be Scott, our Party Helper. He seems rather panicky, as well he might be, but after a traumatic half hour when we get them undressed while Scott keeps blowing his whistle, suddenly they're all in the pool having a brilliant time, climbing onto the inflatables and trying to get on the pirate island. They've even put inflatable dolphins and crocodiles in the shallow pool, so the ones who aren't quite ready for the big slide are happy bashing each other with dolphins. I'm taking pictures and trying to keep an eye on Archie, who's insisted on wearing his snorkel after a special dispensation from Scott.

There's a great deal of screaming and splashing, and when it's time for tea, Scott blows his whistle and announces there's a prize for the first person to get changed, and before we know it they're all sitting round the table in the café with their party hats on, although not necessarily wearing the socks they arrived in.

Gran's pouring juice while Scott writes down pizza or nuggets on his pad; they don't seem to have a middle-class mothers' menu option, so there's no pretending anyone will eat carrot sticks or a fruit medley, and everything comes with chips. But since I'm not going to have to cook it, or clean up afterward, I really don't care.

Connie and I are putting the candles on the cake. Mark's made a beautiful fish-shaped cake with silvery icing for the scales, and pink-shrimp sweets round the base, which are Jack's favorite. I'm telling her about lunch and Gran's outburst with Fiona.

"Brava, and now you must go there with the bambino, and walk around the village."

"Only if the boys want to."

"Of course. Horrible cow pig."

"Just cow is fine, Con."

"Here, light the candles."

"Can Nelly really not have any?"

"No."

Nelly has disgraced herself by making a run for it and doing a perfect dive off the middle board, really high up, when everyone was lining up to get dressed. The lifeguard nearly had a heart attack, and Scott nearly swallowed his whistle, but she swam to the side and was completely fine. Unlike Connie, who's still furious with her and has told her she's not getting any birthday cake.

"If she says sorry again? Please, it'll be so horrible making her just sit there; it'll upset Jack. Go and talk to her and see if she's really sorry?"

"Okay, okay. You're worse than Mark."

"You weren't really going to make her sit there without cake, were you?"

She smiles. "No, but she frightened me."

"I know, Con. I think Scott could have done without it too."

Reg is taking more photographs as I kneel down beside Jack.

"Make a wish, sweetheart."

He closes his eyes as we all sing "Happy Birthday."

"This is my best party ever, Mum, and I can have one the same next year, can't I?"

"Yes, if you want to."

"And Dad would be proud of me, wouldn't he? Of my swimming. I'm much better now, aren't I?"

"Yes, you are."

"And do you know something else, Mum?"

Please don't let this be another I'm Missing My Lovely Daddy moment, not right now when he looks so happy.

"What, love?"

"I've still got all my party presents to open when we get home, haven't I?"

"Yes, you have. Let's cut the cake. Who gets the first slice?"

"Me, because I'm the Birthday Boy. And then Archie can be next."

"Okay."

"And next year, the baby can come to my party, can't it?"

"Yes, love."

"But it won't have cake, because it'll be too little."

"That's right."

Archie nods. "And I'll be the big brother, for the baby, won't I, Mum?"

"Yes, love."

Jack smiles. "Yes, but not to me. I'll always be the oldest."

Archie sighs.

We're having a lazy day on Sunday while Jack plays with his new birthday toys and Archie tries not to mind, but by lunchtime we're all a bit bored, so we head off

for a picnic lunch on the beach. I'm doing a casserole for later, but I've made a few sandwiches and I can sit in the beach hut while they have a final session running around in the sunshine. It's a bit warmer today, but I think this might be one of the last days before autumn really sets in.

I'm on the parrot lounger reading the Sunday papers with a cup of tea, feeling very pleased with myself. The boys are playing quietly, and we're all out in the fresh air. How Top Mother of the Year is that?

It's all going rather well until Trevor bounds onto the beach and races into the sea and then races out again, showering water everywhere. The boys are thrilled.

"Hello, Martin."

"I thought I'd better take him for a proper walk. I haven't taken him out for ages."

"Elsie said you'd been in Birmingham."

"Yes. Dad went in and fed him for me; the new kennel's working really well."

"That's good."

"How was the birthday party? Mum said it was yesterday."

"Yes, it was, and he loved it."

"Good."

Actually, I'm still a bit narked that he didn't return my call.

"Did you get my message?"

"What message?"

"I left a message on your voice mail."

"Oh. No, sorry. Trevor ate it."

"He ate your mobile?"

"Most of it."

I can't help laughing.

"It's not funny."

"Sorry."

He smiles. "I think I'll have to go to some of those special help-me-my-dog's-completely-bonkers classes."

"Good plan."

"I'd ring up and book if I still had a phone. So what
was the message?"

"I thought we could fix up a new time for you to come
round to cook that chicken."

"Oh, right, well, that would be great. Any time, if you're
sure. How was your lunch?" He's not looking at me.

"Fine, thanks. It was useful, to talk about the baby. He
might visit, or something. There's no definite plan yet. But
we'll see."

"But just to see the baby?"

"Yes."

"Right. Well, that sounds good."

"Mum, Archie's gone in the sea again."

"Christ."

"Sorry, Jo. Trevor, come here. Look, I'll take him home,
get him out of your way. Trevor, heel. *Heel.* Bloody dog. Oh,
sorry, Jo. Pretend you didn't hear that, Jack, would you?"

Jack nods, looking thrilled.

Bloody, and his brother in trouble again: it's all too perfect.

Trevor stays in the sea, but Archie comes back, with
soaking-wet trouser legs.

"That's very silly, Archie."

"I know, sorry."

"Stand still while I get your socks off."

I'm drying him in the beach hut when Martin finally gets Trevor back on the lead.

I think he's trying to look stern.

"Bad dog. Very bad dog." Trevor's licking his hand. "Sorry, Jo. And you promised, Archie; you told me you wouldn't go in the sea again."

"I know, Martin, and I'm very sorry. Double sorry. But sometimes I just can't help it. I don't mean to, and then the waves just come up, when I'm not looking. They do that sometimes, you know."

Martin's trying not to smile. "Come on then, Trevor. And behave. Walk, okay, no pulling. I mean it." He's whistling as he walks back up the steps from the beach.

The casserole is at the perfect sticky-and-soft stage by the time we're home and desanded. I've lit the fire in the living room, and I'm having a calming moment with *Antiques Roadshow* before I start on another quest for missing PE kit. I seem to have become lost-property monitor again, endlessly rounding up jettisoned socks, but I've already made the packed lunches for tomorrow, so all systems are go for a painless school run, if I can track down Archie's PE shirt.

I'll give them ten minutes before I go up and start tucking them in. I might even get an early night with the rest of

the papers. I've got a magazine I haven't read as well, and my feet are sore and my back's aching, so a bath and then an early night might be my best bet. The baby can have its nightly stretching session while I catch up on what I could be wearing if I still had a waist. Perfect.

needles
and pearls

October

It's the first week of October, and my list of vital things to do before D-Day and my hospital date is getting longer. I'm trying to keep Calm, but the nesting thing still hasn't kicked in yet, although I did manage to get the cot up at the weekend, with Jack and Archie "helping." And I'm knitting like a woman possessed; it's about all I can manage at the moment. Baby blankets and teeny tops with extra-wide necks so we don't have too many of those newborn screaming fits when you try to get something over their heads and they try to stop you by shrieking so loudly you think you must be traumatizing them for life.

We're walking back from school, and Connie's telling the kids all about her uncle's ice-cream parlor in Florence.

"So we'll have our own ice-cream shop, Mum?"

"Yes, Archie." He's skipping. "And we can have ice cream every day?"

"Maybe not every day."

"But nearly every day."

"Maybe."

I wonder if you can go off ice cream, like people who work in sweets factories go off chocolate. Although as far as Archie's concerned, probably not.

"When will it be ready?"

"What, love?"

"The ice-cream shop."

"A while yet; we've got to finish all the tidying up, and get the shop fixed first."

"At the weekend maybe?"

Possibly a bit longer than that.

"After Christmas."

"Well, hurry up, Mum, I can't wait. What's for tea?"

"Omelets."

"Yuck."

It's just past midnight, and I'm having one of my I'm-very-pregnant-and-it's-only-going-to-get-worse panic attacks. I can't do all of this, not with the shop and everything, I know it will all end in tears, and I still haven't heard anything from Daniel, so God knows if he's told Liv yet. And Christ knows what I think I'm doing trying to expand in the shop; I can barely cope as it is. I need to find somewhere quiet

and hide, that's what I need. Somewhere safe and dark and quiet.

"Mum."

Great. That's all I bloody need.

"Yes, Jack."

"I had my bad dream again."

"Did you, love? Well, come and tell me."

"It was horrible."

"Say it out loud and it'll go away."

"I was looking for you, in a sort of forest, and I couldn't find you, and Archie was being really silly and shouting."

So no change there then.

"And then there was a wolf."

"Oh, dear."

"Yes, but then it was Trevor and it was all right. But it was still scary."

"Never mind. It won't come back now."

"Can I stay here?"

"Yes, if you're very quiet."

"Mum."

"Yes?"

"I think the ice-cream shop will be brilliant."

"Good."

"Mum."

"Jack. Go to sleep."

"It's much better here than when we lived in London, isn't it?"

"Yes."

"Because we've got all our friends."

"Yes."

"And now we're going to have an ice-cream shop."

"Yes, now go to sleep or you'll have to go back to your own bed. Think about all your favorite flavors of ice cream and go all floppy. You'll be asleep in no time."

Actually, I might give it a go myself.

Coffee and hazelnut. Proper raspberry ripple, with real vanilla. Orange sorbet. And that honey one, with bits of crunchy honeycomb. Maybe I can do this after all. Maybe the boys will grow up to be Broadgate's answer to Ben and Jerry and they'll transform the family ice-cream business and go global. What was that one I had in Venice? Pistachio—that was lovely—and the pale creamy peach one, with bits of meringue in it.

I'll add it to my list.

It's Wednesday evening, and I'm sitting knitting a soft Aran jacket with a hood for the baby while the boys watch telly and I try to summon up the energy for bath time when Mum calls.

"I just wanted to check you hadn't changed your mind about Christmas."

"No, Mum, sorry, especially not now with the shop."

"Best thing that could happen, if you ask me—burn it down and start again in a proper job, something more suitable."

"Mum, we've had this conversation."

"I don't know how you can be so selfish, Josephine, I really don't."

"I've got to go now, Mum. I'll call you later."

"M um."
"Yes, Archie?"

"Can we have toasted cheese now? You said we could."

"Yes, we can, and then baths."

"And, Mum, you know I'm being an aubergine in the play. Not tomorrow, tomorrow is just stupid singing."

Christ, I'd forgotten about the Harvest Festival at school tomorrow and I'm meant to be taking fairy cakes in, for the PTA stall afterward. Damn. I think I've got flour and eggs. I'll make them while Mummy's little helpers are asleep. Bugger.

"Mum?"

"Yes, I'm listening, Archie."

"Well, I'm not being an aubergine anymore, because I broke it. I'm being a carrot."

"Okay."

T he phone rings at just after one in the morning. Bloody hell, if this is another emergency fire or flood moment, I'm asking for my sodding money back. And if it's Mum on about Christmas again, I'm putting the phone down on her.

"I've left Harry."

"Ellen, where are you?"

"Outside."

"What?"

"Wake up, darling. I'm outside and I need you to let me in. This is my hour of need."

Ellen was always turning up in the middle of the night when we lived in London and she'd had a fight with the latest man. Nick used to get the phone and hand it to me without even waking up. But this is different. God, I wonder what's happened. I hope Harry's not having an affair. Or maybe she is? No, I'd know if she was.

She's cold, and a bit shaky.

"Tea, or hot chocolate? I think there's some left."

"Tea, please."

"What's happened?"

"Nothing."

"Okay."

"I'm bored, that's all. I know I shouldn't be, but I am. I wanted the big wedding, I pretended I didn't, but I did, and now I'm bored. It's all so fucking boring. He's not right for me—he's always off with his bloody mates. It's like nothing has changed."

There's something else, I know there is. But she'll tell me when she's ready.

"It can't be that bad."

"It is. God knows why I married him; I'm hopeless. What was I thinking?"

"Ellen, you're the opposite of hopeless."

"And I'm really sorry I haven't been around much lately, over the fire and everything."

There's definitely something else going on here.

"I don't know what you mean."

"I was good over Nick, though, wasn't I?"

"You were brilliant."

"And that time you thought Jack had something hideous and we took him to the hospital at midnight and it turned out to be chicken pox—I was good then, wasn't I? So two out of three isn't bad."

"What do you mean, two out of three?"

"I haven't been there for you, about the baby, or the fire, not really. I'm too selfish. That's the problem."

"Ellen, stop it. Tell me what's really bothering you."

"I was jealous."

"Jealous of a fire?"

"Things are always happening to you. Nothing happens to me. God, I'm so fucked, what am I going to do? It's not his fault, you know. He loves me, in his own low-maintenance kind of way. And if you say something crap like happiness comes from within, I'll hit you."

"Fair enough."

"So?"

"Happiness comes from within."

"Thanks, that's great."

"It's down to you to make it happy; that's what you said to me, when Nick died."

"Well, it was crap."

"No, it wasn't."

"Remember when we moved down here and you said how much you envied me, having a new start?"

"Yes."

"Well, if that's what you want, chuck in the job and do something else. It's got to be worth a try."

"I like the job. It's my life I don't like. I miss having a new man on the horizon, all the flirting and wondering what he'll look like with his clothes off. Same old same old."

"Are we talking about Harry now?"

"Yes."

"Ellen, you love him, you know you do."

"Yes, but that's part of the problem. Christ, what are we going to do?"

"Muddle on, like we always do?"

"With our knitting?"

"Yes."

"Great. No news from Daniel, I suppose?"

"No."

"Wanker."

"What else is the matter, Ellen?"

"Nothing. Just my life. You're definitely opening this café then? You don't want to run away with me and live in a vineyard in France or something? Set up a farm? We could have sheep and you could spin the wool. Keep the knitting thing going."

"No, thanks. Sheep are very stupid, you know."

"So are most of the people who work in television, darling, you know that. And your ice-cream parlor will probably have one or two dull moments."

"I know. But I'll be able to have an ice cream to cheer myself up."

"God, I need a drink."

"Have one then. There's some of that vodka you left in the cupboard, I think."

"No, I'm all right."

I think I may have just guessed what's put her into such a tailspin.

"Ellen, you're not pregnant, are you?"

"I don't want to talk about it."

"Oh my God, that's brilliant. Why didn't you say?"

"Because I'm bolting, that's why. It's all too real for me, and I'm terrified." She starts to cry.

"Sweetheart, it'll be fine."

"It might not be."

"Then I'll be there and we'll get through it somehow, just like we get through everything else."

"Promise?"

"I promise."

She puts her cup down. "Don't you ever feel trapped?"

"No, not trapped. Panicked sometimes. Actually, quite a lot of the time."

"Panicked about what?"

"Money, keeping the kids safe, stuff like that. But nothing that makes me feel trapped."

"That's because you're happy."

"I suppose I am, yes."

"So you think I should go back to Harry and muddle through?"

"When did I say that? No, I think you should be honest, and if it's not what you want, then don't waste your time, or his. Life's too short."

"How will I know?"

"I've got no idea."

"Thanks, that's brilliant. We should get you a bloody column."

"I didn't say I've got all the answers."

"But you can help me knit a sweater while I'm trying to work it out for myself?"

"Something like that."

"It's a start."

"It's a bloody good start."

"Pass the fairy cakes."

"They're for the Harvest Festival."

"Sorry?"

"At school, tomorrow. Come, if you like. Actually, please come. It would really piss Annabel Morgan off if I swan in with Britain's Favorite Broadcaster."

"Sure. I'll probably still be bolting then anyway."

"Does Harry know where you are?"

"No."

"Ring him."

"No."

"Ellen, ring him. He'll be worried. Or I'll ring him."

"Christ, you're bossy."

"Ring Harry, and I'll put the kettle on."

I'm lying in bed listening to the sound of the waves; it's stormy tonight and my back is throbbing. Nothing serious, just niggling throbbing. God, I'm so looking forward to being able to knock back a couple of aspirin again, without worrying that the baby will have six legs due to a drug-abusing

mother. Actually, even half an aspirin would be a treat. The midwife at the clinic said my blood pressure was up a bit this week, so I've got to try to relax. Although it's easier said than bloody done. Right. Back to inventing new ice-cream flavors. So far I'm thinking bread-and-butter-pudding ice cream would be good, and I've got high hopes for chocolate and walnut.

"Mum."

Jesus.

"Yes, Archie."

"I'm starving hungry."

"No, you're not."

"And I need a drink."

"Archie, please, it's sleep time. Go back to bed, and be quiet. Aunty Ellen's here tonight."

"Okay, but it's not fair, Mum. I'm really hungry."

"Stop fussing, Archie."

"Is Archie sleeping in your bed, Mum?"

Great. A full house.

"No, he's not, and neither are you."

"I might have my dream."

"You won't. Now listen, both of you, back to bed, and be quiet. Quiet as a mouse, and no squeaking, Archie. Promise."

He tuts.

Gran and Reg are taking the boys for a walk while I'm in the shop on Saturday morning when Mum calls.

"I need to talk to you about Christmas."

Oh, dear.

"Can we do it later, Mum? I'm a bit busy."

"I think it would be so much better if you came here for Christmas, darling, I really do."

To a dilapidated palazzo with no proper heating or hot water, which they only get to use because the Milanese banker owner uses them as free caretakers. Perfect choice with a new baby.

"Yes, but—"

"We had such fun last year; it was lovely having you all here. You can ring Vincent and tell him, and lots of my friends want to see the baby. I thought I could have a series of little drinks parties."

In other words the baby will get passed round like a parcel while I act as a waitress.

I don't bloody think so.

"No, thanks, Mum. I think we'd—"

"Sorry, darling, I can't hear you—this line is terrible. Let me know what flight you're on and your father will meet you. Or shall I book for you?"

"I really think we'd all prefer a family Christmas here this year. You and Dad are welcome to join us, though."

"Honestly, Josephine, how selfish; it's not as if I ask for much, and it would mean a great deal to me. I've told people you're coming now. Why can't you be helpful for once in your life?"

Right. That does it. Time for a bit of call my bluff.

"Maybe you're right, Mum. Gran will need a rest, and I suppose all I need to do is get there and then you can take care of everything else. Look after the boys for me, and make all their meals, and help me with the night feeds and nappy

changes, while I get some rest, and have a few lie-ins—that would be great. If you're really sure? I'm sure I could manage to get up for a drinks party or two, as long as I'd slept all day."

There's a silence.

I think she might have just gone off the idea.

"I'll have to talk to your father, darling. You know what he's like. And of course the flights might be booked. Leave it with me and I'll look into it, shall I?"

"Great."

Excellent. Problem sorted.

I think I'll celebrate with a doughnut.

M y phone beeps. I didn't think she'd get back so quickly. I'm guessing the flights are all booked, but let's see.
It's from Daniel.

SORRY. STILL NOT HAD CHANCE TO TALK.
WORK BEEN CRAZY. HOPE ALL WELL.
CALL ME WHEN ANYTHING HAPPENS. DANIEL.

I'm not going to make a big deal about this. I haven't got the energy. But a text? How pathetic is that? Somehow I'm not terribly surprised.

I text back.

ALL FINE. CALL ME IF YOU WANT UPDATE. JO.

"Mum."

"Yes, Jack? Did you have a lovely walk?"

"Yes, but I'm starving. Can we have doughnuts?"

"Yes, love, we can."

Oh, God. It's Tuesday morning, and it's D-Day tomorrow, which I still can't quite believe. I'm due in at nine at the hospital, and the cesarean is booked for eleven and I'm finishing packing my bag. It's all so unreal. I'm half looking forward to not being so huge anymore. I want to be able to bend down to pick things up without having to think about it, get in the bath without worrying that I might not be able to heave myself out again. It was bad enough with Jack and Archie, but this time I feel even bigger, and much slower, somehow. All I've really been able to manage for the past few days is knitting and waddling.

But part of me wants to stay like this; I can do this. God knows how I'm going to cope with a new baby—I've forgotten what they're like. All those midnight moments and walking them up and down. I've never done that on my own. Not that Nick did much, but he was there, some of the time, even if he was asleep. Christ, I'm so not ready. Ellen's due down first thing and she'll come in with me, and I've been shopping and stocked up the fridge for Gran, so in theory I'm all set. Or I would be if I could get to the end of my bloody list.

I'm ready for the school run in plenty of time, for once; the new shower is really great for waking you up, although I managed to do something to the nozzle that meant it

went onto full throttle by mistake yesterday and a jet of water shot across the bathroom and knocked all the bottles off the windowsill.

"Come on, Jack. Where's your book bag?"

"I don't know."

"Well, find it, love, and Archie, you can't take that to school."

"It's for playtime."

"No swords at school, Archie."

"But—"

"Come on, get in the car or we'll be late. Let's decide what to have for tea. You can both pick your best thing and then we'll decide."

"Not horrible macaroni."

"Okay."

After rejecting Archie's choice of oysters, which he's never actually eaten and would hate on sight, and Jack's chicken pie, because I'm too tired to stand rolling out pastry and getting it stuck to the board, we settle on prawn tagliatelle.

I'm in the shop, trying not to panic, but there's still an awful lot to do. I want to sort out the wool for Connie to give to Angela at Thursday's Stitch and Bitch. Stanley's having a new blanket for his bed with animals on, only I didn't have all the colors; and then I need to check the computer. And I need to get the back door sorted at the house. It keeps sticking, so it's really difficult to shut, and I've practically dislocated my bloody shoulder on it a couple of

times already. Actually, maybe Martin could have a look at it for me. I think he's due in at some point this morning. He's getting his quote sorted for all the carpentry work, so he's been in measuring up. I must remember to call Mr. Prewitt about Elsie's wages; she's doing more days over the next few weeks, and I want to pay her a bit extra on top of that too.

I keep getting those sharp little cramps you get in the last few weeks, which is annoying. I know it's just the practice ones; I had them for days with Archie, but I wish they'd pack it in. Okay, let's find the note I put in the order book about the colors Angela needs, and then I should order some more mohair—we sold loads at the weekend.

Martin's upstairs poking bits of the ceiling when I go up to make tea.

"This isn't too bad, you know."

"Good. Oh, and I meant to ask you, our back door at home has gone funny. You couldn't have a look at it, could you? It keeps sticking."

"It'll be all the rain we've had. Easily sorted; it probably needs a bit of adjusting, that's all. I'm finished here, so we can go round now, if you like."

"Oh, right. Okay."

"I'm just popping home for a bit, Elsie. I'll be back later."

"All right, dear. Make sure you rest. Don't start doing your housework."

As if.

We walk home slowly, with me doing my waddling.

Martin gives me a slightly anxious look. "Are you all right?"

"Yes, why?"

"You seem quiet."

"Bit tired, that's all. I'll be fine once I've had a sit-down."

"Tea?"

"Please."

"You have to push it really hard, sort of lean on it and push."

"Right."

"It's a bugger to shut as well."

"I can imagine. So tomorrow's the big day then?"

"Yes."

"Well, good luck, although I'm sure you won't need it. Have you got everything ready?"

"I think so. Well, most of it."

He smiles.

"Actually, not even half."

"Half is better than nothing."

"True."

I'm pouring tea from the big blue teapot, leaning forward slightly.

"Are you sure you're all right?"

"Yes."

"You're not having, what do they call them, contractions?"

"No, of course I'm not. I'm having the baby tomorrow in hospital. I told you."

"Right."

I'm putting a load of washing on.

"Right, that's it."

"Sorry."

"I'm phoning an ambulance."

"Don't be silly, Martin."

"You're making weird noises."

"No, I'm not."

"You bloody are, and you keep zoning out, like you're in another world, and I bet that's a sign too."

"It's just a sign that I didn't sleep much last night."

Christ. Here comes another one.

"Actually, maybe I should go in, just to get checked over. I can—"

Oh, God. Either there's wee all over the kitchen floor or my waters have broken.

I am not doing this. This isn't part of the plan. Right. I'll drive to the hospital, and it'll all be fine. Although maybe driving isn't such a clever idea. Martin can drive. Calling an ambulance seems a bit excessive.

"Martin."

"I'm on the telephone."

"Martin."

"I know. . . . Try to stay calm, they said, and an ambu-

lance is on its way. Right. Stay calm. Christ almighty, how do they expect people to stay calm? What, sorry, I'll ask her. They want to know how many minutes apart."

"Not many."

"She says not many. That's not good, is it? Yes, I'm staying bloody calm, but to be honest it's not very easy. Can you hurry up, please? Tell them to hurry up."

Dear God. This isn't like I remember with Jack and Archie. This is so much stronger, more brutal. I can't get my breath back. Something must be wrong.

"The ambulance will be here in a minute. They say you've got to keep talking to me. What's happening now?"

"I'm washing out the kitchen cupboards. What do you bloody think is . . . happening?"

I'm making weird grunting noises now; I can hear myself, and I can't stop. God in heaven, please let the baby be all right.

" Shall I boil some water?"

"What?"

"Boil some water, get towels, anything like that?"

"Martin."

"Yes."

"Shut up."

"Okay."

"Oh, God."

"Martin?"

"Yes."

"You're so not helping."

"Sorry. Okay. Stay calm. Breathe. Are you breathing?"

"Yes, Martin, I'm breathing."

"Good. That's good . . . Oh, God . . ."

"Oh, thank God. The ambulance has arrived; they're pulling up outside. Just hang on, I'll go and get . . . Hang on, okay?"

Jesus. Where does he think I'm going to go?

There are two ambulance men standing in the kitchen now, while I'm crouching by the fridge making involuntary noises. Damn. I wish I'd washed the kitchen floor. There's all sorts down the side of the fridge; it's really embarrassing. If only I wasn't such a slob, it would be sparkling clean. If I can just . . .

Christ, here comes another one.

I'm doing my grunting thing again as the ambulance men start unzipping their nylon bags.

"You stay where you are. Bob, go and get the other bag. Thought you'd start without us, did you, love? Where are you off to then?"

Martin is halfway out of the kitchen door. "I'll just be outside, Jo, okay?"

The ambulance men exchange glances.

Actually, I think I recognize one of them; he's the same one who took Mr. Pallfrey in, the one who predicted I'd go into labor on the High Street. Great.

"It's going to be fine, love. Let's just have a look, shall we? Can you move a little bit?"

I grip on to his arm.

"Right, I'll take that as a no then, shall I? Thought I recognized you—you're the lady who was with the gent who took a tumble, aren't you? The one with the dog. Dave will be so annoyed. It's his day off. He loves it when we get home births. I'm John, by the way." He smiles.

Home births? Jesus fucking Christ, why won't anyone believe me? This is not going to be a home birth.

I'm crying now, and I want to punch somebody. This is so unfair. I had my slot booked and everything. I've packed my bloody hospital bag.

I am not having this baby here and that's final.

"You're all right, love, it's going to be fine. If you could let go of my arm for a minute, we can try to get you more comfy."

Comfy. That sounds good. Although unless he's got a sledgehammer or an anesthetic in one of those bags, I've got a horrible feeling we're way past comfy. God in heaven, here we go again. This is so much stronger than with Jack. The epidural was wearing off by the time I had him, but it was nothing like this. This can't be right. Something terrible is happening.

"Okay, let's set up for a delivery, Bob. Get the kit in, would you?"

"No. I'm not. Not here. I'm having a cesarean."

"I don't think so, sweetheart."

"I bloody am."

"Right, okay, you are, love, and you're doing fine. Just let's get you kneeling over a bit so I can have a quick look. Can you do that for me? No need to stand up, but it's a bit tricky for me to help you with you like that. Can you do that for me, poppet?"

Great. I'm about to give birth with someone calling me poppet.

"Don't."

"Sorry?"

"Don't. Call me. Poppet."

He grins. "Sorry. My wife hates it too. You're doing so well. Here, hold Bob's arm—he does weight training. Grip as hard as you like."

Bob gives him a Look but takes hold of my hand and squeezes.

"You're doing grand. Is that another one starting?"

Starting? The last one hasn't finished yet. Bloody hell, I'm frantically trying to remember the classes I went to with Jack and Archie: breathe out and count, visualize a beautiful object, which is easier said than done when you're clinging on to your fridge. Well, bollocks to that. I want my cesarean.

"I want. Cesarean."

"I know. We'll sort that later, my darling."

I nod and put my chin down.

"Shall we get him back in for you, love?"

"Who?"

"His Lordship. He's outside, pacing up and down your back lawn. Fat lot of good he's doing out there when he should be in here helping you."

I think Bob would probably like to be released from my gripping his arm.

"I'm. He's. Not."

Oh, sod it. I haven't got time for this.

"No."

Actually, I think I might be dying.

There should be longer gaps between contractions. I remember with Jack thinking how strange it was: one minute you're clutching the gas and air and trying to go with it, like a huge wave coming toward you that you have to try to swim through, and not hold your breath, and then it's over and you're back to normal. Feeling nothing, chatting before the next one. Nick and I did the crossword and made up rude limericks and all sorts, but there's no time, there are no gaps this time. Something must be wrong.

No. I can do this. I know I can. I will do this.

"Try not to push yet, love. I haven't got the sheet out."

Try not to push? Is he mad?

"Can you, right, okay. Well, you just carry on—that's it. Bob, pass me the . . . I can see the head, lots of hair. That's

it, hang on, pant. Can you pant for me? That's it. We need to slow down, just for a minute. Try to hang on, love."

I can't see anything now, just blackness and stars, but that's probably because I've got my eyes shut. Everything's squeezing, every single bit of me. And then it's not. Someone is holding my shoulders, supporting me, and suddenly, for a second or two, I feel light and calm and everything stops.

I open my eyes and I look down. And there's a baby. A real baby, covered in blood, and I'm shaking. Like I'm freezing cold, but I'm not. She's moving. And opening her eyes. She's. Christ, it's a girl. She's a girl.

I'm crying now, and so is Bob, quietly, still holding my hand.

"Sorry, love. Gets me every time."

John looks up.

"She's lovely. You did a grand job. Quickest I've ever seen, but you're fine and she is too. The midwife will be here any minute. You just stay where you are. Do you want to cut the cord?"

My hands are shaking, so he puts his hand over mine.

"There you go."

He hands me the baby, wrapped in a green blanket.

The baby. My baby. She's looking at me, with those navy blue newborn eyes, locked on to mine.

"Hello."

She moves her fingers.

"Hello, sweetheart."

She's perfect. Absolutely perfect.

She's here. And she's safe. And it's all over. Thank God.

I'm so happy, so deep down happy I really don't know what to do with myself.

"The midwife will want to check you over, but I'm pretty sure she'll be happy for you to stay here, if you'd like to. Or we can take you into hospital. Let's wait and see what she says. Bob, put the kettle on. Handy us being in the kitchen, isn't it? Get your husband back in now, shall we, love?"

"Sorry?"

"Tower of strength he's been out in the bloody garden. Oh, sorry, I didn't mean—"

"He's not my husband."

"Right, sorry, your partner. He'll want to see the baby, won't he?"

Martin has briefly appeared at the kitchen window and made a choking noise before he disappeared again.

Bob's smiling.

"He looked pretty pleased. Give him a minute and then I'll go and get him. Takes a bit of getting over, seeing the woman you love going through something like this. Took me weeks with my wife. There, that'll be the midwife. I'll go and let her in."

She's very impressed.

"Let's get you upstairs and pop you into bed, shall we, my love?"

I try to stand up.

"Actually, could I stay here a bit longer?"

She smiles.

"Come on, chaps. Help her up the stairs, would you; this woman deserves a nice comfy bed. And a medal."

I'm lying looking at the baby. She's so like Jack, I can't get over it.

"Are you all right?"

"Yes, Martin, thanks."

"God. It's unbelievable—one minute there was just one of you and now there's two."

"I know."

"She's beautiful."

"She is, isn't she?"

The ambulance men are both standing smiling, looking very proud.

"Is there anyone you need to call?"

"Gran."

Martin smiles. "Here, use my mobile. I called Mum, I couldn't help it, I was in such a state, but she's promised not to say anything."

"Gran."

"Yes, pet? Are you all right? I was going to pop round. I got you some of that body lotion you like. Hospitals are always too hot and—"

"Could you come round to the house?"

"Of course I can, pet. What's the matter? You sound

odd. You're not having twinges, are you? Reg, get the car out, she's starting. *Reg.*"

"Gran."

"Yes, pet."

"Actually, I've finished. The baby's here."

"What? Oh my Lord, I'm coming, I'm on my way. Just hang on, pet. Reg, Reg, get the car."

"Gran."

"Yes, pet?"

"Here, talk to the midwife. Everything's fine, I promise."

G ran arrives just as the midwife has finished washing the baby. She's still got her plastic pinny on when Martin brings Gran upstairs.

"Here she is."

Gran's smiling but looking pretty frightened. "Oh, pet, are you all right? I was that worried. Are you sure she's all right, Audrey?"

The midwife smiles; I'd forgotten Gran knows everybody round here.

"She's fine, right as rain. She did very well. Quick deliveries can be complicated, but not this one, and her scar's fine."

She's been telling me there's always a worry about old cesarean scars when you have what she says is called a precipitous birth, but everything's fine, and I can stay here, which is great.

She puts her blood-pressure box back into her bag.

"Just keep an eye on her, Mary. She'll be tired."

"I should think she will."

"And if she starts any big bleeding or anything unusual, ring me. But I'm sure she'll be fine, and I'll be back later on this evening. But call me any time if there's anything worrying you. I've left the number by the phone downstairs. I'll let the hospital know, and the GP—he'll probably pop along later. Congratulations, my dear. I'll let myself out."

"Oh, Gran." I'm crying again, which is so annoying but I can't seem to stop. "I'm so happy, I don't know why I keep bloody crying."

"It'll be the shock, pet, but it's all over now."

Actually, it's only just beginning, but never mind.

We both look at the baby. She's fast asleep in her Moses basket, wrapped up tight in the new sheet with rabbits on, and the cream cotton blanket Audrey found in the drawer in the spare room. Her room now. The baby's room.

"She's perfect, isn't she?"

"She is. I was sure she'd be a boy."

"I know, your first great-granddaughter. Maybe your only one, unless Vin gets a move on, so you'd better make the most of her."

"I will, pet. Aren't you clever?"

"Aren't you going to pick her up for a cuddle then?"

"I thought you'd never ask. Shall I bring the things up first?"

"What things?"

"Just a few bits and pieces, and—"

"Gran."

"Yes?"

"Just give her a cuddle."

She picks her up, ever so carefully.

Great. I can sleep now. Gran's here, and she's got the baby. Now I can sleep.

"Are you hungry, pet?"

"Starving. What time is it?"

"Nearly three. Reg has gone to get the boys from school. Let's get you fed, then, before she wakes up. What do you fancy?"

"Tea and toast?"

I had tea and toast on the recovery ward after I had the boys, and I really fancy it now.

"That's not a proper meal. What about if I do you some nice scrambled eggs, and Reg is getting you a steak for your tea. We've got to keep your strength up. I'll do you chips too, if you like; Reg can go home and get my chip pan."

"Lovely. But just toast for now, thanks."

Gran brings the boys straight upstairs when they get in from school, and Archie sits eating my toast while Jack kneels down by the Moses basket and looks at his sister.

"Mum?"

"Yes, Jack."

"So it's a girl, the baby?"

"Yes, love."

"It doesn't matter, Mum. She can still play with us. When she's bigger. What's her name?"

"I don't know. I couldn't decide without you two here."

He smiles, and Archie leans forward to peer into the Moses basket.

"What about Galadriel? She's a queen, in *The Lord of the Rings,* and she's great. That would be a good name."

"I was thinking about Mary."

Gran makes a small noise and steps backward in the doorway as Reg puts his arm around her.

Archie sits down on the bed. "That's quite nice. What other ones?"

"What about Pearl?"

Jack nods. "She is quite pearly."

"So shall we call her Mary Pearl then?"

"Yes."

Archie nods. "Yes, and we'll call her Pearly. Pearly girl, because she's a girl."

"Or maybe just Pearl."

I pat the bed. "Come on then, I'm waiting for my cuddle."

Actually, I must try to remember not to move my legs so quickly.

They both wriggle up next to me and start off very gently, before they relax and snuggle in.

"Do you want to cuddle the baby?"

"Pearl, Mum, you should call her Pearl. She won't like being called the baby all the time."

Archie's clearly enjoying his newly elevated Big Brother status.

"Okay. Do you want to cuddle Pearl?"

"No, thanks."

Jack smiles. "I would. A bit."

Gran puts her on my lap, and she brilliantly stays asleep while Jack has his first tentative cuddle.

"Her hands are so tiny, Mum."

"I know."

"Because she's only little."

"Yes."

Actually, eight pounds four ounces, so not so little, thank you very much.

"Were my hands that tiny?"

"Yes, love. And you had the same hair. Lots of black hair."

"But now it's brown."

"It changes."

Actually, it's uncanny how like Jack she is; she's got the same long, thin feet, and long fingers, and the same-shaped head. Archie was more rounded, and had less hair. Please God she takes after Jack and sleeps sometimes. But actually, even if she doesn't, I don't care, not really. She's here, and she's perfect. Absolutely perfect. All three of them are here, and everything's fine.

I'm going to cry again if I'm not careful.

"Tell us about when we were born, Mum."

"Can we do it later? I'm a bit tired now and you need your tea. After bath time?"

"What's for tea?"

"I don't know, Archie. Gran's in charge. Probably anything you like."

"Yes! Anything we like. I want a lobster. Cooked. With sauce."

I think I'll leave Gran to sort that one out.

"Will you be coming downstairs later?"

"I'm not sure, Jack. Maybe not tonight. I'm a bit tired now."

"But I've got a new reading book."

"Come on, boys. Your gran's got a surprise for you. Let's leave your mum to have a rest. And your new sister. She's had a busy day too, you know." Reg has already had a quick cuddle earlier and seems tickled pink with his new great-granddaughter.

Archie nods.

"See you later, Pearly."

I'm dozing when Gran comes up with the phone.

"It's Ellen. I thought you'd want to talk to her."

"Thanks, Gran."

"Hello, darling. God, you don't hang around, do you? What's that all about, giving birth on the floor? Christ. I can't believe you went for it at home."

"I didn't have much choice in the matter, trust me."

"How is she? And how are you? Was it awful?"

"She's perfect and it was completely terrifying, but weirdly okay as well. It was so quick I didn't have time to get totally freaked out. Thank God Martin was here."

"Good old Dovetail—I knew he'd come in handy. Have you called Daniel?"

"No. It's weird, but it's right in a way that he doesn't know she's here. And if I call him it's like I want him to want him to know, like it'll make a difference, which it won't."

"You could always text him."

"True."

"You don't really care, do you?"

"No."

"Good."

"Now she's here the only thing that matters is that she's safe."

"True. And you're okay, really?"

"Fine. And she's very clever. Already had two feeds."

"What a surprise."

"Are you implying she might take after her mother in the piglet department?"

"I think it's a pretty safe bet, darling. She certainly takes after her mother in the not-hanging-about department. Great name, by the way. I wonder who'll be the first person to buy her pearls? Actually, why don't I do that, as my first godmotherly thing?"

"That would be lovely, Ellen."

"Your gran said she's Mary Pearl, yes? Sweet."

"The boys are already calling her Pearly. I'll have to sew pearl buttons on her coat and get her a tambourine."

Ellen laughs.

"I'm so sorry I wasn't there, sweetheart. You must have been so frightened. Not that I'd have helped much. I'd probably have been totally hysterical, but still. You're amaz-ing. You know that, don't you? And I'll be there first thing

tomorrow. I'll get her loads of girlie stuff. I thought that could be my new role, Fairy Shopping Godmother. Because let's face it, darling, someone's got to teach her how to shop. Anything you need?"

"Twelve hours' sleep."

Gran's holding court downstairs, with Betty making tea and popping up on tiptoe with tasty snacks, and standing looking at the baby with a huge grin on her face. Elsie burst into tears, and so did Connie, and there's been a steady stream of visitors by the sound of the knocking on the door, but Gran's not letting many of them up until tomorrow, and I'm too tired to argue.

And anyway, the only person I really want to see her, now the boys and Gran have seen her, the person I most want to show her to in the whole world, is Nick. Which is daft. But I know how knocked out he'd be with her looking so like Jack, and he'd hold her, like he held the boys when they were tiny, and he'd sing to her, in that deep voice they used to love so much. "Daisy, Daisy, give me your answer do."

Damn. I'm definitely crying now. The hormonal maelstrom is definitely kicking off, and it's completely ridiculous, but I want him here, just for a little while, so he can see her, just once. She's my bonus baby, the one I never thought I'd have. And what's really odd is how she feels far more related to him than to Daniel. She's ours. Part of our family. The moment I saw her, I recognized her, like I'd known her

for ages. And I want him to see her, because I know he'd recognize her too. It's like magic.

M artin's sitting by the bed when I wake up, holding Pearl.

"Your gran said it was okay."

"Of course."

"She started waving her hands, so we picked her up. Was that all right? Your gran said I should just sit and hold her."

"It's fine, Martin."

"She's so tiny. And so beautiful. So how are you feeling now?"

"Completely exhausted. Actually, beyond completely; it's almost scary."

"I'm not surprised. It's so like you."

"What is?"

"To just get on with it. You're extraordinary."

"I think that poor ambulance man might feel differently. I bet he'll have his arm in a sling tomorrow."

"Your gran's in seventh heaven. She was showing me all the flowers. It's like a florist's downstairs; why haven't you got any up here?"

"Gran thinks flowers suck the air out of a room."

"Do they?"

"Not as far as I know. Although maybe that's why most film stars are usually so daft. Too many flowers."

He laughs. "It would explain a lot. The boys seem pretty

thrilled too. Archie's been telling me he's got a new baby so he might not go to school tomorrow."

"Right."

"I've fixed the back door, by the way."

"Thanks, Martin."

"So, have you called him?"

"Who? Oh, sorry. No, not yet. He knows the baby's due around now, and he's got my number."

He smiles. "Well, I'd better be off. I just wanted to make sure you were both okay. I might pop back later on, if that's all right? I've got something I want to bring round."

"Of course. We'd both love to see you."

He's whistling as he goes downstairs.

The midwife comes back, and then Connie, followed by the boys with their reading books.

"Mum?"

"Yes, Archie?"

"When Pearly gets bigger, who do you think she'll like best, me or Jack?"

"She'll love you both the same, because you're her big brothers."

"And who do you love the best?"

"All three of you."

He nods.

"So all the love you have gets shared out between all of us?"

In other words his half share in the maternal devotion stakes has just gone down to a third.

"Actually, it's better than that, Archie. You don't share it out, you just get more. When Jack was born I loved him millions, and then when you were born I loved you millions too, and now we've got Pearl it's happened again. Isn't that clever?"

He smiles. "It's millions to the moon and back again."

"Yes, that's right."

Jack nods.

"But she'll have her own toys."

"Yes, love, she will."

"We can share sometimes. But not all the time."

"Okay."

Archie giggles. "We probably won't want to share her pink girlie stuff."

"She might not be a pink girlie girl, Archie. Not all girls are."

All three of us look at her.

She's on my lap, half asleep, head to toe in pink. Gran changed her earlier and put her in the pale pink Babygro Connie brought.

He tuts. "Well, if she's not, she's going to be very cross when she sees all her clothes."

Gran comes up with Martin, who's carrying what looks like a small sideboard.

"I thought I'd have a few more days to get it finished, before you came out of hospital."

It's a cradle, a beautiful old-fashioned cradle that rocks gently from side to side when you push it. The boys are very impressed.

"I measured the Moses basket with your gran, ages ago, so it should fit. Shall we try it?"

The Moses basket fits inside perfectly.

"Isn't that lovely, pet?"

"It's great, Martin. Thank you so much."

"You're welcome."

"I'll put the kettle on. Would you like a cup of tea, Martin?"

"Yes, please, Mary."

"Come on, boys. You can have a tiny bit more telly if you're quiet."

"Thanks, Martin, really. It's lovely."

"I'm glad you like it."

There's a silence.

"Well, I should be going. Oh, I meant to say. I should be able to start work on the shop next week."

"Great."

There's another silence.

"I've been meaning to talk to you, actually, about putting things on a more official basis."

"Like a board outside saying 'Carpentry by Martin Trent'? That's a good idea. It would be great for your new business."

He sighs. "No, I meant, well, I thought I should ask you."

"Sorry, Martin, I'm still not sure I follow you."

"No, well, that's the point. I mean I don't want you following me, or me following you, but I'd like us to have an understanding."

At this precise moment, so would I; I'm still not sure what he's trying to say.

"An understanding?"

"Yes. I didn't want to say anything until the baby was born, it didn't seem right, but now she's here . . . well, I thought I should ask you."

"Ask me what, Martin?"

"Look, I know I'm not very good at this sort of thing, and things are complicated and this probably isn't a good time, but I'd like it if we could have an understanding. I know it sounds old-fashioned."

"No, it sounds rather nice."

He smiles.

"Well, that's great. Excellent, actually. And I don't want you to think you're getting mixed up with someone useless. And I'm glad he's not going to be around, her biological father. I know it's probably not the right thing to say, but I am."

"You make him sound like a box of washing powder."

He smiles. "I didn't mean—"

"Actually, so far he's been a lot less useful than washing powder."

"That might change."

"Maybe."

"And?"

"And nothing. I'll do what's right for Pearl, but there won't be anything else."

He looks at his feet. "You'll want new skirting boards, I take it?"

"Will I?"

"Yes. In the shop."

"Okay. There is one tiny problem I can see on the horizon, though."

"No, I've thought of that. We can match them, in both shops."

"I meant your mother, Martin."

"Right. Sorry. Well, don't worry about that. Just leave her to me."

"How?"

"Never you mind."

"I think I preferred it when you were all nervous."

"I'll alternate then. I'll be bossy about the stuff I know about, like why you can't have MDF and why you need to spend money on proper oak for those shelves. And you can be in charge of, well, everything else really. I'll spend half my time at your feet, and the rest of the time I'll be up a ladder."

"My God, I think I've finally stumbled across the perfect man."

He laughs. "Sorry to blurt all this now. I should probably have waited."

"No, I'm glad you did."

"Still, I should be off, leave you to rest."

"Okay."

"Night then."

"Night."

He leans over and kisses me on the cheek, bending forward slightly so as not to squash Pearl.

"I'll see you tomorrow."

"Great."

He's whistling as he goes out.

Crikey. I really didn't expect that, and who knows what will happen? But it's a good start. And even though I'm not sure I'd have chosen someone with quite such a pronounced interest in wood, or with Elsie for a mother, there's always a cloud to every silver lining, as Gran would say.

Crikey.

The boys come in for a good-night kiss, in their pajamas. Gran's washed their hair, and they've both got unusually neat center partings.

"Are you going to sleep now, Mum?"

"Yes, Jack."

"Can we sleep with you and Pearly tonight?"

"No, Jack. We all need to sleep in our own beds."

"Just for a little bit?"

"Okay. But only for a little while."

They snuggle in.

All three of them within arm's reach, and everyone being quiet.

It doesn't get much better than this.

Perhaps I should learn to whistle.

reading group guide

ABOUT THIS GUIDE

In this witty and charming follow-up to *The Beach Street Knitting Society and Yarn Club*, Gil McNeil brings readers back to the scenic English village of Broadgate and into the life of its harried yarn shop owner, Jo Mackenzie. A year after her husband's death, Jo feels like she has finally found a groove: her boys are thriving in their new home, her store is doing well, and she has begun to navigate—with some success—the complicated social circles that rule her seaside town. But just when her life seems settled, it once again gets complicated: between several unexpected developments, a budding romance with a local carpenter, and a piece of shocking news, Jo needs a lot more than knitting to keep from completely unraveling. *Needles and Pearls* is full of entertaining and interesting topics for discussion, and this guide is designed to help your book group start a lively dialogue.

ATTENTION: SOME PLOT SPOILERS IN THIS GUIDE.

QUESTIONS FOR DISCUSSION

1. Based on the author's depiction of a seaside resort town, what do you find most, and least, appealing about life in Broadgate? Could you live in such a place?

2. How would the novel have been different if it were set in the United States and featured American characters? In other words, what role does British culture and sensibility play in the book? If you had to pick another location within which to set *Needles and Pearls*, what would it be?

3. "I should be the grieving widow, but I'm still so furious with him" (page 10). Consider the circumstances surrounding Nick's death. Do you sympathize with Jo's mixed emotions at his passing? How is a grieving widow supposed to act? Does grief sometimes go hand in hand with anger? Why?

4. Talk about Gran and her suitor, Reg, and how their decision to marry affects different members of the family. Can you understand why Jo's mother wasn't happy with this turn of events? Do you have a friend or relative who remarried after the death of a partner? What did you think of their decision?

5. The women of *Needles and Pearls* are in various stages of "moving on" from different things. Pick a few characters and discuss their individual situations. What are these women trying to change? How will their lives be better once they take a step forward?

6. If you had to pick which suitor to root for, who should Jo have chosen, Martin or Daniel? Why?

7. While considering Daniel and Martin, which do you think is a more unfortunate position for a women to be in:

to be involved with a man who has a girlfriend or wife, or a man who has a difficult mother?

8. In the chapter "The Thin Blue Line," Jo makes the shocking discovery that she is pregnant. Did this revelation surprise you? What did you think of Jo's decision to keep the baby, given all she had going on in her life?

9. In chapter 9, Ellen shows up fraught and upset at Jo's door. Did you expect that Ellen would have trouble with being married? Were you surprised to learn the root of Ellen's distress?

10. After the fire, Jo decides not only to rebuild the shop, but to expand it. Did you expect this? What did you think of her rationale for doing so?

11. When Jo finally gives birth, it's at an unexpected time and in an unexpected place. Do you think that Pearl's delivery might be a metaphor of some kind for Jo's life?

12. If you had to predict events after the novel's end, what would happen?